DEEP READING

Deep Reading

Teaching Reading in the Writing Classroom

Edited by

PATRICK SULLIVAN
Manchester Community College

HOWARD TINBERG
Bristol Community College

SHERIDAN BLAU
Teachers College, Columbia University

National Council of Teachers of English
1111 W. Kenyon Road, Urbana, Illinois 61801-1096

Figures 13.1–13.6 reprinted by permission of Michelle Chiles and Emily Brown.

Staff Editor: Bonny Graham
Interior Design: Jenny Jensen Greenleaf
Cover Design: Pat Mayer
Cover Art: *Jubilee*, 2017, ink on paper, Bonnie Rose Sullivan

NCTE Stock Number: 10638; eStock Number: 10645
ISBN 978-0-8141-1063-8; eISBN 978-0-8141-1064-5

It is the policy of NCTE in its journals and other publications to provide a forum for the open discussion of ideas concerning the content and the teaching of English and the language arts. Publicity accorded to any particular point of view does not imply endorsement by the Executive Committee, the Board of Directors, or the membership at large, except in announcements of policy, where such endorsement is clearly specified.

NCTE provides equal employment opportunity (EEO) to all staff members and applicants for employment without regard to race, color, religion, sex, national origin, age, physical, mental or perceived handicap/disability, sexual orientation including gender identity or expression, ancestry, genetic information, marital status, military status, unfavorable discharge from military service, pregnancy, citizenship status, personal appearance, matriculation or political affiliation, or any other protected status under applicable federal, state, and local laws.

Every effort has been made to provide current URLs and email addresses, but because of the rapidly changing nature of the Web, some sites and addresses may no longer be accessible.

Library of Congress Cataloging-in-Publication Data

Names: Sullivan, Patrick, 1956– editor. | Tinberg, Howard B., 1953– editor. | Blau, Sheridan D., editor. | National Council of Teachers of English, publisher sponsor.
Title: Deep reading : teaching reading in the writing classroom / edited by : Patrick Sullivan and Howard Tinberg and Sheridan Blau.
Description: Urbana, Illinois : National Council of Teachers of English, [2017] | Includes bibliographical references and index.
Identifiers: LCCN 2016055603 (print) | LCCN 2017016252 (ebook) | ISBN 9780814110645 ( ) | ISBN 9780814110638
Subjects: LCSH: Reading (Higher education) | English language—Rhetoric—Study and teaching (Higher) | Academic writing—Study and teaching (Higher) | Reading comprehension—Study and teaching (Higher) | College reading improvement programs.
Classification: LCC PE1404 (ebook) | LCC PE1404.D3875 2017 (print) | DDC 428.4071/1—dc23
LC record available at https://lccn.loc.gov/2016055603

To Susan, Bonnie Rose, Nicholas, and Marigold Hope
—Patrick

For Toni, Miriam, Leah
—Howard

To my students
—Sheridan

And to Louise Rosenblatt,
one of our heroes,
an inspiration and exemplar
who has written so eloquently
about the things that matter most

*While reading, we can leave our own consciousness,
and pass over into the consciousness of another person,
another age, another culture. "Passing over," a term
used by the theologian John Dunne, describes the process
through which reading enables us to try on, identify with,
and ultimately enter for a brief time the wholly different
perspective of another person's consciousness. When we
pass over into how a knight thinks, how a slave feels,
how a heroine behaves, and how an evildoer can regret
or deny wrongdoing, we never come back quite the same;
sometimes we're inspired, sometimes saddened, but we are
always enriched. Through this exposure we learn both the
commonality and the uniqueness of our own thoughts—that
we are individuals, but not alone.*

*The moment this happens, we are no longer limited by the
confines of our own thinking. Wherever they were set, our
original boundaries are challenged, teased, and gradually
placed somewhere new. An expanding sense of "other"
changes who we are, and, most importantly for children,
what we imagine we can be.*

—MARYANNE WOLF

CONTENTS

III Practical Strategies for Teaching Deep Reading in the Writing Classroom

Contents

INTRODUCTION

PATRICK SULLIVAN
Manchester Community College

HOWARD TINBERG
Bristol Community College

SHERIDAN BLAU
Teachers College, Columbia University

We began this project with great enthusiasm—and with perhaps an even greater sense of urgency. We have grown concerned with the lack of attention given to reading in our disciplinary conversation about the teaching of writing, and we are alarmed by the impoverished and reductive understanding of reading that has worked its way into curriculum and state standards by way of the Common Core State Standards (CCSS) and the widespread use of standardized tests to measure proficiency in English. The theory of reading enacted in these state standards and in most standardized testing positions readers as passive recipients of information and defines reading primarily as a kind of text-focused close reading (Dole, Duffy, Roehler, and Pearson). Unfortunately, as Ellen C. Carillo has noted, "a foundational element that has infused literary study since at least the 1970s, but one that the Common Core largely ignores, is that the reader plays a role in the construction of meaning" ("Reimagining" 31). While text-centered close reading must certainly be an important component of any individual's repertoire of literacy skills, this approach to reading draws on a traditional, outmoded, and simplified understanding of the reading process and the nature of reading itself. It is also difficult to find ways to link this type of reading activity to meaning-making and authentic intellectual work because the reader is left almost entirely out of this process. This approach to reading thus serves to disconnect reading from the important academic and human activities of exploring problems (Wardle), thinking critically and creatively (Facione; Sullivan, "UnEssay"), and producing knowledge.

This theory of reading also ignores decades of reading scholarship that positions readers in more complex relationships with the texts they read. Louise Rosenblatt's important transactional theory of reading, for example, first formulated in 1938, positions individuals in a dynamic, reciprocal relationship not only with texts but also with "the natural and social environment" (Rosenblatt, *Reader* xiv). Rosenblatt theorizes reading, famously, as "an event in the life of a reader, as a doing, a making, a combustion fed by the coming together of a particular personality and a particular text at a particular time" (*Literature* xvi). Transactional theories of reading provide abundant opportunities for students to engage in authentic intellectual work, and they connect reading to writing, critical and creative thinking, and the production of knowledge in deep and powerful ways. This theory of reading also enacts the production of knowledge in personal, academic, and vocational contexts, in which the value of an act of reading is intimately connected to the character traits, habits of mind, and ethical commitments of the persons who read (Blau). Key habits of mind, like those articulated in the "Framework for Success in Postsecondary Writing," that we seek to privilege in our classrooms can also be actively nurtured. These habits of mind include curiosity, openness, engagement, creativity, persistence, responsibility, flexibility, and metacognition (Council of Writing Program Administrators; Costa and Kallick).

Marcel Proust may have provided the most eloquent formulation of this theory of reading in his essay "On Reading," first published in 1905. Proust positions the reader as central to the meaning-making process and formulates a complex transactional understanding of how readers produce meaning:

> Indeed, this is one of the great and wondrous characteristics of beautiful books (and one which will enable us to understand the simultaneously essential and limited role that reading can play in our spiritual life): that for the author they may

be called Conclusions, but for the reader, Provocations. We can feel that our wisdom begins where the author's ends, and we want him to give us answers when all he can do is give us desires. He awakens these desires in us only when he gets us to contemplate the supreme beauty which he cannot reach except through the utmost efforts of his art. But by a strange and, it must be said, providential law of spiritual optics (a law which signifies, perhaps, that we cannot receive the truth from anyone else, that we must create it ourselves), the end of the book's wisdom appears to us as merely the start of our own, so that at the moment when the book has told us everything it can, it gives rise to the feeling that it has told us nothing. (23)

The key moment for us—and a formulation of vital importance for our discipline as we seek to theorize a deeper, more integrated understanding of the reading–writing relationship—is this phrase: "our wisdom begins where the author's ends."

Nationally, the widespread acceptance among school policymakers and politicians of a traditional and radically simplified theoretical understanding of reading appears to have produced an epidemic of what Kelly Gallagher has called "readicide"—"the systematic killing of the love of reading, often exacerbated by the inane, mind-numbing practices found in schools" (2). Gallagher suggests that readicide is caused by educational practices that value the development of test takers over the development of lifelong readers (5). This understanding of "valuing reading" (7) may help to explain the disturbing results reported on the Nation's Report Card, a congressionally mandated project administered by the National Assessment of Educational Progress (NAEP) through the National Center for Education Statistics. As Patrick notes in his essay in this volume, in 2015 only 37 percent of twelfth-grade students performed at or above the Proficient achievement level in reading (Nation's Report Card). The remainder of students in this testing cohort tested below Proficient, with what NAEP identifies as either Basic or Below Basic reading skills. NAEP found comparable levels of low achievement in math, science, and writing. A simplified approach to reading may well help to explain poor student performance in these subject areas as well. Two reports about reading from the National Endowment for the Arts—*Reading at Risk* and *To Read or Not to Read: A Question of National Consequence*—document the scope of this problem. Dana Gioia acknowledges in his preface for *To Read or Not to Read* that "the story the data tell [about reading] is simple, consistent, and alarming" (5). Reading comprehension skills are eroding, and these declines have "serious civic, social, cultural, and economic implications" (7).

Building on the work of Elizabeth Wardle, we must theorize the approach we take to reading in the writing classroom as a high-stakes enterprise. Wardle theorizes two very different kinds of learning dispositions that we can privilege in the classroom: "problem-exploring dispositions" and "answer-getting dispositions." A problem-exploring disposition inclines students "toward curiosity, reflection, consideration of multiple possibilities, a willingness to engage in a recursive process of trial and error, and toward a recognition that more than one solution can 'work'" (n.p.). An answer-getting disposition, in contrast, inclines students toward seeking "right answers quickly" and actively encourages students to be "averse to open consideration of multiple possibilities." Wardle warns that

> the steady movement toward standardized testing and tight control of educational activities by legislators is producing and reproducing answer-getting dispositions in educational systems and individuals and . . . this movement is more than a dislike for the messiness of deep learning; rather, it can be understood as an attempt to limit the kind of thinking that students and citizens have the tools to do.

As Pierre Bourdieu and Jean-Claude Passeron have demonstrated, language skills reside at the very core of thinking, learning, and cognition itself: "Language is not simply an instrument of communication: it also provides, together with a richer or poorer vocabulary, a more or less complex system of categories, so that the capacity to decipher and manipulate complex structures, whether logical or aesthetic," depends significantly on the complexity of a student's language (73). The unsettling findings of the National Commission on Writing, therefore, may have as much to tell us about *reading* as they do about writing. The commission found, unfortunately, that twelfth-grade students currently produce writing that is "relatively immature and unsophisticated" (17).

Like Gallagher, a number of reading scholars and expert class-room practitioners have been actively at work seeking to offset this movement toward a simplistic and mechanical understanding of reading, but their work has been slow to be embraced by compositionists (Atwell; Miller; Newkirk; Smith and Wilhelm; Wolf). Much of this work is written by and for secondary school teachers, and this has helped perpetuate the idea in our discipline that reading instruction is the concern of K–12 educators only and does not require the attention of college instructors. This has also contributed to isolating college compositionists from reading theory and instructional strategies, even though college writing teachers routinely acknowledge the need to improve the reading skills of students in their writing classes. As David A. Jolliffe has noted, "At every college and university where I have taught in the past twenty-five years—and this list includes four state universities, a private liberal arts college, and a large Catholic university—the talk about student reading is like the weather: Everybody complains about it, but nobody does anything about it" (470).

We suspect that one reason for the neglect of reading within composition and rhetoric is the well-documented tension within English departments between those whose expertise is literary (including critical theory, historical criticism, gender studies, and other areas of specialization focusing on the reading of canonical, literary texts) and those whose professional expertise is with composition and rhetoric. As Sheridan notes in his essay in this volume, the parting of the ways between teachers of literature and teachers of composition is rooted in a tradition within literary studies of privileging authoritative readings produced by literary specialists and devoting only limited attention to the experience of actual student readers as they engage with texts. In this instructional model, readings communicated by literature teachers to their students become the primary focus and product of instruction. Student writing about literature in this model is often evaluated largely on the basis of its "correctness" in reproducing someone else's knowledge, thereby ignoring what Proust calls in his essay "On Reading" a "providential law of spiritual optics," a "law which signifies, perhaps, that we cannot receive the truth from anyone else, that we must create it ourselves" (23).

As composition began to consolidate into a discrete discipline, however, it shifted from a focus on the product (text) to the process of composing and an understanding of the writer as a maker of meaning. Tensions between literature specialists and composition specialists in English departments thus grew from the fundamental differences in their assumptions about how a text and meanings are produced, taught, and evaluated. The famed Lindemann–Tate debates of the 1990s, which both Sheridan and Howard reference in their essays in this collection, exemplify the intensity of this theoretical difference and its practical focus on the question of whether—or to what extent—the study of literature could continue to command any curricular space in a modern and professionally well-informed first-year composition class. The increasing disciplinary respectability of composition as a field with its own research traditions, theoretical frames, and pedagogical principles eventuated the wholesale removal of literary study from first-year writing classes nationally.

Without literature and the range of interpretive possibilities generated by literary texts and genres, many first-year writing classes and programs have focused instead on teaching students to read rhetorically (Bean) and to employ rhetorical analysis when reading nonfiction texts, particularly in relation to argumentative writing, which in secondary schools and many first-year composition programs has became the dominant genre of writing (Sullivan, *New* 11–118). The popularity of rhetorical reading may help to explain why it occupies such a prominent place in the description of reading skills and competencies emphasized in CCSS documents, where the analysis of texts tends to be reduced to an examination of a text's formal properties and leaving largely unengaged a confrontation with a text's meaning, the problems a text invites readers to consider, and the wisdom it might offer.

For writing specialists, like most academic professionals, keeping up with scholarship outside of their area of specialization is often challenging, and within the field of English, reading specialists and writing specialists often inhabit very different professional and educational spaces, teach different kinds of courses, and perhaps naturally converse primarily with members of their own professional discourse communities. One of our goals with this book is to help address this disciplinary segregation and to help restart our disciplinary conversation about reading and writing that was begun in the 1980s and flourished for about fifteen years before declining precipitously. This conversation was led by scholars such as Patricia Donahue, Mariolina Rizzi Salvatori, David Bartholomae, and Anthony Petrosky. Alice Horning, along with Donahue and Salvatori, have done the important work of keeping this conversation alive since the blossoming of interest in reading in the 1980s. Unfortunately, however, the assessment of our discipline voiced by Marguerite Helmers in 2003 still holds: "the act of reading is not part of the common professional discourse in composition studies" (4; Salvatori and Donahue, "Guest"; Horning and Kraemer; Horning and Gollnitz). Although there has been a recent resurgence of interest in reading by scholars including Ellen C. Carillo (*Securing*), Daniel Keller, Michael Bunn, and Patrick (*New*), there is still much to say about this subject as we develop a theory of writing that is informed by the central role that reading plays in the production of knowledge and meaning (Salvatori and Donahue, "What"; Smith; Jolliffe and Harl). This book seeks to contribute to this reawakening of our professional interest in reading and to help advance our theoretical and practical understandings of the essential connection between reading and writing.

In many important ways, this volume is a continuation of our series of books focused on college-level writing: *What Is "College-Level" Writing?* (Sullivan and Tinberg) and *What Is "College-Level" Writing? Volume 2: Assignments, Readings, and Student Writing Samples* (Sullivan, Tinberg, and Blau). We would like to suggest—after many years of reflection and research on the complex question that frames these two books—that reading must be theorized as foundationally linked to any understanding of college-level writing. As Maryanne Wolf notes in her book on reading and the science of the brain, the invention of writing and reading some 10,000 years ago required us to restructure the physical properties of our brains, creating new neural pathways and the development of important new cognitive functions. This process "rearranged the very organization of our brain, which in turn expanded the ways we were able to think, which altered the intellectual evolution of our species" (3; Kandel, Schwartz, Jessell, Siegelbaum, and Hudspeth). A great deal is at stake, therefore, as we seek to deepen our understanding of the vital role that reading plays in teaching and learning in the writing classroom.

We also seek in this book to affirm the value of reading for pleasure and the importance of developing pedagogies and classroom practices that communicate to students the many aesthetic and affective joys to be found in reading. This is an approach to reading perhaps best captured by the title of one of Louise Rosenblatt's most widely known essays: "What Facts Does This Poem Teach You?" We also believe there is great value in Marcel Proust's understanding of reading as a "pure form of friendship" (34) and, to borrow Maryanne Wolf's memorable phrase about Proust's understanding of reading, as a kind of "intellectual 'sanctuary,' where human beings have access to thousands of different realities they might never encounter or understand otherwise" (6). Wolf has suggested that this "expanding sense of 'other' changes who we are" and "what we imagine we can be" (8). Following Proust, we believe that "it is through the contact with other minds which constitutes reading that our minds are 'fashioned'" (36–37). We also embrace one of Nancie Atwell's key formulations:

> For students of every ability and background, it's the simple, miraculous act of reading a good book that turns them into readers, because even for the least experienced, most reluctant reader, it's the one good book that changes everything. The job of adults who care about reading is to move heaven and earth to put that book into a child's [or high school student's or college student's] hands. (27–28)

Overall, our primary goal with this book, following Atwell, is ambitious: to help nurture skilled, passionate, habitual, critical, joyful, lifelong readers across all grade levels and especially across institutional boundaries in US high schools and colleges.

Part I of this book attempts to clearly define the many challenges we have before us as we seek to integrate reading into the writing classroom and as we develop a theory of reading that honors it as a richly complex social, cognitive, and affective human activity. We begin with a chapter by David A. Jolliffe, which updates his important review essay about reading that was published in 2007 in *College Composition and Communication*. We follow this with a chapter by Sam Morris, a former high school English teacher, who takes us into his high school classroom as he works to teach reading and writing in progressive ways while also struggling to satisfy state and local curricular requirements. Kathleen Blake Yancey, Jacob W. Craig, Matthew Davis, and Michael Spooner follow with an essay about the effects of new technology on reading and writing practices. We conclude this section with Jason Courtmanche, who is director of the Connecticut Writing Project and has been working with high school English teachers for many years. Courtmanche offers a cross-disciplinary perspective on the value of reading from his experience teaching an Honors First-Year Experience course at the University of Connecticut that enrolled primarily non-English majors.

Part II features three essays written by college students about their development as writers. As it turns out, their testimony documents the integral role that reading has played in this development. Significantly, standardized tests such as the SAT, ACT, and K–12 state-mandated proficiency tests played no role whatsoever in nurturing their interest in reading and writing. It appears that standardized tests can, perhaps, certify a certain narrow kind of reading and writing proficiency (Klausman et al.; Hillocks; Sacks), but they cannot nurture or create this kind of proficiency—or a deep love for reading and writing. Instead, our student contributors point to a whole range of experiences inside and outside of the classroom that have kindled and sustained their passion for reading and writing.

We can learn much from these experiences that can inform the activities and pedagogies we privilege in our classroom as we seek to nurture this kind of interest and passion. These activities focus on choice, freedom, autonomy, deep learning, creativity, writing across disciplines, and pedagogical strategies that introduce students to disciplinary knowledge. Overall, these student essays provide a fascinating glimpse into the teaching and learning process in action in the lives of real students. The essays also highlight the many different ways the process of literacy acquisition can unfold as students work their way to becoming strong readers, writers, and thinkers. They also help us see how pedagogical choices, theories of reading and writing, and classroom practices affect real students in real classrooms right now.

Each of our student contributors worked with a sponsor and mentor, and each mentor was given the opportunity to reflect on this collaboration in a brief commentary that follows their student's work.

Because we know that classroom English teachers grades 6–13 will be the primary agents helping students become college-ready readers and writers, Part III of our book focuses on the practical and the pragmatic. This supersized section of our book offers teachers a rich variety of pragmatic approaches to teaching deep reading in writing courses that can be put immediately to use in the classroom. These chapters deal with the widest possible variety of approaches to teaching reading in the writing classroom. We begin with Patrick's essay, which seeks to theorize an approach to teaching writing based on "deep reading"—a process of inquiry built around "challenging questions" and "troublesome knowledge" as well as caution, humility, and open-mindedness. Kelly Cecchini, a high school English teacher, then reports on an innovative collaboration between a high school English department and a local college English department. This chapter reports on precisely the kind of collaboration and bridge building across institutional boundaries that we hope to foster with this book.

We then move on to a group of chapters that explores a variety of approaches to teaching deep reading. Ellen C. Carillo discusses classroom strategies related to "mindful reading" that will help students read and write across disciplines. Katie Hern examines the important role that reading and "big ideas" must play in the basic writing classroom. Muriel Harris offers advice to writing teachers about teaching reading based on more than thirty years of experience as a writing center tutor, director, and advocate. Howard Tinberg explores the many challenges of teaching reading in a first-year composition class in a community college setting. Sheridan Blau proposes that a return to the study of literary texts in first-year writing classes can offer the richest possible opportunities for strengthening the capacity of college students to read deeply. Rebecca S. Nowacek and Heather G. James draw on the practices of expert readers in the STEM disciplines, and through this framework find that they understand student struggles in writing classes in new ways. Patricia Donahue and Mariolina Rizzi Salvatori conclude this section with a chapter that theorizes an approach to teaching reading and writing—"unruly reading"—that bypasses the restrictions of certain established reading patterns to uncover "zones of possibility, provoking, even encouraging, the element of discovery."

Part IV concludes the book with two short letters written for students, one by Patrick and the other by Alfredo Celedón Luján. It is our hope that these two letters, which seek to translate disciplinary knowledge about reading and writing for student readers, will help classroom instructors initiate productive conversations with *their* students about reading and writing.

We have had the great honor of developing this book in consultation with Alice Horning, Deborah-Lee Gollnitz, and Cynthia Haller, who are also editing a volume of scholarly essays about reading that focuses on reading across the disciplines. The title of their book is *What Is College Reading?* (ATD Books and the WAC Clearinghouse). We have developed these two books collaboratively, and we offer them to readers as companion volumes. Although we have pursued different editorial objectives, both collections arose from a similar impulse—the need to address the importance of reading in the teaching of writing. Alice has kindly provided an afterword for this collection, which includes a brief preview of *What Is College Reading?* and the book's table of contents.

We dedicate this book to Louise Rosenblatt, one of our heroes. Like Rosenblatt, we believe that a great deal is at stake when students read—for individual development and growth, for the health of our communities, and for the strength of our democracy. Like Rosenblatt, we believe that

> democracy is not simply a structure of political institutions but, as Dewey said, "a way of life." Democracy implies a society of people who, no matter how much they differ from one another, recognize their common interests, their common goals, and their dependence on mutually honored freedoms and responsibilities. For this they need the ability to imagine the human consequences of political and economic alternatives and to think rationally about emotionally charged issues. Such strengths should be fostered by all the agencies that shape the individual, but the educational system, through all its disciplines, has a crucial role. (*Literature* xv)

Rosenblatt's belief that "the teaching of literature could especially contribute to such democratic education" (*Literature* xv) was the inspiration for her landmark book on reading, *Literature as Exploration*. A similar impulse to communicate the vital importance of reading has been the source of our inspiration as well.

We warmly welcome readers to this collection and its celebration of literacy, intellectual generosity, and classrooms alive with deep reading and deep learning.

Works Cited

Atwell, Nancie. *The Reading Zone: How to Help Kids Become Skilled, Passionate, Habitual, Critical Readers*. New York: Scholastic, 2007. Print.

Bean, John C. *Engaging Ideas: The Professor's Guide to Integrating Writing, Critical Thinking, and Active Learning in the Classroom*. 2nd ed. San Francisco: Jossey-Bass, 2011. Print.

Blau, Sheridan. "Performative Literacy: The Habits of Mind of Highly Literate Readers." *Voices from the Middle* 10.3 (2003): 18–22. Print.

Bourdieu, Pierre, and Jean-Claude Passeron. *Reproduction in Education, Society and Culture*. 2nd ed. Trans. Richard Nice. Thousand Oaks: Sage, 2000. Print.

Bunn, Michael. "Motivation and Connection: Teaching Reading (and Writing) in the Composition Classroom." *College Composition and Communication*. 64.3 (2013): 496–516. Print.

Carillo, Ellen C. "Reimagining the Role of the Reader in the Common Core State Standards." *English Journal* 105.3 (2016): 29–35. Print.

———. *Securing a Place for Reading in Composition: The Importance of Teaching for Transfer*. Logan: Utah State UP, 2015. Print.

Costa, Arthur L., and Bena Kallick, eds. *Learning and Leading with Habits of Mind*. Alexandria: Association for Supervision and Curriculum Development, 2008. Print.

Council of Writing Program Administrators, National Council of Teachers of English, and the National Writing Project. "Framework for Success in Postsecondary Writing." *Council of Writing Program Administrators*. 2011. Web. 30 Dec. 2016.

Dole, Janice A., Gerald G. Duffy, Laura R. Roehler, and P. David Pearson. "Moving from the Old to the New: Research on Reading Comprehension Instruction." *Review of Educational Research* 61.2 (1991): 239–64. Print.

Facione, Peter. "Critical Thinking: A Statement of Expert Consensus for Purposes of Educational Assessment and Instruction." *The Delphi Report Executive Summary: Research Findings and Recommendations Prepared for the Committee on Pre-College Philosophy of the American Philosophical Association.* ERIC Document Reproduction Service, No. ED315423. 1990. Print.

Gallagher, Kelly. *Readicide: How Schools Are Killing Reading and What You Can Do about It.* Portland: Stenhouse, 2009. Print.

Gioia, Dana. "Preface." *To Read or Not to Read: A Question of National Consequence.* Research Division Report 47. Washington: National Endowment for the Arts. Nov. 2007. 5–6. Web. 15 Jan. 2017.

Helmers, Marguerite. *Intertexts: Reading Pedagogy in College Writing Classrooms.* New York: Routledge, 2003. Print.

Hillocks, George. *The Testing Trap: How State Writing Assessments Control Learning.* New York: Teachers College P, 2002. Print.

Horning, Alice, and Elizabeth W. Kraemer. *Reconnecting Reading and Writing.* Anderson: Parlor P, 2013. Print.

Horning, Alice, and Deborah-Lee Gollnitz. "What Is College Reading? A High School-College Dialogue." *Reader* 67 (2014): 43–72. Print.

Jolliffe, David A. "Review Essay: Learning to Read as Continuing Education." *College Composition and Communication* 58.3 (2007): 470–94. Print.

Jolliffe, David A., and Allison Harl. "Texts of Our Institutional Lives: Studying the 'Reading Transition' from High School to College: What Are Our Students Reading and Why?" *College English* 70.6 (2008): 599–607. Print.

Kandel, Eric R., James H. Schwartz, Thomas M. Jessell, Steven A. Siegelbaum, and A. J. Hudspeth. *Principles of Neural Science.* 5th ed. New York: McGraw-Hill, 2012. Print.

Keller, Daniel. *Chasing Literacy: Reading and Writing in an Age of Acceleration.* Logan: Utah State UP, 2014. Print.

Klausman, Jeffrey, Christie Toth, Wendy Swyt, Brett Griffiths, Patrick Sullivan, Anthony Warnke, Amy L. Williams, Joanne Giordano, and Leslie Roberts. "TYCA White Paper on Placement Reform." *Teaching English in the Two-Year College* 44.2 (2016): 135–57. Print.

Miller, Donalyn. *The Book Whisperer: Awakening the Inner Reader in Every Child*. San Francisco: Jossey-Bass, 2009. Print.

National Commission on Writing in America's Schools and Colleges. *The Neglected "R" : The Need for a Writing Revolution*. Princeton: College Board, 2003. Web. 24 Aug. 2010.

National Endowment for the Arts. *Reading at Risk*. Research Division Report 46. Washington: National Endowment for the Arts, 2004. Print.

———. *To Read or Not to Read: A Question of National Consequence*. Research Division Report 47. Washington: National Endowment for the Arts. Nov. 2007. Print.

Nation's Report Card. "Nine Subjects. Three Grades. One Report Card." *National Assessment of Educational Progress,* 2016. Web. 2 Jan. 2017.

Newkirk, Thomas. *The Art of Slow Reading*. Portsmouth: Heinemann, 2012. Print.

Proust. Marcel. "On Reading." *On Reading*. Ed. and trans. Damion Searls. London: Hesperus, 2011. 3–43. Print.

Rosenblatt, Louise. *Literature as Exploration*. 5th ed. New York: MLA, 1995. Print.

———. *The Reader, the Text, and the Poem: The Transactional Theory of the Literary Work*. Carbondale: Southern Illinois UP, 1978. Print.

———. "What Facts Does This Poem Teach You?" *Language Arts* 57.4 (1980): 386–94. Print.

Sacks, Peter. *Standardized Minds: The High Price of America's Testing Culture and What We Can Do about It*. Cambridge: Perseus, 1999. Print.

Salvatori, Mariolina, and Patricia Donahue. "Guest Editors' Introduction: Guest Editing as a Form of Disciplinary Probing." *Pedagogy* 16.1 (2016): 1–8. Print.

———. "What Is College English? Stories about Reading: Appearance, Disappearance, Morphing, and Revival." *College English* 75.2 (2012): 199–217. Print.

Smith, Cheryl Hogue. "Interrogating Texts: From Deferent to Efferent and Aesthetic Reading Practices." *Journal of Basic Writing* 31.1 (2012): 59–79. Print.

Smith, Michael W., and Jeffery D. Wilhelm. *"Reading Don't Fix No Chevys": Literacy in the Lives of Young Men.* Portsmouth: Heinemann, 2002. Print.

Sullivan, Patrick. *A New Writing Classroom: Listening, Motivation, and Habits of Mind.* Logan: Utah State UP, 2014. Print.

———. "The UnEssay: Making Room for Creativity in the Composition Classroom." *College Composition and Communication* 67.1 (2015): 6–34. Print.

Sullivan, Patrick, and Howard Tinberg, eds. *What Is "College-Level" Writing?* Urbana: NCTE, 2006. Print.

Sullivan, Patrick, Howard Tinberg, and Sheridan Blau, eds. *What Is "College-Level" Writing? Volume 2: Assignments, Readings, and Student Writing Sample*s. Urbana: NCTE, 2010. Print.

Wardle, Elizabeth. "Creative Repurposing for Expansive Learning: Considering 'Problem-Exploring' and 'Answer-Getting' Dispositions in Individuals and Fields." *Composition Forum* 26 (2012). Web. 24 August 2015.

Wolf, Maryanne. *Proust and the Squid: The Story and Science of the Reading Brain.* New York: Harper, 2008. Print.

I

THE NATURE OF THE PROBLEM

"Learning to Read as Continuing Education" Revisited: An Active Decade, but Much Remains to Be Done

David A. Jolliffe
University of Arkansas

A decade ago, *College Composition and Communication* published my review essay "Learning to Read as Continuing Education." Shortly after its publication, my former student and, at that time, director of composition at the University of Wyoming, Mary P. Sheridan, accused me of being a bit sneaky. She recognized my gambit right away: I wasn't merely reviewing four important books, all of which touched on issues related to the teaching of reading in high schools and colleges and to fostering a better "reading transition" from the former to the latter. Under the guise of a book review, I was assaying what I perceived to be a substantial problem in composition studies, which I now refer to simply as "the reading problem": the failure of the field in general to interrogate the roles that reading plays in high school and college writing and to recognize the paucity of theories, methods, and materials teachers have in both settings to develop more informed perspectives about themselves as teachers of reading. As I noted in the review essay, "the topic of reading lies outside the critical discourse of composition studies," so instructors do "not have access to ample resources to help them think about a model of active constructive reading in their courses or about strategies for putting that model into play" (478). Given that lacuna, I wanted in 2007 to jumpstart a conversation about reading in composition studies, to contribute to the incipient impulse at that moment in the profession to bring reading to the fore. I'm delighted to report that Mary almost immediately understood my call for more extensive discussions of the reading problem and invited me to come to Laramie to talk about the issue with her and her colleagues.

In the ten years since the publication of "Learning to Read as Continuing Education," the conversation has become slightly more vigorous, if not necessarily more focused, and I am honored that the editors of this volume have invited me to reflect on how the terrain of the reading problem has changed in the ensuing decade. In what follows, I describe the contributions of some new participants in the discourse—important new documents and new scholarship—and I conclude by raising questions I hope the profession will continue to address in the coming years. Because, ideally, students' acquisition of college-level reading abilities exists on a continuum, I begin with the new action in the K–12 scene and then move to new developments at the postsecondary level.

The Reading Problem Confronted, K–12

There can be no doubt that, for K–12 educators, a seismic shift in the reading problem's center of gravity came about with the famous—some would say infamous—Common Core State Standards (CCSS). The standards, a joint venture of the National Governors Association, the Council of Chief State School Officers, and Achieve, a not-for-profit education-reform organization, emerged very quickly between early 2008, when the three sponsoring organizations released a report calling for the development of a "common core of internationally benchmarked standards" (*Common Core State Standards Initiative*), and late 2009, when the first draft of the actual standards was released.

The standards are cast as instructional guideposts for teaching English language arts and mathematics in grades kindergarten through 12, and the English standards hold the potential to significantly affect both the ways students are taught to read in elementary and high school and the reading habits, practices, and states of mind they bring to college. The jury is still out on the question of "significantly affect" for good or ill.

The English language arts standards are subdivided into categories of reading, writing, speaking and listening, and language, and there are four sub-subdivisions for reading: "reading-literature," "reading-informational texts," "reading-foundational skills," and "literacy in science, social studies, and technical fields." (Some teachers initially objected to the label "informational texts," wondering whether they would be required to teach students to read, say, technical manuals.) The sub-subdivisions are then sub-sub-subdivided into grade-level bands—for reading literature and reading informational texts, for example, there are standards for each grade from kindergarten through grade 8 and then standards for grades 9–10 and 11–12. The CCSS document clarifies that the "reading-foundational skills" standards are relevant only in grades kindergarten through 5, and the literacy in the content areas standards pertain only to grades 6 through 12.

Each of the sub-sub-subdivided sets derives from the same ten "anchor standards" for reading:

◆ Anchor standard 1: Read closely to determine what the text says explicitly and to make logical inferences from it; cite specific textual evidence when writing or speaking to support conclusions drawn from the text.

◆ Anchor standard 2: Determine central ideas or themes of a text and analyze their development; summarize the key supporting details and ideas.

◆ Anchor standard 3: Analyze how and why individuals, events, or ideas develop and interact over the course of a text.

◆ Anchor standard 4: Interpret words and phrases as they are used in a text, including determining technical, connotative, and figurative meanings, and analyze how specific word choices shape meaning or tone.

◆ Anchor standard 5: Analyze the structure of texts, including how specific sentences, paragraphs, and larger portions of the text (e.g., a section, chapter, scene, or stanza) relate to each other and the whole.

◆ Anchor standard 6: Assess how point of view or purpose shapes the content and style of a text.

- ◆ Anchor standard 7: Integrate and evaluate content presented in diverse media and formats, including visually and quantitatively, as well as in words.

- ◆ Anchor standard 8: Delineate and evaluate the argument and specific claims in a text, including the validity of the reasoning as well as the relevance and sufficiency of the evidence.

- ◆ Anchor standard 9: Analyze how two or more texts address similar themes or topics in order to build knowledge or to compare the approaches the authors take.

- ◆ Anchor standard 10: Read and comprehend complex literary and informational texts independently and proficiently.

At first blush, these standards might seem relatively unobjectionable. They essentially call on students to learn old-fashioned, New Critical close reading—what's the main idea of a text and how do the parts of the text work to flesh out, to instantiate, this main idea?—and a few other things: how to read "diverse media and formats" and how to make what Ellin Keene and Susan Zimmerman call "text-to-text connections" (55).

There are a couple of odd blemishes in the reading standards. The collocation of "point of view" and "purpose" in standard 6 has always struck me as odd, as an apples-and-oranges juxtaposition. And I have often wondered why standard 8, on delineating and evaluating the argument, is so far down the line since it seems so directly related to standard 2, determining the central ideas. (Plus, I find myself completely befuddled by the way anchor standard 8 appears in the standards for reading literature: "Does not apply to literature" is what it says. How, I wonder, am I going to teach act 3, scene 2, of *Julius Caesar* ["Friends, Romans, countrymen, lend me your ears . . . "] without delineating and evaluating the argument and the specific claims in the text?) Now in my forty-first year in the classroom, having taught everything from tenth grade through graduate school, on the one hand I see these standards as a potentially salutary assurance that students whose teaching has been guided by them will at least be able to encounter a text on my syllabus, take a stab at constructing a statement of what they think it means (and, yes, the opinions of sundry literary theorists be damned, I do think texts actually *mean* something), and justify their interpretation by referring to specific elements of the text.

On the other hand, I share many of the qualms my colleagues have expressed about reading as outlined in the Common Core State Standards. The problems can be represented in three categories, two of which are not immediately evident in the anchor standards. First, given the inclusion of a set of standards for reading informational texts, high school English teachers have been concerned that the important primary texts of fiction, poetry, and drama they are prepared to teach—and perhaps have taught for years on end—will be elbowed out of the curriculum by nonfiction texts, especially those that might deserve the ungainly name of "informational texts." These teachers' fears have been exacerbated by the allusion in the standards document to the "distribution of literary and informational passages by grade in the 2009 National Assessment of Educational Progress reading framework" (*Common Core State Standards Initiative*). That framework proposed that the entire reading "menu" for fourth graders should be 50 percent literature and 50 percent informational texts; for eighth graders, 45 percent literature and 55 percent informational texts; and for twelfth graders, 30 percent literature and 70 percent informational texts. The standards document attempts to assuage these fears of the death of imaginative literature by arguing that the teaching of reading should not be the sole responsibility of English instructors and that literacy instruction should be spread across the curriculum—hence the inclusion of reading standards for literacy in science, social studies, and technical subjects. If a typical high school senior is expected to read 30 percent literary and 70 percent informational texts, so the thinking goes, the bulk of the 70 percent will be shouldered in the non-English courses. Most high school English teachers I know, however, understand the pedagogical realpolitik of their schools and concede that they are usually the only faculty members who in practice attend to the teaching of reading. If any administrator in their district believes in those NAEP percentages, these teachers surmise, they're going to be teaching lots less literature and lots more "information." Seasoned English teachers have nightmares about being required to explicate refrigerator repair manuals.

Second, teachers wonder whether the CCSS provide a de facto reading list—one, moreover, they don't like much. The hotly disputed Appendix B of the standards document offers 183 pages of lists of "exemplar texts": fiction, poetry, drama, and informational texts for English language arts in all the grade levels and for history and social studies, science, and technical subjects in grades 9 through 12. To be sure, the standards document clarifies that these are not recommended reading lists, but instead simply collections of texts that are appropriate in "complexity, quality, and range of date, authorship, and subject matter" (*Common Core State Standards Initiative*) for the grade levels. But Appendix B has agitated teachers for a handful of legitimate reasons. First, even the literary selections are often texts with which teachers are not familiar and which seem to be beyond the comprehension level of their students. Few teachers of English language arts in grades 9–10, for example, could envision themselves teaching (and their students understanding) Turgenev's *Fathers and Sons* or Ionesco's *Rhinoceros*. Second, the informational texts selected for English language arts and for the other content area courses seem even odder choices than the literary texts. The informational texts for English include a number of mainstream American history and government works—for grades 9 and 10, for example, Patrick Henry's "Give me liberty or give me death" speech, Washington's Farewell Address, and Lincoln's Gettysburg Address and his Second Inaugural—but also some quirky suggestions like Margaret Chase Smith's "Remarks to the Senate in Support of a Declaration of Conscience." And one has to wonder if any teacher in the content areas would actually assign some of the informational texts recommended for them: at grades 9–10, for example, Mark Kurlansky's *Cod: A Biography of the Fish That Changed the World* for history and social studies and the Environmental Protection Agency pamphlet "Recommended Levels of Insulation" for science. Third, almost predictably, some high school administrators apparently do view Appendix B as comprising recommended reading lists and actually require teachers to add selections from the appendix to their courses.

Finally, the most problematic aspect of the Common Core reading standards is adumbrated in the anchor standards, but it's made explicit in the sample "performance tasks" that accompany the lists of exemplar texts in Appendix B. Simply put, the reading standards have heralded a solitary—some would say a manic— focus on close reading, on what the professional development mavens have come to call "text-based responses." These tasks operate on the assumption that texts have stable, determinate "meanings"; that the component parts of a text, also stable and determinate, combine to forge these meanings; and that readers' responses to the texts play no vital part in their comprehension and evaluation. Critics of this "text-based" focus call attention to the operative verbs in the reading anchor standards: *cite, determine, summarize, analyze, interpret, assess, integrate, evaluate, delineate.* Notably absent are verbs that might signal what many teachers believe to be appropriate starting points for reading comprehension: *respond, react, connect.* Personal response—and some would add personal engagement—is verboten.

Even a cursory examination of the sample performance tasks reveals the standards' "just-the-texts, ma'am" approach. Consider this task for a grade 9 or 10 English language arts course: "Students analyze how the Japanese filmmaker Akira Kurosawa in his film *Throne of Blood* draws on and transforms Shakespeare's play *Macbeth* in order to develop a similar plot set in feudal Japan." Similarly, look at this sample task for a grade 9 or 10 science class: "Students cite specific textual evidence from Annie J. Cannon's 'Classifying the Stars' to support their analyses of the scientific importance of the discovery that light is composed of many colors. Students include in their analyses precise details from the text (such as Cannon's repeated use of the image of the rainbow) to buttress their explanation" (*Common Core State Standards Initiative*). Nowhere in the Kurosawa-*Macbeth* question are the student readers encouraged to position themselves in relation to the central themes of both the film and the play: ambition, regicide, marital relations. Nowhere in the Cannon question are the student writers invited to consider why the "repeated use of the image of the rainbow" might actually be engaging to Cannon's audience.

Scholars and teachers of reading at the college level decry the mindsets, habits, and practices that students taught under the CCSS might bring to higher education. Taking a pragmatist's perspective, Hephzibah Roskelly offers this indictment:

Reading, it's implied, consists of knowing "what a text says explicitly." Experience as a part of reading is absent in this construction of values. Absent as well is recognition of how one makes meaning from texts. If a reader reads the text *explicitly*, the assumption is, she should have no difficulty reading. What's left unsaid in this set of reading desiderata is significant for teachers. How do readers attain these skills? How do they come to interpret words and phrases? How do they recognize genres? There is no mention of the process of reading, much less the experiences readers bring with them or the role of experience in reading at all. Without that help or suggestion, many teachers are left to understand that "what they think, what they feel" doesn't matter. Or shouldn't. (123)

Sean Connors and Ryan Rish see the CCSS focus as a call to an elitism that plagued English studies for much of its history:

> [The] CCSS's myopic emphasis on close reading . . . constitutes a social justice issue in so far as this emphasis validates and sanctions certain texts, types of readers, and sets of literacy practices while marginalizing others. Through the CCSS keyhole, texts are considered for their complexity divorced from social contexts in which they were written (and are read), students are considered through a deficit lens based on the extent to which their knowledge of text conventions assists in determining the meaning of the text, and students' literacy practices are considered invalid and deficient if they do not map neatly on to school-sanctioned ways of reading and determining meaning from texts. (96)

In short, educators who worry about the completely depersonalized and decontextualized definition of reading tacitly developed in the CCSS ask the simple question, "Is this the way we want to teach reading?"

The future of the Common Core movement is uncertain. As I write, the movement is taking flak from both sides of the political spectrum: right-leaning politicos and educators influenced by them are claiming that it represents a federal government takeover and therefore an abrogation of states' right, while more progressive thinkers are calling into question the developmental appropriateness of the standards, the excessive amount of testing time they will entail, and the labyrinthine bureaucracy that surrounds the entire process—as well as their elimination of personal, experiential response as an entrée to reading. Also as I write, several states have withdrawn their support for, and participation in, the standards movement and are in the process of rewriting their own state standards—many of which resemble the CCSS, only with the state's label on them. It will bear close watching over the next several years to see if the states generate guidelines for the teaching of reading that will result in students' coming to college prepared to engage with texts personally and intellectually and to read them closely and critically.

In Colleges and Universities: A Few, but Important, Movements

I would be hard-pressed to assert that the postsecondary concern about the reading problem has really caught fire. But even though the college-level interest in reading has not been as visible as the one prompted by the CCSS at the K–12 level, there has been a slight uptick in activity among college and university scholars and teachers in the past decade. Specifically, the Council of Writing Program Administrators (CWPA) has revised its "Outcomes Statement for First-Year Composition" in a way that reflects a sharper emphasis on reading, and a small but energetic group of researchers has honed in on the problem.

I think it's no exaggeration to say that the CWPA has become an increasingly important organization—I might even hazard to call it the intellectual and professional center of gravity—in the teaching, administration, and scholarship of first-year college and university writing. While some of the early work of the CWPA— for example, the Wyoming Resolution of 1988 that advocated for better working conditions for college composition teachers and the Portland Resolution of 1992 that aimed to clarify the duties and status of directors of college composition programs—was more political than pedagogical, the salient influence of the CWPA really coalesced, I maintain, with the publication in 1999 of the original "WPA Outcomes Statement for First-Year Composition." The Outcomes Statement represented a clear opportunity for the CWPA to offer a unified vision of what college composition courses should be and do—and to recommend the roles that reading should play in them.

Reading and the reading problem barely made it on the radar screen in the 1999 document: Readers are portrayed as people with "expectations" that writers must understand and meet. Reading is something that one "uses," along with writing, "for inquiry, learning, thinking, and communicating." Students are expected to learn about the "interactions among critical thinking, critical reading, and writing" (61–62). One would scarcely know from this document that a great majority of the papers students write in first-year composition courses are based on the readings contained in the myriad textbooks, anthologies, and whole texts taught in these courses.

In the 2014 revised "WPA Outcomes Statement for First-Year Composition (3.0)," reading rises to a somewhat more prominent role. Readers are still cast solely as people with "expectations" in their fields. (For more about that designation, see discussion below.) As part of their acquisition of "rhetorical knowledge," students should "[g]ain experience reading and composing in several genres to understand how genre conventions shape and are shaped by readers' and writers' practices and purposes." To develop abilities with "critical thinking, reading, and composing," students should "[u]se composing and reading for inquiry, learning, critical thinking, and communicating in various rhetorical contexts." But more vitally—and this is a new emphasis in the revised statement—students should "[r]ead a diverse range of texts, attending especially to relationships between assertion and evidence, to patterns of organization, to the interplay between verbal and nonverbal elements, and to how these features function for different audiences and situations." To foster these abilities, "faculty in all programs and departments" can help their students learn "[s]trategies for reading a range of texts in their fields." Perhaps motivated by composition studies' strong interest in genre as a rhetorical construct that shapes the discursive work of different fields (see, for example, the work of Carolyn Miller, John Swales, David Russell, Amy Devitt, and Anis Bawarshi) and possibly spurred by the slight rise in scholarship about the reading problem in college composition, the authors of the new Outcomes Statement aim not only to associate reading with critical thinking but also to advocate for a productive version of close reading, both in composition and in courses across the curriculum. It remains to be seen whether the revised Outcomes Statement will lead to an even stronger emphasis on addressing the reading problem in first-year composition.

The aforementioned new scholarship on reading in college writing attempts to flesh out just such an emphasis, but the researchers' foci have tended more toward the applied and pedagogical than toward the conceptual and theoretical. One scholar who has taken up the challenge of definition is Alice Horning. In a range of articles, Horning has developed a theory of "expert reading" that she believes should sit at the center of postsecondary pedagogy. As she writes in a 2011 article, for example,

> Expert readers are meta-readers who have awarenesses and skills enabling them to read texts efficiently and effectively. The awarenesses of experts include meta-textual awareness of organization and structure, meta-contextual awareness of how the text fits into its discipline or area, and meta-linguistic awareness of the linguistic characteristics of the text such as specialized vocabulary. The skills of expert meta-readers include analysis of main ideas, details and other aspects of the substance of the points presented, synthesis of points in a single text or multiple texts on the same point and issue, evaluation of authority, accuracy, currency, relevance and bias, and application or creation for the readers' own purposes. ("Where to Put the Manicules" n.p.)

In a later work, Horning amplified that characterization with her definition of *"academic critical literacy"*: "the psycholinguistic processes of getting meaning from and into print and/or sound, images, and movement, on a page or screen, used for the purposes of analysis, synthesis, evaluation, and application" (*Reading* 14). Perhaps even Horning herself would concede that college writing teachers might need help translating these definitions into curricula and pedagogical practices.

Fortunately, the new scholarship that specifically considers issues of assigning and explicitly teaching reading in college composition, while slight in quantity, is rich in concept and content. Linda Adler-Kassner and Heidi Estrem, for example, investigate "how 'directions' for reading attempt to shape the roles that students play in reading and what ideological implications accompany those attempts" (40). Adler-Kassner and Estrem identify three such roles for reading that assignments, usually tacitly, convey:

> Content-based reading . . . asks students to summarize and interpret, to consider connections between ideas, and to use reading to develop ideas. Process-based reading focuses on the work of the writer/researcher, scrutinizing the text to look at decisions made by the writer in the process of textual production as a possible model for students' own writing/research work. Structure-based reading asks students to focus on the conventions reflected in and used to shape content; the attempt is on developing genre awareness so that student writers can make conscious decisions about how to use different genres and conventions, and can make conscious choices about how, when, or whether to use them. (40–41)

Adler-Kassner and Estrem consider these purposes through the lenses of

> three conceptions of language running through 19th and 20th century linguistics outlined by William Hanks in his book, *Language and Communicative Practices*: "irreducibility," or the idea that language is a self-contained structure that "cannot be explained by appeals to nonlinguistic behavior" or "to emotion, desire, psychology, rationality, strategy, (or) social structure"; "relationality," which holds that "language and meaning are grounded in specific circumstance"; and "practice-based," which "acknowledges that language is a system that contains and generates meaning, while at the same time users employ that system based upon their understandings of the contexts where it is used." (40–42)

All three reading roles can potentially reflect each of these conceptions. Adler-Kassner and Estrem conclude: "Articulating the kinds of reading that are enacted in classrooms and the roles that readers are expected to perform within them can open important conversations that enable instructors (and/or programs) to more productively approach reading. At the most basic level, it can help instructors develop their pedagogies for reading in first-year writing" (44).

I also find great encouragement in the work of two young scholars in the field who urge their colleagues to develop more sophisticated theoretical perspectives on the teaching of reading in college courses. For his dissertation at the University of Michigan, Michael Bunn studied "the extent to which composition instructors theorize and teach reading-writing connections" (496). Bunn argues that "explicitly teaching reading-writing connections may increase student motivation to complete assigned reading" (496). He shows that instructors purport to believe that reading and writing are connected activities but that "this belief doesn't always translate into pedagogy" (502). Bunn urges developing a "pedagogical awareness" wherein students would learn to recognize reading and writing as connected activities. He urges teachers to explain specifically the scaffolding they expect students to use to connect the assigned reading to the writing assignment, and he argues that "[w]e must teach students how to read model texts in ways that will inform the eventual writing they must do," encouraging teachers as well to show students how "to read in ways that help them develop their understanding of writerly strategies and techniques" and "to help them identify genre conventions so that they are better prepared to write in those genres" (512).

Drawing on her dissertation at the University of Pittsburgh, Ellen C. Carillo develops a pedagogical strategy that she labels "mindful reading," which is

> best understood *not* as yet another way of reading, but a *framework* for teaching the range of ways of reading that are currently valued in our field so that students can create knowledge *about* reading and *about* themselves as readers, knowledge that they can bring with them into other courses. I use the term "mindful" to underscore the metacognitive basis of this frame wherein students become *knowledgeable, deliberate,* and *reflective* about *how* they read and the demands that context place on their reading. (3)

One hopes that the work started by Adler-Kassner and Estrem, Bunn, and Carillo will be extended and applied, bringing even greater salience to the reading problem among college composition scholars and teachers.

At the risk of self-promotion, I must mention a special issue of *Reader* that my colleague Christian Goering and I coedited and that came out in fall 2014. Our editors' introduction calls for a "revolution in high school to college reading instruction" similar to the "teach process, not product" paradigm shift that emerged in composition studies in the 1960s and 1970s. The issue contains articles by Alice Horning and Deborah-Lee Golnitz, aiming to define what college reading is, and by Alesha Gayle on digital reading practice as critical literary; an annotated bibliography by J. P. Watts; a review essay by Anna Soter; and the articles critical of the Common Core State Standards, cited earlier, by Hephzibah Roskelly and Sean Connors and Ryan Rish. Perhaps the quirkiest—but we hope useful nonetheless—piece in the issue is an extended "polylogue" about the teaching of reading in college that my coauthors Jennifer Mallette and Eli Goldblatt and I titled "The Longest Conversation about Reading You've Never Heard." Our goal with this article was to try, in a substantial collective, to raise and reflect on a wide range of issues—definitional, conceptual, and political—all related to the reading problem.

To produce this piece, Goldblatt, at that time director of composition at Temple University, and I convened a group of teachers and scholars, all with an informed interest in the teaching of reading at the high school and college levels: Douglas Hartman, at the time a professor of literacy instruction at the University of Connecticut; Deborah Holdstein, at the time the outgoing editor of *College Composition and Communication;* Kathleen McCormick, at the time director of first-year writing at Purchase College of the State University of New York; Hephzibah Roskelly, professor of English at the University of North Carolina at Greensboro; Jennifer Wells, at the time a teacher at Mercy High School in Burlingame, California; and Kathleen Blake Yancey, at the time incoming editor of *College Composition and Communication.* We had invited Howard Tinberg of Bristol Community College to represent the two-year college perspective, but a recent tennis injury prevented his attending the meeting.

To prepare for this confab, Goldblatt and I sent the participants a challenging reading-and-writing assignment from the Temple University first-year composition program and a set of five very open questions:

1. What are your perceptions of attitudes among college faculty about how and what college students read?

2. When you think about the conjunction of reading and writing at the college level, what theoretical work do you see as the most important and productive for thinking through the issues?

3. We've given you one example of a first-year writing assignment that involves engaged reading. If you were to give this to your students, what challenges would it present to them? Please describe how you might go about teaching reading in connection with this assignment.

4. What down-and-dirty pedagogical advice can you give college faculty—either in composition or in the disciplines—about the teaching of reading within the typically packed course syllabus?

5. What issues have we left out? If you can imagine a true confluence of reading and writing research, what would be the most pressing areas to explore? (30)

Digging into the assignment and these questions, participants talked for nearly five hours. And, as we note in the article reporting the meeting, "the discussion did not proceed with 'here's question 1, so now everyone say what he or she has so say about it and then we'll go on to question 2.' Instead, the colloquy was wonderfully associative, digressive, anecdotal" (14). It took the outstanding efforts of Sabine Schmidt and Jenn Mallette, both graduate students at the University of Arkansas at the time, to produce a 65-page, single-spaced transcript of the conversation and then to organize a great deal of the talk under fourteen propositions that the participants' contributions to the conversation fleshed out and responded to:

1. It's extremely difficult, even for scholars in composition, literature, and literacy, to define reading.

2. An array of conditions in contemporary schools and colleges contributes to a kind of "pseudo-reading."

3. Both within and beyond academia, the teaching of reading is perceived to be either elementary or remedial or both.

4. Two institutions—schooling and government—seem to have a strong, often insurmountable influence on the ways reading is

taught and studied by educators and perceived by the general public.

5. As with all academic subjects, the teaching and study of reading are affected by conditions of race, class, and ethnicity.

6. The teaching and study of reading are often impeded by the dichotomizing "silos" of education.

7. Nearly every segment of the educator population in high schools and colleges needs to be prepared to teach reading—and anecdotes and strategies of effective teaching abound.

8. Textbooks generally fail in some way when it comes to the teaching of reading.

9. Teaching reading as inquiry can be valuable but can also generate resistance from both faculty and students.

10. Compositionists at the high school and college levels ought to pursue a more unified view of reading and writing in their teaching and scholarship.

11. Standardized testing and large-scale assessments represent impediments to be overcome.

12. Technology offers a new world—perhaps a "brave new world"—for the teaching and study of reading.

13. Questions about whether, and how, students' development of reading abilities in one course, discipline, or context transfers to another need to be addressed.

14. Establishing reading as a legitimate field of research among high school and college compositionists would be a worthy goal.

As we concluded our polylogue, we noted that "the participants found that we have much work to do among our own colleagues and peers. As a field, composition and rhetoric must come to new terms with those researchers who have focused on reading. . . . Eight of us came together and learned a little more about each other and a lot more about the enormity of the job ahead. We hope this article provokes much further productive conversation" (29). We shall see.

On Revisiting the Reading Problem: Where Will the Next Decade Lead Us?

So what exactly is this additional work to be done? The new attention being paid to the reading problem notwithstanding, I can't help but think that the essence of the problem is still eluding us. Let me conclude by ruminating on two big questions that still fester, at least for me: What exactly are the definitions of readers and reading that our students are developing in high school and bringing to college? What should be the focus of a course (or sequence of courses) in which students in both high school and college continue to develop mastery of reading?

At both the high school and the college levels, we need to think more deeply about what we mean by readers and reading. The past decade has provided us with two potential guides for this inquiry, the Common Core State Standards and the revised CWPA Outcomes Statement, but is either fully sufficient? Clearly, if we look to the CCSS for answers, we get something like this: readers are dispassionate, objective processors of texts, and reading is a simple matter of examining the stable and constant parts of a text in order to generate a stable and constant answer about the text's main ideas and arguments. One hopes that the several efforts aimed at rewriting the CCSS so they are more palatable to critics will generate a richer view of readers, one that acknowledges that reading is a constructive activity that begins with a reader's experience and personal response to a text.

At the postsecondary level, if we take the Outcomes Statement as our guide, readers are people with "expectations." But what does that mean? Are these expectations a static, immutable list of actions a text must accomplish in order for it to be successful with readers? Can writers always know what those expectations are? How? How are these expectations triggered? Do they emerge for each new reading experience a reader has? Do they evolve over time? How are they shaped by experience, by age, by sophistication of thought, by field or discipline? And if we can think about all these things, will we get a clearer idea of what reading is—i.e., the thing that readers do? The potential promise of the Common Core State Standards (and the revised documents that might result from the standards' demise) is that high school students might come to college with different practices, habits, and mindsets about reading than they have done for the past several decades. I think it incumbent on those of us at the postsecondary level to meet these students with a well-thought-out vision of what exactly college readers and reading are.

Second, in our efforts as composition scholars and teachers to understand the roles that reading plays in our projects and courses, must we always take up the reading problem solely in relation to writing? This is now the third piece I've written about reading in the past three years in which someone involved in the project has said, "Be sure to connect what you say about reading to writing." Why? Can't we simply be conscientiously curious about how people read, just for the sake of reading? Or are we so driven by what amounts to an institutional mandate to produce students (and citizens?) who are capable of clear expository and forceful persuasive writing that the only focus we allow ourselves to have vis-à-vis reading is one that contributes to our fulfilling that mandate? Can we study, for example, how and why folks just read—cereal boxes, novels, webpages and blogs, real honest-to-goodness essays with no thesis statements, Bibles and Bible study guides? Is it time to have a course in secondary and postsecondary settings that's just called Reading and isn't seen as remedial? What would such a course look like? What would college and university retention and success rates look like if we had a curriculum that said, essentially, "Here's a course designed to equip you to *read* in college, and then here's a course designed to equip you to *write* about what you read?"

Ideally these questions would be enough to keep the current scholars of the reading problem busy for the next decade and bring new ideas about research, curriculum, and pedagogy to the fore.

Works Cited

Adler-Kassner, Linda, and Heidi Estrem. "Reading Practices in the Writing Classroom." *WPA: Writing Program Administration* 31.1/2 (2007): 35–47. Print.

Bawarshi, Anis S. *Genre and the Invention of the Writer: Reconsidering the Place of Invention in Composition.* Logan: Utah State UP, 2003. Print.

Bunn, Michael. "Motivation and Connection: Teaching Reading (and Writing) in the Composition Classroom." *College Composition and Communication* 64.3 (2013): 496–516. Print.

Carillo, Ellen C. "Creating Mindful Readers in First-Year Composition: A Strategy to Facilitate Transfer." *Pedagogy* 16.1 (2016): 9–22. Print.

Common Core State Standards Initiative. 2015. Web. 1 September 2015.

Connors, Sean P., and Ryan A. Rish. "Problem Solving and Modding: Two Metaphors for Examining the Politics of Close Reading." *Reader* 67.1 (2014): 94–118. Print.

Devitt, Amy. *Writing Genres.* Carbondale: Southern Illinois UP, 2008. Print.

Horning, Alice S. *Reading, Writing, and Digitizing: Understanding Literacy in a Digital Age.* Newcastle-Upon-Tyne: Cambridge Scholars, 2012. Print.

———. "Where to Put the Manicules: A Theory of Expert Reading." *ATD: Across the Disciplines* 8.3 (2011): 1–21. Print.

Jolliffe, David A. "Learning to Read as Continuing Education." *College Composition and Communication* 58.3 (2007): 470–94. Print.

Jolliffe, David A., and Christian Z. Goering. "Guest Editors' Introduction: A Call for Revolution in High School to College Reading Instruction." *Reader* 67.1 (2014): 3–11. Print.

Keene, Ellin Oliver, and Susan Zimmerman. *Mosaic of Thought: Teaching Comprehension in a Reader's Workshop.* Portsmouth: Heinemann, 1997. Print.

Mallette, Jennifer, David A. Jolliffe, and Eli Goldblatt. "The Longest Conversation about Reading You've Never Heard." *Reader* 67.1 (2014): 12–36. Print.

Miller, Carolyn R. "Genre as Social Action." *Quarterly Journal of Speech* 70 (1984): 151–67. Print.

Roskelly, Hephzibah. "Reading Like a Pragmatist." *Reader* 67.1 (2014): 119–35. Print.

Russell, David R. "Rethinking Genre in School and Society: An Activity Theory Analysis." *Written Communication* 14 (1997): 504–54. Print.

Swales, John. *Genre Analysis: English in Academic and Research Settings*. Cambridge: Cambridge UP, 1990. Print.

"WPA Outcomes Statement for First-Year Composition." *WPA: Writing Program Administration* 23.1/2 (1999): 59–70. Print.

"WPA Outcomes Statement for First-Year Composition (3.0)." 17 July 2014. *Council of Writing Program Administrators*. Web. 1 September 2015.

CHAPTER TWO

From Twilight *to* The Satanic Verses: *Unexpected Discoveries about Reading and Writing in the High School Classroom*

SAM MORRIS
University of Arkansas

During the summer after my first year as a high school teacher, I decided to read Stephenie Meyer's novel *Twilight*. My reasoning was that I might be able to capture some sense of the zeitgeist of teenage culture, which could in turn increase my ability to interact with some of my students. In addition to accomplishing that goal, the decision to read *Twilight* eventually led me to clearer ideas of why I became a teacher and how I believe reading and writing should be taught to high school students as well as to lots of questions about why reading is approached the way it is in the secondary classroom.

To back up a bit, I began teaching at a large high school in North Carolina in 2007 after a few years of teaching postsecondary first-year composition, business writing, and public speaking at two schools in Tennessee. At the time, the state of North Carolina mandated that all sophomores take a timed standardized writing assessment in March. This assessment required students to write either a definition or a cause-and-effect essay. Some of the topics of this assessment were the definition of human rights, the effects of technology on everyday life, and the definition of responsibility as it relates to being a high school student. As one might expect, sophomore English classes became largely devoted to the teaching of writing (a particular kind of writing, that is) in preparation for this assessment, often at the expense of teaching reading. After all, students had already been tested on reading comprehension and knowledge of key terms related to reading during their ninth-grade year—so what more was needed?

To complicate matters, the literature component of the sophomore English curriculum in the state of North Carolina at the time was World Literature. For my first year of high school teaching, the school's administration assigned to me all Standard English classes, which meant I had the same three groups of students from August until June. Many of these students were unmotivated, at-risk, non-native-speaking, or had disabilities (documented or undocumented). I was responsible for coaching these students to a passing score on the writing test as well as teaching works by Chinua Achebe, Elie Wiesel, and Leo Tolstoy. These texts often did not exist in the quantity necessary to allow several hundred sophomores to take a copy of the book home to read, which, as my colleagues pointed out, was fine since many of them would either not read the book or simply lose it (and any funds the school recouped for a lost book would *not* go to purchasing a replacement). Therefore, students in Standard English had to read these works of literature in the classroom—often in the less-than-ideal states of sleepiness, hunger, boredom, and excessive noisiness. I wondered how we expected students to read—to comprehend, to engage, to develop a relationship with the text—given these conditions. Alas, books are expensive, and half of the English department's supply budget regularly went to Scantron forms for testing.

The one bright spot for teaching reading that year came by way of a pilot program established by the College Board called SpringBoard, an adapted version of AP English for lower-achieving students. Not only did the College Board design the curriculum, the methods of instruction, and the consumable workbooks for the students in our Standard English classes, but they also purchased a few hundred copies of Chinua Achebe's *Things Fall Apart* so that we could all teach the same text to all of our students at the same time. The school's administration was happy to be part of this program because of the injection of resources and the possibility of uniformity of instruction across all classrooms teaching Standard English.

As a new high school teacher, I was suffering from information overload, so I did not pick up on two major problems with SpringBoard and the teaching of reading in general until much later. The first problem is the method of instruction that the creators of SpringBoard preferred and with which many of my colleagues were comfortable: graphic organizers. Acronym-laden charts such as KWL (What I Know, What I Wonder, What I Learned), RAFT (Role, Audience, Format, Topic), and SOAP-STone (Subject, Occasion, Audience, Purpose, Speaker, Tone) help students break down and categorize different elements of a text. The theory here is that by identifying individual elements of a text and summarizing them in the appropriate boxes of a graphic organizer, even a student who reads below grade level can work through a piece of literature as complex as a Nobel Lecture written by Aleksandr Solzhenitsyn.

While there is nothing wrong with these graphic organizers, they are just that: organizers. They have to organize *something*. That *something* should be a better understanding of reading and the skills inherent in becoming a better reader. Too often, however, graphic organizers are used by teachers as an end rather than as a means. If a student can fill in a graphic organizer, that demonstrates that the student has some grasp of a particular concept or an element of a specific text—but not necessarily a grasp of the text as a whole or reading skills that can be applied to other texts. Moreover, graphic organizers reinforce the basic comprehension and terms that were tested the previous year, which tends to make administration happy, so there is no motivation for most teachers to investigate whether these organizers actually help students become better readers. Even though the College Board provided assessments that attempted to "put it all together" at the end of each unit, my colleagues often chose different assessments that usually took the form of multiple-choice tests (graded by Scantron), essays to further prepare for the state writing test (graded for form rather than content), or art projects.

The art projects in particular underscore the second problem I discovered, which was the essential goal of the selected readings. The College Board contextualized World Literature through a lens of "understanding culture"; some of my colleagues contextualized it through what I eventually termed "world atrocities."

In short, we were not teaching students how to read; we were teaching students how awful people have been to one another throughout history. Teaching students to read and teaching them about history or current events are not mutually exclusive, but I found that they became so when classes spent entire days (or, in one extreme case at another school, entire weeks) creating posters and displays that depicted scenes from *Night* or *Things Fall Apart*. SpringBoard did include art projects as *part* of a more comprehensive assessment, and the goal of these projects was to allow students to demonstrate comprehension of what went on in the text as well as to serve as a creative outlet to express their reactions to the text. Too often, though, teachers latched on to art projects as the *primary* means of assessment because they made grading easier (as opposed to tackling stacks of essays) and created a tangible product for administrators to see. Perhaps these art projects helped students understand the Holocaust or the colonialization of Africa, but had the students become better *readers*? During my first year of teaching at the high school, that question never quite bubbled up to the surface.

The one thing that helped me get through that year was my naiveté in thinking that postsecondary teaching skills would transfer handily to the high school classroom. Thus, when we were not actively engaged in a SpringBoard unit, instead of doing things that most of my department colleagues were doing, I tried classroom activities that might be considered by some to be harebrained, including reading and interpreting song lyrics (even having a student who was considering dropping out share some of his raps with the class), parsing the text of presidential candidate websites, and dramatically re-creating action scenes in the short stories from the textbook. I also began to approach teaching as a performance in order to keep students engaged, which worked for me as a short-term strategy. By the end of the year, I had succeeded on more days than I had not, and the majority of my students had achieved the state's prescribed learning outcomes. I, however, was exhausted.

That summer, I knew I had to improve on what I had done during the previous year, especially when it came to teaching reading. In addition to my Standard English classes, I was going to be teaching one section of Honors English. I assumed, somewhat correctly, that most Honors English students would have better reading skills than their Standard English counterparts and that it would be my responsibility to challenge them to improve those skills. For example, as opposed to Standard English students, who were expected (but never held accountable) to read some slim volume of summer reading that had been provided in bulk to the school system, Honors English students were expected to read *The Count of Monte Cristo* (an abridged version, which I thought defeated the purpose of reading the novel in the first place; I subsequently advocated for its replacement on the summer reading list) as well as another book from a list of approved classics. It was during this same summer of contemplation that I made the decision to read *Twilight*.

A few weeks into my second year of high school teaching, after testing students on their summer reading using a department-approved test with as few non-multiple-choice questions as possible, I found myself being stared at by a classroom full of extremely bright yet unmotivated Honors English students. The topic of the day was characterization; the text was Isak Dinesen's "The Ring." Things were not going well, and I was frustrated with the students. That frustration eventually led me to ask, "How many of you have read *Twilight*?" Immediately several hands shot up. The eyes of most students, even the ones who did not have their hands raised, were instantly more engaged. Something *different* was happening here. For the next five minutes, I taught those students characterization based on my memory of how Meyer consistently describes Bella's clumsiness. During those five minutes, I riffed on how awful I felt the plot of the book was as well as how poorly the book was written. At the end of that five minutes, something great had happened: I had an engaged classroom, and the students had a teacher who, on some basic level, *got* them. We went back to "The Ring" after that; they learned characterization, and I learned what I still consider to be the most valuable lesson about teaching.

Many teachers, including me, believe that students *want* to learn what we have to teach them. We believe that a thirst for knowledge is somehow innate. Where I realized that I differed from some of my peers is my belief that this thirst for knowledge does not necessarily predispose students to sit in a classroom and write what we tell them to write and read what we tell them to read. I am reminded of this fact when I think about my own experiences as a student: in the sixth grade, I got into trouble for reading more than the assigned first chapter of *Bridge to Terabithia* for homework—I had actually finished the entire novel during my other classes before the end of the school day. Truly, I am my own case study in student engagement! Now, as the teacher rather than the student, I realized that my performed persona in the classroom my first year was part of intuiting what was necessary for student engagement, and I also realized that what I taught and how I taught it must be derived from the goal of student engagement as well.

Then a funny thing happened: I began to assign *more* work to my students than most department colleagues assigned to their students. Most of my students did not complain. Some students in other teachers' Honors English classes, though, did begin to complain—they wanted to be in my class. (Professionally, this is not something a teacher actually wants to hear.) I created an independent reading assignment; with parents' permission in place, each student would select a contemporary piece of world literature from a list I made, read it on his or her own, and write a literary analysis essay. Some of the books I chose for the list were *Dreams from My Father* by (newly elected) Barack Obama, *The Shadow of the Wind* by Carlos Ruiz Zafón, and *Night Watch* by Sergei Lukyanenko. I had one particularly precocious student who I suspected would pick the most challenging book on the list, so I included Salman Rushdie's *The Satanic Verses* just to see if I was correct. I was, and she produced an essay that was easily on the level of a *college* sophomore.

After I taught my students how to write a basic literary analysis, the majority produced essays that were beyond anything I had expected from them. Furthermore, when their writing test scores came in from the state, they had better scores as a class than any other sophomore English class in the entire high school. For me, it was a personal triumph; however, anyone can do what I did—it takes just a small step in the students' direction to accomplish it. During that year, I read *Dune* because the student who wrote about Rushdie recommended it to me. She then lent me her copy of *Pride and Prejudice and Zombies* and insisted that I read it as well. Before class, I had begun playing popular music that I liked; both Honors and Standard English students were shocked and elated when I played a song from my iPod that they had on their own iPods. They began to suggest their own favorites for me to listen to, and some of those have in turn become my favorites. These were small acts, but they occurred often enough to put students in a mindset that allowed them to be more willing not just to read and write, but also to actively think about what they were reading and writing.

After that year, teaching became more difficult. Now that I had students engaged, I realized that I had to do something more with that engagement. What did it matter that the Honors English students were willing to read independently and to write a literary analysis? What did it matter that the Standard English students liked me and would not skip my class? What was my responsibility to them? Just because I believed that I had some understanding of the problem and had stumbled onto a few short-term solutions did not mean that I was fully equipped to leverage that student engagement to help them develop better reading skills. One thing I did realize, though, was how anathema the writing test was to actual learning. Going into my third year, I decided that I was going to spend far less time on preparing students for the writing test and more time on reading. In my Honors English classes, I spent a third of the time other teachers did preparing my students for the writing test. When the results came in that year, my instincts were proven correct: we were wasting our time overpreparing our students for that test.

Curiously, I discovered that I really had no idea what to do with the overabundance of time that resulted from not overprepping for the writing test. Yes, I could assign students more reading and writing about reading; I had a plethora of writing tools, activities, and assessments from classes I had taken, from peers, and from my own design. But I was not an expert on teaching reading. I relied primarily on discussion (class-based and group-based) and reflection writing, but those activities all assume on some level that the students have already successfully read and understood the text. As a teacher, I realized that I was making this assumption at both my own and my students' risks.

The other difficulty I was beginning to experience was that the administration was taking notice of the nonconformity of my classroom. Up to the beginning of my fourth year, when I began teaching Senior English, I assumed that the results I was achieving more than justified the deviations from the classroom norm I was incorporating to achieve those results. I then discovered, at least at my high school, that this was an incorrect assumption. During a conference following a classroom observation that year, an assistant principal told me that my way of conducting class (i.e., what I believed was my ease of communication with the students and approach to the material) looked like "you have no plan and are making things up as you go along." Looking back now, though it seemed personal at the time, I think what happened was anything but personal. Administrators and most teachers are obsessed with learning outcomes and test scores, and it is difficult to blame them for this obsession since jobs and funding are determined by those outcomes and scores. I am not sure that many administrators are ready to take risks that might jeopardize those outcomes and scores, even if the result might be better-educated students.

The next year I moved to another high school in another system. At first it looked like I would have more freedom there than I had had at my first school. Soon, however, I discovered I was mistaken. This system had a few vocal parents who had bullied the school board into limiting the amount of nontextbook reading students could do. (It seems one mother in particular had taken offense that her daughter's *nonrequired* AP English class had been assigned Toni Morrison's *The Bluest Eye*.) Assigning an independent reading as I had done before would become a Kafkaesque struggle I did not want to participate in. In this school system, just half an hour from where I had taught previously, I found students who were raised by parents who claimed to want their children challenged but complained when those challenges were assigned. After two years of living in what I liked to call "the town from *Footloose*," I decided, to my chagrin, to leave secondary education.

It turns out that I miss teaching high school students a great deal. I am, however, no longer that naïve teacher; I am aware of the problems that keep secondary teachers from teaching students good reading and writing skills. Unfortunately, I left before I became the expert on teaching reading that I wanted to become. When I talk with people about my experiences, though, I choose not to talk about the small, practical solutions to the problems of secondary education that *might* be possible within a broken system. Instead, I talk about the paradigm shift that has to occur regarding how our culture views education. As long as we allow education to be quantified in terms of graduation rates and test scores that can be used to justify a job title, a department, or a curriculum, this shift cannot occur. We should not be teaching students to value education purely as a means to the end of employment, particularly in a STEM field (though, yes, education should be able to help accomplish that goal). People who devote their lives to education should react strongly and vociferously against the idea that education is somehow a business—or anything other than the pursuit of a quality of life. Sure, there are *simple* solutions to the problems in education today: More money for resources. More respect, trust, and encouragement (and pay) for an increasingly thankless job. Less classroom overcrowding. Less administrative interference. Nonrestrictive curricula. But these are only parts of a bigger solution, a solution that requires us to challenge the idea of what education signifies, both for ourselves and for our society.

Then, and only then, can we begin to make progress toward the second part of the solution: teachers must take it upon themselves to hold one another up to a higher and more rigorous standard. The difficulty of teaching skills, especially ones associated with reading and writing, is often overlooked. Unlike static knowledge, mastery of skills cannot be easily tested. Unfortunately, what I have seen by many teachers (at the behest of administrators) is an attempt to treat reading (and writing) skills as testable knowledge, and that has to change. We have to commit to teaching reading as a unique process that can involve multiple approaches, which will lead to eventual and *real* mastery. Many of those approaches will undoubtedly involve putting a variety of texts in the hands of students; some of those approaches might even involve texts that are noncanonical or controversial. Some of those approaches might be unwieldy and defy the self-contained lesson model, stretching across multiple class periods without a looming summative assessment. Some of those approaches might be loud and chaotic or completely silent, both of which might make the administrator peering through the window of the classroom door nervous. We must recognize that each effective teacher teaches differently from the effective teacher in the next classroom; "best practices" is a dangerous misnomer.

Regardless of what the approach looks like, the teacher must be the arbiter of the process, the approach, and even the texts. For this paradigm shift to be successful, the community of teachers has to be responsible and vigilant in order to keep and uphold the respect this authority necessitates; they must constantly share and work to improve pedagogy. Our current educational system has made committing to a process that is not easily quantified in the short term through testing and statistics a frightening endeavor. However, I believe that the long-term results of a paradigm shift that moves away from testing as the goal of secondary education to one in which learning is the goal would be staggeringly beneficial.

CHAPTER THREE

Device. Display. Read: The Design of Reading and Writing and the Difference Display Makes

KATHLEEN BLAKE YANCEY
Florida State University

JACOB W. CRAIG
College of Charleston

MATTHEW DAVIS
University of Massachusetts Boston

MICHAEL SPOONER
Utah State University Press

It is commonplace for students in first-year composition (FYC) to conduct research, and often—given writing programs' increasing reliance on students' bringing their own devices to class, a situation characterized as BYOD—to read the texts they are researching on a dizzying array of digital devices. Some students research texts in print, but increasingly, they read on desktop or laptop computers of multiple kinds, others on Kindles, others on iPads, and others on phones. Some students conduct the bulk of their research on one of these devices; others use multiple devices simultaneously and/or sequentially to complete their writing task. Interestingly, because of responsive Web design, mobile apps, and ebook reading platforms, the ways in which a single text is displayed on these diverse surfaces vary, which speaks directly to the relationship of form and content. If form and content are unrelated, such difference in "display" may not be a problem. If they are related, it is a problem, but even then, is it a problem that teachers of writing need to consider or address? Here, synthesizing a good deal of the relevant research, we take up this issue, focusing our chapter on three questions:

- ◆ How do texts vary according to display and device, and what difference does such variance make in texts and in the ways we read them?

- ◆ What underlying design issues inform both print and electronic texts, and how do they influence the ways we read?

- ◆ What do these differences and similarities mean in the classroom, and how can we help students as they read in the current multimedia landscape?

How We Read

Perhaps not surprisingly, the field of rhetoric and composition hasn't fully attended to the teaching of reading, instead preferring to focus interest in reading on how better instruction in reading can support writers. Moreover, while there is scholarship focusing on the intersection of reading and writing, it hasn't taken hold, as Patricia Donahue explains:

> When it comes to reading/writing, several people have been working consistently since the 80s. Mariolina [Rizzi Salvatori] and I published an essay in C[ollege] E[nglish] relatively recently discussing the long lineage and referencing the names that deserve attention (including Alice's [Horning] and ours, along with David Joliffe, Donna Qualley, Dave Bartholomae, and numerous others). Yet repeatedly, when the subject of the "reading/ writing connection" comes up (as it does repeatedly), previous work (and even relatively recent scholarship, like Horning's and Salvatori/Donahue's and others) rarely is mentioned. Not only is foundational work ignored, but the thinking about certain issues goes in circles because of the emphasis upon duplicating rather than building. (n.p.)

Just as important, when reading is addressed, typically in three terms—(1) what we read, (2) how we read, and (3) how faculty incorporate reading instruction in a writing classroom—the operative condition for reading tends to be print. In some ways, this isn't surprising: our interest in the role of reading in facilitating writing has a historical basis. As Naomi Baron explains, citing the work of famous writers like Coleridge as well as that of everyday readers, "In the act of reading, many readers become writers. They underline passages, draw arrows, and doodle. They write in margins, revealing their own thoughts or objecting to what authors have said" (*Words Onscreen* 27). In other words, reading practices invite writing practices; both are material practices, and for most of history, those material practices have involved print of some kind.

Moreover, our observations about the material practices of reading haven't caught up with our pedagogy. In "Motivation and Connection: Teaching Reading (and Writing) in the Composition Classroom," for example, Michael Bunn calls on his research to make three suggestions for facilitating student reading, none of which attends to the material practice of reading or writing:

◆ Design reading and writing assignments simultaneously.

◆ Help students by talking in class about the connections between reading and writing assignments.

◆ Assign model texts *and* teach how to read them in ways that address not only content but writing. (512)

Such advice is no doubt helpful, but it doesn't consider the myriad texts principally available in digital form and useful to students conducting research—archives of historical materials, for example, data collected by state and federal governments, and digitally native materials. Put simply, those of us interested in assigning such materials to our students haven't explored how we and our students read them. Of course, the jury is out as to the impact of device-display reading practices on our cognitive processes, an important question we hope cognitive scientists will explore. In the meantime, however, the varieties of texts, devices, and displays have multiplied, and a critical question they raise—how we read such materials as they are displayed on different devices—is the focus of our chapter.

Our first question—how we read digital materials—has received some attention, but again, somewhat intermittently. In 1993, for instance, Stephen Bernhardt's "The Shape of Text to Come: The Texture of Print on Screens" identified "nine dimensions of variation that help map the differences between paper and on-screen text," differences including what he calls nine on-screen tendencies: screen texts are situationally embedded, interactive, functionally mapped, modular, navigable, hierarchically embedded, spacious, graphically rich, and customizable and publishable (151). Several years later, James Sosnoski, in "Hyper-Readers and Their Reading Engines," focused specifically on what he calls hyper-reading and the differences between hyper-reading and reading in print, those differences numbering eight.

- Filtering: The reader has an individual focus/goal based on key words or other selection criteria (169).

- Skimming: Web documents are meant for people with too much information to skim, much like a proposal or prospectus (169).

- Pecking: The text is given coherence by the readers who combine the fragmentary text into something useful to their goal (169).

- Imposing: "Hyper-readers impose their frameworks on the texts they peruse. . . . The information available on the Web holds little significance until hyper-readers search it for items relevant to their inquiries" (169).

- Filming: "Graphics often play a more meaningful role than words" (169).

- Trespassing: "Hyper-readers are textual burglars. They break into electronic texts and once they have found the source codes hidden from sight, steal them away with their cut and paste tools and reassemble them" (170).

- De-authorizing: "By virtually reassembling texts, they dismiss the authors' intentions by replacing them with their own, thus de-authorizing texts altogether" (170).

- Fragmenting: Fragmented texts are preferred over linear ones, making organization an activity determined by the individual's needs or purposes (170). (Sosnoski qtd. in Loftin, Carter, and Lewis-Qualls n.p.)

Collectively, these reading practices seem to define what Baron calls "reading on the prowl," reading that is oriented toward gathering information quickly, which she contrasts with a deep, continuous reading historically associated with critical thinking. Baron's perspective, put as a proposition: "We teach the next generation to decipher words on a page, but as the form of what constitutes a page shifts, so does the nature of reading" ("Why Reading" n.p.).

The idea of what constitutes a page is also an intriguing one, especially given the way different pages display information and thus the way that information is presented. It's also worth noting that texts themselves evoke different reading practices: the case of the *New York Times'* "Snow Fall" provides a case in point. Much like an electronic portfolio, this account of backcountry skiing gone bad includes on its "page" multiple kinds of texts—linguistic, graphic, video, and audio—enlarging the print-based reading experience to include listening, interacting, and viewing. In reading this text, the reader needs to make two decisions: (1) how to "read" each kind of text and (2) how to read those texts in sequence; do we read the linguistic text and then watch the video, or do we intersperse the linguistic reading with video viewing and graphic interpretation, or do we follow another path altogether in what Yancey, Powers, and McElroy call "viewer/reading" (n.p.)? Likewise, with multiple kinds of texts embedded within it, what kind of reading does the "Snow Fall" page encourage? One might make the argument that it's not Baron's reading on the prowl, but rather a *different* kind of deep, continuous reading from that we see in print, one more oriented to our *experiencing* the text—and thus what it portrays—in multiple, layered, overlapping ways. But of course this assumes, first, that the reader is able to access the text and, second, access the text as it was designed to display.

Given the relationship between what and how we read, it's not surprising that the ways texts are "displayed" is relevant. In 1993, for example, Bernhardt could confidently assert that "readers become participants, control outcomes, and shape the text itself" (154), although then, as now, readers' participation always operates within a finite set of choices defined by both publisher and device maker. This becomes ever more obvious as the varieties of reading devices proliferate, including smartphones, tablets, e-readers, laptop computers, and notebooks. Indeed, devices themselves now cooperate with or even substitute for the reader in controlling textual display (see Figure 3.1). In some cases, the device and the reader work together, as when a reader adjusts the size of letters on an e-reader, a material practice impossible in print and one that seems generally helpful. In other cases, the digital text has been "optimized" for the device, with the device itself determining the shape of the page. Given this context, a significant question concerns what happens to a text when it is optimized: suppose, for instance, that visuals in the print version, which are optimized out, disappear. Is a richly illustrated historical text like *Alice in Wonderland* the same text if the visuals are shrunk, moved, or erased altogether? Is *Woody Plants*, a field guide to plants in the western mountain filled with photos of plants useful for identification, as useful without the photos? Put baldly, how useful is a text designed to include visuals if it no longer includes them? Another important question is what difference, if any, such questions make for a class of twenty, with students reading the same text on three or five or ten different devices? In this situation, Stanley Fish's question about whether there *is* a text in the class resonates in new and disconcerting ways.

FIGURE 3.1. *Display comparison: smartphone (left), iPad (center), 21" monitor (right), all displaying "Snow Fall."*

How We Got Here

Beginning in 2007, two technology companies, Apple and Amazon, released devices that fundamentally changed the technological landscape and consequently what it means to read electronic texts. Amazon released the Kindle (2007), and Apple released both the iPhone (2007) and the iPad (2010). In the years since, the device market has diversified significantly. While Amazon and Apple continue to create new models and release updated generations of the Kindle, iPhone, and iPad, other companies have released rival devices, many of which now come in different models and generations themselves. Moreover, ownership of these devices has increased significantly over a period of just a few years. In a 2014 survey, for example, Pew reported that 42 percent of adults own a tablet (up from 3 percent in 2010), and 32 percent of adults own an e-reader, up from 4 percent in 2010 (Zickuhr and Rainie, "Tablet"). In a different study, released in 2015, Pew reported that 64 percent of Americans own a smartphone, a 29 percent increase from 2011 (Smith). Perhaps not surprisingly, Pew reports a parallel trend in digital reading; people are using their mobile devices to read: 57 percent on e-readers, 55 percent on tablets, 29 percent on computers, and 32 percent on smartphones (Zickuhr and Rainie, "E-Reading"). Although these figures may not completely represent US adults' device ownership and reading habits, they do suggest that people are using multiple and different kinds of digital devices for accessing, storing, and viewing texts.

Although printed works have always come in multiple versions and sometimes with significant differences in layout from one version to the next, the electronic texts displayed on mobile devices take a markedly different approach to display: responsive design. Rather than coming in a handful of versions like the different editions of works that appear in print, electronic texts vary from device to device. In 2010, Web designer Ethan Marcotte conceptualized this design philosophy based on an emerging discipline called "responsive architecture." The physical spaces designed by this school of architecture reimagine the relationships between people and entities: rather than requiring people to adapt to its material constraints—size, temperature, lighting, etc.—a responsive building "respond[s] to the presence of people passing through it" through "wall structures that bend, flex, and expand as crowds approach them" and through climate control that can "adjust a room's temperature and ambient lighting as it fills with people" (n.p.).

Identifying this approach to architectural design as a way forward in an increasingly device-specific digital landscape, Marcotte reimagines the relationship between users, devices, and texts for Web design. Rather than viewing a webpage as an extension of the printed page with its definite, static dimensions, Marcotte designs webpages as fluid texts that flow into and out of the screens of various devices, scaling up and scaling down based on the specific dimension of each device. This new approach to Web design has led to a new breed of texts that not only can be viewed "along a gradient of different experiences" and "within different viewing contexts," but that also has become a standard approach to Web and ebook design. Most websites and ebooks include multiple style definitions specific to common device dimensions and to whether the text is viewed in landscape or portrait, and such style definitions have improved the readability of digital texts on smaller devices such as smartphones and some tablets.

In addition to the differences in display resulting from a device's dimensions, individual customization of display can contribute to differences in display; such individual customizations include changing fonts, font size, margins, background color, and font color, options that often come as standard features on dedicated reading devices like the Kindle and in reading apps such as iBooks or the Kindle app. Thus, while one reader might opt to leave the default settings of a device or app intact, another reader might alter the appearance of the text displayed on the screen by making fonts and margins larger or smaller and by brightening or darkening the text displayed on the screen.

Taken together, both the responsive design of the electronic file and the options for reader customization point to an important aspect of electronic reading: the malleability of form. In print texts, the publisher designs aspects of a text's form such as paper weight, font choice, margins, or paper brightness; these are static features of a particular copy or version. In digital texts like ebooks, however, form is contingent on the dimensions of a particular screen and a reader's preferred settings, reinforcing Lanham's prescient claim about digital texts as "both creator-controlled and reader-controlled" (Lanham 4). Further, and in addition to customizations Lanham describes such as changing font and enlarging "the print," readers are altering colors, adjusting layouts, enlarging or reducing margins, and displaying one or two "pages" at a time (5). Given the multiplicity of devices used to read texts and the opportunities for customizing displays, Gunther Kress's multimodal theory of reading—reading as design—takes on new meaning. Where Kress emphasizes the reader's ability to order digital texts according to the reader's individual interests and needs, *"(ordering-as-)design,"* however, responsive design "embodies and assumes the necessity of the reader's semiotic work" in two more ways (38, emphasis in original): readers can exercise choices about both device and display. Given these opportunities for choice in device and display, a classroom of twenty-five students with a blend of tablets, e-readers, smartphones, and computers in different brands and generations may be looking at twenty-five different versions of the "same" text and may be having different, possibly competing, interpretive experiences.

Screen Reading: More Than about Electronic Space

Digital devices—whether laptops, smartphones, or e-readers—create an embodied reading experience, an experience sometimes similar to and sometimes different from print. Sometimes we engage with digital devices in ways similar to print: turning page animations in full color, using bookmarking and annotation with just a click, while expanding on the affordances of print—searchability, indexing, and backlighting. Other times, as in the case of the *New York Times's* "Snow Fall," given its video, animations, and audio, the experience of reading digitally feels very different from reading in print. This observation is especially telling in the case of books. A print book has heft in relation to its contents; its cover and apparatus hint at what's inside and how it is to be read; it smells like a book. Those who prefer the affordances of print can find e-reading distracting, fragmented, and an abstraction—or, worse, a mere shadow of the real thing. Those who prefer e-reading find electronic texts more flexible—the font resizable, the content scrollable, the whole text easily searched, indexed, bookmarked to social media. These affordances are especially valuable for conducting research. And for those on connected smartphones, the pull of the Web provides access to supplementary material just as it provides the interruption of calls, emails, and texts. The book, in contrast, offers no such distractions, no accompanying dictionary.

As it turns out, students have documented preferences when it comes to the differences between print and digital reading, especially of school-related texts. In "Redefining Reading: The Impact of Digital Communication Media," Naomi Baron reports on two 2010–11 surveys regarding US undergraduate students' reading practices for course materials. The first survey, of about 100 undergraduates, found:

◆ About half (48%) of students reported that they "occasionally" or "never" annotate their textbooks (usually because they are either renting them or plan on selling them back after the semester).

◆ With two exceptions—academic journals and newspapers—students prefer reading in print rather than online.

◆ Over half (55%) of students preferred having course materials online, but 40% of students print those materials out to read them. Only 6% read the materials online.

◆ Students were almost 10 times as likely to read an article if they were "handed a copy" instead of being provided online access.

◆ In terms of remembering what they read, about half of students said the medium didn't matter; about half said they remembered things better in print. Only 2% said they retained more online.

◆ 90% of students reported multitasking while reading online; 1% reported the same while reading in print. (195)

Though the number of students is small, the findings are interesting. Students want to be able to access readings online, but they don't prefer to *read* most texts online. Instead, they prefer to read in print, and they are more likely to read material if it's in print. That said, students report that they are not taking advantage of one of the chief affordances of print—space for annotation and marginalia. Their reasons have nothing to do with reading or learning: they want to sell back their textbooks.

In Baron's second study, with a sample about twice as large as the first, students were asked which of two reading options made it easier to concentrate in a forced-pair comparison:

◆ Ninety percent of students chose hard copy over a desktop or laptop computer.

◆ Two-thirds (67 percent) chose hard copy over an e-reader.

◆ Two-thirds (64 percent) chose an e-reader over a tablet computer.

◆ Two-thirds (68 percent) chose a tablet over a desktop or laptop computer.

These findings point to two observations. The first is that students have a relatively stable hierarchy of preferences when it comes to school-related reading. They prefer, first, a hard copy, second, an e-reader, third, a tablet, and fourth and last, a desktop or laptop computer. The second is that students' preference for print is directly linked to their perceived ability to concentrate.

While these data emerge from only two surveys and a small sample size, Baron's findings highlight the challenges that teachers face as they attempt to engage and expand students' reading experiences, and they raise three questions about the ways teachers must negotiate the extent to which they try to balance students' reading preferences with encouraging new ways of reading.

1. Students are comfortable with print; as teachers, we're often comfortable with print as well. To what extent, then, should we rely on those preferences over and above others in our classrooms?

2. How does that answer change given that reading in electronic formats is a reading practice more and more common outside our classrooms?

3. How do we help students develop reading practices that, to return to Lanham and Kress, evidence purposeful choices about device and display?

Information Shape as Interface Metaphor

A process of expanding outward from a comfort zone, ours or that of our students, can be eased if we carry with us familiar principles from the comfortable to the less comfortable. So it can be useful to help students notice that print and electronic texts rely on similar principles governing how we read, principles directly related to the visuality of the text. In a study of the impact of text shape on readers' comprehension, for instance, Elaine Toms and D. G. Campbell, Canadian scholars in information science, write: "We suggest that a digital document typically has a configuration of visual features that characterize it as a particular genre, and that *the relationship between visual appearance and semantic content is relevant* as an instrument both of document presentation and of document retrieval" (370, emphasis added).

To establish their point, Toms and Campbell offered a set of study participants a look at the same visual appearance inhabited by two different texts, and the same text designed into two different visual appearances. (Figure 3.2 re-creates their visuals, but with our own texts.) Participants were able to perceive from visual cues alone that panels A and B represented the same textual genre. They could not perceive from visual cues that panels A and C did as well. A compositionist might point to the rhetorical canons as an ancient codification of the idea that a text's visual appearance matters, and although one should say that genre is a far thicker and more layered idea than visual shape alone, their central conclusion is agreeable: the materiality of a text might be relevant to the presentation and retrieval (interpretation) of that text.

Another study from outside composition is also informative. Aaron Fry, Jennifer Wilson, and Carol Overby, who study financial behavior among adults in marginalized populations, advocate deploying what they call "narrative visualizations" to trigger metaphors that resonate with learners. Their interest in exploring these behaviors is to isolate effective means to help learners recognize and abandon self-destructive financial habits they have unwittingly established. By narrative visualization, Fry and colleagues mean visually depicted narratives—resonant metaphors

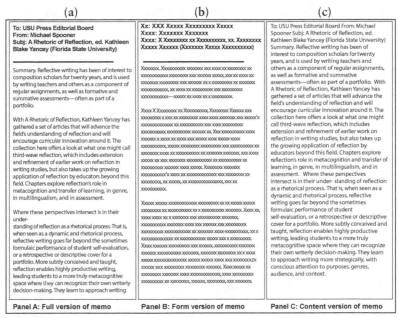

(a)	(b)	(c)

FIGURE 3.2. *Form and content versions of the same text (adapted from Toms and Campbell).*

or visual enthymemes, one might say, or Burkean representative anecdotes rendered visually. To illustrate their process, Fry et al. consider an article from *The Economist* about the implications of aggregate spending and saving, and they compare the article's accessibility with a particular image in the same article. The image depicts a man whose coins are rolling willy-nilly into a gaping hole in the street as he kneels at its edge. From their study, conclude Fry and colleagues, the narrative made visual is more accessible and more emotionally powerful than all the carefully discussed information on implications of aggregate spending and saving in the text of the article. The researchers conclude that the primary cognitive drivers of behavior change are not the cool, rational, neoclassical ones we might hope for; instead, they are "system one" styles of thinking and decision-making—i.e., intuition-based cognition. Because human rationality is bounded on many sides, and because we never have ideal conditions (such as full information) for decision making, we resort to heuristics, rules-of-thumb, intuition, and habit.

And what does all this mean for reading, especially e-reading? These two simple studies at some distance from teaching writing suggest that comprehending the meaning of differences and similarities in textual display between one device and another isn't only a cognitive process; it's also a behavioral process. Like recognizing a memo or engaging a welter of financial decisions, design comprehension is laden with culturally inscribed metaphors, and it proceeds more often intuitively than rationally. As we think about the possible effects of text shape, color, navigation, and delivery device, we might ask: what intuitive associations are at work within the condensed narratives of visual design?

Principles of Design

Students of document design have traditionally been taught four design principles: contrast, repetition, alignment, and proximity. We could put them in any order, but students enjoy pointing out the acronym CRAP, and designers use the acronym as a quick point of reference. Interestingly, artists like Barbara Yale-Read, the calligrapher who created Figure 3.3, think that text and image are both essentially visual phenomena. Those who design book interiors or websites or blog templates feel the same. That is, designers (at least while designing) don't engage with text textually. Nevertheless, with these principles, designers actually frame a metanarrative for the interpretation of a page of text or image. Intuitively, the principles are metaphoric and heuristic. They express interpretive valences (or narratives visualized) that students, with a little help, can recognize as familiar to their own reading of print or digital texts: ideas such as connection, balance, difference, equivalence, emphasis, hierarchy, sequence.

We can help students think of concrete examples. Boldface or italics in a text suggest *emphasis*. The running head at the top of this page is a navigational cue; not only that, but it also appears in a size and a font that connect it visually to other navigational elements throughout the book—perhaps the subheadings. As

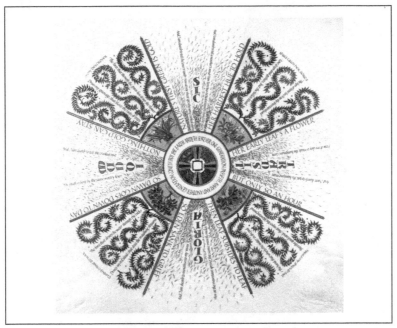

FIGURE **3.3.** *"Nothing Gold Can Stay" (Yale-Read). Used by permission.*

another example, indenting a short paragraph like a blocked quotation offers a visual metaphor of hierarchy or ordination; the indented text is a subordinate unit within or under the "normal" text. The visual differences between a first-level heading and a second-level heading (by designers often called A-heads, B-heads, etc., or H1, H2, etc.) constitute a narrative about the structure of the text. Any of these valences might be at work in any designed display, whether printed text, digital device, or mandala created in sand (see Figure 3.4).

Book designers would seldom discuss what they do with anything like this explicit an analysis. But on reflection, one can see that what they create does indeed trigger these resonant associations, these kinds of metaphors and narratives. The success of the design actually depends on how designers orchestrate all this. The perspective becomes useful and revealing as we approach a diversity of devices and as we design our texts for them, too. Because as we move from device to device in our reading and

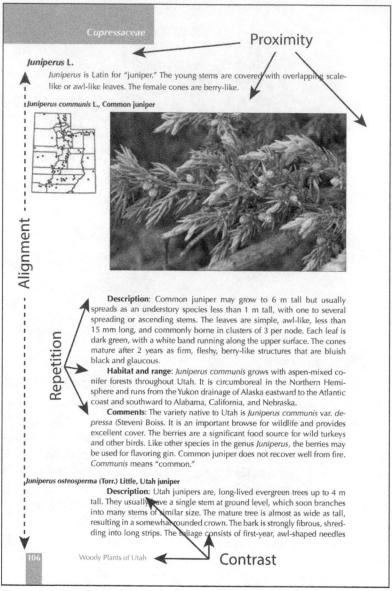

Proximity

Alignment

Repetition

Contrast

FIGURE 3.4. *Traditional design principles.*

writing, what we experience is deeper than a change in visual shape (as relevant as that is) and less obvious than a change in usability—e.g., the convenience of navigation. And it's probably important for us to acknowledge this in the metalanguage we use. We need to notice that when we describe this experience in, for example, the language of "information" or "behavior" or "science" or "content" or "platform" or "container" or "object" or "device," we are also activating for ourselves a set of resonant metaphors. We are triggering in ourselves interpretive behaviors grounded in cultural meanings and framing a narrative for the interface experience. The more we can refine our understanding of that narrative, the better we will comprehend our literacy.

Having students encounter a page or screen with the concept of visual narratives in mind encourages them to unpack the designed meanings they probably already process automatically when reading. Equipped with a better understanding of design principles, they are better able to improve their own composition efforts and to understand those of peers or professionals.

Pedagogical Implications

Although it is beyond the scope of this chapter to detail a pedagogy emerging from this wide array of texts, we do want to make some suggestions to show what such pedagogy might look like. Reading, of course, has always been a material practice, historically involving a material (print) artifact, bodies, accessories (such as desks, pencils, etc.), and manipulations (such as page turning and annotation), and we know something about the teaching of reading (e.g., Horning). And while e-reading currently involves many of the same practices—positioning devices, manipulating displays, and inputting notes—the practices and concerns unique to e-reading suggest that e-reading is a material practice of a different kind. Because texts can be displayed on a range of devices, each with distinguishable characteristics that affect the display of texts, and because texts increasingly depart from the conventions of print texts through responsive display and the inclusion of multiple media, e-reading involves practices and concerns unique to digital media and digital devices. We need look no further than our own classrooms for evidence of new material practices made possible, in part, by the implementation of responsive text design.

In some classrooms, especially those where students are invited to bring their own devices, it is not surprising to see a range of textual displays sitting on students' desks: laptops, smartphones, e-readers, and a handful of print copies, each medium and device having a unique set of material affordances and constraints. Those reading in print have a rich set of spatial and material affordances: 6 × 9 inches or perhaps 8.5 × 11 inches of page space and a range of possibilities for annotation. Those using laptops and e-readers have a similar set of affordances: adequate screen space for reading the text and options for annotating the text depending on the kind of digital file. For those students using smartphones, however, it is not uncommon to see a different set of practices emerge as students try to read on a screen about 3 × 5 inches: craned necks and clawed fingers used to resize the text and focus in. Thus, just as a text's design, responsive or not, provides one context for reading, so too do the material affordances and limitations of the media and devices students use to read.

Given the issues we have raised here, there may be reason enough to consider classroom policies restricting digital devices, if only to mitigate issues that can arise when students are given license to read in their preferred media and on their preferred devices. Rather than advocating such a policy, however, we suggest that inviting students to examine their reading preferences more explicitly and to articulate what effects those preferences have on their meaning-making is a more productive approach. More specifically, we suggest three activities to help students consider how media and devices figure into their reading, researching, and meaning-making: one focused on how the design of a text shapes their experience, a second focused on device preference, and a third focused on annotation. The activities can be used separately or together.

The first exercise asks students to use principles of design to render a common syllabus more accessible to readers: to do this, students work with a syllabus that is largely verbal, as we see in Figure 3.5. Then, using the principles of contrast, repetition, alignment, and proximity, students design a text so that it is more meaningful. Discussion can then focus on choices students made

```
ENC
Visual Rhetoric
Kathleen Yancey (kyancey@fsu.edu)
T 6:45-9:30
Fall
Hours: Mon 4:30-6 and by appointment
Williams 223B
Phone: 645-6896
Purpose
Using several frames of reference and several kinds of visuals, Visual
Rhetoric will explore three related questions.
First, what does it mean to know through visuals—be they pictures,
images, maps, or photographs?
Second, what is the relationship between what we know and how what we
know is represented: do we know and then represent and/or do we know
through the process of representing, or both? And what difference does
the answer to this question make?
Third, what are the richest contexts for visual rhetoric? Contexts for
consideration include the visual display of information, particularly as
seen in an historical context; photography, with its claim of represen-
tation and its function of construction; and multimodality, with its
multiple semiotic systems working sometimes together, sometimes at cross
purposes.
To answer these questions, we will read widely and look closely and
```

FIGURE 3.5. *Text of a syllabus ready for enhancement through principles of design.*

and rationales for such choices and, of course, on the relationship between form and content, the very relationship that e-reading highlights but that is not unique to it.

The second exercise functions like an inventory of reading practices that first asks students to identify the media and devices they use to read (items 1–8) and then asks them to identify what annotation and note-taking practices they use while reading (items 9–14).

1. _____ Reads in print

2. _____ Reads on a laptop

3. _____ Reads on a desktop

4. _____ Reads on an e-reader

5. _____ Reads on a smartphone

6. _____ Reads on a tablet

7. _____ Most often reads in print

8. _____ Most often reads electronically

9. _____ Annotates when reading electronically

10. _____ Annotates when reading in print

11. _____ Takes notes on reading in print when reading
electronically

12. _____ Takes notes on reading in print when reading in print

13. _____ Takes notes on reading electronically when reading
electronically

14. _____ Takes notes on reading in print when reading
electronically

After each student individually identifies his or her preferred media for reading and note taking, students are then prompted to discuss the reasoning behind their preferences. The concepts of affordance and limitation can be helpful here: (1) What's the reasoning behind your preference? (2) How does the medium or device help you while reading and note taking? (3) How does the medium or device limit your reading and note taking? The goals of this exercise are to bring to students' attention their own reading practices and to encourage them to consider how the technologies involved in those practices are beneficial or detrimental to the meanings they make while reading and researching. In other words, students are asked to identify their own reading practices, with special attention given to the technologies involved in reading; and having identified their practices, students are asked to theorize if and how their preferred technologies support them while reading.

While the first exercise is oriented toward design and the second is reflective in nature, the third functions as a kind of pseudo-experiment with emphasis on annotation. In this third exercise, students have three tasks. First, they are asked to annotate a short selection (two to three pages) from a single text in three different iterations: a first page in print, a second page on a laptop or workstation (such as those provided in computer labs), and a third page on a mobile device of their choosing (smartphone, e-reader, or tablet). Second, having annotated the reading in print, on a full-sized screen, and on a mobile device, students compose a summary of the text using all of the annotations they generated while reading each version. And third, having composed the summary, students are asked to identify which set of annotations—those generated in the print version, the full-sized digital version, or the mobile version—were most helpful for their summary and why. This final part of the activity could be accomplished through writing, small-group discussion, guided class discussion, or all three. Although this third exercise is less attentive to students' preferred technologies and existing practices,[1] it shares a goal similar to that of the second activity: to identify which technologies best support the meanings students make through reading, and why.

Students' reactions to this activity focused on their ability to annotate the text and on their experience of interacting with the text relative to device and display. Initially, students found they had trouble orienting themselves to digital versions of the text, with some reporting technical difficulties: "It took a long time to download" or "I couldn't open the file." Others had trouble with the interface of the text: "I can't figure out the formatting," reported one student, and therefore she "couldn't 'get in the groove.'" Even without technical or interface issues, students often found that the texts provided a difficult visual experience: "I felt like I had to re-read much more with the electronic device," one student reported. Another suggested that this re-reading was the result of "a lot of visual disorientation" on mobile devices. In general, students said that screens made it hard to concentrate, that they were distracting (especially mobile devices, which are flooded with constant updates, text messages, and alerts), and that screens quickly lead to "reading fatigue."

Students also reported having to think carefully about textual navigation in digital formats; in particular, students had strong responses to scrolling. Some found it "annoying" or "clunky," while others found that scrolling itself influenced how they read: "It makes me more likely to skim because I want to move the progress bar down." Still other students were happy for a quicker way to move through the text and reported a pleasurable experience with their screens and trackpads. In sum, as one student summarized, "What some people found encouraging—like the progress bar on electronic texts or swiping—other people found distracting."

Finally, students reported that physically interacting with text took on new dimensions in digital formats and that exploring these interactions led them to think differently about print. The initial reaction for most students was that digital texts lack the haptic dimensions of print—the feeling of the heft of a book in your hands; the texture of good-quality paper. As one student put it, these haptic dimensions make print "feel like it has 'notability'—that you can write on it." Some students were simply nostalgic for touching print: "I missed that interaction." Others responded to the need to adjust one's annotation practices: "My reliable techniques for print—like highlighting and underlining—are integrated [in the digital devices], but my techniques are less reliable [in digital devices]." In other words, students find a familiar pleasure in the kinesthetic reinforcement provided by their naturalized ways of interacting with print; in digital formats, they miss that feeling. However, students did find new ways of interacting with online texts: "I found all these highlighting and notation tools and how to look up words—actually, there was so much functionality and I was so excited to try it out that I didn't get much reading done." In short, this activity led students to focus more on the *how* of reading and less on the *what*.

In reflecting on the activity, students turned again to print and reimagined their relationship with it. One student commented that print always required him to go elsewhere to look up words and concepts—he couldn't just right-click and look something up right on the page. Another student framed the limitations of print in relatively humorous terms: "It made me a little sad that pictures and video couldn't be viewed on paper." In general, though, students began to have a stronger sense that they had choices to make among texts, devices, and interfaces, and that those choices related to both their own reading practices and to the purpose for that reading. As one student put it, "There was definitely a most fitting reading experience for the text. Different genres have different purposes and audiences, which would affect the format [of the text] and my reading, I think."

In sum, given the variety of texts, devices, and displays available to students, our best opportunity to help students make good choices as they read and research is to engage them in considering how we tap each of these texts to make meaning—for ourselves and for others, now and in the future.

Note

1. This exercise assumes that students have sufficient access; if not, it can be adapted, students can work together, or a library's media center may be of help.

Works Cited

Baron, Naomi. "Redefining Reading: The Impact of Digital Communication Media" *PMLA* 128.1 (2013): 193–200. Print.

———. "Why Reading on a Screen Is Bad for Critical Thinking." *Huffington Post.* 19 Apr. 2015. Web. 9 Dec. 2016.

———. *Words Onscreen: The Fate of Reading in a Digital World.* New York: Oxford UP, 2015. Print.

Bernhardt, Stephen. "The Shape of Text to Come: The Texture of Print on Screens." *College Composition and Communication* 44.2 (1993): 151–75. Print.

Bunn, Michael. "Motivation and Connection: Teaching Reading (and Writing) in the Composition Classroom." *College Composition and Communication* 64.3 (2013): 496–516. Print.

Donahue, Patricia. "Scholarship scholarship." 19 July 2015. WPA listserv. Web.

Fish, Stanley, *Is There a Text in This Class? The Authority of Interpretive Communities.* Cambridge: Harvard UP, 1982. Print.

Fry, Aaron, Jennifer Wilson, and Carol Overby. "Teaching the Design of Narrative Visualization for Financial Literacy." *Art, Design & Communication in Higher Education* 12.2 (2013): 159–77. Print.

Horning, Alice. "Reading Across the Curriculum as the Key to Student Success. *Across the Disciplines* (2007). *The WAC Clearinghouse.* Web. 29 July 2016.

Kress, Gunther. *Multimodality: A Social Semiotic Approach to Contemporary Communication.* London: Routledge, 2010. Print.

Lanham, Richard. *The Electronic Word: Literary Study and the Digital Revolution.* Chicago: University of Chicago P, 1993. Print.

Loftin, Lynley, Shannon Carter, and Chandra Lewis-Qualls. "Review of *Passions, Pedagogies, and 21st Century Technologies.*" *Kairos* 6.1 (2001). Web. 22 Dec. 2016.

Marcotte, Ethan. "Responsive Web Design." *A List Apart.* 25 May 2010. Web. 16 July 2015.

Pew Research Center. "Device Ownership." *Pew Research Center.* 28 Nov. 2012. Web. 12 July 2015.

Salvatori, Mariolina, and Patricia Donahue. "What Is College English? Stories about Reading: Appearance, Disappearance, Morphing, and Revival." *College English* 75.2 (2012): 199–217. Print.

Smith, Aaron. "Chapter One: A Portrait of Smartphone Ownership." *Pew Research Center.* 1 Apr. 2015. Web. 12 July 2015.

Sosnoski, James. "Hyper-Readers and Their Reading Engines." *Passions, Pedagogies, and 21st Century Literacies.* Ed. Gail E. Hawisher and Cynthia L. Selfe. Logan and Urbana: Utah State UP/NCTE, 1999: 161–77. Print.

Toms, E. G., and D. G. Campbell. "Utilizing Information 'Shape' as an Interface Metaphor Based on Genre." In *Proceedings of the Annual Conference of CAIS/Actes du congress annuel de l'ACSI.* 2013, October 2013. Print.

Yancey, Kathleen, Elizabeth Powers, and Stephen McElroy. "Composing, Networks, and Electronic Portfolios: Notes toward a Theory of Assessing ePortfolios." In *Digital Writing: Assessment and Evaluation.* Ed. Heidi McKee and Danielle DeVoss. Logan: Computers and Composition Digital P/Utah State UP, 2013. Web. 9 Dec. 2016.

Zickuhr, Kathryn, and Lee Rainie. "E-Reading Rises as Device Ownership Jumps." *Pew Research Center.* 16 Jan. 2014. Web. 12 July 2015.

———. "Tablet and E-reader Ownership." *Pew Research Center.* 16 Jan. 2014. Web. 12 July 2015.

CHAPTER FOUR

Why Read? A Defense of Reading and the Humanities in a STEM-Centric Era

JASON COURTMANCHE
University of Connecticut

Background and Context

> "Remember, the firemen are rarely necessary. The public itself stopped reading of its own accord."
> —Faber to Montag, *Fahrenheit 451*

Because I am the director of the Connecticut Writing Project, the editors of this volume asked me to comment on what I have found in my fieldwork as I visit high schools around the state and work with high school and college English teachers and students. The editors asked for gritty detail and a candid assessment. One of the reasons I developed the course on reading that I describe in this chapter is because I have found a great deal of intellectual complacency among students in the high schools I have visited. I have found this complacency in first-year college students as well here at the University of Connecticut. One of my favorite questions to ask new college students is, "How many of you can write a five-page paper the night before it is due and still get an A or a B?" I consistently get large numbers of students raising their hands in agreement. Some even admit being able to complete ten-page papers the night before that earn a passing grade. These students have obviously figured out a formula and are just repeating it. I have also found that the literacies that excite students often reside outside the classroom, as Jolliffe and Harl have noted. Many students I have talked to also report that they loved reading until they got to high school. We obviously have to think carefully about our readicide problem (Gallagher) and begin to create meaningful classroom activities that will be of value to students beyond the fourteen weeks of the semester. This chapter attempts to address this issue.

When I began teaching at UConn in the fall of 2007, English was the second largest major after psychology. We had more than 700 declared majors, plus a graduate program of 115 MA and PhD candidates. After the Great Recession of 2008, the English major plummeted in popularity, the result of a panic fueled by the mistaken belief that an English degree was not valuable in the new economy. Today in 2016, we have just slightly more than 400 majors and 70 graduate students.

While students were fleeing English as a discipline, the Connecticut legislature approved Next Generation Connecticut, a $1.5 billion "investment in building new scientific laboratories, purchasing advanced equipment, constructing new classrooms, and adding housing," along with an additional $137 million for the hiring of new STEM faculty (Reitz). This was coupled with an initiative to expand the incoming first-year class beyond 5,000 students, with the increase being mostly STEM students.

Related to this initiative was an expansion of the Honors Program. Part of that initiative involved efforts to bring first-year students into direct contact with faculty members. Toward this end, the Honors Program recruited faculty who were interested in teaching and who had received high Student Evaluations of Teaching (SETs) to teach one-credit Honors First-Year Experience (FYE) courses. Despite being in the English department, I was among the faculty members who received an invitation to teach an Honors FYE course. I was promised that I could teach just about anything my heart desired and that the students enrolled in my section would be interested in my field.

While I saw this as an opportunity to teach a fun course of my own design and earn a little extra travel funding, I also viewed it as an opportunity to attract students into the English major. And since there are many good and great teachers in my department, I thought that my experience might persuade colleagues to offer their own sections of Honors FYE as a way of recruiting more first-year students into the major.

The Design of the Course

I created a course called Why Read? A Defense of Reading and the Humanities in a STEM-Centric Era. My students were to read Ray Bradbury's *Fahrenheit 451*, Mark Edmundson's *Why Read?* (from which I bold-facedly appropriated the title of my course and this chapter), Thomas Foster's *How to Read Literature Like a Professor: A Lively and Entertaining Guide to Reading between the Lines*, and several current articles and podcasts about books and reading by Charlie Rose, Neil Gaiman, Emanuele Castano and David Comer Kidd, Laura Schocker, Micah Mattix, Annie Murphy Paul, Bijan Stephen, Michael Rosenwald, Julia Ryan, Lauren Martin, Frank Bruni, Laurel Killough, Colin McEnroe and colleagues, and David Masciotra. These dealt with issues as diverse as reading's relationship to cognition, memory, morality, empathy, censorship, identity, education, lovemaking, and more. I also assigned sources such as the Library of Congress's "Books That Shaped America," the American Library Association's "Frequently Challenged Books," and "Leisure Reading: A Joint Position Statement of the International Reading Association, the Canadian Children's Book Centre, and the National Council of Teachers of English."

Each student would have to lead discussion once, each time taking responsibility for a section of one of the longer works by Bradbury, Edmundson, or Foster, along with one of the shorter articles, Web sources, or podcasts. The Honors Program assigned two sophomore mentors to the course, and one of their responsibilities was to post a weekly prompt related to that week's assigned readings. Half the students in the class would have to respond to the prompt with a 300-word post, and the other half would have to reply to two of these posts with 150-word responses, all of which functioned like a blog with a comments section. There would also be a final paper in which students had to answer the essential question—"Why read?"

Best Laid Plans

To paraphrase Robert Burns, the best laid plans of mice and men often go awry. Despite the assurances (and surely the intentions) of the folks in the Honors Program office, I did not end up with a classroom full of would-be English majors. I had one young woman interested in special education, a classics major, and fourteen students in STEM or related majors: geoscience, biological sciences, environmental sciences, civil engineering, electrical engineering, chemical engineering, computer engineering, pharmacy, and accounting. If I had had a roomful of English majors or education majors, I might have been preaching to the choir, but what this course became was a journey for each student to find the role of reading, particularly reading literary fiction, in a life dominated by the sciences.

What Worked and What Did Not in Year One

Interestingly but not surprisingly, every one of the students had taken an advanced English class the year before as a high school senior, so all were "good" readers and had read many canonical texts. Therefore, they were, by and large, not averse to reading, but they were concerned that the reading of literary fiction would drop away from their lives as their majors and then their careers would demand too much of them to leave room for pleasure reading. And at least initially, they valued reading differently than the English majors I typically taught.

During the semester, my experiences with the students led me to see how important it was to offer a course to our future scientists (and accountants and pharmacists) that gave them opportunities to experience the types of reading that Louise Rosenblatt might call "aesthetic reading." At semester's end, according to their responses to questions I included in the Student Evaluations of Teaching, the students, to a person, defended the reading of literary fiction, asserted its value and importance, and vowed to preserve a place for it in their private lives. They all felt that literary fiction struck a chord in their being that science could not.

That does not mean they enjoyed every aspect of the course. Foster's and Edmundson's books were by and large not very well received. Foster's suggestions for reading like an English professor struck the students as too limiting considering they were not going to be English professors. They were more interested in reading for pleasure, recreation, and escape. Edmundson's book patently offended many of the students. His Romantic call to arms struck at least some of the STEM students as adversarial and self-righteous, even self-important. One student diplomatically suggested that perhaps I could change that text, as it "was met with the most resistance." The supplementary articles also fell flat for many of these students. Likely because they were future scientists, the students viewed most of the articles as too popular, in the pejorative sense of the word. For these students, the science behind the articles was not rigorous enough to be truly compelling. The students did, however, love reading *Fahrenheit 451*. The chance to read a work of literature and just talk about it was welcomed with the warmest of metaphorical embraces.

Redesigning the Course

Preparing this course for the fall 2015 semester, I made several changes. First, anticipating another roomful of STEM majors, I dropped both the Foster and Edmundson books. Second, I altered my approach to the supplementary readings. Rather than require these of the students (besides being not well received, they added a lot of content to a one-credit course), I shared them with the two sophomore mentors, and through both the prompts the mentors created for the blog-like discussion board and then in the class discussions, the three of us were able to introduce many of the ideas from those readings into the conversation. Last, I reconceptualized the course so that the students would read three works of fiction, each of which dealt with book banning and censorship in some way. I retained *Fahrenheit 451*, since it had been so popular, and I added *Brave New World* (Huxley) and *The Giver* (Lowry). I chose fiction over nonfiction texts mainly because I teach literature and because my students were reading a lot of nonfiction for their majors. Other aspects of the course, like the blog discussions online, the student-led discussions in class, and the final essay, remained the same.

For the sake of this chapter, I also submitted a research proposal to our Institutional Review Board (IRB). I received permission to survey the students after grades were recorded, as well as permission to request and use samples of their writing. I also received permission to survey and request writing samples from the previous year's students. (Use of comments from SETs was permissible because these are anonymous.) Every student in the current class responded to the survey questions, and all but one granted permission to use samples of their writing. The students from the previous year were harder to contact, but four students from that year agreed to participate in the survey and granted me permission to use samples of their writing.

What I Learned in Week One of Year Two

> "Life is immediate, the job counts, pleasure lies all about after work. Why learn anything save pressing buttons, pulling switches, fitting nuts and bolts?"
> —Beatty to Montag, *Fahrenheit 451*

In the second iteration of the course, I had more students and a slightly more diverse set of majors. Of the eighteen students, two were history majors and four were undeclared. Of the remaining twelve, there were two accounting majors, two actuarial sciences majors, a finance major, a business management major, two computer sciences majors, two biological sciences majors, a biomedical engineering major, and a molecular and cell biology major.

Weekly discussion posts covered topics such as the effects of social media on reading practices, the effects of reading on empathy, book banning and the reasons books are challenged, literature's relationship to both political propaganda and consumerist culture, literature as social satire and critique, the role reading plays in creating a meaningful life, literature's relationship to free will and social engineering, the impact of schooling on reading practices, and reading's role in complex phenomena such as friendship, memory, and love.

I began the course by asking students on the first day how many books they had read *for pleasure* in the past year. Most students said they had read four to six books for pleasure; only a couple had read none. One young woman, an accounting major, estimated she had read more than thirty, but no one else in the class was even close to that. (Last year, I had another statistical outlier who reported having read more than sixty books for pleasure.) Then I asked the students to speculate as to why they did not read more books for pleasure.

Overwhelmingly, students said that the demands of school-work and the allure of social media were the greatest deterrents to more frequent pleasure reading, and that these two things were directly related. For starters, being honors students, their workload for school was significant, so when they did have some downtime, they chose the relatively mindless escape of social media. As one finance major said,

> After finishing all of my homework, it was much easier and a lot more relaxing for me to surf the web or watch Netflix. Both of those options require little to absolute no thought, which is why both of them served as an ideal escape from schoolwork. Reading is great, but the last thing I want to do after spending hours of homework is to continue thinking by reading. I honestly wanted to be able to mindlessly escape.

Other distractions from reading were socializing, working, and volunteering, all of which this population of students saw as important forms of building a résumé for college and career—what one of the history majors termed as characteristic of a "preprofessional attitude" toward school. One undeclared major wrote,

> There is a constant pressure, especially for ambitious students, to get the best grades, with the most extracurricular activities, to be the most "well-rounded" person you can be, to get into a good college, to get a good job, to have a good life; and for some people, trying to achieve this fabled dream necessitates cutting out things that they truly enjoy, such as reading.

Despite these observations, students were quick to point out that they were depicting reality and not an ideal. Most had a very clear sense that these attitudes were suspect at best and perhaps downright unhealthy. One future dentist said, "I've heard 'Put your phone away,' too many times from my father to ignore how terrible screen time is for my self-esteem and productivity. Each minute spent on social media, I was comparing myself to others, feeling bad about how much fun I wasn't having." A biomedical engineering major wrote that prior to receiving her first cell phone as a ninth grader, she

> spent most of my free time reading to my heart's content. I would be reading at least three books a week (yes I really had that much free time). But now with a cell phone and about 16 different social media accounts, reading a whole book is almost a daunting time consuming task. . . . It's almost as if society tells us we *have* to be constantly checking in on news and updates from friends. If we don't do it constantly, we might miss out on something really big and important.

Many students wrote or shared nostalgic or even elegiac reminiscences of a time when they read a lot and loved it. But for most, this period was prior to high school, after which the academic stakes increased *and* most of them got their first cell phones and social media accounts. A perfect storm for the death of reading.

Where to Go from Here

> "There must be something in books, things we can't imagine, to make a woman stay in a burning house; there must be something there. You don't stay for nothing."
> —Montag to Mildred, *Fahrenheit 451*

These realizations were eye-opening for me, and I suspect for the students as well. Even within the first week, many spoke or wrote of a reawakening of their dormant love of reading, and many of them pledged their commitment to do less social networking and more reading. For me it was a great beginning for the rest of the course. Over the next thirteen weeks, we read the three assigned novels and had many fruitful discussions both online and in class. For the sake of brevity, from the students' responses to the weekly discussion posts and from their final essays, I have identified three prevailing strands of thought about the reading of literary fiction. These deal with identity and empathy, success and happiness, and power and authority.

Identity and Empathy

> "When the individual feels, the community reels."
> Lenina to Bernard, *Brave New World*

The focus on identity began in response to the students' initial discussion of the distractions of social media. One of the first posts in the strand titled "Screen Addiction and Reading" was from an actuarial sciences major who wrote, "[W]e all suffer from screen addiction. The urge to constantly visit different websites consistently interrupts our ability to concentrate on long term projects. Even as I am writing this response now, I have fourteen other tabs open." But the focus quickly shifted from screen addiction to broader issues of identity when one of the young women wrote about the dangers of social media to her sense of self-worth:

> [I]t [was] absolutely harmful to my self-esteem and self-assurance to compare my life to the lives of others. Throughout high school, I struggled every day with a negative body image, envying the thinner girls that walked the hallways around me. . . . Social media worsened my harsh feelings because all I saw was what I didn't have: the perfect body.

This post about body image was relevant to some of the issues central to *Brave New World* and prompted an extended discussion between the students about the uses of social media. Many observed that although social media could be used to communicate an honest portrait of one's self, in general it was not used this way. Most people use social media to project an image of themselves that is more aspirational than accurate and sincere. Several students mentioned the case of Madison Holleran, a nineteen-year-old first-year student at the University of Pennsylvania who threw herself from the rooftop of a parking garage only hours after posting a happy Christmas photo on Instagram.

One student shared an ESPN story on Madison in which author Kate Fagan's analysis confirmed their shared understanding of the dangers of social media. Fagan wrote:

> Everyone presents an edited version of life on social media. People share moments that reflect an ideal life, an ideal self. . . . Young women growing up on Instagram are spending a significant chunk of each day absorbing others' filtered images while they walk through their own realities, unfiltered. In a recent survey conducted by the Girl Scouts, nearly 74 percent of girls agreed that other girls tried to make themselves look "cooler than they are" on social networking sites.

By contrast, the students saw literary fiction as a counter to the more pernicious aspects of social media. Rather than create competition between individuals and damage to self-esteem, literary fiction was a source of identification and empathy, an opportunity to see the world through others' eyes and thereby learn about and appreciate other ways of being.

Writing about empathy, an actuarial sciences major emphasized the greater power literary fiction has over other forms of writing to make readers not just understand a historical event but also feel its effects and empathize with its participants. He wrote, "You can read a historical textbook on any war throughout history, but numbers and statistics themselves won't give you the same feeling" as a work of fiction. An electrical and computer engineering major wrote eloquently on this subject in his final paper: "[R]eading is essentially a way to communicate with a little piece of what makes up the collective human experience. . . . The more we read, the more we become aware of this cumulative human experience, and the better we understand what it means to be human."

Writing about identity during our discussion of *The Giver*, another student wrote beautifully about the important role literary fiction plays in our creation of our personal identity. We need the multiple perspectives provided by literary fiction, she wrote, because "in reality we are all reimagining and recreating ourselves every day."

Success and Happiness

> [T]he purpose of life was not the maintenance of well-being, but some intensification and refining of consciousness, some enlargement of knowledge. Which was, the Controller reflected, quite possibly true. But not, in the present circumstance, admissible. He picked up his pen again, and under the words "Not to be published" drew a second line, thicker and blacker than the first, then sighed, "What fun it would be," he thought, "if one didn't have to think about happiness!"
> —Mustapha Mond, *Brave New World*

This emphasis on "what it means to be human" was directly related to the students' concerns with success and happiness. As I mentioned earlier, many of the students perceived school as an exercise in not just education but but also résumé building and networking. Many felt incredible pressure to keep up and excel, but many also questioned the ultimate purposes or outcomes of this emphasis on overachievement. While no one was unaware of the need to find a degree of educational, professional, and, ultimately, financial success, almost all felt that the reading and discussion that took place in our class emphasized human relationships and emotional depth as the most important characteristics of success and happiness. They also felt that literary fiction was crucial to these goals because it both fostered the empathy necessary for meaningful relationships and cultivated an emotional depth that was difficult if not impossible to attain in their chosen fields. A chemical engineering major discussed in his final paper how literary fiction provides knowledge of human relationships that readers can transfer to real life, so that "[i]f we integrate reading into our lives . . . we [will] be able to create better relationships with others."

Once again, the future dentist catalyzed a great discussion. In response to a prompt that asked the students what they thought made life meaningful, she wrote that "overcoming obstacles makes life meaningful," and she elaborated on both personal and family obstacles she had experienced, as well as on other serious obstacles experienced by friends and acquaintances. While books and reading did not in and of themselves solve any of these problems, she and her classmates felt that literary fiction helped nurture the emotional depth necessary to overcome obstacles by providing examples of how to do so.

The novels we read in class provided great examples of the importance of relationships, including the influence of John the Savage on Lenina Grove or Helmholtz Watson in *Brave New World,* the relationship between Clarisse and Montag or between Faber and Montag in *Fahrenheit 451*, and the love between the Giver and Jonas and then Jonas and Gabriel in *The Giver*. One undeclared major wrote that reading literary fiction "provides emotion, beauty, pain, but also ways to deal with pain and imperfection, a way to make it sufferable."

The students were aware, however, that this emphasis on the importance of overcoming obstacles posed something of a challenge. No one wants to seek or prescribe obstacles for the sake of encountering obstacles, and certainly some obstacles are overwhelming and we wouldn't wish them on our worst enemy, but nonetheless, the students felt that reading literary fiction helped them to be aware that instant gratification and perpetual happiness are not only unrealistic but undesirable. The wall-sized televisions of *Fahrenheit 451,* the promiscuity and soma consumption of *Brave New World*, and the genetically engineered emotional flatlining and cultural sameness of *The Giver* convinced students that life perfected would be shallow and without purpose. Obstacles are inevitable in life, and while job and financial security are important, emotional depth and human relationships are going to be more important when one encounters these obstacles.

A special education major wrote that while "emails and chores and jobs and the stressors of humdrum life" can create a gaping void in people, reading can help us to envision ways of dealing with this reality by "opening our eyes to how we fit into our own world." Using strikingly similar language, an undeclared major wrote that "while it is perfectly possible to live a happy and fulfilling life [without reading], there will always be some holes in our souls left unfilled by things undone, unlearned, and unvisited. . . . Books, however, can help fill the void."

Power and Authority

> "I want to wake up in the morning and decide things! . . . I can
> see that it [is] a dangerous way to live."
> —Jonas to the Giver, *The Giver*

A third but less extensively explored course strand was the subject
of power and authority, which actually began with an unintended
discussion of religion. Influenced by these dystopian novels, one
of the mentors posted a discussion question asking students, if
they could eliminate one thing ("an idea, institution, custom,
product, etc.") from society, what would it be? Several responded
that they would eliminate religion; this produced a discussion in
which other students defended religion, or pointed out that much
of religion is narrative and thus similar to literary fiction, or simply pointed out the impossibility or undesirability of completely
eliminating anything from society. From there and over several
other discussion strands in the following weeks, students discussed
the broader issues of power and authority—not just religious but
also technological, corporate, and political.

Technology was a big concern of many of the students. This
was of course evident in all the novels we read in class, and it
related directly to our earliest discussions of social media and
screen addiction. A biomedical sciences major wrote about the
authority afforded technology for its own sake and, as a future
scientist, cautioned her classmates that the fast pace of evolving
technology, coupled with the "slow fade" of art and literature,
presented a threat to our ability to "think more critically and
objectively about our technological 'reality.'"

Consumer culture was a related concern, as students thought
about the ways corporations used technology to market their
products but also shape our consumer desires. One student offered
a caveat when she wrote, "I am growing up in a world dominated
by cell phones and television, where we don't even need someone
to tell us not to read in order for reading to fall to the wayside."

We also talked about the upcoming presidential elections,
which for all of the students would be the first they would be
able to vote in. Many found a number of the candidates quite
disturbing and were upset with the level of public support offered

to some of the most frightening of the candidates. The fact that Americans read so little and yet would be voting in November was particularly upsetting to many students. One of the history majors wrote that "[i]n this day and age, reading literary fiction is more important than it ever has been, mostly because mindless and consumer-driven drones are replacing people who know how to think and lead, just like our dystopian texts predicted."

"Major" Concerns

> [Jonas] looked around the walls of books. "Reading? That's it?" The Giver shook his head. "Those are simply the things that I do. My life is here." "In this room?" The Giver shook his head. He put his hands to his own face, to his chest. "No. Here, in my being. Where the memories are."
> —The Giver to Jonas, *The Giver*

When the students were surveyed at the end of the course, most said they did not find that the course made them think differently about their majors, although the history majors found the social critique within the dystopian novels to be relevant, and two of the future scientists said that the "futuristic themes and STEM things" and the "emphasis on technology" in the novels appealed to their interests.

However, many remarked on the influence of the course as a whole on them. They felt like the special education major who said that "the course revived [her] dormant love of books" and that she was "reminded . . . that perhaps [she] could accomplish two goals at one time—satisfying [her] love of literature" and pursuing her specialized major. At the very least, for most of the students the course reinforced the importance of engaging in the "practice of reading regularly and critically" and fostering the "habit of thinking creatively and analyz[ing] literature intelligently."

The most eloquent response was about intellectual laziness. One student wrote:

> Although this course did not particularly help me in my major, it did provide a valuable lesson for life in general. In modern society, where entertainment is available literally at your fin-

gertips, it is easy to become lax and let yourself be satisfied by whatever takes the least effort. Activities like reading that take a fair amount of time and effort fall to the wayside in favor of five minute videos and endless streams of social media posts. In the books we read, we saw the disastrous consequences of a mentally lazy society: that as people choose to think less, create less, feel less, and form less meaningful relationships, the less of a choice it becomes. Those abilities are diminished, either by the force of unchecked powers, by social norms, or by habit. Because of this, we must strive never to let our society become that sick, and the first step to that is to not let ourselves be satisfied with the cheapest path to pleasure.

The Liberal Arts and "Real" Education

"The magic is only in what books say, how they stitched patches of the universe together into one garment."
—Faber to Montag, *Fahrenheit 451*

When the students were asked to define a "real education," the most honest among them wrote, "I don't know." That said, pretty much all of the students defended a liberal arts education as "real" education, and many offered very good explanations. One wrote, "I think it is important to have knowledge in a wide array of courses so we are able to think across all disciplines." Another wrote, "I believe that there is value in the liberal arts education because it allows you to think very critically about your life and society as a whole."

As future scientists, many had interesting insights about specialization that, in some sense, actually answered the question about their majors. One response effectively sums up what many said: "I think a 'real education' should allow an individual to specialize in a field of his or her interest while also giving students ample opportunities to broaden their knowledge in various disciplines."

The greatest insight on this question may have been from the student who wrote:

In the three books we read in this course, the education received by the characters was limited. They were either taught only what they needed to perform a specific job, or only "practical" subjects like math, science, and grammar. The result of this overly specialized or overly pragmatic education was disastrous: it created populations of people who had no idea how to think critically about the world around them, or how to empathize with others. This should be kept in mind in real life, where the arts and humanities are increasingly criticized as being impractical, and are increasingly taking a backseat in (or even being cut from) curricula across the country. Though scorned, these subjects are invaluable. Through art, music, history, literature, and other mediums, people learn to express themselves, and to care about the direction in which our society is headed. Specialization in a certain technical area is important, but it is just as important to learn about subjects outside your area of study.

Literary Fiction and Life

"Everyone must leave something behind when he dies, my grandfather said. A child or a book or a painting or a house or a wall built or a pair of shoes made. Or a garden planted. Something your hand touched some way so your soul has somewhere to go when you die, and when people look at that tree or that flower you planted, you're there."
—Granger to Montag, *Fahrenheit 451*

In their end-of-course survey responses, not one student concluded that reading literary fiction should not have a place in his or her life, but the perceived roles for reading were incredibly (I might even say wonderfully) varied. Student responses included "pleasure," "entertainment," and "pastime," all of which were consistent with the emphasis on "pleasure, recreation, and escape" that so many of this and last year's students expressed at the outset of the course. But students wrote other, more critical responses too, such as "stimulating thought and discussion," "fostering knowledge," "sharing ideas," "becoming informed," "formulating opinions," and "a lesson in patience."

The most common response about what students learned that they hadn't anticipated at the beginning of the course was a version of what one student wrote—that "literature is a form of empathy." One of the essays I assigned the first year was Emanuele Castano and David Comer Kidd's study "Reading Literary Fiction Improves 'Mind Reading' Skills Finds a Study from the New School for Social Research: 'Theory of Mind' Fostered by Challenging, High-Quality Literature." And although this essay was not assigned to the 2015 cohort, its central ideas were introduced to the class by the sophomore facilitators and me. As I mentioned earlier, much of the social science material we read in the first year was met with skepticism by the STEM majors; by contrast, this article's ideas held remarkable sway with the students in the second year. On just a subjective, qualitative level, the students felt that the conclusions of this study jibed with their personal experience with literary fiction, particularly the works they read outside of school. One student wrote:

> [B]ooks allow us to live vicariously through the words on the page and experience things that we never would otherwise. In this way, reading exposes us to countless ideas, feelings, and situations, giving us a new lens through which to view the world. By learning to see things from the perspective of others, we can become more open-minded, empathetic, and more likely to question the state of the society we live in. This is something I knew, but through discussion I realized the sheer scope of what reading can offer.

Among the more Romantic responses, one student replied that "this class helped me imagine a world without books, and I saw in that world that something was missing."

Books in School

> "Words can be like X-rays, if you use them properly—they'll go through anything. You read and you're pierced."
> —Helmholtz to Bernard, *Brave New World*

Although I had not intended this course to serve as a critique of education or pedagogy, the subject of how reading is taught in school was a pervasive one that cropped up again and again in various strands of our discussions. As already noted, many students wrote achingly nostalgic posts about how much they loved reading fiction as children but that the teaching of literature in middle and especially in high school had altered their interactions with books in ways that damaged their love of reading. Many blamed school for lessening their love of reading and described issues of curriculum and instruction that contributed to what we might call readicide, to borrow Kelly Gallagher's terribly apt term. In sum, the students indicted the content of the high school literature curriculum, as well as both the pace of instruction and the overanalysis of literature in high school English classrooms.

I decided to include this last section because I hope this collection will have an influence on how we teach literary fiction at all levels of education going forward. My students' comments should give us pause, and perhaps give us insight into ways we might change our approach to the teaching of literary fiction.

A love of fiction and reading was instilled in most of these students at a young age. A chemical engineering major wrote about the "awesome power" of books and the "privilege" of having had such extensive "access to books" throughout his childhood. The special education major wrote about the beauty of growing up in a home filled with lifetime readers—those "smart, stubborn, passionately curious individuals who maintain and uphold the sacred search for knowledge." One of the undeclared majors wrote that when she was young, "reading was my life."

But while these sentiments were common among the students of both years, equally common was the experience of the student who found himself one day asking, "What happened? Do I not like reading fiction anymore? Have other things come up that I like more? Personally, what I thought happened was something called middle school and high school."

The actuarial sciences major bemoaned a curriculum filled with irrelevant texts. The future actuary wrote that in his high school, "we had books that we had to read in a curriculum. And I'm going to be honest, a majority of these books were either boring, outdated, or a combination of both." This was seconded by another student who said, "'[T]he canon' . . . is too strict, making it too difficult to adjust it to make books for school applicable to the times or to the special needs/interests of students. . . . [C]onsequently, reading is the last thing teenagers want to do in their free time, and this problem is magnified in high school."

Regarding the pace of the curriculum as well as the approach to teaching literature, the future dentist wrote that she

> despised reading 60 pages each night in English classes through-out high school because we overanalyzed each novel and the curriculum was too fast-paced. I couldn't read leisurely because I had to cram four chapters in each night, five nights a week. If I fell behind at all, I'd never finish the book in time.

Another wrote:

> In many schools, an inordinate amount of reading is assigned, such that most students find ways to skip the reading, making students think of reading as laborious instead of enjoyable. Reading should be difficult in the school environment in order to provide a challenge, but this has been pushed too far.

This same student wrote that she looked forward to summer as a time when she could actually enjoy reading with passion and for pleasure. Similarly, another student wrote that during high school, reading for him had become a divided subject. There was reading for school and then there was "legitimate" reading. As opposed to reading for school, he defined *legitimate reading* as that which happens "when a person will open a book, without being told to do so, and start reading simply because they like to."

Despite these experiences, students retained in some part of themselves a love for reading—even if for most of them it had become separated from school or had lain dormant for a time. In one end-of-semester response to a weekly prompt, the students began offering one another suggestions of books they loved, and it's important to note that these were mostly books they had read outside of school. *The Fault in Our Stars* and the Harry Potter series were overwhelming favorites, but others included *An Imperial Affliction, The Book Thief, Never Let Me Go,* The Lord of the Rings trilogy, *A Game of Thrones, Gathering Blue, The Storyteller, Oryx and Crake, Salem Falls, Speak, Nineteen Minutes, The Glass Castle, Ready Player One, The Virgin Suicides, The Kite Runner, Elsewhere,* The Unwind Trilogy, *The Search for Delicious, The Maze Runner, The Things They Carried, Howl's Moving Castle, Mermaid in Chelsea Creek, The Devil in the*

White City, Looking for Alaska, A Song of Ice and Fire series, *The Help, Divergent,* and *Under the Dome.*

Also interesting, however, was how many canonical texts the students loved, although many described for their classmates the practice of returning to these canonical works *on their own* and reading them more leisurely outside of school. The canonical works students praised included *Anna Karenina, Passing, The Awakening, Pride and Prejudice, Jane Eyre, Anne of Green Gables, Frankenstein, One Flew Over the Cuckoo's Nest, 1984, Animal Farm, One Hundred Years of Solitude, Lord of the Flies, The War of the Worlds, Gone with the Wind, The Count of Monte Cristo, The Adventures of Sherlock Holmes, Adventures of Huckleberry Finn, The Catcher in the Rye,* and *Of Mice and Men.*

The students who recommended these canonical works struck a chord with their classmates when so many of them suggested that so-called boring canonical texts might not be so boring if the books were read outside of school. Influenced by this suggestion, one student wrote in his final evaluation for the course:

> I think everyone should read literature *leisurely* in their lives. I personally want to continue to read literary classics, so I am able to say that I read these classic books. For example, I asked for *Madame Bovary* for Christmas so I can continue to expand the number of classics that I have read. I think reading is important and reading is the way that [you] can expand yourself and continue to grow your ideas. This class has taught me how important books are for the movement of ideas across the world, which is why these societies [of the novels read for class] wanted to control that. Therefore, if we continue to read *for ourselves* we can continue to increase our flow of ideas. I think the expansion of knowledge is one universal truth I learned in this course. (italics added)

Conclusions

A recent study from the U.S. Bureau of Labor Statistics has found that the average American spends only 19 minutes a day reading; young people read less than ever, apparently, with people ages 25 to 34 reading eight minutes a day on weekends and holidays, while those 20 to 24 average around 10. This, of course, is a decline: a report from Common Sense Media found that 45% of 17-year-olds admit only reading for pleasure a few times a year—up from 19% in 1984.

—Bijan Stephen, "You Won't Believe
How Little Americans Read"

When I was a high school English teacher, I created a creative writing elective because it was my firmly held belief that we neglected creative writing in our high school English curricula. But what I didn't anticipate when I began the course was how powerful creative writing would be for so many students. The course became the most popular elective we offered. I taught four sections a year, and students from all academic tracks wrote and published alongside one another.

Sometimes the best consequences are unintended.

Something similar happened with this course. The intention was to recruit a few students to the English major. Instead, a bunch of future scientists, engineers, businesspeople, actuaries, pharmacists, and dentists came to the conclusion that reading literary fiction not only could offer them pleasure, recreation, and escape, but could actually improve their critical understanding of the world, deepen the emotional experience of their relationships, and foster empathy with other human beings. And truly, this is nothing I did, but rather something that happened as a result of putting sixteen or eighteen young people in a room together to talk about books with some minimal guidance and direction from the one adult in the room. The course, like the high school creative writing course, seemed to tap into an unmet need.

Why read? Because, as one of the actuarial sciences majors wrote, "I need the extraordinary."

Works Cited

"Books That Shaped America." *Library of Congress*. Web. 9 Dec. 2016.

Bradbury, Ray. *Fahrenheit 451*. New York: Simon and Schuster, 2013. Print.

Bruni, Frank. "Read, Kids, Read." *The New York Times*. 13 May 2014. Web. 9 Dec. 2016.

Castano, Emanuele, and David Comer Kidd. "Reading Literary Fiction Improves 'Mind Reading' Skills Finds a Study from the New School for Social Research: 'Theory of Mind' Fostered by Challenging, High-Quality Literature." *The New School*. 3 October 2013. Web. 9 Dec. 2016.

Edmundson, Mark. *Why Read?* New York: Bloomsbury, 2004. Print.

Fagan, Kate. "Split Image." *ESPNW*. 7 May 2015. Web. 9 Dec. 2016.

Foster, Thomas C. *How to Read Literature Like a Professor: A Lively and Entertaining Guide to Reading between the Lines*. New York: Harper Perennial, 2014. Print.

"Frequently Challenged Books." *American Library Association*. Web. 9 Dec. 2016.

Gaiman, Neil. "Why Our Future Depends on Libraries, Reading, and Daydreaming." *The Guardian*. 15 October 2015. Web. 9 Dec. 2016.

Gallagher, Kelly. *Readicide: How Schools Are Killing Reading and What You Can Do about It*. Portland: Stenhouse, 2009. Print.

Huxley, Aldous. *Brave New World*. New York: Harper Perennial, 2006. Print.

Jolliffe, David A., and Allison Harl. "Texts of Our Institutional Lives: Studying the 'Reading Transition' from High School to College: What Are Our Students Reading and Why?" *College English* 70:6 (2008): 599–607. Print.

Killough, Laura. "Role Modeling Reading—How to Reverse a Trend of Kids Who Hardly Read." *BlogCEA*. 13 May 2014. Web. 9 Dec. 2016.

"Leisure Reading: A Joint Position Statement of the International Reading Association, The Canadian Children's Book Centre, and the National Council of Teachers of English." Newark, DE: International Reading Association, 2014. Print.

Lowry, Lois. *The Giver*. Boston: Houghton Mifflin, 1993. Print.

Martin, Lauren. "Why Readers, Scientifically, Are the Best People to Fall in Love With." *Elite Daily*. 9 July 2014. Web. 9 Dec. 2016.

Masciotra, David. "Pulling the Plug on English Departments: The Armies of Soft Philistinism Are on the March and Eager to Ditch Traditional Literature Instruction in Favor of More Utilitarian Approaches. To the Barricades!" *The Daily Beast*. 28 July 2014. Web. 9 Dec. 2016.

Mattix, Micah. "Why Read Literature?" *First Things*. 30 August 2013. Web. 9 Dec. 2016.

Paul, Annie Murphy. "Reading Literature Makes Us Smarter and Nicer: 'Deep Reading' Is Vigorous Exercise from the Brain and Increases Our Real-Life Capacity for Empathy." *Time*. 3 June 2013. Web. 9 Dec. 2016.

Reitz, Stephanie. "Connecticut Legislature Approves Transformational $1.5 Billion Investment in UConn." *UConn Today*. 5 June 2013. Web. 9 Dec. 2016.

Rose, Charlie. "A Discussion about the History and Future of Books." *YouTube*. 20 November 2012. Web. 9 Dec. 2016.

Rosenblatt, Louise. *The Reader, the Text, the Poem: The Transactional Theory of the Literary Work*. Carbondale: Southern Illinois UP, 1978. Print.

Rosenwald, Michael. "Serious Reading Takes a Hit from Online Scanning and Skimming." *Washington Post*. 6 April 2014. Web. 9 Dec. 2016.

Ryan, Julia. "Reading a Novel Changes Your Brain: College Students Experienced Heightened Connectivity in Their Left Temporal Cortexes after Reading Fiction." *The Atlantic*. 9 January 2014. Web. 9 Dec. 2016.

Schocker, Laura. "*6 Unconventional Reasons Why You Absolutely Should Be Reading Books*." *The Huffington Post*. 12 October 2013. Web. 9 Dec. 2016.

Stephen, Bijan. "You Won't Believe How Little Americans Read." *Time*. 22 June 2014. Web. 9 Dec. 2016.

II

LISTENING TO STUDENTS

CHAPTER FIVE

The Unschooled Writer

MEREDITH ROSS
Tallahassee Community College

Driven, highly educated, and inclined by both profession and personality to manipulate systems to her advantage, my mother fit the media portrait of a "millennial parent" in many ways. She was armed with the will and the knowledge to ensure that I got the best possible education, and she was disinclined to leave anything to chance. So, when I was five years old, we drove five minutes to the well-considered elementary school we were zoned for. That was what was done, the universally accepted first step on the road of suburban, upper-middle-class success.

I don't remember much about the woman we spoke to there. What I really remember are the buses and the Abbott-and-Costello-style conversation they forced me into. Toward the end of the tour, the woman led us to the fleet of shiny yellow school buses in order to explain to me the complexities of arriving at school each morning.

"You'll be riding in on the black bus, honey," she told me, in what may have been the only part of the conversation directed at me the entire day. "But they're all yellow," I pointed out. "Nono-nonono," she corrected, indicating the large signs in the window of each bus. "See how this bus has a picture of a black bus in the window, and this one has a picture of a red bus in the window? You'll be on the yellow bus with the picture of a black bus."

"Yes," I agreed, "I understand that; I just think it would be less confusing if you used numbers instead of colors." Though it would be ten more years before I learned about Magritte, I already knew that *c'est ne pas un bus noir,* and I wasn't sure why anyone would design a system with such layers of needless complexity. Later, I would realize that just because I knew how to recognize numbers did not mean that all five-year-olds knew how to recognize numbers.

My mother spent the tour learning about what five-year-olds could and could not do in elementary school. Five-year-olds could not leave kindergarten during naptime to have storytime with the first graders, even if they could already read and hadn't taken a nap in three years. Five-year-olds could not take Friday off so their families could get a head start on the drive to Disney World, or just because they wanted to spend the day at home. Five-year-olds had to come to school every single day unless they were legitimately sick. Five-year-olds had to do homework every single night, even if everyone agreed it was stupid, and carry backpacks with them to school every single morning, no matter how concerned their mothers might be about the effect heavy loads might have on developing bodies. Perhaps most egregiously, five-year-olds' mothers had to fill out lots of paperwork, in triplicate, identifying a variety of different phone numbers for each parent, even if they weren't divorced, a point my mother insists on emphasizing every time she tells the story.

In the car on the way home, both of us were uncharacteristically silent, me mulling over the kind of people who would create such a preposterous method of bus classification, my mother considering the inflexibility of systems.

"Meredith," she said, "would you like to just stay at home for another year?"

"Yes."

"Good," she said, and we went home to stay.

Homeschooling, then, started as a kind of accident, something my family chose without exactly meaning to. Over the following twelve years, as we continued to choose it with greater and greater intentionality, homeschooling grew into an educational and life philosophy, a day-to-day reality that changed everything. It wasn't intended as a revolutionary act, or a prescriptive exercise for the world at large; my parents wanted to tailor my education to me, to give one very specific child one very specific educational experience, and used homeschooling as their mechanism. That singular experience—marked by independence, encouragement to immerse myself in reading and writing, and the freedom to make mistakes—prepared me to become the writer I am today and provided the foundation on which I built my undergraduate and graduate degrees.

John Holt and Unschooling

I anticipate that folklorists will someday classify the specific story structure of the "homeschool reveal"—that is, the cautious apologia engaged in by homeschoolers when they tell someone that they're homeschoolers. In my experience, the stories homeschoolers tell others to explain themselves almost invariably include negative identity creation, describing what they are in terms of what they are not. An ideal example of this reveal is performed by Tina Fey's formerly homeschooled main character, Cady, five minutes into the film *Mean Girls:* "I know what you're thinking: homeschooled kids are freaks. Or that we're weirdly religious or something. But my family's totally normal."

In this chapter, I have to engage with that means of identity creation, in part to more precisely articulate how my background helped me become a writer, and in part because I engage it every time I discuss my background with anyone, even as an adult. My family and I weren't exactly "freaks," and we weren't religious fundamentalists—we began as uncommitted Presbyterians and slowly faded into relaxed atheists. But contrary to what I told other kids when growing up, we weren't exactly normal, either.

My mother has a doctorate in education administration and made her career in educational policy in 1980s North Florida, first as a lobbyist, later working for the Florida Department of Education. This meant that, even though she may have wound up homeschooling by accident, she had a strong education background from which to draw. Though I have no idea how early she consciously began implementing his ideas, she'd learned about John Holt and his "unschooling" movement somewhere in her graduate work. Holt, a former teacher whose books *How Children Fail* and *How Children Learn* caused a stir in the late 1960s and early 1970s, was originally interested in public school reform. However, by 1976, when he published *Instead of Education: Ways to Help People Do Things Better,* he had given up on reform and instead began advocating that children not go to school at all, going so far as to suggest the implementation of a "children's underground railroad" to "save" young people from "compulsory schooling" (218). Holt's central philosophy was that humans are creatures who love to learn, who will seek out learning, who do not need to be forced to discover. He argued that the traditional school model set children up for failure by emphasizing memorization and busywork rather than real hands-on learning. He also posited a simple idea that remains controversial: that children (and people in general) should focus on learning things that interest them rather than things that don't. Trying to learn things you don't care about, Holt thought, was inherently pointless because you would never learn it very well and have a miserable time in the process. "Unschooling," as he eventually came to call his philosophy, was quite simply exactly what it sounded like. It wasn't homeschooling; it wasn't school at home; it was raising independent, free-range children in what we might consider the Atticus Finch model.

We were unschoolers—trivia I learned to slowroll as I grew up, since saying it out loud made me sound insane. Had social scientists come by to collect the data, I'm sure they could have produced a long paper focusing on me as a controlled experiment in Holt-ism. There were no "school hours," no division between "free time" and "learning time." No textbook or workbook ever cracked, no homework ever assigned, no test ever taken. My mother was not my teacher, but my facilitator. She kept the lines of communication open, discovering what I was interested in and excited about, and then she found ways to help me experience it. If I was unexcited about or averse to something, she wouldn't push; she would simply wait and then revisit the issue to see if I had changed my mind.

When I was a child, my mother was fond of telling people that our family "learned from the world around us." It was a pat answer, but it was true. Holt believed the experiential would always beat the theoretical, another point that made him controversial: he advocated the removal of a minimum voting age, along with the repeal of many child labor laws. If children wanted to work, that was their business, as far as John Holt was concerned. While my mother didn't plan on sending me to the looms, she agreed with Holt's basic idea and told me and my brother that we should live lives rich with experience. Though my family walked under the dubious banner of homeschooling, we were rarely at home. We were at libraries, museums, scientific talks, music lessons, art lessons, dance lessons, fencing lessons, nature preserves, meetings of the state legislature, Girl Scouts, community theater productions, concerts, the movies, and a host of esoteric summer day camps (North Florida History Camp being perhaps the most oddly specific).

It was on this uniquely eccentric stage that I would begin to become a writer, almost without noticing.

Reading Like a Writer

I became a writer by first becoming a reader. Like the rest of my generation, I fell in love with a certain boy wizard, but he was neither my first love nor my last. To suggest that reading was encouraged in my house would be akin to suggesting that air was encouraged. Books were a simple fact of life that predates memory; my first memory, in fact, is recognizing the word *the* in a Richard Scarry book as my father read it aloud to me. The works of Maurice Sendak were perennial favorites in early childhood, with E. L. Konigsburg, C. S. Lewis, Louisa May Alcott, Frances Hodgson Burnett, and Madeleine L'Engle replacing them as I grew older. My parents, exhausted by my constant demands to be read to for hours every single night (because who doesn't like being read to, even if she can already read?), bought me a cassette player so I could listen to audiobooks every night as I fell asleep. They tried to draw the line at "no books at the dinner table," but that rule was eventually abandoned due to my inventive sneaking.

"I know you said I couldn't leave the table to get *The Cat in the Hat,* but I just happened to spot it on my way back from the bathroom, and I really wanted to show you this illustration of the Cat balancing the fish on his umbrella, because I was reminded of it when you mentioned fish before."

I was three.

Because reading was what interested me, it was what I did, and because my parents' highest law was that I do what interested me, no one demanded that I stop or focus on something else. When I was thirteen, I started riding my bike to the nearby branch of the public library, where I became a serial browser, plucking books off shelves because I appreciated their titles or was drawn by their cover art. I knew how to use the library catalog, but I was rarely looking for anything specific; I took a fierce pride in browsing, in shelf scanning, in stumbling across something I might not have known to look for. I delighted in exploring with no guide, no frame of reference, a one-girl Lewis and Clark making a study of the northeast branch. The only real challenge was getting the books home on the bike.

Not only were we a family that read, but we were also a family that talked about reading, almost incessantly. We would recommend books to one another, read them together or separately, and talk and talk and talk. What did we like? What did we dislike? Why? How did what we'd read work (or not) with other things we'd read? There were no wrong answers, only discussion and a shared enjoyment in interpretation—although there were some heated moments. I am reminded particularly of a discussion my mother and I had of *The Wind Done Gone* in relation to *Gone with the Wind,* in which my mother posited that the mere existence of the former was an insult to the latter and essentially ruining her childhood. I doubt I could have gotten away with yelling "You are totally missing the point of reappropriation of harmful tropes!" in a traditional high school English class, but my mom forgave me relatively quickly, partly because she was glad I was passionate and partly because I was eleven.

"Oh, my god," an acquaintance said recently on hearing about my background, "did you grow up in a doctoral program?" Essentially, yes.

My freedom of reading, unconstrained by summer reading lists or even a working literary canon, allowed me to jump wildly and unsystematically through books, interpreting them myself and creating my own points of connection, bounding from *Jane Eyre* to *The Color Purple* to the Discworld series to *The Great Gatsby* to *The Handmaid's Tale* to the His Dark Materials trilogy to *Dave Barry Is Not Making This Up.* I was thinking about words and stories and books all the time and discussing those books with my parents—a nonmandatory but enjoyable activity that imbued them with meaning and even greater value. It wasn't just that reading made me want to write, although it did. It was that I was exposed to the contours of rhetoric early and often, and developed a reverence for the elegance and power of the written word. By the age of eight, I had clearly formed, if not easily articulable, ideas of what writing could be, what it could do, and why it mattered. Because I was a reader, I believed in writing's capacity to develop and communicate thought in the transcendent connection between writer and reader. And I wanted in.

Thinking Like a Writer

It's something you don't notice unless you're a homeschooler, but the first question adults ask unfamiliar children is always about school. "How's school?" "What are you studying?" "What grade are you in?" When you explain that those questions are irrelevant to your life, the next default question is, "So, what are you planning on doing when you grow up?"

"I'm going to write the great American novel," I said. People usually stopped asking questions after that.

When I was very young, my father was a working journalist, and I told him I wanted to be just like him when I grew up: a writer. While John Holt might have suggested signing me up as a stringer at the paper, my dad took the less radical step of giving me old reporters notebooks, the small ones with the pages that flip over the top and make you feel like you're in a 1940s gangster flick. Some weekends he would take me to his office so that I could type my stories on the real electric typewriters, their resounding clickety-clacks giving the words weight, assuring me that I'd made it to the big time. If I was good, my father would take me into the briefing room, a special treat. The game we played was simple but elegant: one of us stood behind the podium, playing the role of President of the United States, issuing statements and answering questions, while the other sat in front, playing the Ace Reporter, not letting the President off the hook. While other fathers and daughters played pretend in the world of fantasy, peopled with unicorns, princesses, and incorruptibility, my dad instead invited me into the world he lived in—a world of tough questions and slippery evasions, where the only real virtue lay in uncovering and enunciating the truth. He let me glimpse something of what it was to be a working writer, to feel around the edges of a possible future.

My writing habit began early on and developed hand in hand with my voracious reading. Not long after our ill-fated elementary school visit, I handwrote and illustrated a series of tales about characters I called Catty and Mousey, who, in retrospect, would certainly not have held up under any copyright scrutiny from the *Tom and Jerry* people. My mother explained to me how I could best lay out the pages and balance illustrations with text to make the manuscript look like a "real book," and when I was done she helped me staple my loose pages together in a primitive sort of binding. I recall being concerned that the pages of the finished product were not double-sided, which made it look unprofessional, and resolved to fix the problem next time. My quest for a kind of visual authenticity plagued my later writing as well—as an eight-year-old, I spent hours teaching myself Microsoft Word to ensure that my amateur publications had the spacing, fonts, double-sided printing, and general formatting that I considered the marks of professionalism.

I started a variety of publications when I was middle and high school age. The highest circulation I ever reached was four, and that was only if my grandmother came to visit. Sometimes these publications followed local events, sometimes they were humorous takes on Associated Press stories. Frequently they were attempts at satire that didn't quite land, like the article about Jesus and Judas having a celebrity feud, using only quotes from Lindsay Lohan and Hilary Duff, or the article about the Catholic Church's changing stance on exorcism ("with the ghosts taken care of, the Church will be able to focus on their real adversaries: Protestants"). I was exploring, experimenting with different voices and styles, which alternated between terrible and carbon copies of whomever I was reading at the time.

I also had a blog in which I focused on more esoteric topics, including literature, politics, and snarky teenaged thoughts about my everyday life. When I got my first job, I wrote about the old women who sat in the lobby next to my office and pontificated about their lives. I referred to them as "the Parade of Deranged Hillbillies" and frequently opened up their monologues for discussion among friends, family, and the Internet at large. I also wrote a summary of *Rick Steves Best of Europe* in the "voice of Rick Steves." An excerpt:

> Well, hello, again, it is still me, Rick Steves. Do not fear, I am not the sort of man who would abandon you in a foreign country, and certainly not on a subway. I am in a CAFE, a sort of French restaurant where one can order caff-ay ole-ay and bag-ettes. It is often a fun activity to sit in a cafe and be stared at by disgruntled French people. Oh! I did not mean to confuse you with all those French words all at once. Perhaps I had better explain. I will be using lots of French phrases in this videocassette. But since you are probably too unintelligent to speak French, I will pronounce the words incorrectly in both French AND English, utilizing a special vernacular of my own devising, known only as "Frangalis." This sullen, excessively bearded man is my companion, Francois. He will accompany me in restaurant scenes throughout the videocassette. Francois does not respond to any of my questions in French, English, or Frangalis, so I can only assume that he is a feral man-bear.

My blog helped me to develop a distinctive writerly voice. It gave me a creative space in which to play with different forms of writing, including the personal essay, which served me in particularly good stead in my undergraduate creative writing program at Florida State University. In reviewing my personal essays from that time, I am struck by how clearly they are the descendants of Rick Steves and Francois the feral man-bear, and how obvious it is that my silliness helped me develop serious skills. In my junior year, detailing one of my more colorful family members, I wrote:

> She came bearing gifts, though not gifts in the traditional sense: her offerings were the sort of fare one might wind up with in a secret Santa exchange in which the spending limit was zero dollars. For me and my mother, she brought a paperback which chronicled the rise of the Beatles, but not the fall of the Beatles, because that had not yet happened when it went to print. "I remembered you liked the Beatles," she said, a statement that struck me as the epitome of laziness. Saying you "remembered" that someone likes the Beatles is like saying you "remembered" that someone hates head lice: while it's a safe bet you're right, wrapping a delousing comb in ribbon hardly speaks to your thoughtfulness or ingenuity.

Even though I used blogging to experiment with different forms, that isn't how I thought about it at the time—because, like a child learning to speak in a bilingual home, I made no distinction yet between the different forms I was learning. Language is language, writing is writing, and writing was everything. Blogging helped me grow up fluent in different writing styles, preparing me to be an interdisciplinary writer by freeing me from categories. For me, there wasn't a difference between my personal essay/review/satire of Rick Steves and my nascent political and literary analyses, or my more journalistic accounts of people around me and things I was learning. As a college and later graduate student who moved through several different disciplines, this attitude allowed me to seamlessly transition from writing poetry to writing basic research papers to writing annotated bibliographies to writing academic articles. I never approached new assignments as alien, as puzzles to be solved: they were all writing, weren't they?

Like my reading, my writing was never boxed in, shrink-wrapped, optimized for consumption. It was up to me to decide what good writing was and how to perform it. I didn't learn what a five-paragraph essay was until I got to community college and was expressly told not to write one.

"Well, that was easy," I thought.

The very first time I ever took a test I was ten years old, participating in a regional talent search for a Dick Clark–hosted program called *Challenge of the Child Geniuses: Who Is the Smartest Kid in America?* My mother had tried to explain to the talent scout that I wasn't really what they were looking for; I wasn't used to testing or standards, and I had yet to become the broad-knowledge trivia genius I am today. But the more she protested and tried to explain about my curious upbringing, the more enthusiastic the scout became, probably because of the common perception, to again quote Fey, of all homeschoolers as "freaks, or weirdly religious." It had been established that my family was not homeschooling for religious reasons, therefore it was assumed that I was some sort of mathlete science fair spelling bee champ. I think the Dick Clark people were expecting a diamond-in-the-rough Hermione Granger type, and instead they got me: less of an eager, A+ student and more of a cantankerous emeritus professor who has long since ceased to care about anything outside of his own discipline, and who also doesn't understand why everyone gets so uptight about socks matching. As a ten-year-old, I knew a lot about the things I knew about, but not much else.

I took the test differently than the other kids. They had what I now understand to be good test-taking skills: they all sat up straight, pencils poised, and carefully considered each question before answering it and moving on to the next one. They used all the time that was given to them; if they finished early, they used that time to check their answers. I bet they did great on the SATs. I, on the other hand, sprawled almost my entire torso across the table in an effort to get my face as close as possible to the paper. I don't know why I thought this would help, but it felt right (incidentally, I adopted the same strategy when taking notes as an undergraduate; several professors, I'm sure, thought I was asleep—until they read my work). I flicked through the questions, picking ones to answer largely at random. If I was sure of the answer, I painstakingly wrote it down in my still-bad handwriting; if I had to think about an answer, I simply skipped the question. I intended to come back later, but I was so unsystematic that nine times out of ten I probably didn't. I finished first because I decided I'd done all I could do and that was that and let's move on to the next thing, and I didn't check any of my answers or take my time or do any of the things I would and did do as an adult. The real difference between me and the other kids, though, was that they cared and I didn't. I had been raised to believe that testing wasn't important, and passing or not passing a test had no say over who I was or what I could do. And the way I was raised, this was true. There would be other tests in my life, later, that would matter. Passing a test could show a professor that I understood the material. Passing a test could get me a degree. Passing a test could get me into graduate school. But passing a test could never measure my worth, or make me truly happy on its own, or help me in the real world. Because of unschooling, I saw tests as means, not ends.

No one gave me my score on the fifty-page written test, and that was probably a kindness. I know I bombed it. I skipped all of the math and science questions and answered the art, literature, and history questions to the best of my ability. But I remember being surprised at the flatness of the questions. Sure, I could answer the one question about the Declaration of Independence, but it seemed lonely and insufficient when there weren't any follow-ups about the colonial political situation or the dynamics of the Declaration writing committee, both things I could have happily and competently discussed at length. I knew who shot Lincoln, but wouldn't it have been more interesting (and, I thought, a better indicator of "smartness") to talk to me about why he did it, and what he yelled from the stage after leaping onto it and breaking his ankle? I had grown up in a world of context and complexity, and the trivia questions and the flat answers in boxes just weren't cutting it. If I was going to propose an answer to a question, I wanted it to be a question worth talking about, and I wanted to answer it fully. I was a writer.

The June Mingle: On Being Allowed to Make Mistakes

One of the traditions my mom instituted when I was still elementary-school-age was that I read the news out loud in the car. It was a sly plan; she was able to help me develop my reading skills and keep up with current events while she ran errands. If there was anything I didn't understand, she explained. If I had trouble with a word, she helped me work it out contextually or, sometimes, just read it for me when we stopped at a light.

When I was nine years old, I read her a *Newsweek* cover story on the ongoing Elián González situation, clipping along at a good speed as usual. "The boy's father, June Mingle, said that . . ."

"Wait a second," my mom interrupted. "Elián González's father is named June Mingle?"

"I know, it's weird." I said. "But it's spelled J-U-A-N space M-I-G-U-E-L."

My mother tried really, really hard to hide her smile, but she couldn't quite manage it.

"That's pronounced Huwan Migelle," she articulated carefully, "because it's a Spanish name."

"Oh, that makes a lot more sense than June Mingle."

With that, we both started laughing helplessly, and we didn't stop for quite some time.

"It sounds like some sort of midsummer party, maybe like a family reunion," my mom choked out.

"See you at the June Mingle!" I yelled, and we dissolved in giggles again. This was an in-joke between us for years.

Almost every mistake I made as a child, small or large, was handled this way, as an understandable, easily correctable mistake rather than an insurmountable failure or something that needed to be addressed seriously. There were no grades, no progress reports, no standards to meet. The only questions I had to answer were "What do I want to do?" and "How do I do it?" I wasn't afraid of failing, I wasn't afraid to try things, and even when I elicited laughter, it was laughing *with* rather than *at*. I don't know if there's a better lesson for a writer to learn: do your best, and if it comes out wrong, just laugh and know better next time.

This allowance for mistakes—the understanding that I did not need to be perfect at everything every time—may have helped me become a writer more than anything else. When I was young, it was hard for my mother to get me interested in math. I responded to it with a very specific, panicky aversion that didn't manifest with anything else. Even the gentlest forms of exposure (grocery store and drive-through math, entertainment-driven games and videos, offhand problem solving) could lead to tears. I didn't like it and I didn't get it. Like the Holtian she was, my mother didn't push it. She would revisit the subject every few months to see if I felt differently, but I never did—and so I reached community college with a first-grade knowledge of math. Scoring a 112/120 on the English portion and a 38/120 on the math portion of my placement test, I landed in a remedial arithmetic class. I determined to apply myself; if there was one thing unschooling had given me, it was a confidence in my capacity to learn anything.

As it turned out, that confidence was misplaced when it came to the world of mathematics. After earning Ds and Fs on all of the exams by midterms, I, straight-A honor student, wound up sobbing in the professor's office. I had done all the homework and everything that was asked of me; I had yanked on my own bootstraps until my hands were bleeding. The professor gently suggested that I might have a learning disability, which was confirmed through testing with a psychologist later in the semester.

I had been terrified of math as a child because I had an undiagnosed math-specific processing disorder known as dyscalculia, which gives me trouble with math-related abstractions, processing numbers, and estimating distances. I still use a calculator for everything (except tip math), and I probably always will; it's simply how my brain is wired.

"Thank goodness you weren't in the public school system," the psychologist said. "They would have made you keep doing math, and you wouldn't have gotten any better at it, and you would have wound up in a special ed track."

He was right. Great strengths combined with great weaknesses isn't something well-accounted for in the schooled paradigm: you're a good student or you're not. Poor performance in one area indicates failure in all areas. In unschooling it was expected that I wouldn't be equally good at everything, and that it wasn't particularly helpful to allow my math deficits to compromise my reading and writing. My community college understood this too; after my diagnosis, I was exempted from future math requirements.

Being exempt from the K–12 educational system is what allowed me to thrive in college and graduate school. Not only was I able to focus on reading and writing and developing writing instincts, but I was also saved from being pigeonholed and forced to bang my head against an educational brick wall. I have joked to friends that "I'm just getting my twelve years of school on the back end," and, between us, I think I picked the right half of school to attend.

Me, Matilda, and the Guy in the Bar

My mother read *Matilda*, Roald Dahl's children's classic, for the first time this past spring. This was a bizarre and unacceptable oversight, given that my childhood can be understood as an attempt to correct for everything that plagued Dahl's title character. Matilda, a preternaturally smart little girl, is inexplicably born to cruel and foolish parents whose main interests are television, bingo, and light fraud. Realizing that she will never be valued at home, Matilda takes comfort at the local library, where she reads all of the great classics (plus the entire children's section) by the age of four. Her excitement at starting school is thwarted by abusive headmistress Miss Trunchbull, who delights in torturing children, frequently dangling and throwing them by ears and pigtails. Miss Trunchbull also refuses to recognize Matilda's brilliance, allowing her to languish in kindergarten, where Matilda's underexercised mind develops telekinetic powers, which she ultimately uses to create a happy ending for those who deserve it. I too was a smart little girl, although I am still perhaps not quite as well-read as Matilda. My parents were kind, smart, and supportive—and, wary of real-world Trunchbulls, they never sent me to school.

Homeschooling, or unschooling, isn't a good choice for everyone—it wouldn't have been a good choice for Matilda. Trunchbull aside, school saved Matilda from her awful parents. In her school-sponsored happy ending, Matilda was moved up to the tenth grade, Doogie Howser–style, and was allowed to leave her biological family and come under the guardianship of her kind teacher, Miss Honey. I'm not here to suggest that homeschooling is a foolproof recipe for producing a writer; homeschooling, like any other lifestyle choice, depends on the individual. What I can attest to is that unschooling was the right choice for me. Not only did it allow me to become what I wanted to be, but I was also encouraged to *learn* what I wanted to be, to get to know myself without any distractions. It was understood that traditional schoolwork—standardized tests, assigned reading and writing—would distract from the big picture, and I was the big picture.

My parents gave me all the tools to succeed as a writer, but having a box of tools doesn't mean you know how to build a fence. What it does mean is that, when the opportunity presents itself, you will be able to learn how to build a fence faster and more easily than someone without a box of tools. Furthermore, just knowing that you have a box of tools makes you more enthusiastic about building a fence than you would be otherwise, because, hey, you know you've got everything you need. When I was fifteen, I began my community college career and started using the tools my parents gave me to become a real writer. But—if I may extend the metaphor further than is perhaps wise—all of those tools remained under a guaranteed parental warranty.

Early on in Freshman Composition, I was having trouble crafting thesis statements, as most beginning writers do. Despite the guidance of my experienced and patient instructor, John Pekins (who deserves any and all credit for my writing left to be appropriated), I wasn't getting it. I just wasn't sure what a thesis statement was, a frustration I expressed to my father as he drove me home from school one day.

"Okay, think of it like this," he said "You're writing something, and you've been working on it a long time, so you need to take a break. You go to a bar."

He glanced over at me, and amended, "or a restaurant, I guess. And there's a guy there, at the bar. . . ."

"Restaurant," I corrected.

"Sure, whatever, this place. Anyway, there's this guy, and you know him from around, and he knows you've been working on something, and he asks you what you're writing about."

"Okay. Then what?"

"Then, what do you tell him? What you tell him is your thesis, essentially."

In the intervening years, I have heard theses described as arguments, as aboutness, as the point, and still the thing that makes the most sense to me is that guy in the bar (or restaurant). I introduce him to my students and invite them to share their theses with him. I visit him when I write, venturing into the knotty, wood-paneled bar of my imagination, where it smells like beer and brass and everything is covered in a layer of grime that manages to be inoffensively comforting. Sometimes I have trouble explaining to him what I'm writing about. In my imagination, he scrunches up a fat, red face in confusion, worrying the brim of the worn-out fedora he set on the stool next to him (in my imagination, he's an alcoholic, but a funny, self-consciously Irish one from the imaginary world of 1950s television). When he makes that face, I reframe. And reframe. And reframe, until his round, red face illuminates like the sun, and I can bid him happily goodbye until next time.

By unschooling me, my parents gave me what I needed to be a writer: the freedom to read, to write, to explore, to practice, and, of course, to explain myself to that guy at the bar.

"Faithfully Clinched":
A Response to "The Unschooled Writer"

JOHN PEKINS

Tallahassee Community College

In the final pages of *Walden*, Henry David Thoreau provides this "hammer-and-nails" characterization of good writing: "Drive a nail home and clinch it so faithfully that you can wake up in the night and think of your work with satisfaction" (311). I believe that Meredith Ross accomplishes Thoreau's goal in her "faithfully clinched" article, "The Unschooled Writer," and I am honored to respond. I number Meredith among the most outstanding students I worked with during thirty-five years in the Florida public education system. In 2006 she arrived at my Tallahassee Community College (TCC) ENC1101 class as a dual-enrolled, homeschooling high school junior. Soon after, we worked again in second-semester composition. Finally, before she had reached the usual age for completing high school in Florida, Meredith received funding to help me design and pilot a college composition mentoring course. Her responsibilities included participating in a two-semester brainstorming and design process, mentoring sixty college composition students, and providing valuable editor's input on the various documents I wrote throughout the project. She eventually graduated from TCC with honors and went on to distinguish herself at Florida State University (FSU), earning both a BA in creative writing (summa cum laude) and an MS in library science. She is now completing coursework as a doctoral student in FSU's religious studies program and also teaching classes and mentoring undergraduate student writers as part of her teaching assistant duties. I am grateful for the teacher-student working relationship and now valuable friendship that has evolved over ten years of knowing and working with Meredith. I am also grateful for the opportunity to watch her career unfold in most remarkable fashion, the fulfillment of her parents' decision to homeschool her—a validation of their courage and also of Meredith's own determination to make the most of the opportunity this presented.

The bulk of our collaboration for this project took place during the fall of 2013, my last semester before retirement—the end of a career process that Meredith is just now beginning. May these responses honor both her fine essay and also the efforts of composition educators and their students.

I. What Is "College-Level" Writing?

For three volumes, this publishing project has explored Patrick Sullivan's highly productive question, "What Is 'College-Level' Writing?" Patrick and his fellow editors, Sheridan Blau and Howard Tinberg, demonstrate great wisdom in providing students an opportunity to take the lead in addressing this question and, in so doing, to discuss the influence of reading on their writing practice. As one confirmation of these editors' vision, Meredith offers this insightful narrative of her early encounters with the integral relationship of reading to writing:

> It wasn't just that reading made me want to write, although it did. It was that I was exposed to the contours of rhetoric early and often, and developed a reverence for the elegance and power of the written word. By the age of eight, I had clearly formed, if not easily articulable, ideas of what writing could be, what it could do, and why it mattered. Because I was a reader, I believed in writing's capacity to develop and communicate thought in the transcendent connection between writer and reader. And I wanted in.

So, a question: what is "college-level" writing? Answer: what Meredith began learning between the ages of three and eight. Our field should note Meredith's points, including her emphasis on reading, and we should also note the age and manner in which she arrived at these points. As Meredith's experience testifies, reading as a writer and writing as a reader are reachable goals for students at any level, preK to college. Indeed, these goals are not just reachable, if I read her essay correctly, but also essential if students are to make full use of the written language experiences they encounter throughout their academic years and beyond.

II. "College-Level" Reading/Writing and K–12 Preparation

Earlier in this now three-volume series, I discussed an approach to college-level reading and writing called "reading/writing," suggesting a way to see the two processes as integrated rather than separate. In college one does not only read or write, any more than in breathing one only inhales or exhales. In the end, reading and writing combine to support a larger process, written language, just as inhalation and exhalation combine to support respiration (Pekins 239). Carol Smith, an insightful and generous scholar from Fort Lewis College in Durango, Colorado, was among the first colleagues to expose me to the integral relationship of college-level reading and writing. In writing the following passage for Fort Lewis first-year composition students, Smith provides an important summary of the college written language environment, one which, with her permission, I shared with thousands of my own TCC composition students:

> We are always understanding one text in terms of another, developing our ideas in the context of what has already been thought, and writing our papers in response to others' papers. The concept *intertextuality* describes this cumulative and interactive process through which we attempt to create knowledge and reach understanding through reading and writing. (xiv)

"I became a writer by first becoming a reader," Meredith asserts in the section "Reading Like a Writer." Additionally, these reading and writing experiences took place in an environment Meredith characterizes as "marked by independence, encouragement to immerse myself in reading and writing, and the freedom to make mistakes." She believes that such intellectual freedom is not a luxury, as some might suggest, but a necessity if a student is to explore thoroughly her own mind and determine how best to use it.

As with Meredith's early commitment to intellectual freedom, we find the history of US postsecondary education often characterized as "the struggle for academic freedom," a battle that most, if not all, postsecondary academics view as both ongoing and also essential to ensuring an optimal environment for research, teaching, and learning. In light of this passionate commitment to academic freedom in postsecondary education, one reasonably wonders why such freedom is not as highly valued for K–12 students, many of whom often struggle in learning environments characterized by standardized curricula focused on minimum competencies and/or standardized tests. In the reading/writing area specifically, these tests frequently feature multiple-choice evaluation of reading achievement and five-paragraph writing evaluation involving little to no reference to reading. In her essay, we see Meredith confronting this struggle as a ten-year-old participating for the first time in a standardized testing experience and "being surprised at the flatness of the questions":

> I had grown up in a world of context and complexity, and the trivia questions and the flat answers in boxes just weren't cutting it. If I was going to propose an answer to a question, I wanted it to be a question worth talking about, and I wanted to answer it fully. I was a writer.

In my observation, many K–12 educators would assert that such an attitude toward one's writing represents an ideal outcome of K–12 reading/writing education. If I am correct in that understanding, a reasonable question emerges: why do we find a former homeschooler articulating these values, rather than the many traditional students who have traveled through "the system"? I suggest humbly that herein lies an important question for written language educators to explore.

III. Meredith's Homeschool Experiences and the Support They Can Offer Traditional Classrooms

Some educators might suggest that Meredith's homeschooling experiences are too far removed from traditional classrooms to offer suggestions on how to encourage more effective integration of reading and writing processes in those classrooms. In response, I offer that homeschooling, when approached open-mindedly, can indeed offer many suggestions that could benefit traditional education. What follows, therefore, represents an effort to identify points for educators to consider when exploring how best to build a bridge from Meredith's reading/writing homeschool experiences to traditional K–12 classrooms. While these suggestions are far from comprehensive—nor should they be, given the limited purposes of this short response—perhaps, in combination with Meredith's essay, they present a useful starting point.

A. Background

Before proceeding, I should mention some experiences that came my way during a thirty-five-year career in language education, as these experiences influence the lens through which I read and respond to Meredith's essay. First, from 1979 to 1988, I worked at Tallahassee's School for Applied Individualized Learning (SAIL), a publicly funded alternative school for grades 7–12. As directed by Florida statute, admission to SAIL was limited to students who demonstrated significant lack of success in traditional schools. When I began teaching college composition at Tallahassee Community College (TCC) in 1988, one of my goals was to incorporate into this more traditional setting what I had learned during nine years at SAIL, including extensive student conferencing and an emphasis on intellectual freedom. Also, in 1993 my wife, children, and I joined ten to twelve other families in starting the Tallahassee Homeschool Group, an organization that continues to this day and now includes well over 100 families. As our family's work with the homeschooling group advanced, I sought to incorporate insights from these homeschooling experiences into the TCC environment, encouraging students to ask questions about their own directions as learners and find ways to build meaningful bridges from those directions to priorities required by the institution.

The conclusion I draw from participating in this mix of traditional and alternative educational environments is that whatever the approach, teaching and learning in all environments have more in common than not, and each approach has much to offer the others along the overlapping pathways all approaches tread. Against this background, I will attempt to elaborate on the benefits Meredith emphasizes in her essay, including how adaptation of these benefits, however nontraditionally they may have emerged, might support the efforts of students and teachers in more traditional reading/writing classroom environments.

B. Boundlessness: Homeschooling's Foundation

I am convinced that what Meredith asserts about the benefits of homeschooling is not just "worth considering" or "valuable" in the broad, largely meaningless sense we often use those terms. Meredith sounds an alarm: Wake Up! Offer students fear-free reading/writing environments focused not on boxes to be checked or outcomes to be accomplished in rote sequences, one year to the next. Instead, offer an environment that supports each student in surprising herself or himself, and us as well, with what can be possible when the boxes and lists disappear. We owe students more than checked boxes and crowd-managing curriculum outcomes during the precious years of their youth. We owe them more respect for their journeys through this life than most school systems provide, as well as more accompanying opportunities to explore the open possibilities of their reading/writing experiences and the boundless imaginations these experiences speak to and emerge from.

Some might characterize the previous paragraph as a Whitmanesque "rant" leading to no practical application. In response, I would assert that no change can be accomplished without clear understanding of the foundational principles on which that change must take place. Holt understood that point, and Meredith demonstrates she understands as well when she says that "Holt's central philosophy was that humans are creatures who love to learn, who will seek out learning, who do not need to be forced to discover. He argued that the traditional school model set children up for failure by emphasizing memorization and busywork rather than real hands-on learning." Even as a young child, Meredith understood these important principles. Do I believe that students in traditional classrooms are also capable of understanding and therefore benefiting from these principles? Yes! As occurred with Meredith, if we expose students to these points in both theory and practice, and we treat students with the respect Holt recommends, the rest will take care of itself.

C. Shared Responsibility

The decision to homeschool represents a shared responsibility for all in the homeschooling family, resulting frequently in significant benefits, as demonstrated in Meredith's essay, and resulting also in significant challenges. I have already discussed some of the gains. Concerning the challenges, the first point to make is that, contrary to perceptions sometimes expressed in analyses of the home-schooling movement, these students do not represent a "gifted" or "privileged" class of children. Indeed, in my observation, the decision to homeschool is not undertaken lightly, as sacrifices for all in the family are sometimes extensive. At the financial level alone, homeschooling can be hard going. No social privilege there at all, so much as genuine concern about how the monthly bills will be paid. Still, these families choose homeschooling because they believe this approach offers children the best opportunity to develop their talents and learn how to share these talents with the world. This determined, whole-hearted family commitment to each child's education represents an essential element of any successful homeschooling effort.

When shifting perspective from individual homeschooling families to the larger community, or "extended family," of home-schoolers, one witnesses more opportunities for engagement in shared responsibility. As an example, while some homeschooling parents may be college educated, like Meredith's parents, others are not, a condition that offers many benefits for homeschooling families learning together, such as the Tallahassee Homeschool Group. Shared responsibility provides parents and children alike valuable opportunities to pool resources and draw from the strengths of each family. Knowledge bases are diverse and often shared in creative ways, both within and among these homeschooling families, resulting in special topics instruction, tutoring, field trips, and other experiences designed to support student learning—including individual and group reading/writing activities at every turn. These efforts represent just some of the opportunities homeschooling families encounter when approaching their respective educational decisions as shared responsibility.

One hears of the difficulties public schools encounter when seeking to provide adequate resources that support students' educational needs. Understandable financial obstacles and resource shortages often accompany tight budgets and restrict options available to enrich students' educational experiences. Perhaps an adaptation of homeschooling's individual family or community of families shared-responsibility approach might provide a valuable resource for schools seeking to expand their menus of available resources.

D. Elimination of Standardized Curricula and Standardized Tests

A suggestion discussed often among homeschooling families goes like this: There is no better time than now to abandon our twenty-year national experiment with K–12 competency testing. While consultants, research centers, and software and textbook publishers continue to profit greatly from this trend, in the end, all we have to show for it among our students is, at best, mastery of test-taking skills, a bottom-line competency that collapses dramatically when compared to the values of actual learning emphasized by Holt, Meredith, and others. We can start by formally acknowledging the artificial separation of reading and writing these instruments employ and the equally artificial separation of these processes such testing encourages in classroom instruction. In so doing, we would also make clear, as Carol Smith suggests, that students will rarely, if ever, be asked to engage at the postsecondary level in one process at the exclusion of the other. Instead, we should ensure that K–12 students are provided instruction; practice; and meaningful, supportive, growth-focused assessment in the integrated reading/writing processes they will practice as postsecondary students. These priorities become increasingly relevant as open-enrollment colleges and professional programs expand their presence across the country, and as the numbers of K–12 graduates attending these institutions expand as well.

E. The Importance of Imaginative Literature

Though some argue—and I agree—that the importance of imaginative literature has been downgraded in the standardized testing environment of the last two decades, homeschool advocates still assert that an effective reading/writing environment should include ample exploration of "literary experiences." Young people love stories. The present popularity of films and television programs for all age groups illustrates students' attraction to the pleasures of narrative. The parallel proliferation of recorded songs demonstrates their attraction to poetry. As Meredith suggests, students are not just drawn to these genres; they are fully capable of reading them and writing thoughtfully about their reading experiences as well—including what those experiences say about the world surrounding them. Like Meredith, students will read imaginative works, they will write about what they read when given the opportunity, and they will become stronger in their written language abilities as a result.

F. Two Recommendations for Postsecondary Institutions

Having read and written about Meredith's essay, I offer here these two postsecondary recommendations that emerge from that experience of "intertextuality" (with thanks to Carol Smith):

1. Based on conclusions discussed throughout this response, I recommend that faculty design integrated reading/writing process curricula for postsecondary reading and writing degrees, particularly those degrees related to teaching these written language processes. Not only will postsecondary students benefit from this change, but their future students will benefit as well.

2. I also recommend that college accrediting organizations withdraw their resistance to providing professionals with reading process backgrounds a place at the college composition table. As one who holds a graduate degree in the reading process and has overcome formal credential challenges on two occasions, I know firsthand that these professionals can provide great value to the college-level reading/writing classroom. Indeed, I would say that their contributions to students' reading/writing growth are as valuable as those provided by graduates in literary study, creative writing, and related degree tracks offered in graduate English programs and accepted without question by accrediting organizations.

IV. Conclusion

I thank Meredith Ross and also Patrick Sullivan, Howard Tinberg, and Sheridan Blau for the opportunity to respond to Meredith's essay. As I write, I have not yet read the other student essays. Knowing the editors, though, I am sure these articles are every bit as wonderful as Meredith's, and so I am left with a great sense of confidence in the next generation. I look forward to following their reading/writing adventures, and particularly their efforts to make reading/writing teaching and learning benefit all students in this great, wide world.

Works Cited

Holt, John C. *Instead of Education: Ways to Help People Do Things Better.* New York: Dutton, 1976. Print.

Pekins, John. "A Community College Professor Reflects on First-Year Composition." *What Is "College-Level" Writing?* Ed. Patrick Sullivan and Howard Tinberg. Urbana: NCTE, 2006. 231–42. Print.

Smith, Carol. "Three Questions (and the Answers) about College Composition." *Joining the Conversation.* 4th ed. Ed. Bridget Irish, Molly Costello Culver, Katherine Niles, and Susan Palko-Schraa. Acton: Copley Custom Publishing Group, 2004. x–xv. Print.

Thoreau, Henry David. *Walden.* New York: Fall River Press, 2008. Print.

CHAPTER SIX

Seeing the Differences: Writing in History (and Elsewhere)

EVAN PRETZLAFF

University of California, Santa Barbara

I've learned from working with Linda Adler-Kassner that it's a commonplace for college faculty to say that writing is different in high school and in college. Certainly, that's been my experience. But what I've also realized is that college faculty don't always help students develop lenses to analyze *how* writing is different—what the differences are, why they exist, and what we can do to adjust to them. In this chapter, I discuss the experiences I've had learning to conduct this kind of analysis. First, I describe experiences with high school teachers who helped me realize that writing is, in fact, different in different situations. Then I talk about a framework, called "threshold concepts," that provides a lens that I have used to analyze expectations for learning and writing in a number of college classes with great success.

Writing in High School: Identifying Difference . . . Sort Of

Before high school, *good writing* was consistently defined as writing that included a thesis at the beginning of the essay and a topic sentence at the beginning of every paragraph. This formatting, rather than content, was seen as the most important quality of any essay. When I arrived in high school (which in my district started in grade 10), three teachers taught me that what had seemed so straightforward was actually much more complicated. Mr. Oster, my English 10 Honors teacher and subsequent AP Composition and Literature teacher, guided much of the development of my writing style. Throughout my sophomore year. he honed our ability to analyze characters from the novels we read, the effects of the environment on them, the events that took place, and how those events relayed the importance of the novel itself. More important, he taught me how to make strong arguments by avoiding passive voice and through proper quote integration. What happened to my writing was a shift from simply writing to writing with a purpose. After his class, though, I realized that writing in English should consist of creating argumentative essays that didn't describe a text but instead analyzed it by clearly addressing a prompt and clearly arguing my points.

Mr. Oster's class was rigid. He gave the class a list of thirty rules that we could not break—things like "no passive voice" and "proper quote integration." But while I sometimes chafed at these rules, this rigidity helped me in college because it taught me how to write what the person grading my papers wants to hear. Because we were asked to revise, the class also made me realize the importance of a strong argument and underscoring key points by answering the prompt correctly and thoroughly. It also taught me as the importance of constant revision.

If tenth grade was marked by the realization that writing needed to conform to particular rules and prompts, eleventh-grade English and history classes were where I learned there could be differences between "good writing" from one context to another. Once I entered college, this realization became especially significant. Mrs. Neagley, my eleventh-grade English teacher, sought argumentative papers that clearly hit the main points of the prompt; however, there were no "thirty rules" to constrain my style. I remember one day I asked her how best to format my paragraphs, to which she responded, "I don't care so much about the length or if they're all structured the same. Just do what you need to argue your point. There is no cookie-cutter method for a strong, argumentative essay." A lightbulb went off: I realized that I didn't have to write five- to six-sentence paragraphs with one quote in them and move on. The length could be three sentences or it could be ten so long as the content was proper and thorough. But while these different writing assignments helped me realize that there was no *one* way to write, there were still strong similarities between them—they asked for a clear thesis and topic sentences, proper quote integration, and conclusive evidence arguing and furthering the point of the paper.

At the same time that I was learning about the different ways to write an English paper, writing in my AP US History course, taught by Mr. Lee, helped me realize that writing in history was different, and that the expectations for writing within disciplines spoke to things that were valued *in* disciplines. In English we were given analyses of texts when our teachers discussed those texts with us; in our papers, our job was to develop those analyses. In history we used texts to develop our own analyses about events. Writing these papers showed me how the recontextualization of primary documents provides valuable insight not possible in a simple read-through and taking all the words at face value.

These differences were related to the "threshold concepts" of history, the theoretical framework I want to focus on here. These concepts are critical for epistemological participation within disciplines. Jan H. F. Meyer and Ray Land, education researchers who wrote regarding their research on "threshold concepts," define them as "a portal, opening up a new and previously inaccessible way of thinking about something. It represents a transformed way of understanding . . . without which the reader cannot progress" (1). Threshold concepts play a critical role in shaping expectations for college-level writing because that writing needs to demonstrate the ways in which the writer—in this case, me as a student—understands and is able to employ these concepts and participate, even as a novice, in the discipline. In Mr. Lee's AP history class, I started learning some of these concepts in the discipline of history. For example, I learned that in writing for history classes, it's critical to interpret and recontextualize primary source documents, not just use them to fuel a description of "what happened" in a historical event or situation. It's also necessary to develop a thesis that makes an argument *about* a historical event and to use evidence to support that argument.

Threshold Concepts and College Writing

I came to understand these ideas *as* threshold concepts once I arrived at the University of California, Santa Barbara. In winter quarter 2011, I enrolled in two history courses (because I'm a history major) and Writing 2LK, a required lower-division writing course. Based on my experiences in Mr. Oster's, Mrs. Neagley's, and Mr. Lee's classes, I started to think about differences in expectations for writing between history and English. Because Writing 2LK focused on the study of writing, I learned how to investigate these differences more systematically and consider their implications for my writing. Our section was a special class in which all students were also enrolled in History 17b (American History from 1840–1920).

In Writing 2LK, we used the lens of threshold concepts to analyze expectations for writing in history, especially in the second assignment of the course, which asked us to analyze materials from History 17b (syllabi, assignments, course materials) and to interview faculty or TAs teaching the course in order to identify threshold concepts. Then we had to analyze our own writing from a history course to identify where the concepts were or were not present. This explicit application of the threshold concepts framework encouraged me to think about where threshold concepts were—and were not—present in my essays and in the course itself. It also provided a useful lens for thinking about the expectations for writing in history and their relationship to those threshold concepts.

In my Writing 2LK research, I identified three threshold concepts that are especially important in history, concepts that absolutely must be incorporated into writing in history for students to be successful. These are: (1) history is subjective; (2) context is critical when interpreting primary source documents in history; and (3) revision is essential for the development of historical arguments. I'll include evidence from my analysis of these materials to illustrate these concepts. But in doing so, it's important to point out that this analysis of threshold concepts did double duty. While I was writing about threshold concepts in history, I was also engaging in threshold concepts of composition. One of the threshold concepts of that discipline is that writing is a subject of study. So I was studying writing in two ways as I analyzed threshold concepts in history and analyzed my own writing to find evidence of those concepts. Before taking Writing 2LK, this isn't something I had thought about at all; I understood writing simply as something that students (or others) did to communicate their ideas to others.

Threshold Concepts in History

The first threshold concept I identified in my analysis of history texts is that history is subjective. In other words, history isn't a series of "facts"; it is an interpretation of events, documents, and experiences written through the perspective of informed authors. This concept is really foundational for writing in history because it's the basis of all analysis. It means that as a reader of historical documents, I have to pay attention to the context in which documents were created: Who wrote them? When? And why? And when I write history papers, I need to demonstrate that I am able to interpret primary documents in their appropriate context to create an interpretation. This is very different from just *repeating* what a primary document says, because it requires analytical thinking.

The first paper I wrote for History 17b illustrates how I applied the threshold concept that "history is subjective" in my writing for the course. This paper focused on the sectionalism crisis faced by the United States between 1820 and 1860. My essay argued that slavery was the heart of the sectional tension that tore the nation in two and led to the Civil War. I argued the points in my paper by bringing in documents and playing the role of historian in order to shape this perspective. I interpreted Hinton R. Helper's "The Impending Crisis," from a book that spoke to the Southern white majority about how only abolition could save the South from itself. I specifically focused on one line in the document: "If assaulted, [we] shall not fail to make the blow recoil upon the aggressor's head" (Helper). I argued that Helper meant that the North would not start the war, but should the time for war come, the North would retaliate with full force, crushing the rebellion.

Since historians create interpretations situated in their understanding of the document(s) and their own ideas, it's also critical that they locate documents in the contexts in which they were created. Historians don't just assume that a primary source document represents "reality"; they think about how the documents and their creators were situated within a specific time period. Both of these ideas are conveyed to students when we are told to "think critically" when analyzing historical sources. But this is a fairly general phrase, and it's not always well defined or understood. In history, "thinking critically" means situating primary source documents in their context and then making connections between sources and using them to paint a bigger picture. Once the analysis has yielded fruitful results, the paper more or less writes itself.

For example, in the essay I wrote for Writing 2LK, I identified how I analyzed historical documents in their context and used that analysis to develop my interpretation. First I reviewed how the South's secession document provided reasons for Southerners to staunchly protect slavery and defend their states' rights. I took from George Fitzhugh's "Cannibals All!," a document written by Southern slaveholders, the idea that advocates for slavery would be driven by their personal desire to maintain slavery and to do so through the use of legislation and dominance in Congress. Then I reviewed other documents such as Hinton Helper's "The Impending Crisis." Through reviewing these different documents and thinking critically about them, I gained a deeper understanding of the impending crisis.

A third threshold concept I identified in my analysis of documents from History 17b is one that applies to history, composition, and life as a student more generally: the idea that it's critical to talk with experts—whether a course instructor, TAs, or whoever is outlining expectations for writing in a course—about which ideas are critical and how they should be represented, and then to revise writing with these expectations in mind. Remember, threshold concepts are gateways to better understanding the academic world, and what better way to gain entrance into these doors of knowledge than by developing deeper understanding of academic disciplines in this world. To quote my Japanese history professor: "Your first draft is never going to be your best work. Even your final draft can still be improved upon. Recognizing that revision plays a crucial role makes you guys better historians and writers." I couldn't say it better myself. Revision at its very core is a combination of mucking around, trying again, and constantly improving. The improvement on paper reflects improvement in knowledge, understanding, and conceptualizing.

The importance of revision is evident in the writing I did in History 17b. In the initial draft of my first essay, I wanted to argue that conflicting ideologies of the North and the South led to the Civil War. I wanted to use George Fitzhugh's "Cannibals All!" to demonstrate the North's use of what he called "wage slavery" as both parallel to and more damaging than the South's slavery, which he said was paternalistic. But in a conversation with my TA about my initial draft, he pointed out that I made no connection to the importance of the reading and how it tied in to the prompt. By reviewing the document within my paper, I developed the perspective that Fitzhugh's argument was in fact a biting attack mocking Northern beliefs "in order to debase the North's opinion of the South." A modicum of detail and revision goes a long way in terms of understanding the meaning of a document.

Lessons Learned

What I've learned by thinking carefully about writing in history is that threshold concepts are reflected in the idea that the arguments put forth and the support of the arguments make the paper. Unlike an English paper one might encounter in high school, history papers are not telling a story; there's no argument of the merits of totalitarianism in effectively controlling a society like that depicted in Orwell's dystopian *1984*. An interpretation of hard facts and primary source documents, filtered through the historian's informed perspective, is necessary to make the case. While an individual's argument might not be new, despite the number of people in the lower-division history courses I've taken—more than 450—there's still a chance to make a unique point, to have a different take. Creativity counts for a lot; history writing is as much experimental as it is structured. Paragraphs need not be the standard cookie-cutter five-sentence structure. Nor does a paper need to have a three-part thesis with three body paragraphs and a cute conclusion to tidy it all up. College is a great equalizer, and what you put into your work is actually reflected in your grade. It's a simple truth, but one to live by and keep close, particularly for history writing, in which time is of the essence, and focus even more so.

Now that I've started to recognize threshold concepts in history, I actually see them everywhere. I was working with a friend of mine on a paper for an upper-division religious studies course. As we read through each other's eight-page, single-spaced final essays, we realized that while we were writing about the same thing, we were doing so differently. As a history major with an emphasis on prelaw, I analyzed the documents we were given for the assignment, thinking about the contexts in which they were created and incorporating evidence from them to support an argument about economic, social, and political reform. Dave, a psychology major, viewed the subject through psychological lenses, examining the motivations of individual actors and looking at discrete events. Another friend, Brittany, is a biology major. I read an essay she was writing for her Writing 2LK course, and I could see evidence of her experience with science writing reflected in that paper. Science writing is often about describing activities step by step, clearly addressing what went right and what went wrong, what changes could be made, and how certain results came about. This was also the way her Writing 2LK paper read.

Writing for history courses over the past two years has taught me much about my own writing and how to be a successful writer. I tool my arguments for individual disciplines by identifying their inherent and intrinsic threshold concepts. I'm then able to work with the overlapping basics such as the importance of theses, topic sentences, argumentative language, etc. However, the structure and content of essays, including all the time, effort, and revision put into them, are what make writing for history unique. It takes time and dedication to write history papers. Caring about the topic and really investing the time make a paper the best it can be.

Through formative high school experiences, significant "aha" moments, and the foundation that threshold concepts provide, I sought to situate history as a unique discipline, one in which threshold concepts define much of the writing I've done throughout undergrad and graduate school. Here are my takeaways:

◆ Threshold concepts forever change how the subject, discipline, writing, etc. are seen. They can be a blessing and a curse; once you find them, they are engrained forever.

◆ Creativity serves as perhaps the most useful tool in structuring arguments, particularly for history. Creativity is not a formula; it is a mode of expression that requires much effort, personal time, and, yes, revision. The more creative, the greater the possibility for a good grade and a more fulfilling paper.

◆ Without revision a paper is of little worth. Time and consideration are two of a writer's best friends. Do not, especially for a history paper, make it a last-minute effort.

◆ Never be discouraged by a tough essay topic or final essay topic; those are actually the best challenges because they engage the brain; they take time and really hammer home the core values of the class, the subject matter, and the outer layers of knowledge.

◆ Writing styles will evolve naturally; the specific discipline will determine the views on course material and how best to incorporate (or not incorporate them) into papers.

◆ Easiest isn't always best. While writing is important for papers, it is good to look ahead toward the written finals for history courses, those where you have no material to work with but what is in your head before the test itself. Going the extra mile while working rather than taking the most convenient path will prove better and more useful in the long run.

◆ High school is very different from college in a variety of ways. College is harder and requires much more thinking due to generally more stringent grading and expectations.

◆ Improvements will come over time. I look back on papers and see what I could have done better, what mistakes I could fix, and how I could make my analysis even better for the next essay I have to write. Revision, even after a grade, is important.

In sum, have fun, enjoy your undergrad years, work hard, pay attention, and make time for fun and work. Balance in life counts a lot for your writing as well. As a final note, I'll reveal what I consider the ideal assignment. It's one in which the question is simple yet multitiered. I'm asked to answer rather than tell. I have a rough draft to turn in and then a final draft to turn in a week later. The question should really make me think and force me to use primary sources almost exclusively, for, in my opinion, that's the heart of history and what it means to be a historian. There should be no set amount of sources required, and the page limit should be reasonable. We all have different styles of writing, we all come from different disciplines, and our strengths and weaknesses define the very character of our paper. It is the analysis and structuring of a paper within the framework of threshold concepts, as well as the writer's personal characteristics, that make for a detailed, unique, and strong paper.

Works Cited

Fitzhugh, George. "Cannibals All!" *History of the American People 1840–1920*. 2nd ed. John Majewski. Dubuque: Kendall/Hunt, 2006. 33–36. Print.

Helper, Hinton R. "The Impending Crisis." *History of the American People 1840–1920*. 2nd ed. John Majewski. Dubuque: Kendall/Hunt, 2006. 43–48. Print.

Meyer, Jan H. F., and Ray Land. "Threshold Concepts and Troublesome Knowledge: An Introduction." *Overcoming Barriers to Student Understanding*. Ed. Jan H. F. Meyer and Ray Land. London: Routledge, 2006. 3–18. Print.

Shaping the Lenses: A Response to "Seeing the Differences: Writing in History (and Elsewhere)"

LINDA ADLER-KASSNER

University of California, Santa Barbara

Over the years, in conversations with colleagues inside and outside of the writing program, I've heard what I've come to think of as the "teach up" or the "blame down" countless times. The teach up is captured in the question: "What should I teach students in <my class> to help them be prepared for <your class or program>?" The blame down is a too-frequently expressed lament: "I can't believe I'm teaching my students <this thing>. They should have learned <this thing> in <a class, program, or school that came before their enrollment in my class or program>."

The teach up and the blame down are two sides of the same coin, a currency that reflects a persistent and problematic perspective of not only school, but also learning more generally. It says, in essence, that learning represents a relatively seamless trajectory, a series of steps whereby students amass one type of knowledge or skill in one site and then build on that knowledge or skill. It's not the idea of building and learning that is problematic. Instead, it's the reductive nature of the model of learning and transfer that is so challenging. As teachers and learners ourselves, we know that learning is more complicated. It involves learning knowledge and skills, of course. But the kind of learning that truly dazzles—the kind that causes us to remark on the amazing insights in the artifact we are reviewing that represents learning (whether a paper, a multimedia production, a poem, a work of art, or anything else)—requires engagement at the level of identity. That is: learners must find ways to connect with the epistemologies of the contexts where they are learning. This means, first, understanding what those epistemologies are, those lenses that people who are experts within the context use to see everything around them. Then, learners find ways to use these lenses for themselves, seeing things differently, anew. And then, finally, they represent these ways of seeing, thinking, and interpreting. This development isn't accomplished as a straight, clean line. Instead, it's analogous to the sort of looping, back-on-itself idea of recursiveness that writing instructors think of when we discuss something like the best end point of a well-revised piece of writing: the ideas develop and then the structure and mechanics need more attention; those get attention, and the ideas develop more through engagement with the writing, and so on. Inviting learners into this process is a complicated matter, to be sure. And it happens across *multiple* contexts—in school and out, high school and college, and so on. But understanding learning as something that involves, in part, analysis *of* learning, and especially the expectations for learning within specific contexts, is an important step in that invitation.

Evan Pretzlaff's "Seeing the Differences" remains, to me, a testament to a learner (and writer) who has taken up this invitation and worked through it in the most engaging of senses. I met Evan in 2011, when he was a second-year student enrolled in a section of Writing 2LK (Academic Writing, UCSB's lower-division general education writing course)—the course, in fact, that he's writing about in his piece. During the quarter we worked together, Evan dove into the analysis he outlines here, of threshold concepts in history (and writing). And as he wrote this piece, he started to think about his experiences in high school courses, especially in English and history. His analysis is a testament to his own perception of the connections across those classes, to his ability to conceptualize learning across contexts and to make connections that clearly contributed to a way of seeing learning within both History 17b (the history class he discusses here) and Writing 2LK, and also beyond to other courses. For this, Evan draws on the idea of "threshold concepts" developed by researchers Jan H. F. Meyer and Ray Land. These are concepts required for continued development and learning within specific sites (in this case, the disciplines of history and writing studies/composition and rhetoric). Studying and ultimately hypothesizing what threshold concepts in these areas are (especially in history) enabled Evan to look back on his high school English and history courses to understand how the expectations there led him to develop particular skills and knowledge and to connect those things to expectations associated with threshold concepts in his college courses. These kinds of connections provide a very different view of what learning looks like over time. Evan's careful reflection on his own learning, thinking, and writing, then, might provide a model for rethinking the blame down/teach up.

I should say, too: while this chapter reflects a close analysis of experience on Evan's part (because, after all, it's being published in a book for a broad audience and has been revised based on many rounds of reviewer comments provided over a number of years), his ability *to* analyze this experience is not especially out of the norm for students I've worked with using this approach and assignments like the ones that Evan writes about here. While I see it less often at the college level (and especially in the writing program where I teach—never there, in fact), I know there is still an occasional tendency on instructors' part to wonder if our students can embark on the kind of ambitious thinking and analysis that might be reflected in a piece like Evan's. To be sure, this assignment was given in a first-year writing class at a particular kind of university and is tailored to those students and this context. But for decades I've used assignments that ask students to reflect on the conditions for literacy that shape their experiences, whether they're tests placing students into so-called "basic writing" courses or threshold concepts in other classes in which students are enrolled. Whether at an institution like UC Santa Barbara, where I currently teach, or at Eastern Michigan University, a comprehensive regional university in southeastern Michigan where I used to teach, my experience is that students embrace the opportunity to investigate these conditions with a particular kind of gusto—particularly when the stakes associated with the conditions (as with writing assessments) are high. This kind of work, then, helps both students and teachers reflect on the broader contexts in which ideas of student practices and learning are shaped.

CHAPTER SEVEN

Development and Duality

TARYN "SUMMER" WALLS
University of North Carolina at Charlotte

Reading for Pleasure

In discussing the development of my writing, I must first share my inspirations, as inspiration is where we all begin no matter the art form. The factor that has influenced my writing the most isn't any teacher or professor, nor is it the practice of writing itself. Instead, reading has affected both my style of writing and my perceptions of it. My love of reading began in elementary school. My time there was one of loneliness and ostracism, and so I turned to books. I either had so few friends because I read so much, or I read so much because I had few friends. I think it was a self-sustaining cycle. I've since developed very good friendships, but novels are still my allies. They've been the cornerstone of my identity and the foremost intellectual influence in my life. This has been true from grade school through my time as an English and communication studies major at the University of North Carolina at Charlotte.

The first of these written allies was *Redwall,* by British author Brian Jacques. The adventures of mice, squirrels, and otters who wield swords and bows ignited in me the love of reading. This hunger led me to The Lord of the Rings trilogy by J. R. R. Tolkien. His legendarium has affected me on an intimate level. At first I read solely for the adventure, but as I've grown, I've realized there is an incredible amount of depth to his works. They have taught me concepts beyond the narrative. For example, Boromir's redemptive arc makes me proud to be a human, flaws and all, rather than a heavenly elf or hardy dwarf. His heroic and tragic fall is unrivalled by any other character and demonstrates that true quality comes from the spirit, not physical attributes. The wretched Gollum shows me that promises cannot be broken, and that Good can use Evil to achieve its rightful end. I owe these lessons, my career choice, and my writing aspirations all to Tolkien.

He is my literary idol. Comparing my style to his shows me just how much I have yet to improve in my writing. It pushes me to write to the best of my ability and never lose sight of my potential. Additionally, because of his influence in my life, I chose to study abroad at Kingston University in London, England. Where better to study English than the place of its origin, and the homeland of my favorite authors?

Whereas Jacques inspired me to read and write fantasy, and Tolkien revealed to me the art of prose, my third literary inspiration, Margaret Weis and Tracy Hickman, taught me how to create worlds and expand characters. I found their pioneer work, the *Annotated [Dragonlance] Chronicles*, in a thrift shop. Though I'd never heard of this series before, I couldn't bear to let the 1,312-page monstrosity pass for only ninety-nine cents. I had no way of knowing that *Dragonlance* would show me how deep and complex a fantasy world could be. Because it has, I've developed a greater sense of invention. When I first started planning novels in my spare time, I desperately wanted to be entirely new and innovative. However, after reading hundreds of Weis and Hickman's intimate annotations, which are a critical insight into the writing process as well as comedic relief, I've realized that things loosely based on the known may fare better than those that aren't.

Authors haven't been the sole source of inspiration and growth for my writing. My parents have been supportive from the start. I attribute my success and the spark of my passion to them; for As on my report cards, I earned trips to the bookstore. I can think of no better way to foster education and mental stimulus. Though most children might not appreciate books as a reward, I did. Not only did literature help to increase my intelligence and affinity for academics, but it also provided the escapism I desperately needed in my unsociable school environment.

Reading has affected my life more than any other activity, both in my personal life and in an academic sense. I strongly believe that an individual's writing is mostly influenced by what they read, and that without a solid foundation in reading students can't reach their writing potential. Because of this I think that if students are encouraged to actively read for enjoyment, early on and especially by teachers and parents, they're more likely to continue with it later, and their grades—at least in the humanities—will be higher.

Reading in Class

Sometimes in high school it seemed as though teachers didn't care about our disposition toward reading, only that we accepted a certain symbolism in a classic novel. My friends and I had many conversations about how awful some of the novels in our curriculum were. I know from experience that there are many more students who dislike reading than those who love it, which I suspect is because they're forced to read books they hated in school. A professor in my first year of college let us vote on what novel to study for class, but this has only ever occurred once in my academic career. Maybe if this happened in high school, where not everyone in the class is an English major and therefore more receptive to reading assignments of any sort, it would have been more enjoyable for the students. It may have been more beneficial too, because an appreciation of the subject makes all the difference in a student's effort and quality of work.

The hard thing is literature's subjectivity. I didn't like *To Kill a Mockingbird* at all, but to my surprise, even classmates who don't like reading were able to appreciate it. To find a middle ground, I would suggest voting from a preapproved reading list, encouraging more creative forms of essay writing, and giving students examples of the types of analysis they are required to produce.

Open-Ended Writing and Autonomy

Open-ended writing, as a creative story or as expression through syntax in academic writing, has always been effective in my development and the content I create. Flexibility in writing topics and styles is much more stimulating than a designated task and yields greater productivity on my part. It is, for a writer especially, the ability to explore and therefore grow.

At UNC Charlotte, there was one course in which I had the greatest freedom and motivation to write—Honors Topics: Middle-earth. I was overwhelmed with excitement; taking a course on Tolkien had been on my bucket list for years. The history of Middle-earth had never seemed so tangible and complex as it did to me that semester. Literary analysis was not something I had ever applied to Tolkien before; as a child, I only wanted to read his works for their superficial beauty, but this particular course made me appreciate his craftsmanship more.

I was able to mold my term paper, "On the Nature and Importance of Oaths and Curses in the Works of J. R. R. Tolkien," into a successful and layered essay because the subject was completely of my choosing. There was no constrictive or singular topic, and the class atmosphere was one that encouraged imagination. For example, one classmate produced a paper in journal format from the perspectives of non-central characters. This paper showed me how important and potent an interest in the subject can be, especially in an academic environment.

I don't mean to say that students should be so privileged all the time, because some curricula simply can't offer complete free rein, but a degree of creativity if possible can make all the difference between an inspiring assignment and a dragging bore. I think this is especially true in high school English classes, in which all students, regardless of literary affinity, are required to read, analyze, and write.

I am an advocate of letting a class vote on its reading list (as long as it has been preapproved by the instructor) and the use of imaginative writing styles like my classmate's journal-style essay. However, unorthodox methods should only be used if appropriate to the subject of the analysis, which can be determined by each teacher. An additional suggestion for the practice of writing is to make it collaborative. I experienced this in college, and working in a group or with a partner offered views about the literature that I otherwise would not have seen. If I had worked alone, I would only know my view and the professor's.

Across the Disciplines

I first experienced the effects of the balance between choice and guidelines at Myers Park High School, where the International Baccalaureate (IB) program promotes the crossing and interrelation of subjects. Because of IB's writing-intensive expectations, writing across the disciplines is a given. The IB program basically consists of one landmark paper after another. Each core subject in the junior and senior years requires two moderated papers. The most rigorous of these courses is IB 20th Century World History, which requires two historical investigations. What is interesting about the essay requirements is the balance between a choice of pre-set topics and the student's ability to extract an essay question from them. I chose the topic concerning the relationship between the United States and Japan and developed my own concentrated research area. My exploration of Western imperialism, prior treaties, discrimination, and trade proposals all came to the conclusion that America may have been just as at fault as Japan for the conflicts in World War II.

These investigations are meant to be research-based and focused. I learned how to effectively draw the most relevant and tightly concentrated information from multiple sources and incorporate it into a unified theme. This is different from the literary analysis I was used to, for which I deeply dove into a single work. However, the reading skills that transferred across the disciplines included the ability to skim for specific supporting material, compile notes, highlight valuable information, and plan my writing according to what I was reading.

In addition, the value of the content itself was as important as the research skills involved. I'd never written serious papers outside of English, and this cross-disciplinary approach taught me a valuable concept, ethnocentrism. My exploration of the strained relationship between Japan and the United States that contributed to World War II made plain humanity's tendency to view the world through a single lens. In our history classes, we are taught that Japan was the aggressor, but our nation can be seen as equally guilty. This revelation awoke in me a greater awareness; the world is infinitely complex and we can't hope to understand it from a single viewpoint. This concept has stayed with me in my adult years, especially while I studied abroad.

This cross-disciplinary writing taught me how to critically analyze history and its complexities, especially outside socially and ethnocentrically established views. I am now able to more effectively aggregate information from multiple sources and come to a well-developed and strongly founded perspective.

Though I have taken writing-intensive classes, I've never had a class meant specifically to better my writing; I become more skilled by writing for different subjects and absorbing writing lessons via feedback. This is why I think cross-disciplinary writing is important. Writing class doesn't only have to cover literature; assignments can cover journalistic, scientific, technical, speech, creative, and report writing. This is especially true in high school or general education classes, before students have committed to a major.

IB World Literature marked the beginning of my development as a literary analyst. The first self-guided analysis I did in my career was "Relations of Humanity to Solitude," which compares Aureliano Buendía (from *One Hundred Years of Solitude* by Gabriel García Márquez) and D-503 (from Yevgeny Zamyatin's *We*) and their evolving characterizations in respect to isolation:

> D-503 and the Colonel's involvement with revolutions and rebellions also lends itself to their isolations and developments. "Colonel Aureliano Buendía organized thirty-two armed uprisings and he lost them all" (103). The wars and his long absence from home are what fulfill his de-humanization. In his opinion, "the only effective thing is violence" (98). Later he realizes that "I'm fighting because of pride" (135). His adopted sister Rebeca even calls him a "renegade," no matter what ideals he strives for (157). He "looks like a man capable of anything" (156). This assumption proves correct when he has his bodyguard completely sack and burn a widow's home (165). His close friend, Colonel Geraldino Márquez, warns him to "watch out for your heart Aureliano, you're rotting alive" (165). Aside from the horrendous act committed against the widow, he even refuses to commute a former friend's death sentence. He is able to casually say, "Remember, old friend. I'm not shooting you. It's the revolution that's shooting you," after which the prisoner, the widow's husband, replies, "You'll not only be

the most despotic and bloody dictator . . . but you'll shoot . . .
Ursula in an attempt to pacify your conscience" (158–9). During
the course of endless wars Colonel Aureliano Buendía becomes
the antithesis of a normal human's conduct. He has hardly any
feeling or emotion, especially compassion and mercy. This is
the opposite of his initial characterization at the beginning of
the novel, as shown in the contrast between his conduct with
the prostitute and with the widow.

This analysis lacks qualities of tightness and structure. I included
a large number of distracting quotations and parenthetical citations. These take away from the content and draw too much
attention to the cluttered presentation. Later I developed an
ability to paraphrase a greater amount of information in a more
detailed way but with less dependence on piecemeal quotes. In
high school, the need for "evidence" was emphasized more than
the greater ideas that were welcomed in college classes. I think
that encouraging reflection, discourse, and connections between
ideas on any subject, not only literary analysis, produces better
writing and thinking than does simply supporting a claim with
a barrage of quotes.

I have greatly improved my fluidity since I wrote that com-
parative analysis. English 2100 and 3100 in college called for
exactly the same type of work I did the previous two years in
high school, but I found that I had personally matured in style
and structure. My development is shown in my study on another
Márquez story, "A Very Old Man with Enormous Wings," which
I completed for English 2100:

> Gabriel García Márquez's short story is a social commentary
> dependent on a critical analysis of relationships and symbolism.
> Pelayo and his wife, Elisenda, along with practically every other
> member of their small village, fail to recognize the Jesus figure
> that comes to them in the form of the titular old man with
> enormous wings. Such shortcomings on the villagers' parts are
> the result of an apathy towards religion and the failing structure
> and ineffectiveness of the Catholic Church.
>
> The moral lesson presented by García Márquez is centered
> around the capture of a stray angel-creature and the subsequent
> reactions, consequences, and ethical issues that arise. Though

the angel is not under the organized structure of the Church, his methodology and message is actually more critical. The failure of organized religion is shown through its unreliability and shallowness. A priest named Father Gonzaga (who is supposedly knowledgeable on matters of religion) is summoned to decipher the mysteries surrounding the newcomer. Due to his suspicion of the angel-man being an "imposter," the priest promises to "write a letter to his bishop so that the latter would write to his primate so that the latter would write to the Supreme Pontiff in order to get the final verdict from the highest courts." Irony comes into play here, as the repetitive "latter" is a homonym of (and mirrors) the ladder of the Catholic hierarchy. This cumbersome and bureaucratic ladder is shown to be ineffective in administration. The response from Rome shows "absolutely no sense of urgency" while the religious authority is more concerned about whether or not "the prisoner had a navel" and if "he could fit on the head of a pin." Not only do the villagers display ignorance of who the "captive" really is, but even those who are meant to be in charge of leading thousands of people's lives care not to seriously study religion. They are more concerned with trivial matters. Within the text, authority figures are seriously devoid of earnestness and sincerity; this negligence signals the downfall of the village and spiritual guidance.

This selection is more succinct and visually clean, showing greater control and a sense of direction. There are no distracting parenthetical citations (perhaps due to the lesser complexity of short stories), and the quotes are used more seamlessly than those in the first selection.

I matured with practice and I had very minimal problems transitioning from high school writing to college writing, primarily because the IB program tries hard to uphold university standards. Only two issues come straight to mind. First is the fact that university writing is generally freer than that of high school. Though I consider this open-minded approach to writing an asset, it doubles as a challenge too. It's possible to be stranded without an original topic idea! Second, the word count requirements increased dramatically, but with maturity this is easily handled.

Across the Disciplines and across the Sea

At UNC Charlotte, most of my classes had multiple-choice exams instead of essays, and any papers I *did* have were in English literature. When I studied at Kingston University in London, writing was my only form of assessment.

It was a completely different way of teaching. There were no tests, and I had "modules" instead of classes. Mine were Late Medieval to Early Modern Literature, Science Fiction Television and Short Film, Consuming Cultures, and Writing That Works. Each module met once a week for lecture and once for a seminar in a small-group setting. There were readings every week, but students were expected to do their own research and supplemental study (mostly in preparation for the writing assessments). For example, my Science Fiction module had contact time only during the first five weeks of the semester, and I was completely free to work on my term paper for the remainder of the school year. Personally, I find it odd and uncomfortable to have so little guidance! Even so, my year at Kingston was an opportunity for me to try types of writing that I hadn't done before. Each module was a new subject for me, so it was a sampler of writing styles.

Consuming Cultures looked at society, marketing, and capitalism. I conducted a research experiment on a consumerism subject of my choice. The subject required a new approach to writing; it wasn't about analyzing words or characters, but instead about real people. I had to incorporate external sources, scientific research, and the ability to critically examine details.

In Consuming Cultures, the approach was methodical and scientific, but Writing That Works was on the other end of the spectrum. It was a creative writing class covering a broad range of subjects, from blog posts to dramatic scenes to poetry. Although I've dabbled in storytelling and blogging, I'd never written a poem before. Without this class, I'm not sure I would ever try.

I came away from my Writing That Works seminar with a novel exercise. The first step is to write a paragraph in the first person.

> I'm not sure how I do it, but somehow I am out of bed before my alarm is done with its first beep. Next, within a minute,

> I'm on the computer, checking all my social media sites and my email. What an embarrassing addiction, I think to myself. Breakfast comes next.

The second step is to replace the character of "I" with a name of the opposite sex, and some embellishment, so the blurb becomes:

> David never could figure out how he did it each morning, but somehow he was wide awake before his alarm finished its first beep. Within a minute of rolling out of bed, he was on the computer, checking all his social media sites and email. What an embarrassing and wasteful addiction, he thought to himself. Breakfast came next, a quick batch of eggs and toast.

This assignment taught me three things. First, in only a couple simple steps, something routine and mundane can be transformed into the basis for a story. Second, what seems like very insignificant details can be manipulated to create interest and grab a reader. Third, it is often beneficial to include bits of the author in a story, so long as the characters remain independent.

The broader lesson learned from these classes is that trying a variety of assignments, no matter how long or short, is one of the best ways for a writer to grow. I tried a lot of writing methods for the first time at Kingston: a dramatic scene, poetry, and others. Through this I gained a better understanding of my style and strengths. Variety, combined with newness, is the best method of self-exploration for a writer, it seems.

The method of assessment in England was demanding in a different way from what I am accustomed to. I missed exams, through which objective material is strengthened in my memory, but the intensive writing during my British schooling reinforced time management, long-term planning, research methods, and imagination. However, I think that the specific way I analyzed literature and my essay-writing style remained the same as when I attended UNC Charlotte. I simply took what I learned about writing in high school and at college and adapted it to the system of education in England.

The writing-intensive environment was definitely more conducive to my academic development as a whole. I've always found multiple-choice, exam-based classes incredibly easy, but the self-guided approach to learning forced me to be more responsible and proactive. This was especially true for my Consuming Cultures research, for which I interviewed Internet media creators, and for my long-term Science Fiction Television and Short Film paper. Of course, I still procrastinated, but periodic progress checks kept me effectively updated. My main concern about Kingston's teaching style is that many modules (though not my Consuming Cultures or Writing That Works classes) had a severe delay in feedback. For Late Medieval to Early Modern Literature, I had a three-month gap between submission and grading. Even then, I had to ask for it! In comparing the teaching styles of the United States and England, I would like a combination of autonomous research and writing and timely guidance to bring students to their full potential.

The Editor-Writer

Through my reading and writing in school, I better understand what it means to be an editor, and vice versa. This growth came from considering the thoughts and advice of my teachers as they corrected my writing, my role in peer editing, and my recent internship.

I worked as an editorial assistant on UNC Charlotte's College of Liberal Arts and Sciences magazine, *Exchange*. From my experience, participating in both sides of the writer-editor relationship is key to understanding how to better my own writing during the writing process itself, not only after someone looks at the draft. The interrelations of writing, editing, and thought have changed my approach to life and academia and have prepared me for my career. Perhaps peer editing should be of greater focus in classrooms. It would help students understand the applicability and necessity of writing concepts and help them understand teachers' expectations.

There's a fine conflict between the art of writing and the editing which inevitably follows. It's hard to be corrected, but I appreciate and consider all advice given to me *during* the writing process, and I seek it in order to make informed decisions. The delicate balance between advice and a writer's autonomy requires tact and discernment, acquired from trial and error in the practice of writing.

Conclusion

My recommendations for incorporating reading in class and encouraging pleasure reading include a possible reward system or extra credit for proven extracurricular reading (like the Accelerated Reader program in grade schools) and letting students choose what to read for class from a preapproved list.

For writing itself, I would recommend multiple things. First is the inclusion of peer editing as an integral tool for learning about writing theory and how to better one's own writing mechanics. Second, clearer rubrics or examples of the types of writing expected would also be helpful for any assignment. Third, incorporate cross-disciplinary writing assignments about topics besides literature. This would help students discover their own affinities and prepare them for any field they wish to enter later. Fourth, encourage different creative writing styles when appropriate. I found this to make assignments more engaging and interesting. I'd even want to read classmates' work! Finally, though it requires more effort, the connection of broader ideas and discourse on complex topics or threads in a work of literature makes for better essay quality and deeper learning than does a book report–style quote mash-up.

When considering the marriage of writing and reading in class, encourage or require introspective and metacognitive assignments to help students understand their own reading and writing processes and growth. From my experience, school focuses considerably more on facts than on epistemology, but I think writing can benefit just as much from introspection as practice.

Reading, writing, and words have been central in my personal development and identity. Though I may have been disappointed by some classes, professors, or assignments, the involvement of writing in my academic career has been integral to both my degree and my personality. The dualities of reading for pleasure and work, reading and writing, writing and editing, and American and English schooling have all been instrumental in my development.

I feel considerably more capable and intelligent, I have a greater appreciation for the media I consume, and I hope to make words my life's work. Writing is one of humankind's greatest means of creation, and it is perhaps the most powerful.

Works Cited

García Márquez, Gabriel. *One Hundred Years of Solitude*. Trans. Gregory Rabassa. New York: Harper Perennial Modern Classics, 2006. Print.

———. "A Very Old Man with Enormous Wings: And the Sea of Lost Time." Trans. Gregory Rabassa. *North Dakota State University*. Web. 9 Dec. 2016.

Jacques, Brian. *Redwall*. New York: Philomel, 2003. Print.

Tolkien, J. R. R. *The Fellowship of the Ring: Being the First Part of* The Lord of the Rings. Boston: Houghton Mifflin, 2003. Print.

Walls, Taryn. "On the Nature and Importance of Oaths and Curses in the Works of J. R. R. Tolkien." Essay. University of North Carolina at Charlotte, 2012. Print.

———. "Relations of Humanity to Solitude." Essay. Myers Park High School, 2010. Print.

———. "US-Japanese Relations 1919–1941: To What Extent Did the Commercial Relations between the USA and Japan, from 1919 to 1941, Contribute to the Friction Resulting in the Bombing of Pearl Harbor?" Essay. Myers Park High School, 2011. Print.

———. "'A Very Old Man with Enormous Wings' Analysis." Essay. University of North Carolina at Charlotte, 2011. Print.

Weis, Margaret, and Tracy Hickman. *The Annotated Chronicles*. Renton: Wizards of the Coast, 2002. Print.

Zamyatin, Yevgeny. *We*. Trans. Mirra Ginsburg. New York: Eos, 1999. Print.

Writing with Courage:
A Response to "Development and Duality"

RONALD F. LUNSFORD
University of North Carolina at Charlotte

I have come to know Taryn "Summer" Walls quite well as she has drafted the essay in this collection and completed her undergraduate degree at UNC Charlotte. In this process, I have been impressed by her intelligence, confidence, seriousness of purpose, and, most of all, her determination to be a writer. Summer and I met when I asked the dean of the Honors College to recommend some students nearing the end of their college experience who might be interested in writing an essay for this volume. The dean immediately recommended Summer, and we agreed to ask her if she would be interested. She was eager to accept the invitation, so we set a time to meet in my office for the first time.

My first impression of Summer was that she was a nice but rather meek and diffident student, one who was eager to please and who would strive to give a writing coach exactly what she or he wanted. I was soon to find that, although she is willing to listen to criticism and to accommodate that criticism where she can, there is nothing "meek" or "diffident" about this young writer.

When I received Summer's first draft of the essay included here, I found a narrative of her experiences as a writer that showed her to be confident and opinionated about every aspect of her journey as a writer. Although I was impressed by the voice and convictions I found in that draft, my first responses to Summer's work were meant to suggest that she think more critically about her experiences, in school and out, and that she consider not painting with such a broad brush: I suggested, for example, that she consider whether it would be more correct to identify her readings as "one" of the factors responsible for her love of writing, or that, when interpreting literary events and characters, she might be served well by recognizing the role she, as a reader, plays in constructing the meanings she finds in those readings—rather than assuming the meanings she finds there are really "there" for all to "find." Even though Summer felt strongly about the issues she was dealing with and was not about to retreat from the main points she wanted to make, she was willing to accept specific suggestions. As Summer attempted to accommodate my advice, however, I did not always think her drafts were improved by the changes she made. For example, I had suggested that her agenda of having students choose what they would read was at odds with her belief that "good" literature helps create good writers—since students cannot be counted on to choose the kinds of literature that might be most helpful to them once they are exposed to it. I also pointed out the fact that a class of twenty-five students might well submit twenty-five different reading lists to the teacher. Summer's accommodation was to suggest that the students choose what they wanted to read from a list provided by the teacher. This solution backed Summer into the corner of saying, on the one hand, that it is students' freedom to choose what they want to read that will provide the motivations the students need to succeed, and, on the other, that students can't really be trusted to choose their readings. As I reflect on the corner I backed Summer into—and on the way I felt when this new draft came to me—I am reminded of the film *Educating Rita* and the comment that Michael Caine's character makes to Rita (played by Julie Walters) when he sees Rita's writing after he and Rita have spent several tutoring sessions together: Caine's character tells Rita that "it [her paper] wouldn't look out of place with these [the other students' papers]." Caine's character means the comment not as a compliment, but rather as a lament of the loss of voice and verve in Rita's writing. Like Rita, whose writing originally had an authentic voice, Summer began writing this essay with a message she wanted to share with her readers: that in writing instruction (in fact, in life overall), too often authority figures try to impose their will on students, with the result being a stifling of creativity. Unlike the Rita character, however, and despite those few places where I see her message diminished a bit by "instruction," Summer's creativity (and iconoclasm) comes through: she tells us she didn't learn to write from teachers, nor did she learn to write in the way that many "process" teachers have encouraged her to (by writing); rather, she learned to write by reading.

As I reflect on this message, and am tempted to suggest she qualify it, I am reminded of how many times, as a writing program administrator, I have said, with no qualifications, that I would rather have, as a placement tool for first-year writing, a list of a given student's readings (a list chosen by the student, not by teachers) than any other placement device. Had I been asked to write on this subject, I would doubtless have qualified my statement to make my writing sound like it belongs in the "stack" of statements on the subject made by other WPAs. Nevertheless, I believed (and still do believe) in the unqualified statement.

As I continue to reflect on the iconoclastic approach Summer brings not just to her writing, but also to her thinking in general, I am reminded of her attraction to the historians offering a counterhistory to World War II. As I read her statement that "[m]y exploration of Western imperialism, prior treaties, discrimination, and trade proposals all came to the conclusion that America may have been just as at fault as Japan for the conflicts in World War II," I am reminded that Noam Chomsky, a person I have had the privilege of writing about, makes the same arguments. And I smile when I think about the similarities between these two very different (in age and professional status) people. Like Summer, Chomsky is soft-spoken and polite in one-on-one conversations, quick to point out the limitations of his knowledge and to acknowledge the possibility of error. Yet the Chomsky that readers find in his prose (both linguistic and political) is strident and uncompromising; one might go so far as to say that he "paints with a broad brush," condemning the terrorism sponsored by his own country just as harshly as that sponsored by enemies of the United States. We call Chomsky a radical, but many of us think he is that type of radical who makes all of us better thinkers by forcing us to face "facts" that we often hide from ourselves. I am glad no one was ever able to stifle his voice. Likewise, I am glad that Summer is dedicated to keeping her own voice.

I am most impressed by what Summer says about editing in her last section. Here I see the seeds of a mature understanding of just how difficult it is to balance creativity and form. She concludes that section in talking about the conflict she finds between:

the art of writing and the editing which inevitably follows. It's hard to be corrected, but I appreciate and consider all advice given to me *during* the writing process, and I seek it in order to make informed decisions. The delicate balance between advice and a writer's autonomy requires tact and discernment, acquired from trial and error in the practice of writing.

I hope my comments make it clear that my work with Summer has been a learning experience for me. I also hope it is clear that I have real admiration for what she has produced here and, perhaps even more, for the way she has done so—for her tact and cooperative spirit and for her tenacity and determination. I salute her at the beginning of what I am sure is a stellar career as a writer.

Epilogue

After I had written and submitted this response, the editors invited me to read a draft of the introduction to this collection and then to make any connections I might see between the thoughts they present there about reading–writing processes and what I have observed and learned in working with Summer. I am happy to do so.

I begin by addressing an important question asked by readers of the manuscript: how might my experience in working with Summer be applied in classrooms comprising students whose backgrounds are very different from that of Summer? As this question makes clear, the readers' assumption was that Summer's background is not representative of the vast majority of students we work with. I readily concede that point: Summer's answers to the question of what she has read voluntarily during the year before entering college would set her apart from most of her peers. That said, I think there are two key elements of my interactions with Summer that are instructive for all of us working in literacy.

The first of these is that Summer's reading process is one by which she "constructs" the meaning in a text, rather than one in which she "finds" the meaning of that text. A corollary to this principle is that, like most students at all levels and from all backgrounds, Summer entered our tutoring sessions unaware of the role she played in creating the meaning in texts. And just as Summer needs to understand the role she plays in creating meaning via her reading process, Summer must develop a sense of what it means to take charge of her writing process. All of us—students, teachers of writing, and professional writers—struggle with the issue of just how to maintain our voices and our perspectives and yet adjust and shape what we write according to feedback we receive on that writing (or in those cases in which we don't receive feedback, on what we "hear" from our internal critic that imagines how others may respond to what we write). Even though she was polite and unassuming in our sessions, Summer came to those tutoring sessions with a strong sense of self and with a strong and clear voice. She had the confidence to hear criticisms and then to sort through them to attempt to find what would help her sharpen and refine her message and what would derail her. That is not to say that she always used criticism to make her writing better; who among us does? But she continued working through the process to create something that, in the end, was true to her self and yet improved by the writing–reading process.

Of course, Summer is unlike many students in that she came to the college writing experience with a strong sense of self and with a strong motivation to continue her development as a reader and as a writer. These qualities made it possible for me to spend less time encouraging her to have confidence in herself and more time challenging her to think about her work in new ways. Less confident students would need different types of interactions with teachers and mentors, but in the end, we must hope that they are working toward the same goals that Summer is working to achieve. I trust that the many helpful chapters on the teaching of reading and writing in this collection will provide insight into just how we can support students in these endeavors.

III

Practical Strategies for Teaching Deep Reading in the Writing Classroom

CHAPTER EIGHT

"Deep Reading" as a Threshold Concept in Composition Studies

PATRICK SULLIVAN
Manchester Community College

Things which matter most must never be at the mercy of things which matter least.
—JOHANN WOLFGANG VON GOETHE

"Troublesome Knowledge"

If we embrace Jan H. F. Meyer and Ray Land's formulation of a "threshold concept" as "akin to a portal, opening up a new and previously inaccessible way of thinking about something" and as "a transformed way of understanding, or interpreting, or viewing something without which the learner cannot progress" ("Threshold Concepts" 3; see also Meyer and Land *Overcoming*), then "deep reading" must certainly be considered a threshold concept for teachers of writing. Theorizing deep reading in this way would allow us to acknowledge the central importance of reading in the composition classroom, in most kinds of mature meaning-making activities, and, indeed, as essential to our understanding of human history and achievement, as Maryanne Wolf demonstrates in her important book on this subject, *Proust and the Squid: The Story and Science of the Reading Brain*. Deep reading as I am theorizing it here is a process of inquiry built around the exploration of what the Association of American Colleges and Universities (AACU) calls "challenging questions" (13) and engagement with what David Perkins calls "troublesome knowledge."

As readers may know, the study of threshold concepts emerged from a national research project conducted in the United Kingdom to study effective teaching and learning practices. This research discovered fascinating new insights into the developmental process of learning and "how we might both render conceptual understanding visible and assess it in a more dynamic fashion" (Meyer, Land, and Baillie xi). As Meyer, Land, and Baillie note in their introduction to *Threshold Concepts and Transformational Learning*,

> For readers new to the idea of threshold concepts the approach builds on the notion that there are certain concepts, or certain learning experiences, which resemble passing through a portal, from which a new perspective opens up, allowing things formerly not perceived to come into view. This permits a new and previously inaccessible way of thinking about something. It represents a transformed way of understanding, or interpreting, or viewing something, without which the learner cannot progress, and results in a reformulation of the learners' frame of meaning. The thresholds approach also emphasizes the importance of disciplinary contexts. As a consequence of comprehending a threshold concept there may thus be a transformed internal view of subject matter, subject landscape, or even world view. (ix)

Threshold concepts are also theorized as "frequently *troublesome*" for students (Meyer, Land, and Baillie ix; Meyer and Land, "Threshold Concepts"), primarily because they often require a new mental model or understanding that replaces a customary way of seeing things. This body of research has been widely embraced in recent years, and scholars in composition studies have just begun to discuss threshold concepts in our discipline. Linda Adler-Kassner, John Majewski, and Damian Koshnick suggest that genre, rhetorical purpose, audience, and situated practice may be threshold concepts for composition (3). The contributors to Adler-Kassner and Elizabeth Wardle's book, *Naming What We Know*, have proposed an additional group of threshold concepts: writing is a social and rhetorical activity; writing speaks to situations through recognizable forms; writing enacts and creates identities and ideologies; all writers have more to learn; writing is (also always) a cognitive activity. I would like us to consider adding deep reading to this list of threshold concepts.

I propose in this chapter that we theorize writing as a form of deep reading and learning—an active, generative process of intellectual inquiry built around reading and sustained engagement with complex, ill-structured problems. This process of inquiry privileges student immersion in confusion, uncertainty, and "chaos" (Blau, *Literature* 21–22; Dewey; Sommers), and embraces engagement with "troublesome knowledge" as essential for the development of mature meaning-making. In this we will be following learning theorists, and their embrace of doubt, uncertainty, and "intelligent confusion" (King and Kitchener 166–67; Perry; Kegan; Sullivan 24–31). Furthermore, I theorize deep reading as a specific type of inquiry and meaning-making activity—an approach that honors the value of caution, humility, and open-mindedness, and that sees learning in general, following Louis O. Mink, as "an invitation to discover and enter into modes of seeing quite different from our own" (qtd. in Wineburg 109). Deep reading is a form of inquiry that is built around the integration of reading, writing, and thinking in ways that are specifically designed to promote the transfer of knowledge to other disciplines and other areas of life beyond the classroom.

Reading became a primary focus of scholarly activity among teachers of writing in the 1980s and early 1990s, but then it virtually disappeared from our scholarship for almost twenty years (Carillo, *Securing* 1–16; Salvatori and Donahue, "What"). During this time, as Mariolina Salvatori and Patricia Donahue note, "reading" became a "complex term that signifies a range of ideas, practices, assumptions, and identities" ("What" 203). The issue for compositionists has now become not whether to teach reading (Jolliffe) but, rather, following Salvatori and Donahue, engaging a much more complicated question: "what does it mean to teach a particular kind of reading, and how is that reading to be connected to which kind of writing?" ("What" 206; Horning and Kraemer; Horning and Gollnitz).

Furthermore, the discovery of the brain's "neuroplasticity" has introduced important new complications into our understanding of reading and writing (Bransford, Pellegrino, and Donovan; Carr; Wolf and Barzillai). As Maryanne Wolf notes in *Proust and the Squid*, her book about the cognitive and biological science of "the reading brain," reading has had a profound impact on shaping the human brain and on human history. Wolf provides a compelling rationale for attending carefully to the kinds of reading—and the kinds of learning activities—we assign to students in our composition classes:

> Reading is one of the single most remarkable inventions in history; the ability to record history is one of its consequences. Our ancestors' invention could come about only because of the human brain's extraordinary ability to make new connections among its existing structures, a process made possible by the brain's ability to be shaped by experience. This plasticity at the heart of the brain's design forms the basis for much of who we are, and who we might become. (3)

Wolf's research suggests there is great value in assigning reading activities that are "time-demanding, probative, analytical, and creative" (16).

Like many thinkers now concerned about the effect of fast-paced reading practices encouraged by the seemingly limitless availability of information on the Internet and by standardized testing regimes in schools, Wolf fears that "our children are in danger of becoming just what Socrates warned us against—a society of decoders of information, whose false sense of knowing distracts them from a deeper development of their intellectual potential" (226). Wolf suggests that we must be vigilant in protecting what she calls "the profound generativity of the reading brain" (23). Unfortunately, it appears that much reading and writing activity in high school and college classrooms actively works against the development of this luminous human capacity.

"An Analogue for Thinking"

The pedagogy of deep reading I am theorizing here is designed to target and engage this "profound generativity" of the mind. This pedagogy is not, therefore, focused exclusively on how we read and decode assigned texts, although devoting class time and attention to discussing reading strategies and decoding assigned readings collaboratively is certainly an essential part of it. Deep reading is also not simply close reading of texts, like those famously championed by the New Critics and scholars like I. A. Richards and William Empson and more recently by Lehman, Roberts, and Antao, although close reading is an important part of it. Nor is deep reading exclusively what Thomas Newkirk calls "slow reading," which focuses on "the quality of attention that we bring to our reading, with the investment we are willing to make" (2), even though this is also an essential component of the curriculum I am proposing here. Deep reading is also not focused only on difficult or challenging texts, although there is considerable value, of course, in assigning readings that may at first appear beyond students' ability and that position students in a "zone of proximal development" (Vygotsky 79–91; Salvatori and Donahue, *Elements*).

The deep reading pedagogy theorized here is most essentially designed to provide opportunities for students to engage in metacognitive thinking about the *process* of learning, and to help students assess and reassess their own mental models for understanding the world. Furthermore, if it is true, as Salvatori and Donahue suggest, that we have perhaps, as a discipline, "failed to take full advantage of reading as an analogue for thinking" ("What" 214), then deep reading pedagogy seeks to position deep reading and thinking at the center of our teaching practice in the writing classroom. If we accept Mark Twain's idea that "[i]n religion and politics people's beliefs and convictions are in almost every case gotten at second-hand, and without examination, from authorities who have not themselves examined the questions at issue but have taken them at second-hand from others," then deep reading is consciously designed as an academic activity and curricular model to offset and combat this kind of uncritical, "automatic" thinking (Bargh; Bargh and Chartrand).

Deep reading is also designed to acknowledge and help promote an appreciation for what Louise Rosenblatt has called the "aesthetic stance"—privileging the pleasure of reading and "what is being lived through under guidance of the text" ("What Facts" 393). Here we are acknowledging and foregrounding the complex, nonlinear, reciprocal processes of affective as well as cognitive meaning-making enacted when we read (Rosenblatt, *Reader*). Following Rosenblatt, this pedagogy is also designed to help students develop a philosophy about how to live in the world and engage its many complexities (*Literature* 3). Here we are following not only Rosenblatt, but also learning theorist Marcia Baxter Magolda and her work on "self-authorship" and educational researchers Patricia King and Karen Strohm Kitchener and their work on developing reflective judgment.

Surface Learning vs. Deep Learning

At the heart of an approach to teaching writing through deep reading is the crucial distinction scholars have made between surface learning and deep learning. Much of this discussion is built around the various ways that students can potentially position themselves *as readers* in the classroom—some of which provide productive and powerful orientations toward learning, while others do not. Obviously, curriculum design and pedagogical approach have a lot to do with how students choose to engage the work we assign. This body of research on deep learning suggests that writing teachers must think very carefully about how they theorize the role of reading in the composition classroom and how they operationalize this theory in their day-to-day teaching practice (Morrow; Salvatori).

In "Deep Reading, Cost/Benefit, and the Construction of Meaning: Enhancing Reading Comprehension and Deep Learning in Sociology Courses," an important essay on this subject, Judith C. Roberts and Keith A. Roberts suggest that the academic culture at many high schools and colleges promotes what they call "surface learning." Much of this hinges on the approach to reading employed by teachers at these institutions. A number of studies that Roberts and Roberts cite, for example, reveal that the instructional and assessment framework in many classes focuses reading and learning simply on "key words and other concepts at the knowledge level of Benjamin Bloom's Taxonomy" (127), thereby promoting a surface learning approach requiring only short-term memory use (what researchers call "episodic memory"). "Big ideas" are often left largely unexamined and unengaged (127). Furthermore, Roberts and Roberts have found that many students see reading as simply forcing one's eyes to "touch" each word on the assigned pages (125). Many students, in fact, candidly admit that they do not read assigned materials at all (127). Students often appear to favor this kind of approach to learning because it requires very little emotional, psychological, or cognitive effort.

Some of this problem Roberts and Roberts blame on "the McDonaldization" of the academy, with its focus on standardized tests, accountability, and "simplistic measures of quality and of competence reduced to efficient scores and numbers" (129; Sacks). Absent institutional support that rewards deep reading and deep learning, Roberts and Roberts conclude that

> the important point here is that it is unproductive to blame either students or public schools for a narrow rational choice focus on technical competence; we in academia have done our share to contribute to this stress on getting the best grade with the least understanding of the larger meaning. (129)

A focus on deep reading pedagogy is designed to address this problem directly.

This approach to deep reading as a design template for high school and college English classes is also informed by John Tagg and his book *The Learning Paradigm College*. Tagg has done important research on curriculum design, and his book includes a lengthy discussion of deep learning and surface learning (67–86). Tagg also sees much in higher education that encourages students to embrace surface learning, a type of learning that privileges memorization, linear recall, "surface-level processing," and "inert ideas"—that is to say, following Alfred North Whitehead, "ideas that are merely received into the mind without being utilized, or tested, or thrown into fresh combinations" (qtd. in Tagg 70). Tagg suggests that there are many "incentives, disincentives, and constraints on choice that act on students in college" (96), and he theorizes these incentives and restraints as a kind of "cognitive economy," a "system for managing and allocating cognitive resources" (96). Tagg's ideal college culture is one he calls the "learning paradigm college," designed to provide the "highest rewards for high cost activities"—to "deep approaches" and "complex cognition" (101). Significantly, Tagg notes that the *approach* students take to learning "largely determines the kind of learning they engage in" (67), citing Paul Ramsden's summary of this research to support this claim: "Many research studies have shown that the outcomes of students' learning are associated with the approaches they use. What students learn is indeed closely associated with how they go about learning it" (67). This research has important implications for teachers of writing and lends support for a curriculum focused on deep reading, which in many ways is perhaps most essentially about what kind of process of learning we want to privilege in our classrooms. As Tagg suggests, deep learning equips students with skills and dispositions that transfer to many areas of their lives (72). Surface learning does not. A significant body of scholarship and research supports this claim (Blau, "Performative"; Bransford, Pellegrino, and Donovan; Weimer).

Problem-Exploring Dispositions

Closer to home, a number of researchers in the field of composition studies have suggested that we have our own surface learning problem to address (Beaufort; Hillocks; Sullivan). Generally speaking, much of this research aligns with a distinction Elizabeth Wardle has theorized between two very different dispositions toward learning: *answer-getting* dispositions versus *problem-exploring* dispositions. Wardle notes that "problem-exploring dispositions incline a person toward curiosity, reflection, consideration of multiple possibilities, a willingness to engage in a recursive process of trial and error, and toward a recognition that more than one solution can 'work'" (n.p.). This is precisely the kind of mature critical and creative thinking endorsed in the Delphi Report by critical thinking scholars (Facione). Answer-getting dispositions seek "right answers quickly and are averse to open consideration of multiple possibilities" (Wardle).

Wardle suggests that schools have helped create a culture of surface learning in the United States and that "the steady movement toward standardized testing and tight control of educational activities by legislators is producing and reproducing answer-getting dispositions in educational systems and individuals" (n.p.). It is important to note that this movement, Wardle suggests, "is more than a dislike for the messiness of deep learning; rather, it can be understood as an attempt to limit the kind of thinking that students and citizens have the tools to do" (see Darling-Hammond; Ravitch; Ripley; Tucker).

Other recent research helps map the landscape of our current surface-learning, answer-getting state of affairs, and much of it is dependent on the way students orient themselves *as readers* as they engage assigned reading materials in classes across the disciplines. There is a great deal of evidence that surface reading—rather than deep reading—is widely practiced across disciplines and across institutional boundaries. Daniel Keller's case study of nine students from a midwestern high school, *Chasing Literacy*, provides a fascinating glimpse into the intellectual reading lives of students, and much of what he discovered suggests a deeply ingrained culture of surface learning in schools. Keller found, for example, that many students "know how to 'game' the system" in school by reading assigned texts "in tactical ways" (130) that often involve doing either very little reading, reading for surface detail only, or avoiding reading altogether. Much of this appears to be dictated by an educational model and curriculum design that puts a premium on quantity and "covering" content in the classroom. Keller's book documents the many ways that students game the system and engage in surface reading and learning practices. He found, for example, that some students "had devised tactics for reading a little bit of the text, just enough to get by":

> Sarah's frustration with the curriculum was a reason for taking shortcuts: "They expect you to love this stuff, to get really deep meaning out of it, but then we fly right through it. Why bother? The tests don't care as long as I get [the answer] right." (78)

Another student, James, reveals to Keller that "there are ways to make it seem as if he had read" a homework assignment: "'You can pick up enough knowledge for a quiz late in the week if you were paying enough attention earlier'" (78). Another student, Amy, acknowledged that she knew students "'who read enough to get their one comment in during class'" (78). And James admits that many times he didn't even bother to do the reading at all because "he didn't like to read and discuss novels and poetry in the shallow ways demanded by the fast pace" (77). This fascinating testimony from students suggests that current curricula across many disciplines and types of institutions foster, as Keller notes, "a particular kind of reading: fast, shallow, and testable" (79; Jolliffe and Harl 611–12). This is a curriculum design in which "homework sheets and tests" provide the "ultimate purpose guiding the reading" (Keller 80). Significantly, "Despite their disenchantment with reading at school, nearly all of the participants—with the exception of David—expressed love and admiration for novels, placing their quality above the magazines and Internet reading" (80). Many of these students, in fact, report spending a great deal of time reading for pleasure. One student reported that he often read for hours, "pulling all-nighters if I really get into it" (80).

We may be seeing evidence here of what Kelly Gallagher has called "readicide"—"the systematic killing of the love of reading, often exacerbated by the inane, mind-numbing practices found in schools" (2). Gallagher suggests that readicide is caused by educational practices that value the development of test takers over the development of lifelong readers (5). This may help explain the disturbing results being reported on the Nation's Report Card, a congressionally mandated project administrated by the National Assessment of Educational Progress (NAEP) through the National Center for Education Statistics. In 2015 only "thirty-seven percent of twelfth-grade students performed at or above the *Proficient* achievement level in reading" (Nation's Report Card "Nine Subjects"). The remainder of students in this testing cohort tested below Proficient, with only Basic or Below Basic reading skills. Two reports about reading from the National Endowment for the Arts, *Reading at Risk* and *To Read or Not to Read: A Question of National Consequence,* provide additional data that confirm the disturbing depth of this problem. Dana Gioia acknowledges in his preface for *To Read or Not to Read: A Question of National Consequence* that "the story the data tell [about reading] is simple, consistent, and alarming" (5). The conclusions reported in this document are indeed sobering:

◆ Americans are spending less time reading.

◆ Reading comprehension skills are eroding.

◆ These declines have serious civic, social, cultural, and economic implications. (7)

Data from PISA, the international test used across the globe among nations to measure educational effectiveness, reveal similar levels of underperformance (Tucker).

Ominously, NAEP reported that twelfth-grade high school students performed poorly in other core disciplines as well. Only a statistical minority demonstrated proficiency in other key academic areas: mathematics: 25 percent; science: 22 percent; and writing: 27 percent (Nation's Report Card, "Nine Subjects"; see also Nation's Report Card "2015"). A simplified, surface approach to reading may well help explain poor student performance in these subject areas as well. As Alice Sullivan and Matt Brown have documented in their landmark study, "Social Inequalities in Cognitive Scores at Age 16: The Role of Reading," reading competency must be understood as much more than simple vocabulary acquisition: it "is actually linked to increased cognitive progress over time" (37). As Pierre Bourdieu and Jean-Claude Passeron have demonstrated, the influence of language skills developed through reading, conversation, and family life "never ceases to be felt" across an individual's life span (73). Language skills affect student performance and cognition in profound ways: "Language is not simply an instrument of communication: it also provides, together with a richer or poorer vocabulary, a more or less complex system of categories, so that the capacity to decipher and manipulate complex structures, whether logical or aesthetic," depends partly on the complexity of the language a student possesses (73). The findings of the National Commission on Writing, therefore, may have as much to tell us about *reading* as they do about *writing*. The commission found, unfortunately, that twelfth-grade students currently produce writing that is "relatively immature and unsophisticated" (17). Obviously, much work remains to be done.

Deep Reading across the Disciplines

Deep reading can be theorized as a form of intellectual inquiry that is practiced across disciplines and across professions. Skilled practitioners across an imposing variety of disciplines must be "deep readers" in some foundational ways. This list would include physicians and health care providers, scientists, attorneys, software designers and programmers, sociologists, mathematicians, and engineers, among many others. They are deep readers in the way they use prior knowledge, extensive subject matter knowledge, systematic and methodical investigation, careful reading and re-reading of primary and secondary sources, critical and creative thinking, and working in response to systems, interactivity, context, and communities of practice. Virtually regardless of major, deep reading skills will transfer to other contexts and activities as students move beyond their English and composition classes. *The Cambridge Handbook of Thinking and Reasoning* offers a rich body of evidence that the best thinking in a variety of disciplines is built around the kind of deep reading practices I am theorizing here (Holyoak and Morrison).

To provide just one paradigmatic example, historian Sam Wineburg theorizes the discipline of history as perhaps most essentially a form of deep reading. In the first chapter of *Historical Thinking and Other Unnatural Acts,* Wineburg examines professional historian Bob Alston's readings of a group of primary and secondary documents related to Abraham Lincoln, providing a fascinating case study of this deep reading process in action. Significantly, Alston's unwillingness to be sure—his caution, his humility in the face of what he doesn't know, and his many questions about Lincoln—leads him to a "nuanced and sophisticated understanding" of Lincoln (Wineburg 21). Questions play a key role in Alston's reading and meaning-making activity:

> The questions Alston asked are the tools of creation, dwelling in the space between his present knowledge and the circumstances of the past. Alston is an expert, to be sure, but not in the sense in which that term is typically used. His expertise lay not in his sweeping knowledge of this topic but in his ability to pick himself up after a tumble, to get a fix on what he does not know, and to generate a road map to guide his new learning. He was an expert at cultivating puzzlement. It was Alston's ability to stand back from first impressions, to question his quick leaps of mind, and to keep track of his questions that together pointed him in the direction of new learning. (21–22)

This is precisely the kind of reading practice I would like to suggest we privilege in our composition classrooms.

Following Lee S. Shulman, we may wish to theorize deep reading as a "signature pedagogy" in composition, as a way we define disciplinary learning in writing classrooms. Should we choose to do so, this is a pedagogy that will obviously have applications across disciplines. This approach to inquiry and meaning-making can also help us frame the deep structures of our teaching practice in accessible and powerful ways. Signature pedagogies, Shulman suggests, "implicitly define what counts as knowledge in a field and how things become known" (54). Shulman notes that signature pedagogies also "simplify the dauntingly complex challenges of professional education because once they are learned and internalized, we don't have to think about them; we can think with them" (56). Such an approach can help focus the day-to-day "concrete, operational acts of teaching and learning" that we privilege in our classrooms (54), while also providing a compelling moral dimension for our work by embodying "a set of beliefs about professional attitudes, values, and dispositions" (55). Significantly, Shulman insists that signature pedagogies must also be "pedagogies of uncertainty. They render classroom settings unpredictable and surprising, raising the stakes for both students and instructors" (57). Learning to deal with uncertainty in the classroom, Shulman suggests, "models one of the most crucial aspects of professionalism, namely, the ability to make judgments under uncertainty" (57).

Big Questions

In his chapter on how skilled teachers prepare to teach in *What the Best College Teachers Do*, Ken Bain discovered that highly successful college teachers begin by asking themselves two questions: (1) What kind of learning do I want my students to experience? and (2) What counts as knowledge and wisdom in my discipline? Bain discovered that the best college teachers moved well beyond the transmission model of teaching, in which "teaching is something that instructors do to students, usually by delivering truths about the discipline" (48). Excellent college teachers focused instead on much broader, more ambitious goals and then on designing learning activities that provided opportunities for students to meet these goals. Bain notes that this becomes

> a kind of epistemological investigation into what it means to know something, pushing far beyond the vague little phrases that often litter discussion of learning objectives ("learning the material," "thinking critically," "engaging the subject matter," "feeling comfortable with the topic," "taking it to a higher level"). (49)

For the teachers that Bain studied, the creation of a successful learning environment was theorized as "an important and serious intellectual (or artistic) act, perhaps even as a kind of scholarship, that required the attention of the best minds in academia" (49). Additionally, Bain found that the outstanding teachers he studied had "an unusually keen sense of the histories of their disciplines, including the controversies that have swirled within them, and that understanding seems to help them reflect deeply on the nature of thinking within their fields" (25).

Bain also discovered that questions were crucial to the approach of the teachers he studied: "In the learning literature and in the thinking of the best teachers, questions play an essential role in the process of learning and modifying mental models. Questions help us construct knowledge" (31). In fact, Bain notes, "some cognitive scientists think that questions are so important that we cannot learn until the right one has been asked" (31). Bain found that the first thing many professors focus on as they are designing courses is "big questions": "What big questions will my course help students answer, or what skills, abilities, or qualities will it help them develop, and how will I encourage my students' interest in these questions and abilities?" (50; Association of American Colleges and Universities 33–34). Perhaps most significantly for our purposes here, Bain also discovered that because the outstanding teachers he studied "recognize that the higher-order concepts of their disciplines often run counter to the models of reality that everyday experience has encouraged most people to construct," such teachers "often want students to do something that human beings don't do very well: build new mental models of reality" (27). Bain notes that mental models become entrenched, often function automatically, and are typically resistant to change (Wardle; Bargh; Bargh and Chartrand). A key question for Bain throughout his book is one I am pursuing here as well: "How can we stimulate students to build new models, to engage in what some call 'deep' learning as opposed to 'surface' learning in which they merely remember something long enough to pass the examination?" (27).

As writing teachers, then, the questions before us are these: What counts as knowledge and wisdom in our discipline? What does it mean to "know" something as a reader, writer, and thinker? What is the history of our discipline and how does this history help us understand the nature of thinking within our field? What are the threshold concepts of our discipline that we want to be teaching in our classrooms? What are the "right questions" for us to ask so that deep learning can take place? What are the "big questions" we want our students to engage? There are also a number of essential questions related to *reading* that require our careful attention: What role does reading play in the construction of knowledge? What role should reading play in the writing classroom? What theory of reading will we privilege in our writing classrooms?

The answers to these questions, I would like to suggest, do not involve grammatically correct sentences, how to produce well organized essays, or even how to craft a strong thesis statement. Instead, the answers might be most usefully framed, quite simply, this way: how one thinks productively about a complex subject. To help develop new mental models for students, we must design learning activities that require them to think deeply, creatively, and reflectively about complex problems.

The pedagogy of deep reading I am theorizing here is built around this essential goal, and it is designed to be applicable in classrooms grades 6–13. I would like to illustrate this approach to writing pedagogy by discussing a deep reading unit I developed for my English 93 class, a developmental writing class I have been teaching now for many years.

"Nations Themselves Are Narrations"

The genesis of this unit began with a novel I was assigned to review for *Library Journal* in 2012. The book was *The Family Mansion*, written by Jamaican novelist and humorist Anthony C. Winkler. Winkler was born in Kingston, Jamaica, and he has written a number of novels about colonial Jamaica, indigenous populations, and the legacy of Christopher Columbus. He has, in effect, been rewriting the history of Jamaica one novel at a time, attempting to offset the grim reality that, as the saying goes, "history is written by the victors." Many of Winkler's novels offer readers a brutal and darkly humorous revisionist history of his homeland and its native populations. Modeling the kind of deep reading practice I am advocating here, I was inspired by *The Family Mansion* to read more of Winkler's work and then to read more deeply about Columbus, early explorers in the New World, and the history of the Caribbean. At first I was doing this reading for personal interest and the pleasure of learning, but at a certain point I began to think, "This would make a great unit for my English 93 class." I wanted to frame the discussion around an important idea, and I settled on a key paragraph from Edward Said's book *Culture and Imperialism* about narrative. I didn't want the unit to end up being a simple moral lesson about Europeans doing bad things to indigenous peoples in the Americas, so the addition to my reading list of *1493: Uncovering the New World Columbus Created* was crucial, as Charles Mann offers readers a scientific, global perspective to consider when assessing Columbus and his legacy, thereby complicating things considerably. Here is the assignment I distributed to the class:

Essay #2: Columbus Sailed the Ocean Blue
Reading Sequence:

1. Excerpt from "Introduction," *Culture and Imperialism* by Edward Said (xi–xxviii)
2. *My First Biography: Christopher Columbus* by Marion Dane Bauer (a children's book)
3. *A Short Account of the Destruction of the Indies* by Bartolome de las Casas

4. *1493: Uncovering the New World Columbus Created*
   by Charles Mann

Using the work of Edward Said, I would like you to write a reflective essay about what we have learned ~~about the~~ importance of "narrative." I would like you to focus your essay around this key passage from Edward Said's *Culture and Imperialism*:

> Readers of this book will quickly discover that narrative is crucial to my argument here, my basic point being that stories are at the heart of what explorers and novelists say about strange regions of the world; they also become the method colonized people use to assert their own identity and the existence of their own history. The main battle in imperialism is over land, of course; but when it comes to who owns the land, who had the right to settle and work on it, who kept it going, who won it back, and who now plans its future—these issues were reflected, contested, and even for a time decided in narrative. As one critic has suggested, nations themselves *are* narrations. The power to narrate, or to block other narratives from forming and emerging, is very important to culture and imperialism, and constitutes one of the main connections between them. (xii–xiiii)

What does this mean, exactly? What is "narrative" and why does Said think narrative is so important? What kind of narratives have we encountered in this unit? What do these different stories say about our shared history and about the writing and understanding of history and the world we live in?

How can a nation be said to be a "narrative"? ("As one critic has suggested, nations themselves *are* narrations.")

Said also suggests that "[t]he power to narrate, or to block other narratives from forming and emerging is very important to culture." What does this mean exactly? Is there any way that we can expand this general principle beyond Columbus to other areas of life and the world right now—or is this just an idea limited to Columbus and the world many, many years ago?

I began this unit by asking students to write down everything they knew about Christopher Columbus. It turns out it wasn't much, and it didn't go much beyond "he discovered America" and "in fourteen hundred ninety-two Columbus sailed the ocean blue." We then moved on to the selection from Said, which baffled everyone in class. As planned, I had successfully positioned my students in a "zone of proximal development." We spent much of the class enacting an eighty-minute version of Salvatori's "difficulty paper" activity in which students talked (and vented) about all the things they didn't understand in the reading, identifying all the problems they had as readers with this text (Salvatori and Donahue, *Elements*, 9–11; Sweeney and McBride).

I told students not to worry, because the remainder of our time in this unit would be spent reading material that would help illustrate and embody what Said was saying. I assured them that by the end of this unit they would indeed be able to "read" this passage and talk about it thoughtfully. I also framed this activity as an important aspect of learning how to be a strong college-level reader, writer, and thinker, especially in terms of not giving up in the face of difficult or challenging readings. I also championed the great value of *re-reading*. I also framed this discussion "expansively," indicating that as college students they were likely to get difficult or challenging readings like this in other courses they took, and acknowledged that part of my job was to prepare them to engage with such readings productively. I was deliberately drawing on "expansive" framing strategies advocated by educational theorists, a key pedagogical strategy that promotes transfer of learning. As Perkins and Salomon note,

> Expansive framing emphasizes the meaningfulness and usefulness of what's being learned and its potential to relate to a range of other circumstances. Bounded framing treats what's being learned as for the unit, for the class, for the quiz. The broad teaching/learning moves that characterize expansive framing plainly put learners in a better position to detect opportunities for transfer. They include cultivating expectations that what's being learned will speak to related settings; treating previous learning as continuously relevant; treating the use of prior learning as desired socially; and, broadly speaking, encouraging students to see themselves as the agents of their own learning and use of knowledge. (254)

I assured the class that we'd have the opportunity to discuss and discover what Said was saying about narrative for ourselves. A fascinating aspect of this process was that we began with a three-page excerpt from Said (I thought it important to provide some context and background for his main idea about narrative in this passage), but as the unit developed our focus grew tighter and tighter. Soon it was just a few paragraphs, then just one key paragraph. By the end of the unit, we were focused on just four words: "nations themselves *are* narrations." I have to admit, this turned out to be the most rewarding time I've ever spent with just four words in my entire career as an English teacher.

After Said, we moved on to discuss the sequence of assigned books, which were selected to illustrate Said's ideas and to present students with a variety of competing narratives about Columbus and America. The children's book, *My First Biography: Christopher Columbus* by Marion Dane Bauer, had the advantage of neatly summarizing one popular kind of narrative still current today about Columbus and the Americas. We followed this with *A Short Account of the Destruction of the Indies* by Bartolome de las Casas, which presents a much less happy picture of this time in our history and offers readers a very different type of narrative about the first meetings of these two cultures. None of my students had ever heard of de las Casas before, and most were shocked by the story he told. They were greatly interested in why this narrative was unknown to them, and this provided an important opportunity for us to reflect on Said's idea about the formation of narratives and also the power to "block other narratives from forming and emerging." Our discussion ranged widely, especially when I asked the class about their family histories and the narratives they have embraced about their families. I asked if any of them had ever learned surprising things as adults about family members that complicated their understanding of their family history, and many had powerful stories to tell. Obviously, someone had shaped these family narratives for particular rhetorical purposes, highlighting certain features and blocking or editing out others. We also talked about narratives related to love and relationships and how the ideal "successful" relationship was supposed to proceed. We also talked about where these narratives that exert such power over our lives might come from.

We concluded this unit with a selection of chapters from *1493*. This reading disoriented students further by turning their attention to science and biology—and mosquitoes, potatoes, and oil. We paid special attention to Mann's claim that Columbus had invented the modern world:

> By founding La Isabela [in what is now the Dominican Republic] Colón initiated permanent European occupation in the Americas. And in so doing he began the era of *globalization*—the single, turbulent exchange of goods and services that today engulfs the entire habitable world. . . . Colón's signal accomplishment was, in the phrase of historian Alfred W. Crosby, to reknit the seams of Pangaea. After 1492 the world's ecosystems collided and mixed as European vessels carried thousands of species to new homes across the oceans. The Columbian Exchange, as Crosby called it, is the reason why there are tomatoes in Italy, oranges in the United States, chocolates in Switzerland, and chili peppers in Thailand. To ecologists, the Columbian Exchange is arguably the most important event since the death of the dinosaurs. (7)

Mann also discusses the controversy surrounding Colón (i.e., Columbus) and the efforts to memorialize his voyages and achievement. Colón has been renounced, after all, as "the exterminator of a race" (23). For Mann, however, these claims are misguided:

> A thesis of this book is that their belief, no matter how understandable, is mistaken. The Colombian Exchange had such far-reaching effects that some biologists now say that Colón's voyages marked the beginning of a new biological era: the Homogenocene. The term refers to homogenizing: mixing unlike substances to create a uniform blend. With the Colombian Exchange, places that were once ecologically distinct have become more alike. In this sense, the world has become one, exactly as the old admiral hoped. (23)

I am happy to report that at the end of this deep reading unit, when we returned to Said to see if our understanding of his ideas had changed, they had. Students were now able to speak thoughtfully about narrative, and most had many interesting and perceptive things to say about the power of narratives to shape our lives and perceptions.

The overall effect on the class was positive. Students understood that they were engaged in real intellectual work and authentic meaning-making, and this helped nurture motivation and commitment to the enterprise of learning. The class also clearly appreciated the challenge I set before them, were motivated by my belief in their ability to engage this kind of deep learning activity, and appreciative of the effort I had put into designing the unit. I have used deep reading assignments like this now for many years (Sullivan 80–97), and they have been well received by students. Deep reading activities have become central to my approach to teaching writing.

Sample Student Responses

Space does not allow me to provide extensive samples of student work, but I would like to share two representative highlights. In each case, I detected hints of a "threshold concept" being engaged—an idea or practice that is "akin to a portal, opening up a new and previously inaccessible way of thinking about something." Part of this is related to the idea of narrative itself and how narratives come to be embraced and for what reasons. This is certainly one kind of portal and threshold concept. Another is related to the enterprise of deep reading itself as a "portal" for the productive engagement of complex problems and authentic meaning-making. Although these excerpts are brief, we see evidence of deep reading being embraced and the development of at least the beginning of "a transformed way of understanding, or interpreting, or viewing something without which the learner cannot progress" (Meyer and Land 3). Both of these writers are working in good faith to engage a form of what Perkins calls "troublesome knowledge." These artifacts also provide evidence of students assessing or reassessing their own mental models for understanding the world—a key goal for deep reading pedagogy. Even if this is only an emerging awareness, with additional exposure to this kind of intellectual practice students might eventually begin to embrace deep reading as their default strategy when they engage complexity—across disciplines and in all areas of their lives. Although both of these students were initially baffled by Said, they worked productively through that confusion and emerged with at least a preliminary understanding of Said's primary point about narrative.

> **Chelsea:** The power to narrate is not just a topic related to Christopher Columbus because that is who we have been talking

about; the power to narrate and block others is something that can pertain to anything, all day every day. This is not just an idea that is limited to Columbus or the world many years ago. The power to create a narrative and block another is happening right now, to every single person you know. It pertains to relationships, family, school, and work. There is a story behind even the simplest of things. There is a story behind *you*. It all comes down to who has the power, who believes what, and whether or not someone wants to share a simple version of a narrative, a selectively shaped version, or the truth where not even the smallest detail is left out.

Alex: We live in a complex world, where narrations are a part of our every day lives. I believe that this relates to our lives on a daily basis, we can't believe the first story we're told, or the most well known. Our world is intense and complex and so is our history behind it. Every nation, family, religion, and person has a story, and although it's easy to believe the first one we hear, sometimes it goes much deeper than we think. While the history behind Columbus shows how easy it is to believe the first thing were told, this happens in our lives all the time. We're all taught to believe that it's supposed to work out, or end up one certain way and if it doesn't, its wrong or there's something wrong with us. We grew up hearing narrations on the "fairy-tale ending," but what we were never told is that it doesn't always end up that way. There are always two sides to a narration, and usually the darker less innocent side is hidden.

Following classic learning theory, this assignment was designed with the goal of "empowering individuals to know that the world is far more complex than it first appears" (King and Kitchener 1)—and both of these artifacts suggest this has been at least partially achieved. In fact, evidence suggests that both writers may be "passing through a portal, from which a new perspective opens up, allowing things formerly not perceived to come into view" (Meyer, Land, and Baillie ix). It is important to note in this regard that both writers are not ultimately even talking about Columbus—they are talking about new mental models and new ways of knowing the world and constructing knowledge and meaning.

Toward a Pedagogy of Deep Reading

The deep reading pedagogy discussed in this chapter theorizes and enacts academic writing as a high-stakes enterprise. This is intellectual work, following Wolf, that honors "the profound generativity of the reading brain" (23). Pragmatically, how might we best operationalize a deep reading pedagogy in our classrooms? I would like to suggest the following guidelines, suitable for writing teachers in grades 6–13:

1. Frame deep reading as a form of intellectual inquiry that is practiced across disciplines and across professions and is "an analogue for thinking."

2. Define reading not simply as a way to decode texts or to encounter received ideas but rather as a valuable process of *constructing* knowledge and meaning. To be a deep reader in this sense is to participate in Bruffee's "conversation of mankind" (see also Carillo, "Reimagining").

3. Theorize deep reading as a form of advanced listening and mature critical and creative thinking that requires important dispositional characteristics and habits of mind such as open-mindedness, intellectual generosity, and humility (Costa and Kallick; Council of Writing Program Administrators), not just decoding skills, although these are important too, of course.

4. Target immersion in confusion, "chaos," and "troublesome knowledge" as key classroom strategies that are essential for the development of mature meaning-making. In this, we will be following learning theorists' embrace of doubt, uncertainty, and "intelligent confusion" (King and Kitchener 166–67; Perry; Kegan; Sullivan, *New* 11–118).

5. Build writing and reading units around "serious intellectual questions" (Beaufort 158) and "complex and rich problems" (Wineburg) that are real, essential, and significant—and that will be a reach for most students, requiring them to work from within Vygotsky's zone of proximal development. If questions are so important that we cannot learn until the right one has been asked, then we must choose our questions carefully, with the research discussed here clearly in mind.

Works Cited

Adler-Kassner, Linda, John Majewski, and Damian Koshnick. "The Value of Troublesome Knowledge: Transfer and Threshold Concepts in Writing and History." *Composition Forum* 26 (2012). Web. 21 June 2015.

Adler-Kassner, Linda, and Elizabeth Wardle, eds. *Naming What We Know: Threshold Concepts of Writing Studies*. Logan: Utah State UP, 2015. Print.

Association of American Colleges and Universities. *College Learning for the New Global Century*. Washington: AAC&U, 2007. Print.

Bain, Ken. *What the Best College Teachers Do*. Cambridge: Harvard UP, 2004. Print.

Bargh, John. "The Automaticity of Everyday Life." *The Automaticity of Everyday Life: Advances in Social Cognition, Volume X*. Ed. R. S. Wyer, Jr. New York: Psychology P, 1997. 1–61. Print.

Bargh, John, and T. L. Chartrand. "The Unbearable Automaticity of Being." *American Psychologist* 54 (1999): 462–79. Print.

Bauer, Marion Dane. *My First Biography: Christopher Columbus*. New York: Scholastic, 2009. Print.

Baxter Magolda, Marcia. *Making Their Own Way: Narratives for Transforming Higher Education to Promote Self-Development*. Sterling: Stylus, 2001. Print.

Beaufort, Anne. *College Writing and Beyond: A New Framework for University Writing Instruction*. Logan: Utah State UP, 2007. Print.

Blau, Sheridan. *The Literature Workshop: Teaching Texts and Their Readers*. Portsmouth: Heinemann, 2003. Print.

———. "Performative Literacy: The Habits of Mind of Highly Literate Readers." *Voices from the Middle* 10.3 (2003): 18–22. Print.

Bourdieu, Pierre, and Jean-Claude Passeron. *Reproduction in Education, Society and Culture*. 2nd ed. Trans. Richard Nice. Thousand Oaks: SAGE, 2000. Print.

Bransford, John D., James W. Pellegrino, and M. Suzanne Donovan, eds. *How People Learn: Brain, Mind, Experience, and School: Expanded Edition*. Washington: National Academies P, 2000. Print.

Bruffee, Kenneth. "Collaborative Learning and the Conversation of Mankind." *College English* 46 (1984): 635–52. Print.

Carillo, Ellen C. "Reimagining the Role of the Reader in the Common Core State Standards." *English Journal* 105.3 (2016): 29–35. Print.

———. *Securing a Place for Reading in Composition: The Importance of Teaching for Transfer.* Logan: Utah State UP, 2015. Print.

Carr, Nicholas. *The Shallows: What the Internet Is Doing to Our Brains.* Norton, 2011. Print.

Costa, Arthur L., and Bena Kallick, eds. *Learning and Leading with Habits of Mind.* Alexandria: Association for Supervision and Curriculum Development, 2008. Print.

Council of Writing Program Administrators, National Council of Teachers of English, and the National Writing Project. "Framework for Success in Postsecondary Writing." 2011. Web. 30 Dec. 2015.

Darling-Hammond, Linda. *The Flat World and Education: How America's Commitment to Equity Will Determine Our Future.* Teachers College P, 2010. Print.

de las Casas, Bartolome. *A Short Account of the Destruction of the Indies.* New York: Penguin, 2004. Print.

Dewey, John. *How We Think.* Mineola: Dover, 1997. Print.

Empson, William. *Seven Types of Ambiguity.* 1930. New York: New Directions, 1966. Print.

Facione, Peter. "Critical Thinking: A Statement of Expert Consensus for Purposes of Educational Assessment and Instruction." *The Delphi Report Executive Summary: Research Findings and Recommendations Prepared for the Committee on Pre-College Philosophy of the American Philosophical Association.* ERIC Document Reproduction Service, No. ED315423. 1990. Print.

Gallagher, Kelly. *Readicide: How Schools Are Killing Reading and What You Can Do about It.* Portland: Stenhouse, 2009. Print.

Hillocks, George. *The Testing Trap: How State Writing Assessments Control Learning.* New York: Teachers College P, 2002. Print.

Holyoak, Keith J., and Robert G. Morrison, eds. *The Cambridge Handbook of Thinking and Reasoning.* Cambridge: Cambridge UP, 2005. Print.

Horning, Alice, and Elizabeth W. Kraemer. *Reconnecting Reading and Writing*. Anderson: Parlor P, 2013. Print.

Horning, Alice, and Deborah-Lee Gollnitz. "What Is College Reading? A High School-College Dialogue." *Reader* 67 (2014): 43–72. Print.

Jolliffe, David A. "Review Essay: Learning to Read as Continuing Education." *College Composition and Communication* 58.3 (2007): 470–94. Print.

Jolliffe, David A., and Allison Harl. "Texts of Our Institutional Lives: Studying the 'Reading Transition' from High School to College: What Are Our Students Reading and Why?" *College English* 70:6 (2008): 599–607. Print.

Kegan, Robert. *In Over Our Heads: The Mental Demands of Modern Life*. Cambridge: Harvard UP, 1994. Print.

Keller, Daniel. *Chasing Literacy: Reading and Writing in an Age of Acceleration*. Logan: Utah State UP, 2014. Print.

King, Patricia, and Karen Strohm Kitchener. *Developing Reflective Judgment*. San Francisco: Jossey-Bass, 1994. Print.

Lehman, Christopher, Kathleen Roberts, and Tobey Antao. *Falling in Love with Close Reading: Lessons for Analyzing Texts—and Life*. Portsmouth: Heinemann, 2013. Print.

Mann, Charles. *1493: Uncovering the New World Columbus Created*. New York: Vintage, 2011. Print.

Meyer, Jan H. F., and Ray Land. *Overcoming Barriers to Student Understanding*. London: Routledge, 2006. Print.

———. "Threshold Concepts and Troublesome Knowledge: An Introduction." *Overcoming Barriers to Student Understanding*. Ed. Jan H. F. Meyer and Ray Land. London: Routledge, 2006. 3–18. Print.

Meyer, Jan H. F., Ray Land, and Caroline Baillie, eds. *Threshold Concepts and Transformational Learning*. Rotterdam: Sense, 2010. Print.

Morrow, Nancy. "The Role of Reading in the Composition Classroom." *JAC* 17.3 (1997). Web. 8 May 2010.

National Commission on Writing in America's Schools and Colleges. *The Neglected "R": The Need for a Writing Revolution*. Princeton: College Board, 2003. Web. 24 Aug. 2010.

National Endowment for the Arts. *Reading at Risk*. Research Division Report 46. Washington: National Endowment for the Arts, 2004. Print.

———. *To Read or Not to Read: A Question of National Consequence*. Research Division Report 47. Washington: National Endowment for the Arts. Nov. 2007. Web. 30 December 2015.

Nation's Report Card. "2015 | Mathematics & Reading at Grade 12." National Assessment of Educational Progress, 2016. Web. 4 Jan. 2017.

———. "Nine Subjects. Three Grades. One Report Card." National Assessment of Educational Progress, 2016. Web. 2 Jan. 2017.

Newkirk, Thomas. *The Art of Slow Reading*. Portsmouth: Heinemann, 2012. Print.

Perkins, David. "Constructivism and Troublesome Knowledge." *Overcoming Barriers to Student Understanding*. Ed. Jan H. F. Meyer and Ray Land. London: Routledge, 2006. 33–47. Print.

Perkins, David N., and Gavriel Salomon. "Knowledge to Go: A Motivational and Dispositional View of Transfer." *Educational Psychologist* 47.3 (2012): 248–58. Print.

Perry, William. *Forms of Ethical and Intellectual Development in the College Years: A Scheme*. San Francisco: Jossey-Bass, 1999. Print.

Ravitch, Diane. *Reign of Error: The Hoax of the Privatization Movement and the Danger to America's Public Schools*. Knopf, 2013. Print.

Richards, I. A. *Practical Criticism: A Study of Literary Judgment*. 1929. New York: Harvest, 1956. Print.

Ripley, Amanda. *The Smartest Kids in the World: And How They Got That Way*. Simon and Schuster, 2013.

Roberts, Judith C., and Keith A. Roberts. "Deep Reading, Cost/Benefit, and the Construction of Meaning: Enhancing Reading Comprehension and Deep Learning in Sociology Courses." *Teaching Sociology* 36.2 (2008): 125–40. Print.

Rosenblatt, Louise. *Literature as Exploration*. 5th ed. New York: MLA, 1995. Print.

———. *The Reader, the Text, and the Poem: The Transactional Theory of the Literary Work*. Carbondale: Southern Illinois UP, 1978. Print.

———. "What Facts Does This Poem Teach You?" *Language Arts* 57.4 (1980): 386–94.

Sacks, Peter. *Standardized Minds: The High Price of America's Testing Culture and What We Can Do about It.* Cambridge: Perseus, 1999. Print.

Said, Edward W. "Introduction." *Culture and Imperialism.* New York: Vintage, 1993. xi–xxviii. Print.

Salvatori, Mariolina. "Conversations with Texts: Reading in the Teaching of Composition." *College English* 58.4 (1996): 440–54. Print.

Salvatori, Mariolina, and Patricia Donahue. *The Elements (And Pleasures) of Difficulty.* New York: Pearson/Longman, 2005. Print.

———. "What Is College English? Stories about Reading: Appearance, Disappearance, Morphing, and Revival." *College English* 75.2 (2012): 199–217. Print.

Shulman, Lee S. "Signature Pedagogies in the Professions." *Daedalus* 134.3 (2005): 52–59. Print.

Sommers, Nancy. "Responding to Student Writing." *College Composition and Communication* 33.2 (1982): 148–56. Print.

Sullivan, Alice, and Matt Brown, "Social Inequalities in Cognitive Scores at Age 16: The Role of Reading." Center for Longitudinal Studies Working Paper 2013/10. *Institute of Education, University of London.* September 2013. Web. 10 August 2015.

Sullivan, Patrick. *A New Writing Classroom: Listening, Motivation, and Habits of Mind.* Logan: Utah State UP, 2014. Print.

Sweeney, Meghan A., and Maureen McBride. "Difficulty Paper (Dis) Connections: Understanding the Threads Students Weave between Their Reading and Writing." *College Composition and Communication* 66.4 (2015): 591–64. Print.

Tagg, John. *The Learning Paradigm College.* San Francisco: Anker, 2003. Print.

Tucker, Marc S., ed. *Surpassing Shanghai: An Agenda for American Education Built on the World's Leading Systems.* Harvard Education P, 2011.

Twain, Mark. "10 July 1908." *Autobiography of Mark Twain, Volume 3.* Mark Twain Project Online. California Digital Library, The Mark Twain Papers, 2015, http://www.marktwainproject.org/xtf/

view?docId=works/MTDP10364.xml;style=work;brand=mtp; chunk.id=dv0071#pa1874. Web. 30 Dec. 2016.

Vygotsky, L.S. *Mind in Society: The Development of Higher Psychological Processes*. Ed. Michael Cole et al. Cambridge: Harvard UP, 1978. Print.

Wardle, Elizabeth. "Creative Repurposing for Expansive Learning: Considering 'Problem-Exploring' and 'Answer-Getting' Dispositions in Individuals and Fields." *Composition Forum* 26 (2012). Web. 24 August 2014.

Weimer, Maryellen. *Learner-Centered Teaching: Five Key Changes to Practice*. San Francisco: Jossey-Bass, 2013. Print.

Wineburg, Sam. *Historical Thinking and Other Unnatural Acts*. Philadelphia: Temple UP, 2001. Print.

Winkler, Anthony C. *The Family Mansion*. New York: Akashic, 2013. Print.

Wolf, Maryanne. *Proust and the Squid: The Story and Science of the Reading Brain*. New York: Harper, 2008. Print.

Wolf, Maryanne, and Mirit Barzillai. "The Importance of Deep Reading." *Educational Leadership* 66.6 (2009): 32–37.

CHAPTER NINE

Getting Our Students Ready for College and Career: It Doesn't Have to Be Greek to Us

KELLY CECCHINI
Manchester High School
Manchester, Connecticut

Several years ago, an assistant superintendent in my district asked whether any Manchester High School (MHS) English teachers would be interested in working with local college professors to reduce the number of our students who are required to take developmental (also known as remedial or noncredit) English and mathematics courses. My response was immediate and enthusiastic; as someone who had been teaching high school English for many years and had also been simultaneously working as an adjunct instructor in a community college teaching both developmental and three-credit composition courses, I could see clearly where the gaps in college readiness existed.

"Sign me up," I said.

When I discovered that in 2009 only about 44 percent of MHS students who showed up at our local community college had tested into credit-bearing English classes, I was both shocked and deeply disheartened. I was also somewhat incredulous—perhaps even indignant.

How can this be? High school English teachers work incredibly hard doing everything we believe we should be doing to prepare our students for college, and then some. That can't be right.

But there were the cold, accusing data, staring me in the face.

So, as a part of the federal College Access Challenge Grant (CACG), I worked closely with members of the Board of Regents; administrators; university, state, and community college professors; high school teachers; and guidance counselors. In my first meeting with this dedicated group of educators, the CACG Partnership, two things became immediately apparent: (1) the lack of communication between grade 7–12 educators and college-level educators had been a major contributor to the readiness gap, and (2) college professors were perplexed about exactly what was going on in high school classrooms in terms of reading and writing preparation. Much like high school teachers who bemoan the fact that middle schools don't seem to fully prepare students for the rigors and academic expectations of ninth grade, college professors were complaining about us.

Why are so many students arriving unprepared for college work? Why can't these kid write? Why don't they have more advanced reading skills? Just what are they doing over there?

I will tell you what we were doing. We were working like Sisyphus, rolling that boulder up the mountain every day, most often in relative isolation, in the face of nearly constantly changing educational policies, initiatives, standards, testing requirements, technologies, and student demographics. The mountain grows steeper, the terrain more treacherous. But we keep rolling that rock. We push as hard as we can despite having to face realities that make it very difficult—some would say impossible—to move our students up and over the top.

Who Am I, Atlas?

As any high school English teacher can attest, despite the fact that literacy is supposed to be the province of all educators, secondary school reading and writing instruction is generally considered to be the responsibility of English language arts (ELA) teachers. While "writing across the curriculum" is a phrase with which we should all be familiar by now (just type it into Google's search bar and marvel at the 10,300,000 results that appear in 0.36 seconds), I doubt very much that our colleagues in the art, physical education, music, or foreign language departments feel the same anxiety we do when standardized test scores are released and widely published. Despite the fact that, as former teacher and vocal anti-testing advocate Alfie Kohn says, the main thing that test scores reveal is "how big the students' houses are," that kind of public shaming continues (7). No offense meant to teachers in those departments; I have nothing but the highest regard for the work they do and consider each one vital to the education of our students, but I believe I can safely say that ELA teachers feel the burden of ensuring reading and writing proficiency most acutely. It sometimes does feel as though it is all on our shoulders. Until attitudes shift so that secondary teachers in every discipline truly embrace the idea that we are *all* responsible for building literacy, the Herculean task of adequately preparing every student for college-level reading and writing will continue to be carried out by a few harried but hopeful lovers of Shakespeare (and, in case you hadn't noticed, Greek mythology).

The Twelve Labors of Heracles . . . or Hercules . . . or Whatever My Name Is Now.

Secondary-level English teachers are not, aside from certain exceptions, reading teachers—and yet we have to be. Even though those of us who have master's degrees in secondary education took only the one required reading course (Issues in Content Area Reading, or some such thing) and the one required special education course, we are expected to teach reading skills to students of all abilities. In some ways, we have an advantage over our local postsecondary colleagues who, like most college English professors, have an MA or PhD in English literature. At least we have had a semester's worth of training in how to teach reading. Middle and high school ELA teachers are held accountable for the reading performance of their students despite the fact that most of us view writing instruction as our primary charge. When our students arrive unprepared or unable to interpret literature or make sense of grade-level nonfiction texts, though, the reading–writing connection becomes strained. We want our students to write with sources, but what if half the class has limited comprehension of those sources? What then? We employ differentiated instructional techniques (e.g., jigsaw groups, think-pair-share activities, Bloom's Taxonomy cubes), communicate the content in multiple ways (written and verbal instruction, note-taking assistance, rephrasing, repetition), plan collaborative learning activities, use scaffolded questioning, and teach our kids to use specific proven reading strategies such as activating prior knowledge, using graphic organizers for note-taking, taking text walks, and employing word attack strategies, and we hand out exit slips that assess understanding. We call on the school's reading specialists for help. If we are lucky, we have a special education co-teacher with a strong reading background, or perhaps a well-trained paraprofessional aide. We modify assignments and assessments when we are mandated to do so—and even when we are not. We make adjustments in both number and length of reading and writing assignments based on learning disabilities, emotional issues, medical concerns, and sometimes simply out of compassion in response to a student's life circumstances. Meanwhile, we must continue to teach writing skills, speaking and listening skills, study skills, time management skills, behavioral and social skills, vocabulary skills—and, lest anyone forget, we are also compelled to prepare students for whatever standardized tests are looming. In their 2006 book, *Change Leadership: A Practical Guide to Transforming Our Schools*, Tony Wagner and colleagues ask us to "[i]magine being asked to rebuild an airplane—while [we] are flying it" (xv). Although this hypothetical scenario was intended to illustrate the complexities of transforming school culture, it speaks to the difficulties of being a secondary ELA teacher as well. Even if we could stop everything else to focus only on improving the reading skills of our students, we could not, in most cases, completely close the readiness gap. Of course, many high school ELA teachers don't believe we should even have to try. This work, they claim, should be the responsibility of teachers in the primary grades. In truth, improving literacy skills *is* the primary focus for elementary educators, but like us they are trying to complete all of their many "labors" simultaneously.

Aeolus, God of the Winds . . . Where to Now?

Testing. Funding. Changes in administration. New initiatives. Old initiatives, but with new names. Social promotion policies. IEP and 504 plans. Socioeconomic disparities. Like Odysseus, we want to say to our colleagues: *Don't open the bag!* But like Odysseus' men, we can't help ourselves. In fact, we have no choice. We have to navigate regardless of the storms by which we are often battered. When all of these things are swirling madly around us, we just want to take cover. These are winds over which we as teachers have virtually no control. No matter how fiercely we rail against the weather, it still rains and storms. It makes little sense to obsess over what we cannot change, or at least not change overnight. So what can we do in our own classrooms today to begin to reduce the college-readiness gaps in reading and writing? There are quite a few things, actually.

The first one may not technically take place in the classroom, but it may be the most important. All teachers, but in this case secondary-level teachers in particular, must collaborate. In my work with the partners in the College Access Challenge Grant, having the opportunity to hear firsthand what college professors wanted my students to walk in the door already able to do was invaluable. Led by former Manchester Community College (MCC) Academic Dean Joanne Russell, the ELA members of the regional partnership were charged with creating and delivering the following:

> Modularized curricular package and training materials [for]: 12th grade ELA curricula addressing English deficiencies that would most likely result in students needing remedial or developmental coursework upon acceptance into Connecticut public two- or four-year higher education institutions immediately following graduation from high school.

So where to begin? Operating within the insular world of high school English, responding to the demands of the now defunct Connecticut Academic Performance Test's Response to Literature subtest by "training" our students in formulaic writing, and continuing to prepare our students for college English classes in exactly the way we ourselves had been prepared (regardless of how long ago that may have been) had gotten us to this place. We had to sit down together, English professors and English teachers, to have real conversations. We had to ask hard questions. We had to look closely at what we were and were not doing, and at what absolutely had to change. We had to figure out what we could do *right now* to close the readiness gap.

Reforms were, in fact, already underway; due to Connecticut's Public Law 12-40 (enacted in 2012), public community colleges and state universities were compelled to reconfigure how remedial and developmental education was delivered. Public high schools were now required to align their curriculum "as described by the Common Core State Standards to ensure that graduates are ready for college level work" (Connecticut PL 12-40). Members of the CACG Partnership realized, however, that positive changes in student performance that might result from the implementation of more rigorous standards would simply take too long to come to fruition. We were not willing to wait two, five, or twelve years to see results. The Partnership used the Educational Policy Improvement Center's *Seven Principles of College and Career Readiness* as a mission statement of sorts. Adopted by Connecticut's P-20 Council and the state's Board of Regents, EPIC's recommendations are as follows:

Principle 1: Create and maintain a college- and career-readiness culture in the school.

Principle 2: Create a core academic program aligned with and leading to college readiness by the end of twelfth grade.

Principle 3: Teach key self-management skills and academic behaviors and expect students to use them.

Principle 4: Make college and careers real by helping students manage the complexity of preparing for and applying to postsecondary education.

Principle 5: Create assignments and grading policies that more closely approximate college and career expectations each successive year of high school.

Principle 6: Make the senior year meaningful and appropriately challenging.

Principle 7: Build partnerships with and connections to postsecondary programs and institutions. (Connecticut PL 12-40 13)

And there we had it: a list of additional things we could begin to do right away to improve the college readiness of our students. I envisioned my role most clearly in the last three principles. Principle 7, *build[ing] partnerships with and connections to postsecondary programs and institutions*, was definitely being strengthened and expanded. At MHS, we had been teaching Early College Experience (ECE) dual enrollment courses for the University of Connecticut (UConn) for decades. ECE teachers attend regular professional development on the types of assignments UConn requires in first-year writing classes. We also offered (and still do) a very large number of AP courses, two of them in English language arts, and AP teachers attend College Board workshops regularly as well. We offered fourteen MCC articulated courses in various subject areas in which students could also earn college credit (we now have fifteen, with the addition of the first-ever Connecticut high school articulation of a community college ENG 101 in 2014). Our ties to postsecondary institutions were already well established; now we were also a part of the CACG Partnership. Principle 7: Check.

Principle 6, *mak[ing] the senior year meaningful and appropriately challenging*, was being addressed by the newly redesigned curriculum. Although twelfth-grade teachers never saw Senior English as a throwaway course, there was sometimes an unspoken sense that the grade 11 American Literature course was the *really* important one, and that it was probably "normal" for seniors to have "checked out." In the new curriculum, seniors complete the most difficult and challenging assignments in the final semester. We frequently talk to them about college-level expectations. We teach them about developmental courses and how students might end up there—something most of them don't know. Principle 6: Check.

Then there was Principle 5: *Create assignments and grading policies that more closely approximate college and career expectations each successive year of high school.* Enter Manchester Community College English professors Steve Straight and David Caldwell. They, along with several other MCC English professors, generously shared their syllabi, assignments, rubrics, and insights. Most important, they shared their time, and a lot of it. We met monthly at the CACG Partnership meetings and separately as an ELA group. They visited my school and worked with our Senior English teachers. They worked closely with me as I made decisions about text selection, reading lists, and pacing, offering helpful feedback on several incarnations of my curriculum, and they helped me to plan writing assignments that would truly prepare students for the next level. Rather than focusing only on literature analysis and traditional research papers, our writing assignments now included essays in which students were asked to deeply explore big questions, to consider their own thoughts in light of multiple complex readings on a given topic, and to explore one text through the "lens" of another (see example in the appendix). We shifted the Senior English curriculum toward argument writing, toward the use of mentor texts (such as Rosa and Escholz's *Models for Writers: Short Essays for Composition*; Colombo, Cullen, and Lisle's *Rereading America: Cultural Contexts for Critical Thinking and Writing*; and DiYanni's *One Hundred Great Essays*) and high-quality nonfiction readings, and away from the formulaic, literature-based thematic responses we had previously been focused on to the exclusion of nearly everything else. We planned with the end goal of college readiness in mind, developing real learning and critical thinking opportunities for students, the rigor and complexity of which escalated appropriately over the course of the year.

In addition to the curricular shifts we were making, we considered the intake assessment practices that were landing many of our students squarely in the realm of developmental, noncredit (but not non*cost*) education. MCC, like many postsecondary institutions, uses the College Board's ACCUPLACER, which is primarily a reading assessment, as a placement test. As an intake assessment, it leaves much to be desired, and so the Challenge Essay Test was created. At MCC, students who test into ENG 93 (or other non-credit-bearing remedial class) may request a Challenge Essay Test as an alternate way of being admitted to ENG 101. At MHS we decided to prepare our students for the Challenge Essay rather than the ACCUPLACER. We did this for two reasons. First, we have a large number of students in our district for whom English is not a first language, and these students were being disproportionately placed in remedial classes because ACCUPLACER did not reveal the depth of their thinking or ideas. The Challenge Essay assessment does reveal those things, and more. Second, the Challenge Essay asks students to demonstrate that they possess the components of the skill set needed not just to get into but to *actually succeed* in ENG 101. We could see that it wouldn't matter if a student tested into ENG 101 if he or she could not then complete the course successfully. The Challenge Essay scoring rubric became a guide not just for preparing students for college placement tests, but also for college reading and writing. In addition to the classroom work we do to teach our students to write with sources, we administer Challenge Essays in class every other month. These are one-hour assessments. Students read a short (one- to two-page) college-level writing excerpt and respond to the following prompt: *Write an essay that in your own words summarizes the author's ideas, and then explain whether you agree or disagree with them and why.* We sometimes use writing excerpts provided by the college; at other times we create our own versions that have similarly high Lexile scores. The essay scoring rubric assesses comprehension, the ability to concisely summarize complex text, the ability to credibly support one's own ideas and to thoughtfully analyze that support, understanding of essay structure and organization, rhetorical skill in establishing a purpose, the ability to create tone to address a particular audience, the ability to "take ownership" of the topic, and, of course, use of the conventions of Standard English. We spend some time "teaching" the rubric itself and a great deal of time teaching the reading and writing skills represented in it. Students use the scoring rubric to self- and peer-evaluate and to analyze growth over time. This is a far better use of our time than preparing students for an ACCUPLACER test would be, and, as previously noted, the work actually contributes to readiness for and success in college courses. It's what we want students to be able to do in their writing anyway.

Without the support of administrators, department leaders, and other powers-that-be, it would be difficult to implement change of this magnitude. Most of the partner schools involved in the CACG work were only able to pilot a new Senior English curriculum in one or two classes; I am lucky enough to work in a district where I was allowed to go "all in" in terms of implementation. My visionary former principal (now superintendent) Matthew Geary could see the potential benefit in challenging the ELA status quo, and, thankfully, he let us run with it. My former department leader, Marsha Testa, was equally supportive, allowing me the autonomy to lead and train a group of teachers who were as committed to making the necessary changes as I was. We began implementation of a revised Senior English curriculum at MHS in September of 2011. All grade 12 students who were not enrolled in AP English, UConn Early College Experience English, or Public Speaking (an MCC articulated communications course allowed for English credit in some of our College and Career Pathways programs) had to take Senior English at either the college preparatory or postsecondary preparatory level. In that first year, approximately 250 students in twelve individual classes were simultaneously immersed in the redesigned curriculum: roughly 175 in college preparatory classes and another 75 in postsecondary preparatory ones. The results speak for themselves: in the fall of 2009, just 44 percent of newly graduated MHS students who enrolled at MCC tested directly into ENG 101; by the fall of 2014, that number had risen to 68 percent. Certainly, some of that improvement can be attributed to PA 12-40 and its effect on the postsecondary developmental education system; however, much of the credit must go to our new Senior English curriculum, to those who taught it, and to the hard work of our students. Steve Straight and the MCC English department monitored the success of MHS students who had been taught in the new curriculum; they were impressed enough that they now allow our Senior English teachers to waive college preparatory students who earn a B or better for the year directly into MCC ENG 101 without additional testing beyond our own in-class Challenge Essays. Clearly there is still a great deal of room for improvement, but an increase of 24 percentage points in just three school years is a noteworthy achievement.

Hermes the Messenger, God of Communication, Shall Now Sum Up.

When I am asked what the single most important contributing factor in reducing the ELA college-readiness gap is, I always have to say *communication*. Aside from the actual work involved in writing the new curriculum, making the change has not been particularly difficult. Once we stopped operating in isolation, once we really listened to what the college professors were looking for in terms of reading and writing preparation experiences, it was a relatively simple matter to begin to provide that for our students. It was a change that had nothing to do with textbooks or technology or even money. The change had to do with openness. It had to do with listening. It had to do with putting aside old, deeply ingrained ideas about what we may have thought "college prep" meant. It had to do with a willingness to accept guidance while we were thinking and planning in ways that would truly prepare students for the next step. Anyone who is serious about improving the college readiness of students must start with open and honest conversations that include educators on both sides of the gap. Every high school should establish a partnership with at least one local college as part of ongoing professional development. The importance of this cannot be overstated.

The communication can't stop there, though. It was easy enough to persuade my former principal and department leader that we should do this; the teachers were a harder sell. Veteran English teachers who had been doing business in a particular way for a very long time were the most difficult to convince. Since English teachers are almost always former English *majors*, they tend to see literature analysis as vital and sacred in the ELA classroom. While I agree that reading, analyzing, and writing about great literature teaches us higher-order thinking skills as well as deeply human universal truths, most of our students are, sadly, not going to be English majors. (Well, perhaps it's not too sad; after all, I'd hate to have an English major trying to do my taxes.) Traditional literature analysis has an important place in the ELA classroom, but it is not the only type of writing we should be teaching. If that is all we do, we are not preparing students for the wide variety of academic writing they will be asked to do in college. Should ELA teachers be taking on academic writing instruction all by ourselves? Of course not. Again, communication is key. If high school social studies, science, and math teachers are not aware of what kinds of assignments are commonly given by college professors in those disciplines, invite them all to join the "gap" conversation. By all means, social studies, science, and math—take some of this off of our shoulders! How nice would that be?

With all of this focus on twelfth-grade ELA courses, it is important to remember that the work of preparing students for college must begin much earlier than senior year of high school. In all ELA classes, well-supported students should wrestle with appropriately rigorous and complex texts as soon as their reading skills allow it. Yes, they should think and write about literature, but they should also explore large, conceptual ideas and support their own original claims. They should be allowed to take risks, make mistakes, and start again. They should have the chance to read and write about things that interest them, about which they have something authentic to say, that "light them up." Too many of our students have written themselves off as readers and writers by the time they get to us, which further complicates the task of preparing them for postsecondary academics.

As Senior English programs go, Manchester High School has reason to be proud of where it stands today. Seniors can choose between AP Language and Composition, UConn ECE ENG 1011, MCC ENG 101 (Composition), or Senior English, which is now *truly* college preparatory. There are currently nine full sections of college credit–bearing English classes running (two AP, five UConn, two MCC). Nearly half of this year's senior class can potentially earn college credit for English before they graduate. But regardless of whether students earn the grade or score necessary to get the credit, they are far better off in terms of college readiness than they would have been had they not taken one of these courses. And if they elect to take regular Senior English, they are taking a course that was thoughtfully and collaboratively designed by educators whose shared desire is nothing less than to see them succeed in college and in life. It is a win-win situation. Surely Athena, Goddess of Wisdom, would approve.

Appendix

Senior English Lens and Artifact Paper Assignment Ms. Cecchini
Course Title: College Preparatory Senior English

Text Titles and Authors*: **LENS**—"The Causes of Prejudice" (Parrillo) and one self-selected **ARTIFACT** from this approved list: "Veiled Intentions: Don't Judge a Muslim Girl by Her Covering" (Haydar); "The English-Only Movement: Can America Proscribe Language with a Clear Conscience?" (Jamieson); "Who Says a Woman Can't Be Einstein?" (Ripley); "From Rez Life: An Indian's Journey through Reservation Life" (Treuer); "The New Jim Crow" (Alexander).

Length: 1,250–1,500 words
Due Date: TBA
[CCSS] Standards Addressed:
W.11-12.1. Write arguments to support claims in an analysis of substantive topics or texts, using valid reasoning and relevant and sufficient evidence.
RI.11-12.1. Cite strong and thorough textual evidence to support analysis of what the [informational] text says explicitly as well as inferences drawn from the text, including determining where the text leaves matters uncertain.
L.11-12.1. Demonstrate command of the conventions of standard English grammar and usage when writing or speaking.

Revision Policy: As always, drafts must be submitted so that all students receive constructive feedback to guide revision. Drafts for this paper will be submitted in three parts: Summary of the Lens, Summary of the Artifact, and Full Draft (includes introduction, conclusion, and application of the lens to the artifact).

Assignment Steps and Guidelines:

◆ Read and annotate the lens (the Parrillo text). You will be using this text to "view" the artifact, so make an effort to "get into the author's head." It is relatively difficult reading, so take your time. Note Parrillo's viewpoints, assumptions, and justifications. It might be helpful to break down and outline the arguments he makes. We will discuss the text at length in class.

◆ Over the span of a week, read and write journals on the five potential artifacts while keeping Parrillo's text in mind. Consider the following: How does the lens serve to **shed light** on the artifact? Does it **"criticize"** it or support it? Does it offer some **new understanding or way of seeing it?** Can the lens be applied to the artifact in **one or more interesting ways?** If the two pieces were written during **different periods in history, consider the implications** of that. **Explore the "tension" that exists between the two texts.** Again, we will discuss each potential artifact in class; be sure to have journals ready.

◆ With your notes in hand, construct your claim (thesis statement). State the connection between the two texts. This forms the basis of your entire paper, so it is always helpful to write it first. Keep it as clear and simple as you can manage. We will discuss what a good claim/thesis might look like in this case, and practice revising and improving some possible ones.

◆ Write! A lens essay is typically constructed on a text-by-text basis. Concentrate on presenting/summarizing the lens in the first paragraph(s). Offer the reader an overview of Parrillo's ideas, and then hone in more specifically on any part of it that will be important to your essay's premise. Next, briefly summarize your selected artifact. In the following paragraphs, present the second text *as viewed through the lens (the first text)*.

Audience: You should write the essay as though your reader is mature and educated but may not be as familiar as you are with either the lens or the artifact. This means that you may, for instance, need to briefly explain key "players," context, or circumstances.

Organization of Assignment: The paper should be organized into three sections: the introduction, body, and conclusion.

> <u>Introduction</u>: Aside from an introduction to the topic, it should include the titles and names of both readings' authors and should end with a clear claim/thesis statement that indicates what you will assert/prove about how the lens plays out in the artifact.
> <u>Body of the essay</u>: Early in your essay, you will need to summarize the lens. Do not provide a summary of the entire text, but instead focus on the text's key points that will be analyzed in body paragraphs. While you may use direct quotations in the summary, use them sparingly: this is your chance to show your reader how well you understand the lens.
>
> In the body of the paper, each supporting paragraph should cover one main idea that supports your thesis. Briefly summarize the artifact only to the extent needed to provide context for analysis within the body paragraph. Transitions should be used as a way to bridge one paragraph point to the next.
> <u>Conclusion</u>: The final paragraph should neatly wrap up your essay and make some final statement about the paper's topic. More on this in class.

Use of Evidence in the Essay: Each body paragraph should use an appropriate number of properly formatted and cited quotations and/or paraphrases. Overall, the paper should use *several* properly formatted and cited quotations and paraphrases in each body section. Direct quotations should be carefully selected, properly contextualized and introduced beforehand, and commented upon afterward.

Use of MLA in the Essay: Essays should be formatted according to MLA style rules. In addition, all quotations and paraphrases should be properly cited, and all texts should be documented on a Works Cited page, properly formatted in MLA style.

Grammar/Correctness: Your writing should be formal (academic style, as practiced previously) and clear, and your essay should contain few errors. You should strive for fewer than one error (average) per page. **Proofread carefully.**

Plagiarism: Plagiarized work will result in a grade of zero. A grade of zero on this assignment may result in a failing grade for the quarter or even the year. All MHS students must pass all four years of English in order to graduate.

Evaluation of Essay: The essay will be evaluated on a 100-point scale according to the following guidelines (**closely adapted from the MCC English department's expected student outcomes**):

Competent essays will do the following:
1. Present information and ideas from texts with accurate quotation, paraphrase, and summary and, when appropriate, enough explication/interpretation/evaluation to develop a coherent analysis or synthesis. This includes:

- Demonstrating a clear understanding of central ideas in both texts
- Using relevant information from texts to support arguments
- Using appropriate number/amount of quotation, paraphrase, and summary

2. Use important conventions particular to expository essay writing, including the use of a clear claim/thesis, effective paragraphing, and an organizational pattern, including effective transitions, that develops an idea over the course of an essay rather than simply listing supporting ideas. This includes:

- Using a writing style that is appropriate for a specific audience
- Developing a clear thesis statement
- Creating paragraphs with central points and clear, relevant details
- Using transitions to bridge paragraph points

3. Use language that generally conveys a meaning to readers, contains few errors, and demonstrates an ability to ethically and accurately use MLA format to cite and document sources. This includes:

- Making few or no grammatical/spelling errors

- ◆ Writing in a way that conveys clear meaning
- ◆ Writing in a formal, academic voice
- ◆ Introducing quotations correctly, per MLA rules
- ◆ Citing quotations and paraphrases correctly, per MLA rules
- ◆ Including a Works Cited page listing all assignment texts, properly formatted per MLA rules

*Text Sources

Colombo, Gary, Robert Cullen, and Bonnie Lisle. *Rereading America: Cultural Contexts for Critical Thinking and Writing*. 9th ed. Boston, MA: Bedford/St. Martins, 2013. Print.

Rosa, Alfred F., and Paul A. Eschholz. *Models for Writers: Short Essays for Composition*. 11th ed. Boston: Bedford/St. Martin's, 2012. Print.

Works Cited

Colombo, Gary, Robert Cullen, and Bonnie Lisle. *Rereading America: Cultural Contexts for Critical Thinking and Writing*. 9th ed. Boston: Bedford/St. Martin's, 2013. Print.

Connecticut Public Law 12-40: An Act Concerning College Readiness and Completion. Substitute Senate Bill No. 40. Connecticut General Assembly. 31 May 2012. Print.

DiYanni, Robert, ed. *One Hundred Great Essays*. 4th ed. New York: Pearson Longman, 2011. Print.

Educational Policy and Improvement Center (EPIC). *Connecticut College and Career Readiness Tookit*. Prepared on Behalf of Connecticut's P-20 Council. Hartford: Connecticut State Department of Education, 2011. Print.

Kohn, Alfie. *The Case against Standardized Testing: Raising the Scores, Ruining the Schools*. Portsmouth: Heinemann, 2000. Print.

Rosa, Alfred F., and Paul A. Eschholz. *Models for Writers: Short Essays for Composition*. 11th ed. Boston: Bedford/St. Martin's, 2012. Print.

Wagner, Tony et al. *Change Leadership: A Practical Guide to Transforming Our Schools*. San Francisco: Jossey-Bass, 2006. Print.

CHAPTER TEN

Preparing College-Level Readers to Define Reading as More Than Mastery

ELLEN C. CARILLO
University of Connecticut

Over the years, Alice S. Horning has described the need for postsecondary institutions to develop reading across the disciplines programs to complement their writing across the disciplines programs. Supporting Horning's call, compositionist Mary Lou Odom recently argued that *all* faculty "must see that they have a role—beyond simply assigning texts—to play in student reading behavior" and "must be willing to provide guidance for students reading complex, discipline-specific texts" (n.p.). Still, reading across the disciplines programs have yet to materialize as faculty are largely unwilling to see reading as writing's equally complex counterpart in the construction of meaning. Robert Scholes blames reading's invisibility: "We accept [that writing must continue to be taught in college] . . . because we can see writing, and we know that much of the writing we see is not good enough. But we do not see reading. . . . I am certain, though, that if we could see it, we would be appalled" (166). Another obstacle prohibiting faculty from recognizing reading as the complex act it is lies in the perpetual association of education with mastery. Reading is perhaps one of the best examples of this, for once students learn or "master" reading in elementary school, they are expected to summon that skill for the rest of their academic careers no matter the context or level. Educational psychologists David N. Perkins and Gavriel Salomon explain this phenomenon:

> For many teachers and students, knowledge of whatever sort is something to "possess," to have in the mental warehouse ready for deployment as required. The key question for these teachers and their students becomes whether students can show knowledge on demand—through assignments and tests that relatively directly call for what hopefully has been learned. ("Knowledge to Go" 256)

They call this familiar conception of education "a learning culture of demand" and while they don't deny its uses, which include preparing students for high-stakes standardized exams, they take issue with its exercises and tests, which are "direct rather than open-ended," and its "courses and units," which tend to be "encapsulated rather than richly cross-connected" ("Knowledge to Go" 257). The reading pedagogy I describe below, intended for high school and college instructors committed to helping students develop as readers, challenges this conception of education. Extending my previous work on reading, this chapter argues for the importance of teaching reading within what educational psychologist Randi A. Engle and her colleagues call an "expansive frame" as opposed to the problematic context that Perkins and Salomon describe.

As Perkins and Salomon's metaphors suggest, teaching for mastery often involves engaging students in activities that ask them to call on their knowledge in targeted, limited, and constricting ways, an approach that does not enable students to engage in more encompassing, critical, and nuanced activities. If our goal is to prepare students to read at the college level, which necessarily means preparing them to read across disciplines, each of which brings with it its own (often implicit) expectations about what it means to read, why one reads, and what that reading looks like, then reading instruction needs to take place in a more open and flexible context. Engle et al. describe these more open and far-reaching contexts as "expansive," while they call the narrower, mastery-driven context "bounded." They have developed these terms to describe which contexts are most conducive to the transfer of learning, which Perkins and Salomon describe as "instances in which learning in one context or with one set of materials impacts on performance in another context or with other related materials" ("Transfer of Learning" n.p.). Describing the difference between bounded and expansive contexts, Engle et al. offer the following examples: "A teacher can frame a lesson as a one-time event of learning [. . .] or as an initial discussion of an issue that students will be actively engaging with throughout their lives" (217). Their findings indicate that bounded frames "tend to discourage students from later using what they learn," while expansive frames "tend to encourage it" (217). Because students need to use what they learn about reading across the disciplines, in other academic contexts, and ideally even beyond academia, I have developed an expansive frame in which to teach reading to foster transfer, a frame that challenges mastery-driven conceptions of reading.

I call this expansive framework "mindful reading." Mindful reading is not another type of reading that might appear on a list alongside rhetorical reading, for example, but a *framework* that contains the range of reading strategies that students might be taught, including—but not limited to— annotation, rhetorical reading, close reading, the says/does approach, and reading like a writer. Within this framework, instructors choose, define, and teach the reading strategies that they imagine will be most useful to students. Mindful reading is the framework in which they do this work, but this framework does not prescribe any specific reading strategies or reading approaches. This expansive framework exists, instead, to provide the context in which students are expected to create knowledge about reading and about themselves as readers, knowledge they can bring with them into other courses. I use the term *mindful* to underscore the metacognitive basis of this frame wherein students become *knowledgeable, deliberate,* and *reflective* about *how* they read and what different reading approaches allow and enable. Mindful reading is related to "mindfulness," a concept often associated with Buddhism and used frequently in the field of psychology. The term *mindful,* when modifying *reading,* describes a particular stance on the part of the reader, one that is open (Shapiro), flexible (Langer), and characterized by intentional awareness of and attention to the present moment and the demands that it makes on reading. This intense awareness—the key to transfer—helps student readers construct knowledge about (1) reading (2) the reading strategies they are practicing and testing out on a range of texts, and (3) themselves as readers.

The reader's/student's stance is crucial, for while various definitions of *metacognitive* and *mindful* often overlap and *metacognitive* is already widely used, the concept of mindfulness highlights not just the task that one does "mindfully," but also the individual, the reader, who is learning *to be* mindful. Mindfulness, unlike metacognition, is a way of being. One learns to be mindful, to adopt certain behaviors such as openness and flexibility when engaging with texts and while testing out various reading strategies. Moreover, the term *mindful* opens up opportunities for talking about ways to cultivate mindful readers, *students* who will potentially remain mindful readers throughout their academic careers and beyond as they negotiate, experiment with, and come to learn about a range of reading approaches and the contexts in which they are most effective. To adapt Stephen North's (not uncontroversial) description of writing center work, we might think about this in terms of producing mindful readers, not just mindful (or metacognitive) readings.

I recommend teaching within this framework either in late high school or early college (in an introductory composition course or a first-year seminar) as a means to prepare students for college-level reading, which puts new demands on students as they are faced with more reading overall, disciplinary-specific readings, and more complex reading than they likely previously encountered. Although the need to prepare students for the transition to college-level *writing* does impact the development of high school curricula, the same is not necessarily true of reading, as David A. Jolliffe explains:

> By the time students are graduating from high school, the course called "reading" has been absent from the curriculum for at least three or four years, having usually made its last appearance in the eighth grade, at the latest. By the time they come to college, then, students haven't had a course called "reading" for five or six years. Oh, to be sure, some of their high school teachers might have tucked something resembling reading instruction into courses or units labeled "critical thinking" or "study skills." . . . But by the time students come to college, it's been a long time since students have had any instructor say to them, "Okay, let's work on how to read this text." (473)

Based on Jolliffe's description, the secondary school curriculum seemingly defines reading in terms of mastery. The curriculum suggests that students master this skill early in their academic careers and thus there is no need to return to it. Neither do college curricula designate a space for this work because "the very thought of what a 'reading class' might be at the post-secondary level has never quite coalesced" (473). Moreover, postsecondary instructors of composition—who might take on this work— lack support and resources for developing reading pedagogies to complement their writing pedagogies. Linda Adler-Kassner and Heidi Estrem explain, "At the same time as instructors ask for more explicit guidance with reading pedagogy, that pedagogy is rarely included in composition research, graduate composition courses, or first-year writing programs' developmental materials" (36). "To put it starkly," Jolliffe agrees, "reading as a concept is largely absent from the theory and practice of college composition" (473). And so to teach reading in a deliberate way, as described in the following section, either in high school or college is to acknowledge that reading is a complex, context-bound practice that defies mastery.

Designing Courses That Support Expansive Frames That Foster Transfer

Reading Selections

Choosing appropriate reading selections is important when teaching within the mindful reading framework. The selections need to support the development and practice of a range of reading strategies to prepare students for the diverse reading experiences college brings with it. Unlike a mastery model of reading, teaching reading within an expansive frame means helping students recognize the importance of moving among reading strategies in deliberate and flexible ways, actually developing the ability to do so, and self-monitoring as they are doing so in order to position themselves to transfer what they are learning about reading to other and future contexts.

While it may be tempting to assign only complex selections that students wouldn't otherwise read, a more realistic approach to choosing readings—and one that better fits within this expansive framework—involves "accommodat[ing] the fact that college students read lots of textbooks, and productive, working adults read lots of reports, manuals, memoranda" (Jolliffe 579). In other words, challenging, virtually opaque essays that demand multiple re-readings offer students a valuable reading experience, but instructors need to prepare students to be "constructive, connective, active readers of *all the material* that comes their way—textbooks, reports, memoranda, and so on, as well as complicated, discursive essays" (Jolliffe 579, emphasis added).

Because this framework is intended to prepare students for reading across the disciplines, the reading selections should not only range in difficulty, but come from a range of disciplines as well. It is a scary prospect, perhaps, for an instructor with a background in English to be expected to teach a piece drawn from the sciences, but this is not about being an expert in the subject matter, or even trying to re-create the discourse community of that particular discipline, but rather about creating opportunities to discuss, practice, and reflect on reading. This framework is about experiencing, trying out, and reflecting on reading texts across disciplines. The framework supports this work because it helps students recognize, understand, and anticipate their relationship to reading in a range of contexts and how that relationship changes depending on whether the context is an English or a biology class. This work has nothing to do with mastery and everything to do with trying, testing, and experimenting. For example, students might have the opportunity to read a scientist's and a historian's take on an environmental issue, as well as a geographical perspective and a human rights perspective on the same issue. Then they can reflect on how best to gain access to texts (i.e., which reading strategies to employ) that are not readily penetrable with their default reading practices, the practices they automatically apply to texts they encounter.

To help students cultivate a rich repertoire of reading strategies from which to draw when faced with everything from literature to textbook chapters to scientific studies, it behooves instructors to provide students with ample opportunities to experience a range of texts and thus a range of reading strategies. Within the mindful reading framework, students have the opportunity to develop knowledge about each strategy individually, their relationship to that strategy, as well as knowledge about that approach in comparison to others. Instructors should also include opportunities for students to experience texts across media since students will likely be expected to do so within and beyond academia. For example, instructors might have students experience the traditional print ways of annotating a text, as well as digital means or applications to annotate texts. Students would then reflect on how this electronic form of annotation affects their reading practices and ways of constructing meaning compared to more traditional methods of annotation. Instructors might also provide students with opportunities to read digital texts, including those with hyperlinks, so they can reflect on how screen reading and reading through hyperlinks are different from reading print sources. Students could then be expected to reflect on those reading experiences, including which reading strategies work best for reading on a screen and what, if any, ways they needed to adapt their print reading strategies.

Writing Assignments

Teaching reading within this expansive frame—as opposed to the more traditional bounded frames—calls for assignments and activities that are designed to "connect the learning environment to other times [and] places" (qtd. in Engle et al., 228) in order to position students to transfer what they learn about reading to other courses and contexts. Therefore, assignments and other prompts need to be developed with these goals in mind. Many of my prompts (see the appendix), whether classroom discussion or short, informal writing assignments, are exercises in reflection that often encourage students to anticipate other and future uses of what they are learning.

Asking students to keep a reading journal, for example, in which they track and reflect on how they are applying different reading strategies to the texts they encounter gives students a place to collect these and other metacognitive notes. In that same journal or in a different space, students might describe how what they bring to the reading experience—"personality traits, memories of past events, present needs and preoccupations" (Rosenblatt 30)—impacts how they construct meaning. This work helps students understand and experience the complexity that characterizes the reading process since ideally (1) they realize that meaning is not hidden in a text (2) they recognize the role the reader plays in the construction of meaning, and (3) they realize that interpretations are not random, but are inflected by a range of factors.

An in-class activity that helps instructors facilitate these three realizations might involve underscoring the range of *different* readings and interpretations that students have developed. This activity highlights that reading is dependent on more than the text itself and that the reader actually enters into a "transaction" (to use Rosenblatt's term) with the text. Discussion about what these different readings mean depends on something along the lines of what Donna Qualley calls "essayistic reading," wherein "readers put themselves at risk by opening themselves to multiple and contrasting perspectives of others [whether within or outside of the text] while reflexively monitor[ing] their own beliefs and reactions to the process" (62). And while some readings will likely be more tenable than others—an important part of the discussion in and of itself—this activity allows instructors to focus on the why (we arrive at different readings) and the how (that happens) of reading rather than the content, the what. Class discussions or small-group work, then, becomes about *how* texts mean rather than mastering *what* they mean as students come to see firsthand how a text "gains its significance from the way in which the minds and emotions of particular readers respond to the verbal stimuli offered by the text" (Rosenblatt 28).

Formal writing assignments are inflected by the work on reading that students complete ahead of time and continue to demand that they reflect on the reading (and writing) they are completing. Just as reading experiences are contextualized as exploratory and reflective, so is the writing I ask students to complete. I develop writing assignments that ask students to explore and illuminate questions that begin with "how" and "why" rather than "what." Students are expected to use writing as a form of inquiry rather than as a way to (re)present knowledge. My assignments expect that students may discover some tentative answers to the question(s) they have posed, but that these should not be thought of answers in the traditional sense. I emphasize the word *tentative* to students to indicate that answers are not answers in the traditional sense since the very act of writing is positioned as the process through which they ponder and respond to these questions. The result, I tell them, may be some answers or recommendations, or the result may simply be more questions. The key is to use writing to learn what it is they think about the subject, to make meaning from the subject, and to develop their own ideas as they think alongside the writers of the reading selections.

More specifically, one formal assignment is what I call the "critical conversation" (adapted from Gerald Graff), in which students put at least two sources into conversation with each other and find a space for themselves in the conversation. Students are expected to contribute at least one idea to the conversation as they think alongside the other writers, but they are not expected to "master" the subject under discussion. This assignment demands that students take time to "understand and sympathize with others" (Rosenblatt 40) just as I expect them to do in their reading and during class discussions of those readings.

While I do use critical conversations to help prepare students to write longer, argumentative essays, students are not expected to "cultivate authority and 'mastery' concerning subjects they typically know very little about" (Sullivan 57) in these essays. Although argument-driven, these pieces remain exploratory. The most successful essays, I explain to my students, are like extended critical conversations in which they develop their argument as they work and think alongside what others have said about the subject. I consistently remind them to avoid thinking of an argument as something to declare and then repetitively defend. Instead, just as their reflections on their reading experiences and the insights they gleaned from other readers often lead to a reexamination of themselves and their reading practices, students should use the other voices in the conversation to help develop and refine their arguments.

The required cover letter (see the appendix for samples), which accompanies these argumentative essays and every formal writing assignment, gives students the opportunity to reflect on their reading and writing processes (among other elements) in relation to the assignment. These cover letters further position students to transfer what they are learning because the letters prompt students to anticipate where they may take this learning as they move throughout their academic careers and beyond.

Expansive Contexts as Motivators

But getting students to readily transfer what they have learned about reading is impossible to achieve if students reject the course, its material, or this expansive context, all of which may be largely unfamiliar to them. Michael Bunn's, David A. Jolliffe and Allison Harl's, as well as my research (Carillo) corroborate that students need to see that the reading they do is directly connected to their writing in order to feel motivated to complete a course's reading assignments. Within the expansive framework of mindful reading, students' reading—or, more precisely, reading knowledge—is overtly and deliberately connected not only to current writing assignments, but also to other and future reading and writing activities. This provides the incentive to engage in the course because its expansive frame consistently reminds students of this course's relationship to other and future courses and contexts. Education scholars and researchers (e.g., Mac Iver et al.) have found that students who expect to need to use what they are learning in the future and develop confidence in those tasks are more likely to spend more time on the material in order to prepare themselves for those future uses. In an effort to gain access to how the expansive framing of my course affected the extent to which students were transferring what they learned about reading in my sophomore-level research writing course entitled Writing through Research, I regularly asked them to answer this very question. They answered anonymously via surveys, and in other instances they were asked to answer this question as part of the reflective cover letters they wrote to me about various assignments throughout the semester (see the appendix for these documents).

Students' Learning Experiences within an Expansive Frame

In reviewing my students' answers to the various surveys and prompts I distributed throughout the semester, I am most struck by how the expansive framing seemed to prompt what has been called "concurrent" transfer, in which connections are made between two simultaneous contexts. Students regularly made connections between the work we were doing in Writing through Research and their other courses, some of which I never anticipated my own course could impact. During a class discussion, one student spoke of using the reading practices we discussed to better understand word problems in math class (math!). Another student anonymously noted that "learning how to pick apart the text has been by far the most helpful. . . . [I]t has made studying for Biology and Accounting much easier." Also in an anonymous survey, another student described using the says/does approach (wherein one goes paragraph by paragraph delineating what each says—its content—and what each does—its function): "In American Studies, I decided to try the 'Says/Does' approach when reading the Dred Scott case proved difficult due to its word choice. Breaking it down paragraph by paragraph proved very useful. If I see another cryptic piece in further history classes, I would return to the method."

In the cover letter of his second, research-driven essay, another student described the benefits of thinking about reading in a more methodical way. He explains the following about his developmental psychology class: "I have noticed how much more efficient and productive I am at evaluating sources and utilizing them." He continues, "I also find myself reading more slowly in general, even when reading novels, as I realized how much depth some writing has and that it needs to be approached carefully and methodically." I appreciate this juxtaposition of a seemingly contradictory new skill set—namely, the ability to read more efficiently—and this newly developed commitment to reading more slowly. I would posit that this student is not contradicting himself here, but rather has recognized that slow, "careful," and "methodical" reading can in fact be more efficient than "mindless" reading. Ellen Langer, who has published widely on mindful learning, describes its opposite, mindlessness, as being "stuck in a single, rigid perspective" and being "oblivious to alternative ways of knowing" (220). "When we are mindless," she continues, "our behavior is rule and routine governed; when we are mindful, rules and routines may guide our behavior rather than predetermine it" (220). The care this student describes echoes Langer's own description of mindfulness as that which is guided by rules and routine but not predetermined by them. Moreover, one of the key assumptions that informs this student's description of reading is that the very practice of reading is a deliberate undertaking and that to be productive reading needs to be thoughtfully approached. Other students described reading this way too, noting, for example, that they will transfer their abilities to "actively read" and "read more slowly."

Many students talk about transferring their ability to productively use sources, which, I would claim, is directly linked to their abilities to read and understand sources. Students commented on this aspect of the course particularly in their end-of-semester anonymous evaluations. One student noted that she will transfer her ability to "utiliz[e] sources," another described transferring her ability to "evaluat[e] sources," and still another commented on the potential in using sources "as more than just support." This is crucial work because recent studies have shown that college students and young adults more generally struggle in this area. Two studies, both conducted in 2006, one by ACT, Inc. and one by the Pew Charitable Trust, found that close to half of the college students in their samples did not meet minimum benchmarks for literacy or lacked proficiency in reading, respectively (Horning and Kraemer 6–7). These conclusions are also corroborated by more recent findings from The Citation Project, a multi-institutional, empirical research project that seeks to understand how students read sources and use them in their writing. With less than 10 percent of students using summary in their writing (as opposed to paraphrasing, copying, and citing), Rebecca Moore Howard and her colleagues noted that their findings raise questions about "whether students understand the sources they are citing in their researched writing" (189). Moreover, "[t]he absence of summary, coupled with the exclusive engagement of text on the sentence level, means that readers have no assurance that the students did read and understand" (186). Although their findings are intended to help educators reconceive how they think about plagiarism, the data suggest that students have difficulty reading and understanding the texts they encounter. Most recently, a study entitled "America's Skills Challenge: Millennials and the Future," published this year by Educational Testing Services (ETS), found that "one half (50%) of America's millennials," defined as those born after 1980 who were sixteen to thirty-four years of age in 2012 (during that year's round of the Programme for the International Assessment of Adult Competencies), "failed to reach level 3 in literacy" (11). Level 3 in the literacy component of this study tests how well respondents "identify, interpret, or evaluate one or more pieces of information, and often require varying levels of inference" (48). Level 3, as the study notes, "is considered the minimum standard for literacy" (11), and only 50 percent of American millennials met this minimum benchmark, highlighting the difficulty young adults have working with "pieces of information" or what we might call sources.

An unexpected form of transfer that the expansive framework seemed to foster is time management skills in relation to source-based research. One student described having learned to "allow myself enough time to read my articles and see how they work together or against each other" and "allowing myself enough time before the due date to look for articles that can either spawn an idea or speak to an idea I already have." The ability to recognize how much time serious reading takes and then transfer that knowledge and practice into other contexts is, I would argue, indicative of college-level reading. Perhaps this is not what I (as the instructor) expected the student to transfer, but from an "actor-oriented perspective" of transfer wherein the "researcher does not measure transfer against a particular . . . target, but rather investigates instances in which the students' prior experiences shaped their activity in the transfer situation, even if the result is non-normative" (Lobato 235), this does reveal an unexpected way in which this student is generalizing her learning experience (235).

Like the students quoted here, most students focused their comments on school contexts even though the questions I asked regularly prompted students to think beyond school, a crucial goal of a truly expansive frame. Still, a handful of students did think beyond academia. One student, for example, explained in a cover letter that making her sources speak to each other in her first essay has been helpful "while watching the news, . . . and I watch both NBC and Fox to get different perspectives." What she seems to be describing is how she now reads these perspectives in relation to each other, recognizing that each has its own biases, an important way of reading her sources that she has transferred from her coursework to her viewing practices. Deborah-Lee Gollnitz has explained the significance of this type of reading: "Reading is crucial to independent learning" as it is through reading that "consumers make connections of their own that are not swayed by another perspective" (Gollnitz and Horning 63). In juxtaposing the different news outlets, this student is becoming that independent learner who will not simply accept what she hears or reads, but will deliberately consider and compare that information to other ideas and perspectives she encounters whether in or outside of the classroom. Also imagining connections beyond academia that have resulted in her ability to think independently, another student explains, "Being able to voice my own opinion . . . will also help me have educated discussions with others throughout my life." Also in a cover letter, another student explains that she has come to realize that she does not "have to agree with everything someone/an article says" and she can "counter their opinions," a skill she uses "in life situations . . . to speak up about how [she] feel[s] about something." This student is alluding to the course's emphasis on reading as an invitation to respond and to make more sophisticated "moves" than simply agreeing with what one reads or mindlessly internalizing someone else's point of view. When reading becomes about more than mastery and is contextualized in this other way, it has value outside of the immediate classroom setting, value that some of my students seem to be recognizing.

All of the students quoted are making important, deliberate connections, some of which even go beyond the classroom setting. Their descriptions indicate that they are experiencing reading as a "dialogic, bidirectional" process in which readers are "both the subject and object of their reading (they read themselves as they read the text)" (Qualley 62). I would posit that this is college-level reading in action. College-level readers reflect on their ways of reading, they imagine and make connections across contexts, they adapt reading strategies to various contexts, and they are cognizant of the time it takes to read actively. In other words, despite what the curricula they experience suggests, they have learned that reading is not about mastery, but, like writing, is a complex process. That in and of itself is a revelation for a lot of them and puts them ahead of many scholars who readily recognize the complex nature of writing but not of reading.

Although reading is writing's counterpart in the construction of meaning, teaching reading or attending to reading in any deliberate way in the classroom is work that has not really been endorsed by either literary studies or composition studies, perhaps because of the legacy of reader-response theory. While reader-response theories from the 1980s brought "significant and respectful attention to student readers," including "the assumptions student readers brought to the reading activity; the ways in which they identified and negotiated textual difficulties; the ways in which teachers could encourage acts of critical self-reflection in student writing based on their understanding of reading" (Salvatori and Donahue 204), "reader response is now a term used most often to refer to a theoretical past" (204), and because of its association with the "anything goes" approach to reading, reading's status as a complex process has all but been forgotten (205). And so for undergraduates (i.e., college-level readers) to recognize and experience reading for the complex process it is, something that some scholars in the field of composition are still not quite ready to do, is an exciting prospect. I would argue that the expansive framework of mindful reading within which I taught prompted this recognition.

But, before I get carried away, I must emphasize that I do not offer this student feedback as proof of anything—not of successful teaching or proof that these students are transferring what they are learning in my course. I am well aware that the nature of self-reporting, on which the student feedback depends, raises limitations since "self-reports may blend respondents' beliefs and intentions with actual practices" (Eblen 347). Moreover, particularly in the nonanonymous prompts, one might suspect students want to please me (i.e., get a good grade) so they invent courses and contexts to which they have transferred knowledge. Without more formally studying the actual practices of my students in the classes and contexts they reference, I cannot know for sure whether transfer is taking place. Still, research on transfer like Rebecca Nowacek's indicates the regularity of concurrent transfer, particularly among linked courses in curricula. Kathleen Blake Yancey, Liane Robertson, and Kara Taczak's research takes Nowacek's findings even further by pointing out that beyond linked courses designed specifically to promote transfer "there are abundant opportunities for concurrent, or cross-transfer, and students do engage in such transfer" (27). I believe that at least some of the students whose responses I have shared are taking advantage of these opportunities and engaging in genuine transfer. And for those who are not being honest about their experiences, I am confident that reflecting on the class's relevance to other contexts is productive in and of itself because the questions about transfer that I prompt students to answer potentially position them to develop the meta-awareness that is so crucial for the transfer of their learning in the future.

Teaching reading within an expansive framework clearly challenges the more common bounded framing, which has become "the working norm" in secondary and postsecondary institutions (Sizer). Instead of framing students' courses "as being completely separate from one another" (Engle et al. 227), the expansive frame of mindful reading offers students opportunities to reflect on their ways of reading, to imagine and make connections across contexts, to adapt reading strategies to various contexts, and to experience firsthand the amount of time it takes to read mindfully. Within this frame, students are not expected to master reading as if it is some compartmentalizable skill that is independent of context or of the reader herself. Until curriculum coordinators and faculty across the disciplines are willing to admit that reading is not "masterable" and that students need instruction in reading as consistently as they need it in writing, those of us who are invested in helping students develop as readers might continue to do so within expansive frames that help cultivate mindful readers—college-level readers.

Appendix

Online Survey for Students Distributed Four Weeks into the Semester (anonymous)

1. To what extent has this course's focus on different reading practices been helpful in completing the readings in this class?
    Very helpful   Somewhat helpful   Neutral   Not helpful

2. Which reading approach(es) has been most useful to you? (Mark all that apply.)
    A. One of the rhetorical reading strategies
    B. Says/Does
    C. Passage-Based Paper
    D. Annotating

3. How helpful were the writing group meetings?
    Very helpful   Somewhat helpful   Neutral   Not helpful

4. What would make writing group meetings more helpful?

5. I have talked a lot about "transfer." How would you describe the role of transfer in this course?

6. At the beginning of the course, we talked about mindful reading. In your own words, describe what that is.

7. Please list other courses and contexts in which you have been able to apply or use anything you have learned in the course so far. Please also describe the specific skill. If there are none, please write "none."

8. Please use this space to offer further comments about the course.

Cover Letter Template for Essay 1, Second Submission (not anonymous)
Compose a letter to me about your second submission. Please attend to the issues outlined below. You will turn it in with your second submission (and your first submission). Please include this letter as an attachment when you email me your second submission. I will take it into consideration as I grade your second submission since this helps you reflect on and understand your process, as well as articulate what it is you need to work on in your writing and what you are doing well in your writing.

Your letter should be about 1–2 pages, typed.

Below is a template for your letter. You need not address these in this order, but you must address all of them. Notice that some have two distinct parts.

Dear Dr. Carillo:
1. For this submission I concentrated most of my efforts on revising the following aspect of my essay . . . because . . . I did this by . . .
2. What I struggled most with was . . .
3. I think that the strongest parts of this submission are . . .
4. On my first submission, my group members' comments focused on . . . . I address these comments by . . . .
5. I use sources for more than just support on the following pages . . . and I use them in these specific ways . . . .
6. I acknowledge and respond to potential objections and questions on pages . . . .
7. I can transfer the following skills/abilities that I honed while completing this assignment to the following classes/non-academic contexts . . . (please be specific about which skills/abilities might transfer and to which contexts/classes). If you have already started transferring this skill, please indicate that, as well.

Cover Sheet for Essay 2, First Submission (not anonymous)

1. Underline your claim/research question in your essay and put the word "claim" or phrase "research question" next to it in your essay.
2. Using language from Chapter 9 in *Writing Analytically*, describe how your introduction introduces your topic in the way that an essay within your field should.
3. Do the same as above, but with the conclusion.
4. Using language from Chapter 4 in *Writing Analytically*, list the types of evidence you use in your paper.
5. Refer to the "How to Make Details Speak" section on page 94 in *Writing Analytically*. Notice examples in your essay where you are doing this work and choose two. Note which approach (#1, #2, #3, or a combination) you are using in those examples and list any examples from your essay where you could do more to make the details speak.
6. What are you most proud of in your essay?
7. What needs more work?
8. What might you transfer from the experience of writing this essay

to other courses or contexts? Be specific. What—if anything—have you already transferred to other courses/contexts? Please describe specific classes/assignments, and so on.

Cover Letter for Essay 2, Second Submission (not anonymous)

Compose a letter to me about your second submission. Please attend to the issues outlined below. You will turn it in with your second submission (and your first submission). I will take it into consideration as I grade your second submission since this helps you reflect on and understand your process, as well as articulate what it is you need to work on in your writing and what you are doing well in your writing.

Your letter should be about 1–2 pages, typed.

Dear Dr. Carillo:

1. For this submission I concentrated most of my efforts on revising the following aspect of my essay . . . because . . . I did this by . . . .
2. What I struggled most with was . . .
3. I think that the strongest parts of this submission are . . .
4. On my first submission, my group members' comments focused on . . . . I address these comments by . . . .
5. I use sources for more than just support on the following pages . . . and I use them in these specific ways . . . .
6. I acknowledge and respond to potential objections and questions on pages . . . .
7. I can transfer the following skills/abilities that I honed while completing this assignment to the following classes/non-academic contexts . . . (please be specific about which skills/abilities might transfer and to which contexts/classes). If you have already started transferring these skills, please indicate that as well.

End-of-Semester Survey (anonymous)

1. What did you expect from this course?
2. What has been the most beneficial to you about this course?
3. What has been the least beneficial or disappointing about the course?

4. What have you learned in the course (list everything you can think of)?
5. What do you think you can transfer from this course to other courses? List everything and be as specific as possible.
6. What—if anything—have you already transferred from this course to other courses or contexts in and out of school? Be specific. Please mention courses, assignments, and so on.
7. Describe what you don't think will transfer from this course to other courses or contexts.
8. What is your major? What—if anything—from this course helped you in your major? What would you like to see included that might help students in your major?
9. What else would you have liked to have covered in the course?
10. How would you define mindful reading?

Works Cited

Adler-Kassner, Linda, and Heidi Estrem. "Reading Practices in the Writing Classroom." *WPA* 31.1–2 (2007): 35–47.

"America's Skills Challenge: Millennials and the Future." *Princeton: ETS.* 20 May 2015. Web. 9 Dec. 2016.

Bunn, Michael. "Motivation and Connection: Teaching Reading (and Writing) in the Composition Classroom." *College Composition and Communication* 64 (2013): 496-516. Print.

Carillo, Ellen C. *Securing a Place for Reading in Composition: The Importance of Teaching for Transfer.* Logan: Utah State UP, 2015. Print.

Eblen, Charlene. "Writing Across the Curriculum: A Survey of University Faculty Views and Classroom Practices." *Research in the Teaching of English* 17.4 (1983): 333–48. Print.

Engle, Randi A., et al. "How Does Expansive Framing Promote Transfer? Several Proposed Explanations and a Research Agenda for Investigating Them." *Educational Psychologist* 47:3 (2012): 215–31. Print.

Gollnitz, Deborah-Lee, and Alice Horning. "What Is College Reading? A High School-College Dialogue." *Reader* 67 (2014): 43–72. Print.

Graff, Gerald. *Professing Literature: An Institutional History.* U of Chicago P, 2007. Print.

Horning, Alice S., and Elizabeth Kraemer, eds. "Introduction and Overview." *Reconnecting Reading and Writing*. Anderson: Parlor P, 2013. 5–25. Print.

Howard, Rebecca Moore, Tricia Serviss, and Tanya K. Rodrigue. "Writing from Sources, Writing from Sentences." *Writing and Pedagogy* 2.2 (2010): 177–92. Print.

Jolliffe, David A. "Learning to Read as Continuing Education." *College Composition and Communication* 58.3 (2007): 470–94. Print.

Jolliffe, David A., and Allison Harl. "Studying the 'Reading Transition' from High School to College: What Are Our Students Reading and Why?" *College English* 70.6 (2008): 599–617. Print.

Langer, Ellen. "Mindful Learning." *Current Directions in Psychological Science* 9.6 (2000): 220–23. Print.

Lobato, Joanne. "The Actor-Oriented Transfer Perspective and Its Contributions to Educational Research and Practice." *Educational Psychologist* 47.3 (2012): 232–47. Print.

Mac Iver, Douglas J., et al. "Explaining within-Semester Changes in Student Effort in Junior High School and Senior High School Courses." *Journal of Educational Psychology* 83.2 (1991): 201–11. Print.

North, Stephen M. "The Idea of a Writing Center." *College English* 46.5 (1984): 433–46. Print.

Nowacek, Rebecca. *Agents of Integration: Understanding Transfer as a Rhetorical Act*. Carbondale: Southern Illinois UP, 2011. Print.

Odom, Mary Lou. "Not Just for Writing Anymore: What WAC Can Teach Us about Reading to Learn." *Across the Disciplines* 10 (4). Web. 24 June 2015.

Perkins, David N., and Gavriel Salomon. "Knowledge to Go: A Motivational and Dispositional View of Transfer." *Educational Psychologist* 47.3 (2012): 248–58. Print.

———. "Transfer of Learning." *International Encyclopedia of Education*. 2nd ed. 1992. Web. 5 May 2015.

Qualley, Donna. *Turns of Thought*. New York: Heinemann, 2007. Print.

Rosenblatt, Louise. "The Literary Experience." *Literature as Exploration*. 4th ed. New York: MLA, 1983. 25–53. Print.

Sizer, Theodore. *Horace's Compromise: The Dilemma of the American*

High School. New York: Houghton Mifflin, 1984. Print.

Salvatori, Mariolina, and Patricia Donahue. "Stories about Reading: Appearance, Disappearance, Morphing, and Revival." *College English* 75.2 (2012): 199–217. Print.

Scholes, Robert. "The Transition to College Reading." *Pedagogy* 2.2 (2002): 165–72. Print.

Shapiro, Shauna. "The Integration of Mindfulness and Psychology." *Journal of Clinical Psychology* 65.6 (2009): 555–60. Print.

Sullivan, Patrick. *A New Writing Classroom: Listening, Motivation, and Habits of Mind*. Logan: Utah State UP, 2014. Print.

Yancey, Kathleen Blake, Liane Robertson, and Kara Taczak. *Writing across Contexts: Transfer, Composition, and Sites of Writing*. Logan: Utah State UP, 2014. Print.

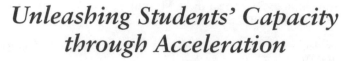

CHAPTER ELEVEN

Unleashing Students' Capacity through Acceleration

KATIE HERN
Chabot College

A few years ago I had the chance to sit in on a developmental reading class at another community college. It was the lowest level of their curriculum, four courses below college composition, and I was curious to see what happened there. The college's demographics were similar to my home institution, Chabot College, serving a poor to working-class community, with a high percentage of students of color and immigrants. But this course has no counterpart at my college. At Chabot, reading and writing are integrated, and most developmental students enroll in just a single course before taking college-level English.

Directed by the instructor, the students took out their reading comprehension textbooks and opened to that day's section. Their job was to read a paragraph. It seems implausible as I look back, but I believe this paragraph involved tulips in fifteenth-century Holland. That's my memory at least. After reading, they were to work in groups to label each sentence in the paragraph as "main idea" or "supporting detail." The groups then reported their answers back to the class, and the teacher noted whether

---

This essay is adapted from a 2011 keynote speech delivered at "Meeting in the Margins: Discourses on Reading and Writing," a conference hosted by the English Council of California Two-Year Colleges. As director of the California Acceleration Project (CAP), Hern was working to mobilize faculty from the state's 112 community colleges to rethink their approach to incoming students. At the time of the speech, 17 colleges were piloting accelerated curricula as part of CAP's professional development program. In 2016–17, more than 80 colleges are implementing new approaches to placement and remediation with support from CAP. Chapter copyright retained by the author. Please direct reprint requests to drkatiehern@gmail.com.

the answers were correct. When they finished, students moved on to reading and labeling another paragraph on a completely unrelated topic—this time, perhaps, social changes brought on by the US industrial revolution.

By some measures, the class I observed went well. The teacher was polite to the students. The students seemed to have a rapport with one another. They stayed on task during the small-group activities. And yet I left that classroom upset and agitated. In describing why, I'm afraid I may offend some of you. By way of explanation, I'll say I am originally from the Boston area, and even by Yankee standards, I'm direct. But more than that, I feel an urgency to name things as unflinchingly as possible here.

The class I observed was on the margins of the college landscape. The students came from underrepresented groups on the wrong side of the achievement gap. Their placement scores put them two years away from a college-level course in English and blocked them from many general education classes. A lot of them likely made it through high school without ever having read a full book, and they no doubt needed to work on the conventions of formal written English.

But what's more important here is that the curriculum itself was marginal. What I mean is it was radically disconnected from the core purposes and habits of mind of a college education. There was no world of ideas in that classroom. No sense that reading was a way to join a larger discussion of issues that matter. No opportunity for students to climb into the upper reaches of Bloom's taxonomy, weigh conflicting evidence, and develop their own well-informed viewpoints. The tasks students were given bore little relation to the kinds of reading, thinking, and writing they would see in a good college-level course—if, that is, they could ever *make it* to a good college-level course.

As community college English teachers, we have a particularly important role in the higher education landscape. We are custodians of the open-door mission of the community college. Our classes provide students access to significant social capital—the ability to understand and engage with complex texts, the confidence to express their own ideas, fluency in the conventions of academic exchange. At their best, our classes can be gateways to expanded educational and career opportunities.

To fulfill this purpose, however, we need to break from the model of education embodied in that reading class, four levels below college English. Some of you have already made this break, but others may be imprisoned inside departmentally approved curricula that look very much like the classroom I described. If so, I hope you'll take this as an invitation to pry apart the bars holding you and your students back.

The biggest problem of these classrooms is that they ask so very little of students. Reading and writing just a paragraph at a time. Focusing not on meaning, but on de-contextualized sub-skills such as recognizing a main idea or writing a topic sentence. These classes start with the assumption that students can't handle academic challenges and then provide such low-level tasks that students never get to show us they can do more. This is a big part of why I've become an evangelist for acceleration. We need to stop teaching down to students and start tapping their capacity.

I'd like to share some video of students in my accelerated, integrated reading and writing course at Chabot (Hern): http://www.vimeo.com/16983253. The class is a one-semester, four-unit course one level below college-level English, and there is no minimum placement score or prerequisite. My classroom includes students who skipped the placement test, students who really should have been in college-level English, students scoring at the very bottom of ACCUPLACER scales, and everyone in between. It's week two, the fourth class of the semester, and they are discussing an excerpt from Paulo Freire's *Pedagogy of the Oppressed*. This is the chapter in which Freire introduces what he calls the "banking model" of education, in which teachers deposit inert information into the empty vessels of their students' minds, and students categorize and store this knowledge for later retrieval. Freire contrasts this approach with what he calls "problem-posing education," a model in which students are fully humanized, active co-creators of meaning, wrestling to make sense of their world in partnership with their teachers. The Freire chapter is challenging, full of abstract language and philosophical terminology, with few concrete examples to ground the discussion, the kind of thing you read in a graduate education program.

Seeing my students grapple with Freire, I'm struck by the capacity they're demonstrating. To be sure, there's a lot they aren't getting in Freire's argument—unfamiliar vocabulary, confusion about what he means by "problem posing." But there is a lot they *are* getting. One student—a Latino guy in a skull t-shirt—applies Freire's concepts to his own experience, and a lightbulb goes off: "Wait a minute! I get what's going on here now!" A young African American woman in his group sums up the banking model beautifully: "You copy. You're just copying. You ain't even taking in. You're just writing down: A, B, C." And a Latina in a baseball cap provides a succinct closure comment about why people educated with the banking model would be easier to oppress: "They just listen and do what they're being told."

Watching this video, I'm aware of ways I've developed as a teacher over the years. It used to make me so tense when students came out with a misreading during class. I'm more comfortable now with the role of coach and facilitator, posing questions, naming reading strategies I see them using, suggesting additional strategies to try, not freaking out when students don't get it right away. But it's a work in progress. There's a moment in this video where I stop in the middle of a sentence, catching myself in the impulse to jump in and just give them the answer.

I'm also conscious of missed moments in my teaching that day. I wished I'd been more dialed in when an African American student launched into wordplay on the meaning of oppression—"you ain't got no jobs, you got a *de*pression, a *re*cession." He was employing a good technique—using word roots to figure out unfamiliar vocabulary—and it would have been great to call that out and celebrate it so that other students could add this strategy to their repertoire as readers.

I wish too that I had been clearer about why students were struggling with Freire's idea of "problem posing." ("I thought about that over and over last night," says one African American woman, "and I couldn't think of nothing.") The issue, I now see, was that they were thinking about one meaning of the word *problem*—a thing that needs to be fixed—and they weren't aware that there is an alternative use of that word in academic circles, where a "problem" is an exciting intellectual challenge. Because of this, they couldn't understand why Freire would find problems liberating. If I could go back, I'd let the whole conversation unfold exactly as it did, but then wrap up by naming what was giving the students difficulty so that they could be more conscious of this as a potential source of confusion in their reading.

This is a class in which students are grappling, imperfectly, with challenging material, and the teacher is grappling, imperfectly, with how to guide them toward better understanding and stronger skills. They may have been placed in a developmental class, but they are capable of discussing substantive issues. In fact, it's the substantive issues that motivate students to care about things like context clues and thesis statements. They are interested in what they're reading. And they feel like they're in college.

For me this is a nonnegotiable part of being an English teacher. We have to provide meaningful content for students to engage with. Our classes can't be *about* topic sentences. Topic sentences just aren't that interesting. And neither are thesis statements, or brainstorming strategies, or subject–verb agreement, or any of the other subskills that, as a field, we tend to fixate on.

Another nonnegotiable for me is that we require students to read and write *a lot*. That's another place where I think we have fallen short as a field. We all know that the only way to become a stronger reader and writer is through practice. Yet the practice our classrooms provide is often sadly limited. It's not enough to ask students to read a handful of short articles and then spend several weeks on an elaborate process for writing a three-page essay.

I need to fess up here that I'm talking about my own former teaching self. For the first ten years of my professional life, I called myself a "writing teacher" and my classes required students to read only short articles and excerpts, probably less than seventy-five pages total. That changed when I started teaching at Chabot College, where reading and writing instruction is integrated, and the English department requires at least one full-length book be taught at every level, including developmental classes. Many of my colleagues have developmental students read two or three books, plus assorted short pieces to complement them.

I have followed their lead and increased the amount of reading in my classes over time. Figure 11.1 is the reading list from my current accelerated course. I've also increased the volume and types of writing in my class (see Figure 11.2). There are in-class and at-home essays, lower-stakes ungraded work, and more formal assignments. Instead of my previous approach of assigning a few papers with extensive prewriting and revising processes, we do more papers with faster turnarounds. You may be surprised by the volume and level of work in this class. It's more than what was required in first-year composition classes at the four-year university where I first began teaching. Plus, this is an open-access class, and my students might be placed two, three, or four courses away from college English courses at your school. You may be thinking about your own developmental students and worried that they'd feel overwhelmed, that they might not be able to handle these demands.

Let me say that I do think we need to be careful about *how* we integrate challenging work into the class. We don't want to just dump a synthesis essay on students without having provided

---

"Reading, Reasoning, Writing (Accelerated)"
Chabot College, Katie Hern, Fall 2011

Theme: Human Psychology & What Makes Us Tick
Total Required Reading: 500-600 pages

3 Non-Fiction Books
1. *Drive: The Surprising Truth about What Motivates Us* by Daniel Pink (Students read 6 chapters)

2. *Opening Skinner's Box: Great Psychological Experiments of the 20th Century* by Lauren Slater (Students read 6 chapters)

3. *One Psychology-Related Memoir* (Students read complete book of their choice from list below)

   Tweak: Growing Up on Methamphetamines by Nic Sheff
   Madness: A Bipolar Life by Marya Hornbacher
   Danger to Self: On the Frontline with an ER Psychiatrist by Paul Linde

Scholarly and Critical Articles
   • From "Social Class and the Hidden Curriculum of Work" by Jean Anyon
   • From "The Perils of Obedience" by Stanley Milgram, along with 2 critical reviews of Milgram's experiment by psychologists Baumrind and Herrnstein
   • Two reviews of the class text *Opening Skinner's Box*
   • Online materials to supplement key chapters of the Slater text

---

FIGURE **11.1.** *Texts assigned.*

1 Group Presentation of chapter from book *Drive*—ungraded
3-4 Reading Quizzes—open book, letter graded re: accuracy and completeness of answers about ideas/info from each unit's texts
8 Papers of Different Types
- Educational Autobiography—ungraded, in-class essay
- Critical Response—ungraded, in-class essay, 1-2 pages
- 3 Synthesis Essays Involving Class Texts—out-of-class essays, 3-4 pages each, assessed *High Pass, Pass, Low Pass, Not Yet Passing, Rewrite*
- 1 Essay Analyzing the Students' Chosen Memoir—out-of-class essay, 3-4 pages, assessed *High Pass, Pass, Low Pass, Not Yet Passing, Rewrite*
- 1 Self-Reflection Paper about Their Learning—ungraded, in-class essay
- Final Exam—in-class essay evaluating primary course text, assessed *High Pass, Pass, Low Pass, Not Yet Passing, Rewrite*

FIGURE **11.2.** *Major tests and assignments.*

in-class activities that help them know how to approach it. I'll talk more about this in a bit. But I want to say here that students are much more capable than our placement tests and low-level courses often lead us to assume.

For evidence, I turn again to my students. I've taught the accelerated class with these materials for a couple years now, and during the last three semesters, 72 to 88 percent of my students have passed the course with a C or better (see Figure 11.3). My pass rates haven't always been this high. I did an inquiry project a few years back into what I came to call the "academic sustainability gap." In 2005, I taught three sections of the accelerated class inside a learning community. I had poured my heart and soul into this program, and at the end of the semester, only 55 percent of the students passed. That 55 percent became my own personal baseline, a number I've worked to improve over the last six years. Two areas have been especially important in increasing my pass rates.

First, I realized that I had been making some unconscious assumptions about my students as readers. I'm almost embarrassed to admit them here, in a room full of seasoned community college

Spring 2010	Fall 2010	Spring 2011
Success rate: 72%	Success rate: 80%	Success rate: 88%
Enrollment at Census: 29 (Week 3)	Enrollment at Census: 30 (Week 3)	Enrollment at Census: 25 (Week 3)
Pass:* 21 No Pass: 4 Withdrawal: 4	Pass: 24 No Pass: 5 Withdrawal: 1	Pass: 22 No Pass: 2 Withdrawal: 1

*Pass = C or higher

FIGURE 11.3. *Success rates in Hern's Reading, Reasoning, Writing (Accelerated) course.*

teachers, but when I began teaching at Chabot, I assumed that my students would: (1) do the reading I assigned, (2) understand it, and (3) ask questions if they didn't understand something. I have learned that these are flawed assumptions.

More important, I've learned that one of the most high-leverage ways to use class time is to give students the chance to actively process what they've read, the way students are doing in the Freire video. They can handle challenging readings, but they need to talk them through, express the author's points in their own words, hear what other students think, and receive occasional guidance and clarification from the teacher.

That's pretty much what we do in class every day. They might work in small groups to collaboratively answer questions. They might get into debate teams and argue that Stanley Milgram's obedience experiment was—or was not—a good experiment. Or they might do "speed dating," where they face each other in pairs and spend three minutes talking about a topic from the reading, then switch partners and topics several times over. For each unit, once we've informally discussed the readings, I give an open book quiz, and then students write an essay integrating those readings. Figure 11.4 features a diagram of the instructional cycle I use in my classes.

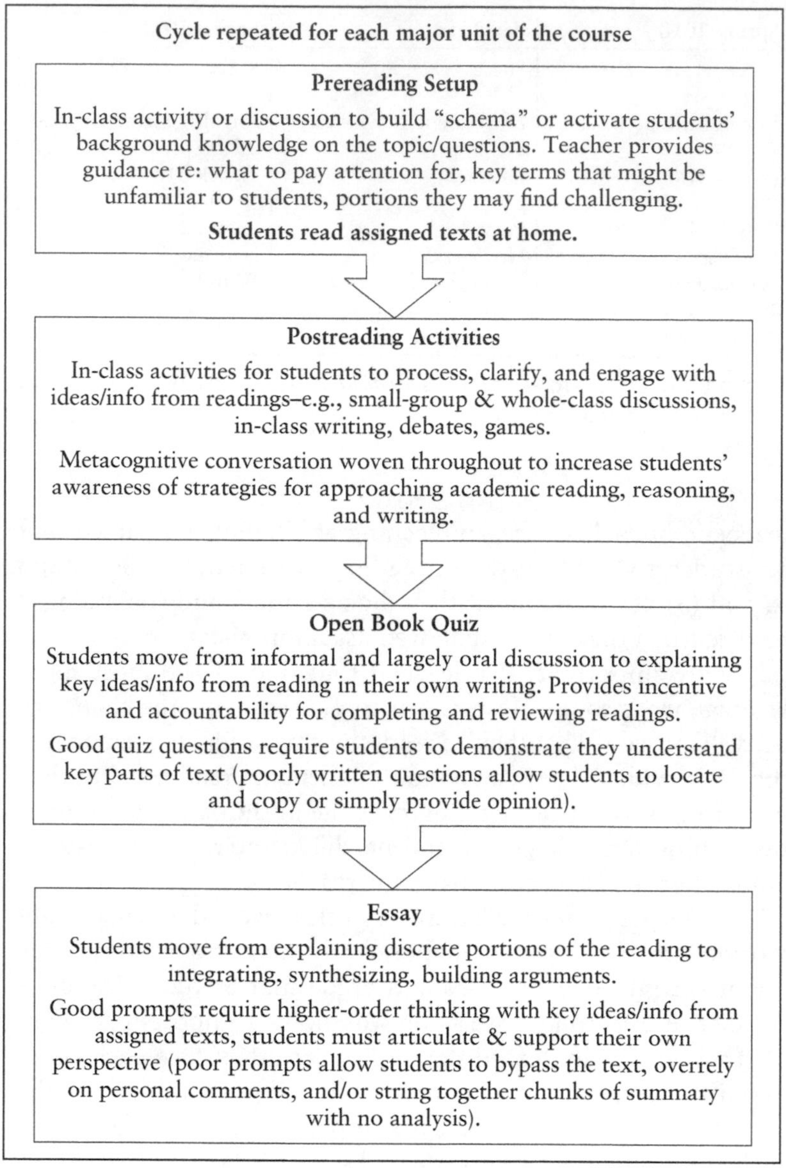

Cycle repeated for each major unit of the course

Prereading Setup

In-class activity or discussion to build "schema" or activate students' background knowledge on the topic/questions. Teacher provides guidance re: what to pay attention for, key terms that might be unfamiliar to students, portions they may find challenging.

Students read assigned texts at home.

Postreading Activities

In-class activities for students to process, clarify, and engage with ideas/info from readings–e.g., small-group & whole-class discussions, in-class writing, debates, games.

Metacognitive conversation woven throughout to increase students' awareness of strategies for approaching academic reading, reasoning, and writing.

Open Book Quiz

Students move from informal and largely oral discussion to explaining key ideas/info from reading in their own writing. Provides incentive and accountability for completing and reviewing readings.

Good quiz questions require students to demonstrate they understand key parts of text (poorly written questions allow students to locate and copy or simply provide opinion).

Essay

Students move from explaining discrete portions of the reading to integrating, synthesizing, building arguments.

Good prompts require higher-order thinking with key ideas/info from assigned texts, students must articulate & support their own perspective (poor prompts allow students to bypass the text, overrely on personal comments, and/or string together chunks of summary with no analysis).

FIGURE **11.4.** *Instructional cycle in Hern's accelerated course.*

The power of this cycle is that students get multiple chances to engage with the readings. They can clarify parts they hadn't understood, develop a sense of ownership over the material, and formulate their own positions on the issues at hand. By the time that essay comes around, they *know* those readings, and their essays are rich with ideas and information drawn from them.

One of the clearest signs that this process works is the virtual disappearance of something that previously had been a chronic problem in students' papers—quotes stuck into paragraphs where they made no sense. I used to interpret this as a writing problem and respond to it by explaining (and reexplaining) the technique for integrating quotes smoothly into one's writing. But I realize now that it was actually a *reading* problem. Students hadn't understood the quote they were using, so of course it didn't make sense in the flow of their paper. Now that so much class time is devoted to actively working with the assigned texts, students are not only less likely to quote randomly, but they also will often choose not to quote at all, instead explaining ideas and information in their own words, a beautiful sign of how deeply they've integrated what they read.

The other big factor in increasing my own pass rates is that I've become better at dealing with the emotional dimensions of student learning, especially student fear. A quick plug here for Rebecca Cox's book *The College Fear Factor*—an incredible qualitative study of community college students' fear and how it plays out in the classroom.

When faculty from other colleges first hear about Chabot's accelerated course, they often have a hard time believing that students can develop the reading and writing skills to move on to college English courses in just one semester. But many of us who teach the course have noticed that students' literacy is usually not the biggest factor in whether they pass. It's more about whether they come to class, do the reading, turn in their papers, and write more than one draft. Sometimes we refer to these as *student-ing skills,* sometimes as *motivation* or *effort.* But all of these terms carry a tinge of moral judgment that can obscure what I think is driving students' behavior.

The video provides a good illustration of what I'm getting at. The day we discussed Freire was amazing (which was lucky, since

I'd forgotten that the student cameraperson was coming). When I did our regular "fess up" at the beginning of class, 100 percent of the students reported that they had read the Freire article for homework. Students were so loudly engaged it was hard to hear the audio. They felt comfortable saying they were lost. They were willing to talk their way through and figure out Freire's meaning as best they could. They demonstrated what is sometimes called "productive persistence," hanging in there and continuing to try when you're not getting something right away.

What's important to know here is what happened in the class *before* this. That day's reading assignment was Mike Rose's "I just wanna be average," and when I asked them to "fess up" if they didn't do the reading, two-thirds of the room raised their hands. My first response was a flare of anger and judgment. It was only the third class of the semester, and already this many students were not doing the reading? Luckily, I caught myself before launching into a tirade, and I asked a follow up question: When they said they didn't read, did they mean that they didn't even try? Or that they started and then gave up? Overwhelmingly, they had tried, gotten discouraged, and stopped.

This is an incredibly important thing to understand about our students. Rebecca Cox's research shows that community college students often arrive at our open doors feeling deeply insecure that they are not really "college material," a feeling reinforced by their placement in remedial courses. They are terrified of being found out, and they will often cope with this fear by evading assessment—not turning in papers, skipping tests. When they encounter a difficult task, or receive critical feedback, or start to feel hopeless, they often disengage and even disappear.

Educational psychologist Carol Dweck's research is also helpful in understanding these dynamics. Students who have what Dweck calls a "growth-mindset" about intelligence believe that intelligence is something they can *develop*, and they are more likely to engage with challenge, invest effort, and learn more. Students with a "fixed mindset," on the other hand, see expending effort as a sign of lower intelligence, avoid challenges they fear may subject them to exposure, and ultimately learn less. The related idea of "self-handicapping" is also relevant here. Not studying, being intoxicated while writing a paper, avoiding the reading—all of these are, ironically, ways students protect their self-worth. After all, it doesn't hurt to fail if you barely tried.

All of this was at play in students' response to the Mike Rose essay, but then two things helped the Freire discussion go differently. First, I gave them some guidance about what I wanted them to pay attention for, a few simple questions about the reading. What does the author mean by "banking model" of education and why does he say it's oppressive? And what does he mean by "problem posing" and why does he say it's liberatory? The questions helped students stay moored when they started to get lost in Freire's language.

More important, though, was that before I sent students home to read Freire, I let them know that I had chosen the article *because* it was difficult. They could all read *People* magazine, but that wasn't going to help them grow as readers and become skilled with dense college-level texts. I said I knew they wouldn't understand everything but that I wanted them to read the whole thing and do the best they could, and then we'd work with it together in class. This conversation defused the reflexive shame that is often triggered when students don't understand something they've read—"I should get this, I'm in college"—and opened up the space for the productive persistence you saw. Instead of withdrawing in the face of difficult material, they engaged with it more deeply.

This is an example of the idea I mentioned earlier—that it's important to be intentional about *how* we integrate challenging material into the class. It's also an example of one of the core principles of Chabot's curriculum—the idea that developmental students should do the same kinds of reading, thinking, and writing they'll do in the college-level course, but with more scaffolding and support to help them be successful.

I want to go back to that list of assignments from my accelerated course (Figure 11.2). Notice that the first few assignments are ungraded and completed in class. This is my response to a pattern I'd seen in my sustainability gap inquiry—that a significant group of students would, as Cox described, try to avoid assessment, missing class on the day of a quiz and not turning in papers. Making the first few assessments ungraded and low stakes—a group presentation, a paper reflecting on their own education, a short summary response—reduces the level of fear in the room, and students begin the semester already on track, having turned in several assignments. It also gives me, as a teacher, the chance to see their work, point out strengths, and encourage them. All of this helps reduce the fear and make it feel safe for students to try.

The other thing I'd like to point out is that papers in my accelerated class are not letter graded; even the formal synthesis essays are assessed on the spectrum from "High Pass" to "Not Yet Passing" and "Rewrite." That was one of the many changes I made after my semester of the 55 percent pass rate. It's an approach adapted from a colleague at Chabot who I noticed had very high student retention at the end of the semester. Before observing her class and asking what she was doing, I'd give weak papers a C, C-, D+, with notes about how to improve them and encouragement to submit a revision. The class is Pass–No Pass, but I wanted to let students know where their writing stood and motivate them to improve. But what happened is that, instead of revising and improving, the C and D students would often just disappear. Under the new system, they stick around and keep trying.

I do other things to help keep affective issues from derailing students in my class, but right now I'd like to shift back to the reading classroom I described at the beginning and the fact that it is *four* levels below college English. This is where I normally begin a discussion of developmental education, making the case that we are dooming students with these long remedial pathways, and that we need to dramatically shorten our sequences. The more developmental levels students are required to take, the less likely those students are to ever complete college-level English, never mind achieve their larger educational goals of transferring or earning a degree (Hern, with Snell).

The reason for this is not simply that students are underskilled and undermotivated. And it's not just that poverty, family issues, and other outside forces pull them away from school (though it's true that these are powerful factors in community college students' lives). The part that's our responsibility—the part that's under our control—is our curriculum. When we place students into curricular structures that offer so many *opportunities* for attrition, we lose a lot of our students.

My math colleague Myra Snell and I have an exercise we do in presentations in which we show that it is just about impossible to have a respectable number of students complete college-level courses when we require them to start two or more semesters below credit-bearing college courses.[1] I'd like to illustrate this point a different way here. A new online data tool is about to become available that enables all 112 California community colleges to see what happens to students as they move through our developmental sequences (Basic Skills Progress Tracker). I'm going to walk you through an example from Yuba College, which has historically placed incoming students in up to four levels of remediation below college-level English.

In fall 2008, eighty-six students began their English course-work three levels below college-level English at Yuba. During the next three years, their pass rates inside each developmental course were solid—more than 75 percent of the students who enrolled in any given developmental level passed the course on a first or a repeated attempt. But because of cumulative attrition in the sequence, just eleven of those eighty-six students got all the way through college-level English in three years—13 percent of the original group (see Figure 11.5). I'm sharing data from Yuba not to embarrass them—in fact, they were one of the first colleges to join the California Acceleration Project and work on redesigning their sequence. I'm sharing Yuba's data because they are typical. If you think your college is different, and that students who start three levels below college level are doing much better than this, I encourage you to withhold your certainty until you've looked at your local cohort tracker data.

My focus here has been on my own classroom practices, but this conversation is part of a larger argument that I'd like to make explicit in closing. In my work with the California Acceleration Project, I'm advocating for three main curricular changes:

1. We need to shorten our English course sequences. We need to let more students enroll directly in college composition, either in regular sections or sections with additional support provided through an attached corequisite. And we need to streamline stand-alone developmental curricula as much as possible. Aside from English language classes for students just learning the language,

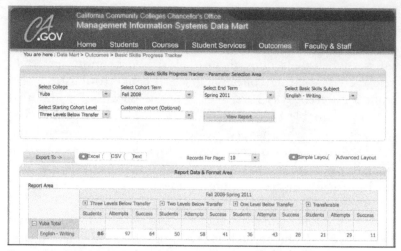

FIGURE **11.5**. *Attrition of students starting three levels below college-level English.*

I argue that English remediation should include no more than a single open-access integrated reading and writing course.

2. We need to make developmental classes more challenging. For me this means giving students the same kinds of reading, thinking, and writing they'll see in the college-level course, but understanding that they won't be as good yet. Instead of grammar workbooks and process paragraphs about how to make tamales, students need to read about substantive issues, engage in higher-order thinking on those issues, and write academic essays integrating what they've read.

3. This increased level of challenge must be combined with high levels of support so that the fear and insecurity students bring to our classrooms don't keep them from being successful. We need to think of support not just in terms of add-ons like tutoring or having a counselor visit the class, but as the environment we create through grading practices, the language of our syllabus, the sequence of assignments, how we use class time, and how we give feedback.

The movement to accelerate developmental English and math has picked up a lot of momentum in the last couple years. Some of your colleges are already trying some form of acceleration:

compressing two levels of a sequence into one intensive course, creating open-access courses like the one at Chabot, mainstreaming students into college-level classes as in the Accelerated Learning Program at the Community College of Baltimore County. If you're at a campus where this work has not yet taken hold, and students are still disappearing inside layers of remedial reading and writing courses, I encourage you to step forward and join the movement.

Students are much more capable than our traditional models of remediation have assumed. And we, as teachers, are capable of supporting them. It's time to change the way we approach incoming students. It's time to believe in student capacity and make our classrooms a place where that capacity is unleashed.

Note

1. A student who begins two levels below college-level English or math faces five exit points before completing the college-level course. They must (1) pass the first developmental course, (2) choose to enroll in the next developmental course, (3) pass that course, (4) choose to enroll in the college-level course, and (5) pass that course. Community colleges lose students at each exit point, which means that the pool of continuing students gets smaller and smaller throughout the sequence. Even if a college had spectacular pass rates in individual courses, attrition would still be high across these five exit points. To illustrate: if 90 percent of students passed each of the three courses, and 90 percent persisted between courses, just 59 percent of the students starting two levels below college level would complete the college-level course (.90 multiplied by itself five times).

Works Cited

Basic Skills Progress Tracker. Management Information Systems Data Mart. *California Community Colleges Chancellor's Office.* 2013. Web. 9 Dec. 2016.

Cox, Rebecca D. *The College Fear Factor: How Students and Professors Misunderstand One Another.* Cambridge: Harvard UP, 2009. Print.

Dweck, Carol S. *Mindset: The New Psychology of Success.* New York: Random House, 2006. Print.

Freire, Paulo. *Pedagogy of the Oppressed.* Trans. Myra Bergman Ramos. New York: Herder and Herder, 1970. Print.

Hern, Katie. "English 102 Freire Discussion." Classroom video. August 2009. *Vimeo.* Web. 9 Dec. 2016.

Hern, Katie, with Myra Snell. "Exponential Attrition and the Promise of Acceleration in Developmental English and Math." *Perspectives: The RP Group.* June 2010. Web. 9 Dec. 2016.

Rose, Mike. "I just wanna be average." *Lives on the Boundary: The Struggles and Achievements of America's Underprepared.* New York: Free, 1989. Print.

CHAPTER TWELVE

Writing Centers Are Also Reading Centers: How Could They Not Be?

MURIEL HARRIS
Purdue University

The old adage that a written text is improved by revision is particularly apt for this chapter. An earlier draft of it lacked some crucial information that, once I learned it, has greatly altered the argument I was planning to make—and has reconfirmed the point that "we write to learn." I had intended to untangle some of the ways in which writing center tutors help students learn how to improve inadequate writing related to inadequate reading skills. I thought it was obvious that many writing problems are intertwined with inadequate reading skills. So my task was merely to delineate some of those connections as I've seen them crop up in writing center tutorials. Some of the college students I have met in more than a few decades of one-to-one tutorials had adequate writing skills but could improve their drafts with closer readings of the texts that informed their essays; other students wanted to revise drafts they weren't content with yet and needed a tutor to help them learn how to be readers of their own writing so they could see what needed to be revised; and others came for tutorial help in improving writing linked to the need to improve reading proficiency. In sum, reading and writing were so closely linked in so many of the cases that I thought those outside of writing centers would profit from knowing how the reading-writing connection plays out in the learning environment of a writing center tutorial.

But as I surveyed the national landscape to find evidence of how college students' reading abilities are factored into writing center theory, research, and pedagogy to inform my assertions, I found two troublesome conditions: first, reading skills are declining more rapidly than I had realized; and second, there is gaping hole in writing center scholarship that needs to be acknowledged and filled. As indicated in a 2015 report by the Educational Testing Service (ETS), "65 percent [of students taking the test] were below proficient in reading" (Coley, Goodman, and Sands).[1] Yet, at a time when more students seeking writing center assistance are in need of improving reading-related writing abilities, there is little in a rather large body of writing center literature or even in tutor training manuals that calls attention to the reading-writing connection and that helps tutors learn how to work with students' reading abilities as an integral part of helping with writing proficiency. It's not a totally empty landscape, as there are a few people in writing centers working on reconnecting writing instruction with reading instruction. G. Travis Adams, Gary Griswold, and Ellen C. Carillo have published articles on the need for more scholarship, and Carillo has guest edited a focused issue on reading for *WLN: A Journal of Writing Center Scholarship*. Still, it is a sparse landscape. And if I cast a wider net, I also see how that lack of attention to the reading-writing connection in writing center studies mirrors how instruction in reading and in writing have parted ways in the larger field of composition studies. Mariolina Rizzi Salvatori and Patricia Donahue, in their introduction to a 2016 special issue of the journal *Pedagogy* focusing on reading, call attention to a resurgence of interest in reading in composition studies in the mid-1980s, only to "fall into relative neglect" since then (2).

Having become aware of the accompanying lack of attention to reading skills in writing center scholarship, I went off to the 2015 International Writing Centers Association conference hoping to learn who else in writing centers is working on tying together the reading and writing so necessary to write competently. Unfortunately, at the one session I found on reading and writing in the writing center, attendance was far less than I would have hoped as the number of empty seats vastly outnumbered the occupied ones. The session should have been standing room only. So this chapter is both a plea for more attention—in the form of scholarship and tutor training methods to work with students' reading-writing skills in the writing center—and also an argument for why such attention is so important. To offer my arguments as to why it's important that we reconnect reading with writing instruction in the writing center, I include here some specific ways in which reading skills impact writing skills as they show up in tutorials. As a way to organize my argument, I attempt to tease out some problems caused by inadequate reading-writing connections that tutors should recognize and be equipped to help the writer with. If tutors focus on discussing students' writing skills without being aware of underlying reading problems, tutors are tending to only part of what the students need to learn. An analogy might be learning how to play the violin using one hand only. A violin player has to have both hands working together to produce a wide range of music, just as reading has to work with writing to produce a variety of genres of competent writing.

The reading-writing connection crops up in numerous ways as writers compose documents. To sort these ways into components of the writing process and to suggest these as possible topics for tutor training and for further research, I offer the artificial categories of (1) reading to write, (2) reading while composing, and (3) reading while revising. These are artificial only in the sense that, as we know, most people's writing processes are far from following such a neat linear progression. Similarly, in tutorials, as student writers and their tutors talk about a paper the student is working on, the conversation may begin with a discussion about revision, go back to reformulating the topic as part of planning, move to re-reading in order to revise, and most probably involve a lot more back and forthing as the paper progresses in the student's mind (or in notes for when she returns to working on the paper later).

Reading to Write

Reading Print-Based Materials

Student writing in college is most often a compilation or a response to what the student has read—as source material for research papers, as literature to respond to, as information gleaned from textbooks, and so on. Students who have not adequately understood what they read cannot competently write informed papers that draw on what they have read. In writing centers, this can cause a student's paper to offer weak, inadequately sub-stantiated conclusions because the student hasn't read the text with the necessary degree of comprehension. Or some students' response to an article or book lead to conclusions or interpreta-tions in students' papers they can't support because they aren't able to locate anything in the text to substantiate their claim or argument. Therefore, after tutorial help in delving into the text more deeply, some students find they need to write a very dif-ferent paper once they have a clearer understanding of the text's content. Sometimes a student's paper wanders around in search of a focus instead of a coherent discussion of the topic. Or the paper includes large chunks of undigested material copied out of a source. Such collages may, of course, be the result of lack of effort or an easy shortcut to finishing an assignment, but this can also happen when students lack the ability to understand the material and explain it in their own words. The hemming and hawing that results when a tutor asks what the paper is about may well be the student's attempt to stumble around trying to understand what he read. Similarly, when Catherine Savini, director of the Westfield State University Reading and Writing Center, observes tutorials in which students have not internally processed what they read, she notes that such tutorials "never get off the ground." Such tutorial discussions go round and round in circles as students grapple unsuccessfully, seeking to land on a topic to write about. Reworking the original draft at this point is counterproductive. To help in these situations, the tutor needs to work with the student on how to read source material with better comprehension. Only after that can they have a productive discussion about how to plan and write the paper.

Another reading skill some students need may be a richer vo-cabulary or a multilayered context from previous reading. In this case, a lack of understanding sometimes begins with a student's inability to know the word choices or terminology used in what they read. Or they may be unable to rise above the details to see the larger points being made. Or their waning attention span as they read causes them to drift over parts of a lengthy piece of prose. Here again the tutor has to focus not on discussing the draft but instead on turning back to the text to learn how to un-derstand what was read. For students whose first language is not

English, there may be idioms, cultural references, or knowledge that has to be explained. In institutions where the majority of the students are not speakers of English as a first language, tutors regularly provide much-needed basic vocabulary assistance to help students understand texts they are assigned to read. Such is the case at Florida International University (FIU) where Paula Gillespie directs their writing center:

> FIU is a minority majority school, with many students whose parents were refugees or in exile from a home country nearby, so they are either ESL students or L1.5. They are not the typical ESL students, though, who have studied English abroad; rather, they are students who learned what English they know in our school systems. Our writing center users will often bring their textbooks or readings with them for help interpreting what they mean. Often the conversation between writer and tutor will start in Spanish and then move back and forth in Spanglish, with the tutor helping writers to understand their readings.

Reading Online Materials

When students read texts with inadequate comprehension of vocabulary, their reading and writing difficulties are further complicated by the fact that many students now read and write primarily online. But, as studies have repeatedly shown, reading online reduces comprehension and memory of what was read. In his study "Reading Behavior in the Digital Environment," Ziming Liu reports his findings as follows:

> With an increasing amount of time spent reading electronic documents, a screen-based reading behavior is emerging. The screen-based reading behavior is characterized by more time spent on browsing and scanning, keyword spotting, one-time reading, non-linear reading, and reading more selectively, while less time is spent on in-depth reading, and concentrated reading. Decreasing sustained attention is also noted. Annotating and highlighting while reading is a common activity in the printed environment. However, this "traditional" pattern has not yet migrated to the digital environment when people read electronic documents. (700)

Because Liu's study is more than a decade old, I am tempted to hope that online reading habits have changed as more people are adapting their reading habits to the digital environment. However, in 2013, in an article in *Scientific American*, Ferris Jabr concludes that after considering many of the studies of online reading and the fact that people are much more used to reading in a digital environment, researchers continue to find evidence that reading online is not as thorough as reading print on paper:

> [E]vidence from laboratory experiments, polls and consumer reports indicates that modern screens and e-readers fail to adequately recreate certain tactile experiences of reading on paper that many people miss and, more importantly, prevent people from navigating long texts in an intuitive and satisfying way. In turn, such navigational difficulties may subtly inhibit reading comprehension. Compared with paper, screens may also drain more of our mental resources while we are reading and make it a little harder to remember what we read when we are done. A parallel line of research focuses on people's attitudes toward different kinds of media. Whether they realize it or not, many people approach computers and tablets with a state of mind less conducive to learning than the one they bring to paper. (n.p.)

Jabr cites other studies, including some that describe attitudes people bring to reading online, while other studies he summarizes explore the physical drain on readers' eyes as they navigate digital text. Reading hypertext apparently fares no better than reading linear text online because, as Diana DeStefano and Jo-Anne LeFevre conclude from their review of studies on reading hypertext, "the increased demands of decision-making and visual processing in hypertext impaired reading performance" (1616). So it is hardly surprising that a company that reports on digital trends notes that four in ten millennials (those in the cohort age 18–34) "say that they would rather communicate with pictures than with words" (qtd. in Ember B4). Therefore, in writing center tutorials, tutors also need to help students read text even more closely when working with online sources. Enlarging text, highlighting, and annotating where possible, even stopping to take handwritten notes or compose summaries aloud, are strategies tutors can explain or model for students as ways to engage more closely with online texts. But it's not evident that there are now well-established methods to help students read texts online with adequate comprehension. Beth L. Hewett, author of *The Online Writing Conference: A Guide for Teachers and Tutors*, notes in a listserv conversation that "my research strongly indicates that students have great difficulty taking what they read [of tutors' and teachers' online response to their texts] and applying it to their own writing."

Reading Assignments

Because most college-level writing is in response to instructors' assignments, student writers also need to read—and read closely and carefully—the assignments they are responding to. Therefore, some writing center tutorials address the question of whether a student's draft has adequately responded to what was asked for in the assignment, usually at the request of the student. John Kneisley, a tutor who surveyed 250 tutorial logs written by tutors after their sessions, noted that 22 percent of the students who came to their writing center "wanted to ensure that they effectively addressed their essay's prompt." Reading and understanding a writing prompt is critically important, yet many students writing in response to an instructor's assignment have not adequately grasped what is asked of them. The assignment can be a class writing prompt, an essay exam question, a group project or report, or a job or scholarship application. So tutors often spend time with students looking at the wording of an assignment and, in particular, discussing the verbs (does the assignment ask to evaluate? argue for or against? analyze? define? reflect on?). Instructors who have asked students to reflect on or analyze a class reading have undoubtedly read too many student papers that, despite careful class preparation, summarize the reading instead. And then there's the problem of wording in an assignment that some students may not understand. As an illustration of this, Travis Adams offers the example of an English language learner who, when asked to write a response to a topic, had no idea what "writing a response" meant (80).

Reading to Gain Genre Knowledge

While students need college-level reading skills to absorb information in order to write in response to various texts, they also need competent reading skills to recognize genre features in assigned texts. As students become aware of genre characteristics in assigned readings, they can respond to such readings by writing in the same genre. If student writers fail to notice how a text is shaped by its genre, a disconnect is the result. As Meghan A. Sweeney and Maureen McBride point out in their study of student responses to "difficulty papers," unless instructors are explicit about asking students to read rhetorically and critically to see models of how they should write, students may not see the difference between how they have been taught to write in other situations and how their assigned readings are organized, present detail, and state a thesis. As a result, they hang on tightly to the models presented in textbooks or classes. This suggests that tutors may need to work with those students who, not having a clear genre model in their minds for what they are being asked to write, will be at a loss for appropriate structures or models and flounder, not sure how to proceed. To compound this problem, some students read texts on writing skills that offer hints and suggestions students internalize as rules to be strictly adhered to in order to produce good writing. If these suggestions are reinforced by teachers' suggestions in class, some students harden them into absolutes for writing—a problem Mike Rose has defined as "rigid rules and inflexible plans" that create dysfunctional writing. These rigid rules are likely to become so deeply embedded that students don't notice that such "rules" are regularly violated or ignored in their assigned readings. Thus, despite assigned readings that do not incorporate the five-paragraph structure, do not place a thesis statement in the first paragraph, dare to use "I" in the paper, do not follow a discernable outline, and do not shape the introductory paragraph like an inverted pyramid or diamond or whatever, students continue to write in ways that are constricted by rigid rules. The list is dishearteningly long.[2] If, during the tutorial conversation, a tutor manages to create a space in which the student can verbalize or defend some aspect of the writing that adheres to one or more of these dysfunctional rules, the tutor takes on the very difficult task of convincing the student that these are rules the writer does not have to follow. Sometimes it is more convincing to go through the assigned reading to help the student see how published writers write. Too often it is only with great reluctance that students realize some absolutes that have governed their writing are not absolutes or do not pertain to all genres (or processes) of writing. They have read and incorrectly internalized advice in their composition handbooks and from their classroom. I offer as an example a bright young engineering student whom I met in a tutorial. He brought along his lab report, which would have gladdened the hearts of some first-year composition instructors. He started with a broad topic, narrowed it down, and announced his point at the end of the introductory paragraph. Sadly, he had no idea why the engineering faculty member indicated that the writing was totally inappropriate and that a rewrite was needed. His rules for writing needed to be put aside as we talked about the genre of lab reports: the need for brevity, the preference for announcing results in the passive voice, and so on. Clearly he needed to have read some lab reports to see what and how that genre is constructed. Reading to gain genre knowledge is important.

Reading While Composing

When tutors assist students with composing processes, they should also draw on reading skills to assist students as they write. This intertwining of reading and writing while writing, as explained by Lynn Quitman Troyka, draws on psycholinguistics, which emphasizes language processes, not products. Troyka summarizes her view of the connection between reading and writing in the form of two propositions:

> Proposition 1: At no time are the acts of reading and writing as inextricably bound to one another as when a person writes.

> Proposition 2: When ineffective writers are helped to become conscious of the interactive language process between writing and reading, their writing quickly becomes more expert. (308)

In particular, Troyka draws on two central psycholinguistics concepts that explain these propositions: prediction and redundancy. Both principles can be explained by tutors and modeled so that writers learn how to use prediction and redundancy as reading strategies while writing in order to produce more skilled writing.

Prediction is the language act of being aware of or able to predict what comes next as we read. Proficient readers are often able to predict what will come next as they read sentences, paragraphs, chapters, or complete documents, and the ability to predict where the reader expects to go next guides the skilled writer as he or she composes. But if student writers do not read their own prose as readers, they are not always aware that what they write builds expectations. Lack of that awareness can lead to organizational problems as well as the absence of connecting information. To help writers see this in action, tutors can demonstrate how they, as readers, respond to a draft the student has brought in. As the tutor reads the first paragraph of a paper, she can stop to tell the writer what she predicts will follow in the next sentence or paragraph. If the prediction doesn't overlap with the writer's prose, then there's a disconnect that the writer needs to rethink. For example, suppose a student's opening sentence of a paper starts as follows:

> The gap year following high school graduation is a growing phenomenon across the United States and has resulted in many benefits to higher education as well as to the student.

At this point, a tutor can offer her prediction that the following sentences will be about the benefits of the gap year to students and colleges. But suppose the next sentence were the following:

> There are numerous ways that students can spend that gap year.

The student writer's text has taken a left turn and wandered off in a slightly different direction. But hearing the tutor-reader's prediction can guide the writer's revision of that part of the essay and help the writer learn to draw on the strategy of reader prediction for all her writing.

Redundancy, the other tool Troyka focuses on, refers to prior knowledge that precedes new knowledge in the structure of a sentence. That is, we bring previous knowledge to bear as we read, and the interaction of reading and writing is apparent when a reader is first introduced to known or "old" knowledge and then the new knowledge is connected to the known knowledge. This principle of redundancy, often referred to in linguistics as the "given —> new" principle, is the basis of a very useful tutoring strategy when talking with student writers about sentence clarity. Often the problem is created when sentences violate this known—>new principle by arranging new information before old. Presenting new before old information can result in sentences such as the following that become momentarily difficult for the reader to track:

> My interest in endangered species began when I was about eight or nine years old. The decrease of available land, due to farmers needing more acreage, as habitat for mountain lions was what first interested me.

The reader would process those sentences sooner and more clearly if the second sentence inverted the information flow and began with the "what interests me" segment, already introduced in the first sentence. This principle of moving from old to new information works on the sentence, paragraph, and whole document level.

Reading While Revising

Re-reading our drafts is an activity acknowledged in the word *"revision,"* the reseeing and reworking of a written draft or a draft in progress. Writers need to gain distance from their own texts in order to read their texts as others will read them. This ability to internalize how other readers will comprehend a text means that writers have to be skilled in reading and comprehending the writing of others as well as reading and re-reading—reseeing—the writing they produce themselves, both during composing drafts and when reading to revise. The most often used strategy at the beginning of a tutorial—though not sufficiently acknowledged as drawing on reading skills—is one that assists writers in gaining distance from their own texts: having the tutor or student read a draft aloud. There is also, of course, the tutor's need to read the text to learn about the contents and think diagnostically about what to work on in the tutorial. As the tutor reads the paper, he can verbalize his responses as he reads. In this way, the student may hear how monotonous a series of sentences sounds or why sentence variety is needed or why the tutor-reader stopped—because either the content or some sentence was difficult to read and/or understand. Or the writer may hear information that is repeated or out of order as the tutor-reader works to make sense of the writing. Or perhaps the writer hears the tutor-reader stumbling over a sentence that needs revising or being puzzled by missing information. Helping students become readers of their own texts is part of what tutors can offer student writers. This ability to read one's own text from the perspective of an outside reader is a basic skill for all writers.

This problem of writers not being able to distance themselves from their writing is what Linda Flower aptly named "writer-based prose"—prose in which writers are writing to themselves and not consciously aware of information or the organization of material that a reader would need in order to follow along. Some of what is missing from the page often resides in the writer's head, and in tutorials this can become evident when a tutor reads a draft a student has brought in and senses some missing connection between one sentence or paragraph and the next. Often, when asked, the student can supply the missing link but has failed to notice that it wasn't written down. Becoming a competent reader of one's own writing means transitioning from composing writer-based prose to reader-based prose. It is an act of reading that competent writers must acquire.

Another reading skill that writers need as they revise is to read—and read with comprehension—instructors' feedback on drafts of papers to understand what or how to revise. As most tutors can attest, some students bring in drafts of papers with instructors' comments that students do not understand. In a study published in *Freshman English News*, Mary Hayes and Donald Daiker asked students to explain what the instructor comments on their papers meant. What Hayes and Daiker found was that, despite the instructor's use of best practices in responding, students didn't understand some of the comments and thus couldn't make use of them when revising. Just as the terminology used in the comments can confuse writers, extensive commenting can simply overwhelm the writer who doesn't know how to prioritize among all the comments, suggestions, and questions an instructor has decorated the paper with. The papers that instructors have labored over to offer fulsome marginal notes and extensive end comments can fail to help writers who lack the ability to critically read and sift through all the comments (Harris). A response I encountered too often from students was that the instructor obviously didn't like the paper because of all that writing. (Apparently, the underlying assumption here is that extensive comments equals extensive negative feedback.) Assisting students with reading skills has many dimensions, including reading texts, reading them online, reading teachers' and tutors' responses, composing written texts, and re-reading those texts.

The Need for Tutor Preparation

Clearly, tutors must learn to recognize students' need for the reading skills that are so integral to writing skills and then have strategies to help students acquire those skills. But some people who train tutors are in institutions where time to meet with new tutors is, for a variety of reasons, severely limited. Plus, tutoring staffs differ in their background knowledge and/or experience, so there's no uniform way to train tutors. Some writing centers are staffed by graduate student tutors; other centers—such as those in community colleges—often have first-year or sophomore students as tutors; some centers can only fund tutors who qualify for work-study; other writing centers are staffed by professional tutors or faculty; and some writing centers within learning centers or student success centers find that their tutors can only be trained along with subject matter tutors, e.g., for math, chemistry, biology, etc. So tutor preparation varies because of the variety of conditions, resources, and available staffing personnel. But in institutions committed to providing adequate resources for writing centers, including training (best offered as a credit-bearing course), there are basic principles that tutors can be introduced to, beginning with recognizing ways that inadequate reading skills impinge on and interact with writing skills. Class meetings can include discussions of the types of writing problems for which tutors can explore underlying causes that involve inadequate reading skills such as those discussed in this chapter. In training courses, tutors learn how to ask students about their literacy histories, how to listen to students explain what they think an assignment asks for, and how to help students become readers of their own writing. In tutor training classes, tutors can be introduced to the types of writing-reading problems discussed here: reading to write, reading while composing, and reading while revising. Moreover, tutors in training classes can review reading skills strategies explained on a variety of websites.[3] But so far, there is not yet sufficient scholarship available for tutors to learn how to recognize interconnected reading skills. As Travis Adams notes, the widely used tutor training manual by Paula Gillespie and Neal Lerner has a chapter on reading, but it limits the examples to close reading of literature. Therefore, Adams complains, "[n]one of the examples is a student who struggled or failed to read because of vocabulary, comprehension, or processing issues" (78). Other tutor training manuals offer brief suggestions for reading assistance but unfortunately lack the kind of in-depth assistance tutors need to learn in order to effectively assist students to read more critically. Adams concludes that there is a need to move beyond generally asking tutors to draw on their own skilled reading habits to assist writers struggling with assigned texts. Affirming the need for all tutors to be trained in how to help with reading, John Kneisley also calls for more training for tutors to assist students with reading skills:

> Successful writers and researchers must be able to identify a text's important points and to synthesize those points into their own writing. But despite the fact that reading and writing are inextricably linked, the tutor training course, as well as many tutoring manuals, fail to demonstrate how tutors can discuss a tutee's critical reading ability. Reading is often labeled as a non-communal activity, yet is an ideal topic for conversation between a tutor and tutee. (n.p.)

In our field, then, some have called attention to the problem, and a few writing centers, such as Delta College's reading-writing center, have worked to develop programs to meet the need. And again, some university websites offer help with improving reading skills. But there is no evidence of a widespread solution or response in published writing center scholarship, in the training of tutors, or in writing centers' descriptions of instructional services they offer. However, there is hope that by calling attention to the vitally important need to reunite reading and writing instruction in the writing center, a new area of scholarship ripe for exploring will eventually become a well-trodden landscape.

Notes

1. In the ETS report by Coley et al., the authors cite a 2013 study by the National Assessment of Educational Progress that concluded that 62 percent of twelfth graders were below proficiency in reading.

2. For those who want to read a list of such perceptions I collected, see "Contradictory Perceptions of Rules of Writing." *College Composition and Communication* 30.2 (1979): 218–20.

3. Tutors can select from a number of websites with extensive information about improving reading skills, e.g., Brookhaven College has a highly useful website, "Reading Skills and Strategies for Students" (www.brookhavencollege.edu/about/readingtheappforlife/Pages/reading-skills.aspx); Dartmouth College's Academic Skills Center has a website with links to handouts, videos, and lists of strategies (www.dartmouth.edu/~acskills/success/reading.html); and St. Mary's College's "Reading Strategies" webpage has an extensive discussion of strategies for active reading, including the widely practiced SQ3R (www.stmarys-ca.edu/academics/academic-resources-support/student-academic-support-services/tutorial-academic-skills-6).

Works Cited

Adams, G. Travis. "The Line That Shouldn't Be Drawn: Writing Centers as Reading Centered." *Pedagogy* 16.1 (2016): 73-90. *EBSCOhost Academic Search Premier*. Web. 9 Nov. 2015.

Carillo, Ellen C. "Reading in the Writing Center." *WLN: A Journal of Writing Center Scholarship* 41.7-8 (2017): 17–24. Print.

Coley, Richard, Madeline Goodman, and Anita Sands. "America's Skills Challenge: Millennials and the Future." *Princeton: ETS.* 2015. Web. 4 Nov. 2015.

DeStefano, Diana, and Jo-Anne LeFevre. "Cognitive Load in Hypertext Reading: A Review." *Computers in Human Behavior* 23.3 (2007): 1616–41. Web. 27 Apr. 2015.

Ember, Sydney. "Brands Woo Millennials with a Wink, an Emoji or Whatever It Takes." *New York Times.* 27 Sept. 2015. B1,4. Print.

Flower, Linda. "Writer-Based Prose: A Cognitive Basis for Problems in Writing." *College English* 41.1 (1979): 19–37.

Gillespie, Paula, "have time to answer a question?" Personal Email. 4 Sept. 2014.

Gillespie, Paula, and Neal Lerner. *The Longman Guide to Peer Tutoring.* New York: Longman, 2007. Print.

Griswold, Gary. "Postsecondary Reading: What Writing Center Tutors Need to Know." *Journal of College Reading and Learning* 37.1 (2006): 59–70. *EBSCOhost Education Source.* Web. 5 Nov. 2015.

Harris, Muriel. "More Comments on Student Papers Results in More Learning." *Bad Ideas about Writing.* Ed. Cheryl Ball and Drew Lowe. Digital Publishing Institute. Web.

Hayes, Mary F., and Donald A. Daiker. "Using Protocol Analysis in Evaluating Responses to Student Writing." *Freshman English News* 13.2 (1984): 1–4, 10. Print.

Hewett, Beth L. "Re" [wcenter] improve the speed and depth of asynchronous consulting. WCenter. Texas Tech U. 11 May 2015. 11 May 2015. Email listserv.

Jabr, Ferris. "The Reading Brain in the Digital Age: The Science of Paper versus Screens." *Scientific American.* 11 Apr. 2013. Web. 27 May 2015.

Kneisley, John. "Exposing the Draft Addiction: Prioritizing Prewriting in the Writing Center." *WLN: A Journal of Writing Center Scholarship.* Forthcoming.

Liu, Ziming. "Reading Behavior in the Digital Environment: Changes in Reading Behavior over the Past Ten Years." *Journal of Documentation* 61.6 (2005): 700–12. Web. 21 May 2015.

Rose, Mike. "Rigid Rules, Inflexible Plans, and the Stifling of Language: A Cognitivist Analysis of Writer's Block." *College Composition and Communication* 31.4 (1980): 389–401. *JSTOR.* Web. 3 March 2015.

Salvatori, Mariolina Rizzi, and Patricia Donahue. "Guest Editors' Introduction: Guest Editing as a Form of Disciplinary Probing." *Pedagogy* 16.1 (2016): 1–8. *EBSCOhost Academic Search Premier.* Web. 1 Dec. 2015.

Savini, Catherine. "A Question about Your Reading and Writing Center." Personal e-mail. 4 Sept. 2015.

Sweeney, Meghan A., and Maureen McBride. "Difficulty Paper (Dis)Connections: Understanding the Threads Students Weave between Their Reading and Writing." *College Composition and Communication* 66.4 (2015): 591–614. Print.

Troyka, Lynn Quitman. "The Writer as Conscious Reader." *A Sourcebook for Basic Writing Teachers.* Ed. Theresa Enos. New York: Random, 1987. 307–17. Print.

CHAPTER THIRTEEN

When Writers Encounter Reading in a Community College First-Year Composition Course

HOWARD TINBERG
Bristol Community College

She is unable to speak, and the text is silent. . . .
—BARTOLOMAE AND PETROSKY,
Facts, Artifacts, and Counterfacts

We have noted that community college instructors do not expect their students to be able to read at the level of their texts or to write very much at all, suggesting that those instructors have very low expectations for their students, expectations so low as to deny many, if not most, students the opportunity to learn skills essential to the careers they have chosen to pursue.
—*What Does It Really Mean to Be College and Work Ready?*

The Resurgence of Reading as a Teaching Subject

It has always struck me as odd that even as we college faculty—especially in English—often complain that our students either are not reading what we assign or simply are not up to the task of reading at the college level, we rarely spend instructional time explicitly teaching what it means to read in our discipline and beyond. It has struck me as even odder that, as a field, composition and rhetoric, which has for decades theorized writing processes and promoted pedagogies that would ground such theory, has not for the most part done as much for reading. And, perhaps oddest of all, is this fact: at community colleges, the separation of reading and writing remains institutionalized, with reading being taught by "reading specialists" in the developmental area and writing by the English department (mostly by contingent faculty), as if reading can occur without an understanding of content.

And yet recent scholarly work on the relationship between English studies and reading reveals a more nuanced narrative than I've suggested. Even as critical theorists in the 1960s were declaring the death of the author, the attention of those theorists naturally shifted to the reader, and, as Patricia Harkin reminds us, reader-response theory radically transformed our notion both of a text (which was no longer stable or defined narrowly by writers' intentions) and what it meant to read that text (with readers shaping its meaning). Yet reader-response theorists were challenged by the same question that troubled the New Critics a generation earlier: Is this concern with reading a privileged and elitist matter or could reading in such a way be generalized and democratized? Could reading, in other words, become a teaching subject, with time spent in class modeling and enacting such activity?

The question became a critical one, especially as composition's consolidation as a discipline took hold within English departments. With its concern fixed on novice students and on the eminently practical and universally required writing course, composition would gladly embrace a literate activity that empowered novice and experienced readers alike and had pedagogical and, indeed, social justice implications. Compositionists such as Ann E. Berthoff posited a view of a constructive composing process that embraced both writing and reading as acts of imagination (*Forming*). Berthoff introduced a new generation of composition scholar-teachers to the challenging works of I. A. Richards and Paulo Freire, among others, as teachable texts. David Bartholomae and Anthony Petrosky would operationalize Berthoff's theory by publishing the still revered reader *Ways of Reading* as well as a scholarly monograph explicitly laying out the readings and rationale for a basic reading and writing course (*Ways of Reading*; *Facts, Artifacts, and Counterfacts*). So clearly tuned in to the challenges that many inexperienced readers face when "silenced" by a difficult text, Bartholomae and Petrosky saw the virtue of having students and teachers explore the silences, buttressed by the theory that while texts are shaped by readers, those readers may bring a range of abilities and experiences to the task. Teachers need to provide, in Berthoff's well-known phrase, "assisted invitations" to those students, facilitating their engagement with difficult readings (*Forming* 8)

As admirable as these efforts were to bridge reader-response theory and classroom practice, composition, still rooted in its democratizing mission of enabling all writers to become literate, would push back against any attempt to create budding English majors or to allow the reading of complex works by published writers to squeeze out the work of student writers. The resistance to what was perceived as an English department takeover of first-year composition (FYC) was played out in reductive but dramatic fashion in two series of debates during the 1990s: the Erika Lindemann–Gary Tate published exchanges (recapping a debate at the 1992 Conference on College Composition and Communication [CCCC] Annual Convention) on whether literature should be included in a first-year composition course, and the Peter Elbow–David Bartholomae sessions at the 1991 Conference on College Composition and Communication Convention (later published) on whether the purpose of the course is to allow space for expressive writing and reading or to prepare students to write and read for the university (Bartholomae).

Near the end of the decade and into the next, scholars continued to do important work on the connection between reading and writing in the composition course, but as composition turned from consolidation (and its focus on the first-year composition course itself) toward expansion into subspecialties (such as new media, queer and disability studies, and more generally a concern for distribution and delivery of communication), discussions about reading became less prominent at the CCCC Annual Convention (as Mariolina Salvatori and Patricia Donahue write) and in print (Salvatori; Joliffe; Salvatori and Donahue, "What Is College English?"). More recently, a national study of reading instruction within composition classrooms does suggest an increasing attention to reading in the FYC course but at the same time revealing a lack of both theoretical and pedagogical knowledge about reading:

> Despite their commitment to foregrounding the practice of reading in their writing courses, 51 percent of the instructors interviewed were not secure in their abilities to teach reading. Marla . . . explained: "I would really like to know more about who our students are as readers, what they're doing as readers, how I can help them more effectively, and what that actually looks like . . . in terms of classroom design. (Carillo Loc. 563)

> It would seem that composition, having achieved status as a legitimate discipline in part by asserting its independence from departments of literature and the privileged status of reader-response theory, now required the very same theory about and foregrounding of reading that it once eschewed. (Harkin 422)

Reading, Remediation, and Reform at the Community College

Four-year institutions have for some time ceded reading instruction of college-age students to the community colleges, where reading departments have been staffed, as I noted earlier, by "reading specialists," typically housed outside of English departments. The creation of reading departments, separate from other areas of the curriculum, reproduced the state of affairs that had occurred at the four-year level: rendering reading as someone else's business. Faculty, outside of the Department of Reading, were disincentivized from giving explicit instruction in reading, with such instruction marginalized as developmental. Moreover, without such instruction, students at the community college inevitably struggle to read in a range of courses, prompting faculty outside of English to forego requiring the reading of challenging texts (*What Does It Really Mean to Be College and Work Ready?* 2).

Pressures to meet international reading standards and the Common Core State Standards for English Language Arts and the well-documented failure of developmental students to complete their goals at the community college have prompted a reexamination of developmental instruction at community colleges (Bailey).

Some community colleges, such as Chaffee College in California, have sought to reintegrate reading instruction within the curriculum and to provide academic support for such reintegration (Grubb and Gabriner 135).

Preparing to Read in First-Year Composition

As I consider the role of reading in my FYC course, the question is not whether to apportion imaginative and informational texts. Rather, the question is, What theories of writing and reading help shape reading selection? Much of this is likely self-evident: If I structure my writing course by way of genre—as I do—then students will be asked to read from a cross section of genres such as profiles, memoirs, trend analyses, and so on. At the same time, students will be producing examples of those genres—in my course, students compose profiles, proposals, annotated bibliographies, and trend analyses. But of course such decisions don't get at *how* students are supposed to read these texts, nor do they get at the essential nature of the texts themselves (rather than their formal characteristics).

Genre theory, crudely applied, would seem to provide a fairly straightforward way of reading: identify the distinguishing characteristics of a genre and allow their deployment to guide students in their reading. For example, students might be prompted when reading a proposal that addresses a community-based problem to look for a fully developed and appropriate solution, or an analysis of costs and benefits. I will admit that for my community college students, such an explicit and grounded approach in the formal features of a text has its advantages. But a more nuanced genre approach to reading (and writing) would see the text as fluid, formed and reformed as it performs certain activities within discursive communities and as a product of readers' sensibilities. Students might then be encouraged to read for difficulty or discrepancies (Salvatori and Donahue *Elements*). They might also be encouraged to monitor their own reading processes and thus engender a deeply metacognitive frame of mind (Tinberg 75).

Bringing Up the Subject of Reading: "Is Google Making Us Stupid?"

To encourage such reflection, I ask my students early in the semester to think about reading and writing in the digital age and at the same time show me how well they read and write with published sources. Students read two excerpted works, Al Gore's "How the Internet Is Changing the Way We Think" and Nicholas Carr's "Is Google Making Us Stupid? What the Internet Is Doing to Our Brains." Like the computer, Hal, in the film *2001: A Space Odyssey*, Carr asserts, "[M]y mind is going," as he speculates that his attention span while reading has diminished. While less polemical and certainly more in awe of what the Web's "World Brain" might enable us to accomplish, Gore's essay does suggest, as does Carr's, that some rewiring of our brain may be occurring due to our addictive reliance on the Web. Both authors foreground the reception of knowledge in the Google Age, principally through reading done via the Web. These are hardly informational texts, but they are texts that build on anecdotal and research evidence to pose speculative questions.

The prompt for the assignment begins with a generalization about time spent (my own and students') online but quickly turns to scholarly commentary on the impact of those experiences on reading and thinking—commentary that most students likely would not have encountered:

> How do you see the impact of online work on the way we read and think? In a clear, thoughtful, multi-paragraph, and well-organized essay, I'd like you to discuss this trend and its impact. To do so, I am requiring you to draw upon the two articles, given below, both from *The Atlantic*, both excerpts.

Anticipating that some students will have difficulty organizing their response, I suggest the following structure, with leading questions:

- ◆ State the trend (What is it? Who is affected?).

- ◆ Describe the evidence that shows the trend's existence (How do we know this is happening?).

◆ Analyze significant causes of the trend (Why now? What has brought the trend about?).

◆ Analyze significant effects of the trend (How is the trend changing us, specifically, changing the way we think, read, and work?).

◆ Reflect on the importance of this trend over time (Why does all this matter?).

I intend students to move from retrieval of information to analysis and then to reflection: a tall order indeed.

Not surprisingly, one student offers, in Rebecca Howard's term, *patchwriting* (with direct quotations highlighted by me in bold but not punctuated as a quotation by the student):

HOW THE INTERNET IS CHANGING THE WAY WE THINK

I call it the internet, some may call it surfing the web. There is an estimated 500 million people in the world that go on at least once per day. Whether its playing online games, checking emails, shopping, etc. 55 percent in the U.S and 60 percent in the U.K are estimated to be women.

The human memory has always been affected by each new advance technology. **Psychological studies have shown that when people are asked to remember a list of facts** in advance, they are not able to remember the list because they can retrieve it on the internet. As things progress technology is becoming more advance, and we can't stop the way of the future. Human beings that have designed all these supercomputers, software and internet mobile devices. **It is beginning to reshape the way we think in ways both trivial and profound.** . . . [sic]

The student continues in the same mode over the next two (and final) paragraphs, showing little evidence of real engagement with either reading (indeed, the student does not draw from the Carr essay at all). The fact that the student uses Gore's title for her own without quotation marks indicates from the start that the student will vacate her own piece, as turns out to be the case. I do not blame the student here: after all, this early assignment is designed to show me where the students are as writers. And this student's writing indicates a lack of confidence in her own abilities as a reader and as a writer.

Reading without Reaching for Certainty or Closure

While not explicitly stated, a key goal in my FYC course is for students to become strategic and self-aware as readers. When reading our textbook, students respond to the following prompts:

1. Please indicate, and elaborate on, three important points made in the week's reading. Please try to use your own words rather than the textbook authors'.

2. Please describe an idea learned from the reading that seems new or unusual or difficult to you. Again, try to use your own words.

3. Please indicate two questions that you have about the reading. There are always questions to ask.

As I reflect on these prompts, I see that I am guided by the following, although unstated, assumptions:

♦ Using "one's own words" when restating accurately what one has read signals genuine engagement with the reading.

♦ Reading well requires an ability to be selective and judicious.

♦ Readers approach a particular text in conversation with other texts previously read.

♦ Dissonance or difficulty that results from texts in conversation may yield new understandings and promote metacognition in readers as they become aware of what "old" understandings they bring to readings.

♦ Reading well does not necessarily translate to closure but in fact is likely to raise questions and to lead to additional reading of other texts.

♦ A text may resist such closure and present meaning that is unstable.

I suspect that I give students the impression, through what Thomas Newkirk calls "our prepared certainty," that reading is effortless, and that if difficulty arises the problem is with the reader (Newkirk 135). Perhaps it is impractical or, indeed, disingenuous to claim to be a novice reader myself, but I can take the time in class to model reading of difficult texts. I might, for example, highlight the title and lede of a profile provided in our textbook—a sample that we discuss in class before students prepare to research and write a profile of their own:

> **The Top Drill Instructor in Boot Camp 101**
> THE BULLWHIP lay on the bookcase, coiled around its wooden handle like a snake around its rattle (Falla in Blau and Burak 193).

Luckily, I often have vets in my classes who can provide a very useful gloss on what boot camp is all about and can also attest to what drill instructors do (many can quote favorite sayings of those instructors). But, of course, the title and the lede present questions that I might raise in class: What comparison is being set up between "boot camp" and "101"? What is a bullwhip doing on a bookcase and why is that detail the first that we see in this profile? A lede, I may remind students, is not a thesis paragraph—a lede does not have to present us with the Big Picture from the get-go but rather can engage our curiosity. The author, in other words, chooses to withhold information from the reader at the start. Difficulty is built in. Readers, if they are to engage the profile to come, must restrain a need to know everything there is to know from the start and be content with uncertainty. Eventually, with readers' help, the author will fill in the gaps, showing us a complex profile of a teacher who challenges and is devoted to his students.

Reading Rhetorically

Students spend a significant amount of their time in the course reading classmates' drafts, either in small groups of two or three or as part of the whole classroom focused on reading and discussing sample works in progress. Crucially, such reading—especially peer review in small groups—needs to be seen as formative, for both the reader and the author of the draft: in other words, the time spent reviewing the work needs to have a payoff for all concerned.

The reader needs to be able to obtain information—including a critical vocabulary about what makes writing "work"—useful for this peer review but also for his or her own draft; the author needs to be able to use reader feedback to improve the draft. All need to benefit. But another principle is at work as well: effective peer review is deeply rhetorical; any reading of another's draft needs to take into consideration the situation that produced the draft and the criteria and set of expectations that helped shape the writing. Hence the first question I ask reviewers to answer in writing is the following:

1. In your own words, fully and with precision, describe what the assignment is asking the writer (your partner) to do. Please use your own words rather than merely quote from the assignment.

Reading, like writing, relies on context, here the assignment itself. Sure, readers can apply what they've learned elsewhere about technically sound, good, clear writing and bring that to a variety of texts to be read. But such reading needs to be cognizant of the criteria the writer intends to meet for this particular situation.

Of course, reviewers need to be able to discern these elements (which I refer to as a "checklist") in order to engage effectively in peer review. The reviewer must demonstrate application of those criteria when analyzing what works well in the piece and what needs attention—and bring textual evidence in support:

1. To what extent has your partner met the expectations of the assignment? **Please pick a passage as illustration** and describe what works well there, **referring to the assignment checklist.**

2. What area needs more work? Why? **Please pick a passage as illustration** and describe what isn't working, **referring to the assignment checklist.**

Peer review rests on the assumption that reading is a shared expertise rather than one owned by the teacher exclusively. Students need to see its validity as they themselves acquire a working, critical vocabulary as readers and writers.

Talking Back to Teacher Commentary

In any writing course, a key reading text is teacher commentary. If teachers intend their commentary to have a formative rather than merely a summative purpose—if teachers wish their comments to have a practical impact on drafts in progress rather than simply provide an after-grade assessment—it becomes terribly important that students read those comments with understanding. I think it also important that teacher commentary be part of ongoing conversation with students about writing, rather than the Last Word. Student post their first two drafts of each formal assignment on blogs. A peer partner comments in writing on the writer's blog to the first draft. I comment on the second draft. When I have responded, students are then required to address in writing the following prompts or Talk Back, an exercise adapted from Kathleen Yancey (37):

1. Please summarize my comments.

2. Please answer: Do you feel that I have missed something that should have been addressed? Is there something you think worked well but that I didn't comment on, or are you unsure about how well something worked in your paper that you would like clarification about? Please explain.

3. Please answer: Do you feel that you can take something of what you've learned from this assignment and transfer that lesson to other writing in this class or elsewhere? Please explain precisely what that transferable element might be.

In asking these questions, I'm attempting not only to engage in dialogue with my students about their writing but also to promote student agency as reader and writer and to offer a view of reading that is deeply rhetorical and resisting closure. I'd like to see students own their writing by demonstrating an awareness of something that I've missed in their work and by achieving some sense of metacognition and becoming what Rebecca Nowacek refers to as "agents of integration": knowing what they have learned and taking that knowledge for application in another writing task (Nowacek 35).

Alas, students often rush to reply without taking the time to summarize my comments or even to address particular suggestions, as we can see in this exchange between me and a student regarding a profile of a man attempting to recover from a terrible accident on the job:

Teacher Commentary

Your title is certainly appropriate for what follows. And you describe the accident in some detail. But until the last sentence you don't really provide an interpretive thesis, which itself should be part of a *nut graf*. In other words, what is the Big Idea or interpretation that you wish your readers to take from this profile? It simply reads like an account of an accident. What are we to do with it?

Here's what I suggest. Ask your subject whether he has had an experience of triumph or accomplishment since the accident—something that he is proud of. Have him give you a particular accounting. And select quotations that suggest his resilience.

Student Talk Back

Hello professor, you are right[.] [A]fter reading it again I noticed the mistakes. Thank you for your input that will help me for next time.

After such a terse response, can I with any certainty assume an understanding between me and the student as to what needs to be done? I think not. Can I assume that the student is ready to assume control or agency over her writing? No. The deference to the Expert Reader (the teacher, who is always right) couldn't be clearer, as is the emphasis on the "mistakes," suggesting the student's lack of confidence. Yet I also see that in referencing the fixed qualities of the profile, I am leading the student to view the genre as one whose meaning is defined by its formal qualities, and, of course, I am inculcating a few of the "teacher as the arbiter of a text's meaning" tropes. In these respects, the student's near silence is almost predictable.

A more substantive exchange occurs here, between me and another student, regarding the profile of a retired coast guard officer:

Teacher Commentary

The writing here is confident, fluent, and patiently descriptive. Nice. And your subject is engaging and honest (almost self-effacing). Correct me if I am wrong but the Big Idea here (judging by your title) is that he found himself and his vocation almost by accident. I wonder, though, if as interpreter you might add this important element: that his character elements include persistence and humility. In other words, he earned the success that finally found his way.

A less significant piece to consider is perhaps a reference to what he did after retirement (seven years just doesn't seem like a long time to me). All in all, I'm impressed by the control that you show here.

Student Talk Back

My summary of your comments:
—You like the way I've written.
—You asked about my interpretive thesis. You aren't wrong in your assumption.
—You suggested that I add information about the subject's persistence and humility in order to highlight the fact that he earned what he acquired.
—Also, you suggested that I add some information about what he did after he resigned.

My biggest concern after writing my second draft of this paper was that the flow of the paragraphs was a little awkward and choppy. It didn't feel like it was incredibly smooth reading. I don't know if you picked up on that at all or if you have any suggestions for how I could make it better.

I think the biggest thing I learned from writing this paper was the importance of finding a focus. Because it was not a biography, it was important to find first the lens through which I would make the readers see the subject's life (which is the thesis) and then pick events that would emphasize that lens, instead of summarizing the most important events of the person's life.

Interestingly and tellingly, the student spends very little time recasting what I had liked about the draft: the confidence, fluency and patient description, an engaging subject. Clearly, for this student and likely for most, a teacher's response is read as geared at what isn't working. That said, I can hardly complain about the remainder of the Talk Back. I was especially pleased to see that the student had picked up on her role as interpreter rather than mere chronicler of her subject's life. The use of the lens metaphor and its application for transfer, while not fully developed, do show a promising self-awareness or mindfulness.

How to Read (and Write with) a Scholarly Article

Like many faculty who teach first-year comp, I consider it important to prepare students for reading and writing with academic or scholarly texts while also preparing them more broadly for the literacy demands that await them. The challenge is that while many FYC students may have used academic databases, few have taken on the challenge of working with bona fide scholarly, peer-reviewed sources.

Prepared by the early semester diagnostic, I require that students engage in a causal analysis of a trend, drawing on two peer-reviewed articles obtained through electronic databases. The assignment is broken down into a two-part sequence. First, students are required to produce a mini-literature review of a single peer-reviewed article focusing on a trend as defined by our textbook. That review should consist of two paragraphs, one a summary of key points in the article, the other an evaluation. I ask students to consider in their evaluations such matters as timeliness of the article, intended audience, and nature and quality of evidence.

For the second part of the assignment, students write a causal analysis of the trend, making sure to identify the trend, provide evidence of that trend's existence (including visual texts), and supply an analysis of causes and effects of the trend.

As I learned during the diagnostic exercise, my students carry varied levels of confidence in working with challenging sources. Now, while I spend a good deal of time in class discussing the mechanics of documenting sources—using signal phrasing, for example, to indicate indebtedness to a source and, of course, using in-text citation in proper bibliographic format—I spend precious little time showing students how actually to read a scholarly essay and how to write with such a source. Over the years, I have called on colleagues from library services to come to class to show students how to conduct a search of the databases. But I have never asked those colleagues to assist in showing students how to engage with scholarly work. I decided it was time to do so.

The colleagues, Michelle Chiles and Emily Brown, began by letting students in on what a scholarly article—in this case, an article on the connection between social media and youths' civic engagement—looks like (Figure 13.1). The titles of academic articles, Chiles and Brown noted, often have limiting subtitles to help focus readers. Moreover, many academics—more commonly in some disciplines than in others—work collaboratively, hence the dual authorship in this example. Another common feature of the scholarly article is the abstract, the purpose of which is to give a preview of what is to come. Experienced readers expect the abstract to provide the research question, the methods used, key findings, and significant implications.

Scholarly articles, Chiles and Brown continued, often provide a literature review early on (Figure 13.2). Reading a literature review, they asserted, carries certain expectations as well, primarily that the authors will reveal current scholarship on the subject so as to position their own work in relation to what has come before. But how do scholars actually do this? Authors demonstrate an ability to synthesize materials. Scholars often group prior research, establishing themes or subtopics, as we see in the example in Figure 13.3. Again, readers bring certain expectations

FIGURE 13.1. *The opening page of a scholarly article accessed through an online database (Chiles and Brown).*

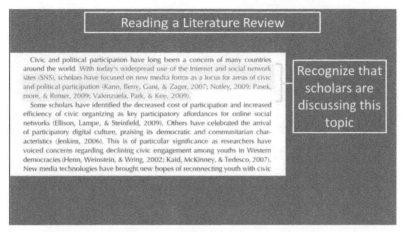

FIGURE **13.2.** *The literature review portion of a scholarly article (Chiles and Brown).*

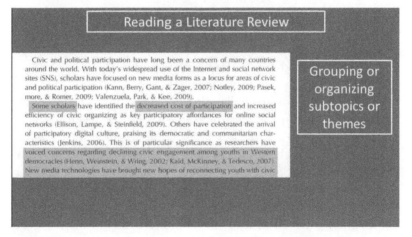

FIGURE **13.3.** *Evidence of synthesis in a scholarly article (Chiles and Brown).*

to a literature review, one of which is that the authors constructing the review will organize prior research in a clear and logical manner. Obviously, we see the convergence of reading and writing here: readers' expectations of synthesis and the writers' methods of grouping sources by similarity. But scholars may also point out differences among the research, as we see in Figure 13.4.

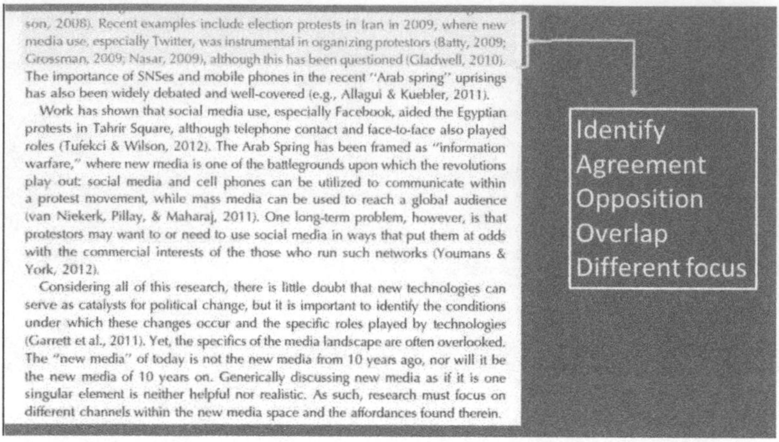

son, 2008). Recent examples include election protests in Iran in 2009, where new media use, especially Twitter, was instrumental in organizing protestors (Batty, 2009; Grossman, 2009; Nasar, 2009), although this has been questioned (Gladwell, 2010). The importance of SNSes and mobile phones in the recent "Arab spring" uprisings has also been widely debated and well-covered (e.g., Allagui & Kuebler, 2011).

Work has shown that social media use, especially Facebook, aided the Egyptian protests in Tahrir Square, although telephone contact and face-to-face also played roles (Tufekci & Wilson, 2012). The Arab Spring has been framed as "information warfare," where new media is one of the battlegrounds upon which the revolutions play out: social media and cell phones can be utilized to communicate within a protest movement, while mass media can be used to reach a global audience (van Niekerk, Pillay, & Maharaj, 2011). One long-term problem, however, is that protestors may want to or need to use social media in ways that put them at odds with the commercial interests of the those who run such networks (Youmans & York, 2012).

Considering all of this research, there is little doubt that new technologies can serve as catalysts for political change, but it is important to identify the conditions under which these changes occur and the specific roles played by technologies (Garrett et al., 2011). Yet, the specifics of the media landscape are often overlooked. The "new media" of today is not the new media from 10 years ago, nor will it be the new media of 10 years on. Generically discussing new media as if it is one singular element is neither helpful nor realistic. As such, research must focus on different channels within the new media space and the affordances found therein.

Identify
Agreement
Opposition
Overlap
Different focus

FIGURE 13.4. *Evidence of authors distinguishing their work from the work of other scholars (Chiles and Brown).*

Letting students in on the varied ways that scholars react to one another's work may demystify academic study and publications and provide models of behavior as students themselves engage in scholarly research and write up their findings.

But how might my students enact some of these behaviors in their own work with challenging sources? The key is making connections as they read from source to source (Figure 13.5). Students' ability to identify key ideas while reading is critical, allowing them to highlight and extract those ideas as they read. Now I have my students work with at least two scholarly sources for their causal analysis. What kind of organizing tool might they use to make the work of synthesizing sources clear and meaningful? Chiles and Brown come up with the matrix illustrated in Figure 13.6. By identifying key ideas in both readings and inserting those ideas in the left-hand column of this matrix, my students are guided in their reading of the sources to fill in the remainder of the matrix, visually demonstrating areas of agreement, opposition, and qualification, if the sources apply: *reading scholarly sources in a knowing way leads to writing effectively with those sources.*

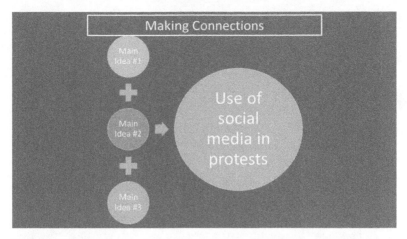

FIGURE **13.5.** *Student readers and writers must be able to make connections between their sources and between their sources and their own writing (Chiles and Brown).*

	SOURCE #1	SOURCE #2
Main Idea #1 Government control and censorship of mainstream media has caused protestors to look for alternative communication tools.	Singapore's government has consistently applied controls on traditional media outlets but has left social media outlets untouched and unregulated.	Online participation in political campaigns and issues was almost five times greater than traditional participation. Researchers concluded that this "could provide the participant with anonymity, in turn less vulnerability to political vengeance."
Main Idea #2 Younger generations find social media and mobile technology to be natural and easy way to communicate.	- *Not all sources will apply to ALL of your main ideas*	According to the survey conducted, 86% of students used their laptops for social media such as Facebook and Twitter.
Main Idea #3 An increase in the use of social media in protests does not necessarily mean a decrease in the use of traditional media outlets.	After studying the survey results, researchers found that "young protestors also had faith in traditional media, believing in its quality and credibility, despite their affinity for online media."	- *Quote* - *Statistics* - *Paraphrased information*

FIGURE **13.6.** *Matrix for synthesizing material from scholarly sources (Chiles and Brown).*

Recommendations for Teaching

Promoting effective reading practices requires time spent giving explicit instruction in reading. Toward that end, I make the following recommendations for my own improvement as a teacher of reading in a writing course:

◆ **Share with students my own experiences as a novice and as an experienced reader.**
We are all novices at one time or another. Posing these questions and sharing with students some of the answers might be helpful: What do I recall about reading scholarly work that was unfamiliar to me? How did I learn to become a better reader? How may I draw on my experience as a reader (and writer) of scholarly work to assist my students?

◆ **Provide students with a road map for reading, especially reading that is difficult.**
Take time in each assignment that involves using sources to articulate a process that will guide students through the reading. Just as I've long been converted to providing incremental steps in the writing process, so I should be similarly committed to reading as a pedagogically grounded process.

◆ **Make a case for the "pleasures" of difficult reading.**
Read a text that is difficult for me in front of my students. Unsettle my "prepared certainty" (Newkirk 135). Show them that all of us who are curious to learn experience the difficulty of the unfamiliar. Explain or provide a rationale for the benefits of difficulty.

◆ **Sing the praises of slow reading and re-reading.**
Debunk the current fetish with accelerated (and multitasked) reading. Show the benefits of reading slowly and of going back to re-read. When assigning reading, try not to pile on reading for the mere sake of apparent rigor: less is likely to be more if instructional scaffolding is provided and the real benefits to good, close, and slow reading are demonstrated.

◆ **Collaborate with colleagues from across the curriculum and in the workplace to find ways to demystify the reading process.**
All of us who are committed to education have a stake in reading instruction, regardless of grade level, institution, or department, whether in academe or in the workplace. I need to engage in conversations with colleagues about the challenges of reading (for themselves and their students or employees) and strategies

for assisting others to improve as readers. No one area "owns" reading: reading matters across contexts and demands special expertise depending on such contexts. I need to read outside my own area. I need to read with others.

Works Cited

Ahmad, Khalil, and Karim Sajjad Sheikh. "Social Media and Youth Participatory Politics: A Study of University Students." *A Research Journal of South Asian Studies* 28.2 (2013): 353–60. *Academic Search Premier*. Web. 20 Apr. 2015.

Bailey, Thomas. "Challenge and Opportunity: Rethinking the Role and Function of Developmental Education in Community College." Community College Research Center Working Paper No. 14. Nov. 2008. Web. 11 June 2015.

Bartholomae, David. "Writing with Teachers: A Conversation with Peter Elbow." *College Composition and Communication* 46.1 (1995): 62–71. Print.

Bartholomae, David, and Anthony Petrosky. *Facts, Artifacts, and Counterfacts: Theory and Method for a Reading and Writing Course.* Portsmouth: Boynton/Cook/Heinemann, 1986. Print.

———. *Ways of Reading: An Anthology for Writers.* 9th ed. Boston: Bedford/St. Martin's, 2010. Print.

Berthoff, Ann E. *Forming, Thinking, Writing: The Composing Imagination.* Rochelle Park, Hayden, 1978. Print.

Blau, Susan, and Kathryn Burak. *Writing in the Works.* 3rd ed. Belmont: Wadsworth, 2013. Print.

Carillo, Ellen C. *Securing a Place of Reading in Composition: The Importance of Teaching for Transfer.* Boulder: U of Colorado P, 2015. Kindle.

Carr, Nicholas. "Is Google Making Us Stupid? What the Internet Is Doing to Our Brains." *The Atlantic.* July/August 2008. Web. 11 June 2015.

Chiles, Michelle, and Emily Brown. "Literature Review." Bristol Community College. 2015. Unpublished *Power Point*.

Falla, Jack. "The Top Drill Instructor in Boot Camp 101." In Blau and Burak: 193–96. Print.

Gore, Al. "Al Gore on How the Internet Is Changing the Way We Think." *The Atlantic.* 25 Jan. 2013. Web. 11 June 2015.

Grubb, W. Norton, and Robert Gabriner. *Basic Skills Education in Community College: Inside and Outside of Classrooms.* New York: Routledge, 2013. Print.

Harkin, Patricia. "The Reception of Reader-Response Theory." *College Composition and Communication* 56.3 (2005): 410–25. Print.

Howard, Rebecca Moore. *Standing in the Shadow of Giants: Plagiarists, Authors, Collaborators.* Stamford: Ablex, 1999. Print.

Jolliffe, David. "Who Is Teaching Composition Students to Read and How Are They Doing It?" *Composition Studies* 31.1 (2003): 127–42. Print.

Lindemann, Erika, and Gary Tate. "Two Views on the Use of Literature in Composition." *College English* 55.3 (1993): 311–21. Print.

Newkirk, Thomas. *The Art of Slow Reading: Six Time-Honored Practices for Engagement.* Portsmouth: Heinemann, 2012. Print.

Nowacek, Rebecca S. *Agents of Integration: Understanding Transfer as a Rhetorical Act.* Carbondale: Southern Illinois UP, 2011. Print.

Salvatori, Mariolina. "Conversations with Texts: Reading in the Teaching of Composition." *College English* 58.4 (1996): 440–54. Print.

Salvatori, Mariolina, and Patricia Donahue. *The Elements (and Pleasures) of Difficulty.* New York: Pearson, 2008. Print.

———." What Is College English? Stories about Reading: Appearance, Disappearance, Morphing, and Revival." *College English* 75.2 (2012): 199–217. Print.

Tinberg, Howard. "Metacognition Is Not Cognition." *Naming What We Know: Threshold Concepts of Writing Studies.* Ed. Linda Adler-Kassner and Elizabeth Wardle. Logan: Utah State UP, 2015. 75–76. Print.

What Does It Really Mean to Be College and Career Ready? The English Literacy Required of First-Year Community College Students. A Report from the National Center for Education and the Economy. May 2013. Web. 11 June 2015.

Yancey, Kathleen Blake. *Reflection in the Writing Classroom.* Logan: Utah State UP, 1998. Print.

CHAPTER FOURTEEN

How the Teaching of Literature in College Writing Classes Might Rescue Reading as It Never Has Before

SHERIDAN BLAU

Teachers College, Columbia University

This chapter begins with an account of the failure of college literature instruction to teach students how to read challenging literary and nonliterary texts. It concludes, somewhat paradoxically, with a modest proposal for restoring an emphasis on the reading of literature as an essential part of the curriculum of first-year composition (FYC) classes. It claims, moreover, that the study of literary texts in FYC classes offers those courses the best possible opportunity to become sites for strengthening the capacity of college students to read deeply (see Patrick Sullivan's essay in this volume), critically, productively, and in a way that will advance their learning across all disciplines and will most surely strengthen their capacity as writers. I intend no satire by referring to my proposal as "modest," but do so to indicate that my proposal will not require a wholesale curricular change in most composition classes, since I am proposing that we define literature broadly to include texts from many disciplines. Nor am I standing up for the "good old cause" (with its largely deserved bad reputation and dubious history) and urging a radical or a reactionary return to the kinds of literature-based writing classes that were the norm for required first-year English classes in the middle of the last century and that persisted—in spite of emphatic and generally well-grounded objections in most precincts of the composition community—on some campuses into the decade of the 1990s. By 1992, it was authoritatively estimated (based on national survey data) that only one in five FYC programs in American colleges and universities still included the reading of literary texts (Tate 317).

Most modestly, perhaps, my proposal builds on the distinctive expertise of most professionally knowledgeable specialists in the teaching of writing and on teaching practices and pedagogically oriented research that have come to represent authoritative knowledge in the field of writing studies over the past forty-five years, at least since the great paradigm shift that moved writing pedagogy from a product-oriented to a process-oriented paradigm (Hairston). Moreover, my proposal is also built on recent cognitive and anthropological research that suggests that a focus on literature in first-year college writing classes will be most efficacious in preparing students for the kinds of complex and nuanced thinking they will be expected to engage in as readers and writers and participants in the discourse of their college classes (beyond their FYC course) across the disciplines, and most especially in the social sciences and humanities.

Reading and Literary Study

To provide a background for my proposal, then, and in anticipation of some well-founded suspicions of any such proposal, I offer a very brief account of the role of reading instruction (or its absence) in college English courses, and I begin with Northrop Frye's axiomatic claim of 1957 in the introduction to his classic and widely revered *Anatomy of Criticism* that "[t]he difficulty often felt in teaching literature arises from the fact that it cannot be done: the criticism of literature is all that can be directly taught" (11). To understand the logic and significance of this statement, we can turn to an earlier statement of Frye's in a 1954 essay in which he insists that

> [e]very genuine response to art . . . must begin . . . in a complete surrender of the mind and senses to . . . the work of art as a whole. This occupies the same place in criticism that observation, the direct exposure of the mind to nature, has in the scientific method. ("Levels" 248)

In other words, it is through the surrender of the mind and senses to a work of literature that the work of literature is experienced, and it is that direct experience of a literary work that teaches its reader the work of art that is the literary text. That experience cannot be taught because it must be lived through, and it can only be lived through by means of the act of reading (or listening to) the literary work itself. But that act of surrender to a text, an act performed through the quality of a reader's attention and engagement in the act of reading, was for Frye outside the concern of the discipline of literary study or the business of a professor of English, occupying "the same place in criticism that observation, the direct exposure of the mind to nature, has in the scientific method." Yet anyone engaged in teaching literature at almost any level of schooling knows that the experience of the literary text itself, which Frye takes for granted as an unproblematic and necessary precondition for instruction in literary criticism, may in fact be the most troubled and problematic transaction of the entire domain that defines the learning and teaching of literature.

Frye's error, of course (though it may not have been much of an error in the context in which he taught), was to think of reading as nonproblematic, but he naturally thought that way because, like most literary theorists, he wasn't thinking about actual readers or the learning experience of a range of typical college students in actual classrooms. The readers he thought about were theoretical and ideal readers like himself and the literary scholars and prospective scholars for whom he wrote. But in treating reading as nonproblematic, Frye ignores the possibility of trying to build a critical discourse on shaky and unreliable foundations and on an enterprise of teaching that addresses readers whose experience of the work of art under discussion may not be answerable at all to the discourse of criticism that putatively gives meaning to that experience.

I have chosen Frye's statement excluding reading from the province of teaching as the starting point for my account of the fate of reading in literary instruction not for its originality or even for its powerful influence on subsequent generations of English professors, but because it is the first and most authoritative statement I am aware of to describe and attempt to explain the reasoning behind what has always been and remains standard practice in teaching literature in college. That is to say, it represents a version (a more conscious one, no doubt) of the way literature appears to have been taught—with virtually no attention to the problem of reading it—by professors who were charged with the teaching of literature from the time literature first became a subject worthy of study in colleges and universities (and even in secondary schools). That history, described authoritatively by Gerald Graff in his now classic study, *Professing Literature*, reveals that the discipline of reading literature has never been regarded as a teachable or a necessary component in courses devoted to literary study, except when reading itself was an oral exercise designed to teach not literature but elocution. Otherwise, literature was itself commodified as an instrument for teaching grammar or rhetoric, until the twentieth century, when it began to be taught as criticism, which is to say the discourse that takes place after the reading of literature and that represents a reflection on the sources and antecedents and cultural models for the literary text and its language and images (the philological tradition of criticism), or on the technical features of the literary text (the New Criticism or formalist criticism). Alternatively, criticism became a way of reading in the service of a commanding discourse or project whereby the text is interpreted to uncover the cultural, ideological, historical, psychological, or political structures and meanings that may be ascribed to or inscribed in it.

Literary Teaching vs. Student Learning: True and False Knowledge

As I have already suggested, however, the problem with any philosophy or method of literary criticism that governs what is taught about the texts that are ostensibly at the center of attention in literature classes is that the critical discourse is predicated on the assumption that the act or process of reading literature is nonproblematic and that the students who are in the classrooms of teachers like Northrup Frye have had for themselves a valid and reliable experience of the literary work that their professors hope to illuminate through a critical or interpretive discourse. But, if the process of reading literature is itself as problematic as it appears to be (and may always have been, as I. A. Richards surely suggests) for a substantial portion of the population of college students in at least their first two years of college, then the literary work of art to which students are asked to submit themselves as readers will not itself be available to teach those readers, but instead some truncated or incoherent and unreliable version of it that cannot be trusted to do anything like valid or valued teaching. And that means that the interpretive or critical discourse about the literary work that is taught to students by their professors (even if the students happen to understand the discourse conceptually) will not interpret or illuminate the text the students have themselves experienced, and for that reason will be more mystifying than illuminating for the students who are expected to learn from it and may even believe they *have* learned from it.

To explain how and why this is so let me describe the substance and the pattern of instruction in literature classes that I have witnessed (in dozens of actual college classrooms and on scores of videotapes of "excellent" teachers), a pattern experienced by most student readers and confirmed by multiple research studies over the past quarter-century of empirical research on the discourse of literature classes in secondary and college classrooms (Marshall; Zancanella; Huber; Nystrand; Bonk). What typically transpires in college literature classes (including those at the first-year and sophomore levels) where complex texts are assigned is for the instructor to present a lecture or perhaps conduct a class "discussion" (in which the teacher does most of the talking and questioning and students give brief recitational responses) designed to lead students to what the instructor understands to represent the standard or correct or authoritative reading (which is to say "interpretation") of the text he or she is teaching. In this way, the instructor meets the responsibility to "teach" the literary works that are central to the curriculum of the course, essentially by following the call by Frye for instruction that is directed to teaching not literature itself but the criticism (usually the interpretation) of literature. What I have just described as typical literature instruction would probably be taken by most school leaders and English department chairs in high schools and colleges across the United States (at least until very recently) as an utterly conventional and accurate description of the job of a proper English teacher (see Huber).

Just as important, that description undoubtedly represents what first-year English instructors (including TAs, contingent faculty, and tenure-track professors) saw as their responsibility as teachers of the literature that was used to generate topics for writing in typical first-year English classes during the six or more decades (Berlin) that preceded the substitution of readings across the curriculum for canonical literary texts in first-year English courses in most US colleges and universities. And it continued to be the pattern for many teachers and college composition programs, even after the decade of the eighties when the teaching of composition had become professionalized and connected to its own research base, yielding the process-oriented instructional emphasis that emerged from that research. With that shift in composition pedagogy, however, the field of English studies more broadly conceived became what Judith Langer referred to as a "schizophrenic" (2) discipline in which writing was taught as a process but literature continued to be taught as a body of fixed knowledge (or authoritative interpretations and literary facts) that responsible teachers were expected to transmit directly to their students. Hence Erika Lindemann, one of the most influential writers of the founding generation of modern composition scholars, could assert in 1993 that virtually nothing that might be taught by a teacher of literature to students in a writing course could be of any value to a student as a human being or to a student's capacity to participate in the literate practices of a college or university. That view, which by the decade of the 1990s was not an unusual one among specialists in composition, may not have been an unfair characterization of typical practice in the teaching of literature, but it reveals a typically limited academic imagination (based no doubt on considerable experience) about how literature might be taught with attention to what students are actually learning.

The problem with teaching literature—or, more precisely, teaching criticism or correct interpretations of literature—is that insofar as instructors teach interpretations to students, they are not enabling those students to learn either how to acquire a valid and accurate experience of a literary text or how to produce such interpretations for themselves. What students learn from their instructors' expertise (when instructors are true experts) is that instructors can produce persuasive and comprehensive readings or interpretations of the texts being studied and that the students themselves can't do it. Which means that from the model of instruction I have described, students are not likely to learn either literature or criticism.

What then do they learn, aside from the false idea that they lack the capacity to produce interpretations on their own? What kind of knowledge do they actually acquire? The answer is either that they acquire no knowledge that counts as knowledge or that they acquire what we can call "false knowledge." Or both. Their knowledge is false insofar as they have learned falsely that they are unable to produce valid interpretations on their own, but (not having had a valid and reliable experience of the text they presumably read) their knowledge is also false in the sense that what they have learned is not what they know for themselves but what they know only by virtue of its having been told to them by their professor. Such knowledge—knowledge that is known by virtue of its having been told to you—is not generally considered reliable or valid knowledge in a court of law and is said to have no evidentiary value since it is not your knowledge at all, but hearsay, borrowed knowledge, unearned knowledge based merely on what somebody else has told you. At best, students might be able to claim they have learned a set of statements they might employ to represent the meaning their instructor attributes to a text. Some students may actually believe they know the meaning of the text, having been taught a meaning by their instructor, and for a very small number this might be true.

But for the majority of students, including most of the graduating college English majors I have interviewed over the years, what they hold as their knowledge of texts they studied in literature courses consists largely of words borrowed from their teachers, words understood so superficially that what these students regard as their knowledge cannot sustain any serious challenge or interrogation by any other reader who is having trouble trying to achieve the same reading. No wonder many English majors who become secondary English teachers feel fraudulent in their early years of teaching and fearful of teaching any text they haven't been taught or for which they don't have a teacher's edition with a script dictating what they should be telling their students about the assigned literary work (Purves 350).

The Alternative Tradition: Louise Rosenblatt and English Education

Ironically, for much of the modern history of the teaching of literature in colleges and universities, while professors of literature paid no attention to how students were reading literary texts and while internecine battles were being waged in departments of English over the most intellectually valid or most illuminating approach to interpreting canonical and modern literary texts, an alternative approach to the teaching of literature and to the reading of literature was being articulated and tested in classrooms by specialists in the field of English education, guided by the writing and spirit of Louise Rosenblatt, the acknowledged matriarch of the field of English education as a distinct academic field for theory, research, and instruction. In her 1938 book, *Literature as Exploration*, Rosenblatt, unlike other critics of her time or any of the mainstream critical schools before or since her time, paid close attention to real readers (including student readers) rather than theoretical ones and to the actual experience of those readers as persons. Most important for literary pedagogy, Rosenblatt focused her attention as a theorist and teacher on the emerging and continually self-correcting, text-attentive, and response-attentive character of the reader's process in a "transactional," mutually informing relationship with a text, as the reader, guided by the text and by the reader's emotional and cognitive experience of the text, construed, constructed, and experienced the text as a literary work of art.

Unfortunately, for almost sixty years after the publication of her foundational book, Rosenblatt had virtually no impact on critical discourse, and her work was ignored by the professoriate in college and university English departments and by the entire academic literary community as represented by the membership of the Modern Language Association (MLA), the principal professional association of college and university teachers of literature. The reasons for such "ignorance" (a word derived from the same root as "ignore") derive almost certainly from the fact that Rosenblatt's book places itself outside the privileged and prestigious arena of professorial literary discourse by focusing on the experience of real readers, including student readers in classrooms, and seems directed to an audience that includes classroom teachers as well as scholars. Such elitism or snobbishness was almost acknowledged in 1995 when MLA published a propitiatory edition of Rosenblatt's 1938 book with a foreword by Wayne Booth in which he apologizes on behalf of his MLA colleagues and acknowledges Rosenblatt's unprecedented intellectual achievement through her entirely original contributions to literary theory and her transformational influence on teaching practice. Yet, in spite of Booth's sensitive and appreciative foreword, there is no evidence that MLA's decision to issue its own edition of her work actually marked any sea change in the pattern of literature instruction in most university departments of English at that time or since. In the meantime, three generations of Rosenblatt's intellectual heirs, who have populated the field of English education since the 1940s and most especially those of her disciples who knew her and worked with her in her later years, have continued to carry on her work, extending, refining, and even proposing revisions to her transactional theory of reading to produce a substantial body of professional literature in the field of English education that has transformed the teaching of literature and the teaching of reading in many secondary schools and in a number of college classrooms.

The most theoretically influential and pedagogically powerful publications from this group of scholars tend to share (1) a commitment to Rosenblatt's emphasis on the reading of literature as an opportunity to undergo an experience in which the reader participates affectively as well as cognitively; (2) an emphasis on reading as a process that resembles writing (see Salvatori) in its construction and revision of a meaning that might be attached to the literary experience; (3) a belief in the intellectual value of discussion and small-group conversation to explore and revise a reader's sense of a text and its possible significance; (4) a belief in the power of writing to explore, test, refine, and revise a reader's thinking about textual meaning; (5) a respect for multiple possibilities in interpreting texts and for the provisionality of every interpretation; (6) a belief in the power of questions and problems and even confusion as a driver of learning through the reading process; (7) a conviction in the capacity of all students to have a productive learning experience through reading; and (8) a suspicion of traditional approaches to literary instruction as the source of student insecurities and defeatist behaviors that must be corrected through therapeutic pedagogical practices (see, e.g., C. Smith; Probst; Pradl; Salvatori and Donahue; Nystrand; Hynds; and Blau). These authors and teachers differ in the degree to which they emphasize such pedagogical practices, as they do in the ways they interpret, extend, and adapt the logic and principles of Rosenblatt's transactional theory, but their practices and the rationales they provide usually reveal their intellectual genealogy (as may be seen in several chapters in this volume) even when they don't self-identify with the Rosenblatt lineage.

Background for a Modest Proposal

I have taken pains to trace the history of college literature instruction and its troubled relationship with English education to make the case that the scholars and English departments charged with the teaching of literature in college have been generally inhospitable (for reasons based on disciplinary norms and values) to the idea of teaching students to be competent, disciplined, autonomous readers of literary texts, and have thereby rendered the teaching of literature for many students an avenue for teaching sham knowledge that is experienced by those students as largely meaningless and disconnected from anything they actually know for themselves. That kind of experience of learning literature has discredited the teaching of literature for a large percentage of college graduates (as is evident from reports of the strong prejudice against literature instruction in discussions of the Common Core State Standards (CCSS) by school administrators and policymakers across the country) and was very likely at least partly responsible for the decision of college curriculum committees and composition program administrators to remove literature as the subject of writing in required FYC classes in most colleges and universities near the end of the last century, when what was needed was attention to reading for understanding and writing to consolidate and communicate knowledge in many disciplines.

But I have also taken pains to describe the alternative tradition of teaching literature that has long prevailed in the field of English education (and surely by now has some proponents among the literary scholars in most professionally active departments of English), a tradition that derives largely from the extraordinary theoretical work of Rosenblatt, who for three-quarters of a century (even beyond her death at age 100 in 2005) has served as the presiding genius for the field of English education with respect to the teaching of literature and reading. Practitioners in the field of English education, however, tend not to teach undergraduate literature courses. Instead they teach preservice and inservice teacher education courses and therefore have been able to have a modest salutary influence on the teaching of literature in secondary schools, but much less influence on the teaching of literature in higher education.

Which brings me to the present moment, when deans and faculty members in various disciplines in many colleges and universities (in a movement reminiscent of the persistent demand articulated by faculty in past years for more effective FYC instruction) are demanding that steps be taken by their institutions to address what they regard as an urgent need to ensure that students in the first year of college learn to function as more insightful and versatile readers than they appear to be when they show up in introductory and advanced college courses across the curriculum. And the logical and most economical place to look for instruction that might ensure such development is in the FYC courses that are typically required of all entering students at most colleges and universities. That it is also pedagogically and intellectually appropriate for teachers of writing to give serious attention to helping their students become stronger readers seems fairly obvious. Most college writing is about ideas and theories and information that students have read in assigned or selected texts. Hence the efficacy of their written discourse depends largely on the quality of their reading of the texts they are writing about or drawing on. Just as important, though perhaps less obvious, insofar as writing is largely a process of revision, entailing a recursive, layered, and self-correcting discovery and refinement of the writer's own meaning, a writer's capacity to discover meaning with precision and clarity is a function of the writer's capacity to read his or her own drafts in progress accurately and insightfully.

Why Read Literature in the Writing Classroom?

Why then should literary texts be not merely included but favored and made the focus of much of the assigned reading for instruction in reading as well as in writing in required first-year college writing courses? First, let me observe that the body of texts that might be selected under the heading of literature would include works that represent not only a number of intellectual and academic disciplines, but those that also, by virtue of their identification as literature, belong not merely to the English department or the field of literary studies or even writing studies, but to all intellectual and academic disciplines at once as the common possession of the wider culture, or at least of the culture that is shared by educated persons. Culturally important classic works such as the novels of Henry Fielding or Ernest Hemingway or Toni Morrison or William Faulkner or Ralph Ellison or Leo Tolstoy, or the short stories of Anton Chekov or William Saroyan or Alice Walker or Flannery O'Connor, or the poems of Langston Hughes or John Donne or Robert Frost or Gwendolyn Brooks, or the autobiographical writing of Benjamin Franklin or Saint Augustine or Malcolm X cannot be said to belong exclusively or even primarily to the discipline of literary studies or exclusively to the particular culture or time from which they emerged. They are cultural resources available to all potential readers both in and beyond the cultural contexts of their production.

And we can probably say something similar about works identified as classics of fields such as economics or political science or psychology or sociology or science: works such as Machiavelli's *The Prince,* Weber's *The Protestant Ethic and the Spirit of Capitalism*, Freud's *Civilization and Its Discontents,* or Freire's *Pedagogy of the Oppressed*. These are texts of broad cultural interest with an appeal to an audience far broader than academic specialists. They are therefore available to become part of the discourse of any educated person and not the exclusive cultural capital of the specialized disciplines within which they were produced. Moreover, what is true of classic intellectual and artistic productions is equally if not more true of contemporary works of fiction and poetry and nonfiction that may have a broader and more popular cultural importance currently and locally. Books by the distinguished cognitive psychologist Steven Pinker come immediately to mind as examples, as do the books and articles by the late neurologist Oliver Sacks, not to mention the novels of Junot Díaz or the stories of Amy Tan, Gary Soto, or Sandra Cisneros or the poems of Maya Angelou or Naomi Shihab Nye. Even texts representing the most advanced literary research—like Stephen Greenblatt's *The Swerve,* which won the most prestigious award for criticism given by MLA yet gained an enormous readership in the United States and England—can be said to belong to the broader cross-disciplinary culture of the educated public as much as they do to the discourse of literary criticism.

Second, I think a good case can be made that written works likely to be identified as literature are also works that can stand as models of the best writing and thinking in their various genres and are therefore the most appropriate of all texts to be assigned for reading in a course devoted to the improvement of writing. For that same reason, of course, they are also the works most likely to reward deep and careful, and repeated, reading. In fact, the best test I can think of as a measure of the quality of writing is the capacity of any written work to retain and to grow in the value attributed to it by its readers as they read and interrogate it with increasingly intense and critical attention. Moreover, since the best writing most rewards the best reading, which is to say the reading that is deepest, most thoughtful, most attentive, most metacognitively conscious, and most persistent in the face of difficulties, these also are the very texts that will provide students with the most rewarding and fruitful opportunities to develop the dispositions and habits of mind (a capacity for close concentrated attention, tolerance for ambiguity, willingness to suspend closure, metacognitive awareness, and so on) that Rosenblatt implicitly identified and that have been explicitly identified through more recent research and theory (California Intersegmental Committee;

Blau 208–14; Sullivan this volume) characterizing the reading performance of strong college readers.

As we consider the case for rehabilitating literary reading in the writing class, we must not forget about the value of pleasure and joy in fostering learning (M. Smith). We need to acknowledge that the compelling narratives and memorable characters and emotionally charged experiences that good literature offers to its readers substantially increase the likelihood that student readers will enjoy such reading and engage in it without having to force themselves to pay attention to it, as they must all too often in reading more specialized disciplinary writing in which they have little interest and less personal connection.

The Misguided Case against Literature for Students Preparing for Advanced College Reading

The counterargument that college students and college prep students need to learn to engage themselves intensely in reading texts that are of no interest to them is entirely specious and a recipe for pedagogical irrelevance. None of us engages very well or very often, if ever, in reading what we have no interest in. Yes, we read clumsily written and soporific prose when we read contracts and directions and many informational texts that we need to read for various reasons, but it is our genuine need and the compelling character of that need that drives us forward. In that sense, our need is an intrinsic motivation, rather different from the motivation that arises from fear of a bad grade or other extrinsic rewards or punishments. Whenever we read what we don't want to read but feel forced to push through, the quality of our reading is compromised by the fact that we must sacrifice some portion of our attentional resources to the work of keeping ourselves on task and focused on our reading in our struggle against our natural inclinations. How different that experience is from reading texts in which we have deep genuine and personal as well as professional interests. And literature, including stories of all kinds, constitutes the discourse in which we all have an interest and expertise as human beings.

The "natural" pleasure that stories seem to offer to virtually all human beings has been in some quarters an argument against a heavy diet of literature for students who, as they progress in their education, need to become, against their natural proclivities, more proficient readers of nonnarrative texts that focus not on actions and characters but on abstract concepts, principles, and complex ideas of the kind characteristic of discourse in nonliterary fields such as philosophy, psychology, sociology, political science, and economics and in such natural sciences as geology, biology, ecology, and physics. In fact, the focus of much of the discourse of the nationally influential Common Core State Standards for English Language Arts & Literacy is on the importance of "text complexity" in measuring the achievement of students in reading, and a major aim of the CCSS document is to ensure that the language arts curriculum provides for teaching students to read increasingly complex texts, which is generally understood to mean reducing the amount of assigned reading in fiction while increasing the amount of assigned reading in informational texts in the various disciplines. (See Appendix A of the Common Core State Standards for English Language Arts & Literacy: http://www. corestandards.org/assets/Appendix_A.pdf.)

Yet such reasoning about the importance of having secondary schools abandon the traditional language arts curriculum that was heavily invested in reading literature (mostly fiction) for a state-mandated program with a new emphasis on reading informational works in order to better prepare students for the complex texts typically assigned in college is based on two misconceptions that have long been widely but uncritically held by policymakers and many reading specialists with powerful influence in the educational community. First is the argument that literature and especially fiction, insofar as it is organized narratively, merely gives students practice in the mode of discourse they are already most familiar with and not in the sorts of abstract and complex thinking that characterize discourse in nonliterary academic disciplines such as philosophy and linguistics and most of the social sciences, where most students will be doing most of their reading throughout their years in college and beyond. Yet this assumption will be difficult to sustain when tested against a content analysis of the discourse of many, if not most, classic and highly respected works of literature.

Consider the virtual course in cetology provided within Melville's *Moby-Dick* or the ethical and moral discourse that fills so many pages of Mailer's classic war novel, *The Naked and the Dead*, where the young lieutenant protagonist debates the morality of war and of command with his crusty commanding officer and mentor. Or think of the deeply philosophical and theological discourse of many scenes in Dostoyevsky's *The Brothers Karamazov* or, for a more popular canonical text widely taught in high schools, look at the legal and moral arguments presented in the trial scene of Lee's *To Kill a Mockingbird*. Or, for an example from a leading contemporary novelist, look at the highly philosophical passages reflecting on politics and historiography in Philip Roth's fantasy of an alternative US history of World War II, *The Plot against America*.

Such nonnarrative discourses are neither rare nor intellectually oversimplified in novels (also see Bakhtin on the novel as a genre that characteristically incorporates other discourses into itself, in "Epic and Novel" and "Discourse in the Novel"), and they are typically of compelling interest to students who read them with the same kind of deep and emotionally charged engagement that those of us who are academics bring to our reading of articles and books in our specialized fields, especially when our reading relates directly to our own research or writing in progress. I will leave it to others to provide statistical data, but my experience as a reader suggests that most serious novels, as Bakhtin insisted, are interlaced throughout with passages that are themselves not narrative, but that are important to the experience of the novel as a structure of meaning and drawn from the discourses of philosophy, theology, ethics, and the various social and natural sciences.

A second and even more significant correction to the reading specialists and Common Core apologists who see the reading of fiction as a poor training ground for reading and understanding complex ideas may be found in recent discoveries in cognitive science and evolutionary biology, along with a new body of cognitive research and theory on the reading of literature. The following brief summary of this research will probably oversimplify and thereby misrepresent it, so I apologize in advance and refer readers to the sources cited.

The relevant research begins with anthropological evidence (Wilson 21–23) that as prehumans (*Homo habilis*) became hunters and gatherers who maintained campsites and organized their families and clans according to different functions such as caring for children and hunting for food, they had to develop a social intelligence unlike that of animals that moved in packs operating as a single organism. The safety, health, and survival of each society now came to depend on how well its members anticipated, understood, and could accurately read the intentions, motives, and behaviors of members who were engaged in different duties for different reasons from one another. In other words, our nearest prehuman and human ancestors, starting about 2.4 to 1.4 million years ago, were required in almost every waking hour to be engaged in a constant process of attending to one anothers' gestures and other behavior (especially when verbal language was almost certainly limited in its expressive capacity) in order to read and anticipate one anothers' intentions and needs.

This means that our closest evolutionary ancestors were engaged fairly constantly (much as we are) in a social process that amounted to a kind of mind reading, and that the capacity to read minds successfully was naturally valued and rewarded through satisfying relationships and other physical benefits. The advent of such complex thinking seems to have been associated with the rapid growth of the brain, as the human cranial capacity more than doubled in the period of human evolution that started with *Homo habilis,* was followed by *Homo erectus,* and ended with *Homo sapiens*—a period during which the human brain appears to have expanded in what amounts to "one of the most rapid expansions of complex tissue evolution in the history of life" (Wilson 23).

Modern humans thus appear to be the cultural and genetic heirs to a cognitive capacity for reading the observable behavior of those around them "in terms of their underlying mental states, such as thoughts, feelings, desires, and intentions" (Zunshine, "Theory" 89), and with this capacity and our cultural and genetic history of employing it comes the innate interest and enjoyment that virtually all human beings appear to demonstrate in stories, myths, fables, chronicles, and other narratives of human behavior. Our capacity for what technical and scholarly articles charmingly and idiomatically refer to as "mind reading" in real human trans-actions and fictional narratives that represent such transactions is what cognitive scientists and, more recently, cognitively oriented literary theorists attribute to the almost universal human posses-sion of a "Theory of Mind," or "ToM."

Drawing on such research in evolutionary psychology, Lisa Zunshine, professor of English at the University of Kentucky, was among the first and most influential narrative theorists to recognize the explanatory power of ToM in accounting for the experience of reading fiction and the fascination that the novel in particular holds for readers (*Why We Read Fiction*). She has been especially influential in demonstrating how the mind reading required in the reading of narratives may be more or less com-plex or nuanced in various narrative works in different genres, in different periods, and by different authors. More recently she has begun to examine some of the pedagogical applications and implications of ToM for adolescent readers of narratives and to speculate about the wider intellectual and academic benefits that accrue for elementary and secondary students who become avid and expert readers of fiction ("What Reading Fiction").

Among the most important findings of Zunshine's current research is evidence of just how complex and nuanced the mind reading demands of fiction are for children and young adult readers of the fiction that is characteristically read or taught or read aloud to children at various ages and levels of schooling. She demonstrates, more specifically, how the forms of thinking children learn to engage in through the reading of fiction are far more complex than the thinking required of them by nonfictional articles or textbooks in any academic discipline or nonliterary subject of study. She also cites related studies with small children demonstrating how their metacognitive thinking and academic vocabulary develop more reliably and with greater intellectual complexity through their independent efforts at making sense of good stories than by any efforts on the part of teachers to teach them academic vocabulary or texts that are designed to teach complex ideas or metacognitive terms ("What Reading Fiction" 87–88).

I will not indulge now in a summary of the main arguments I have presented for teaching literature in the first-year writing class nor of the corrections I have offered to mistaken notions about the limitations of literary texts as preparation for discourse across the disciplines. I will only say that reason and research both make the case that the best way to prepare students to read and understand complex ideas is to have them read literature, and mostly fiction, combined perhaps with selected writing from disciplines such as history, sociology, psychology, or medicine—those with compelling stories to tell, like Oliver Sacks's fascinating medical case studies of various neurological illnesses. Having made that case, I can now conclude this chapter with an explanation of how the professional expertise of specialists in the teaching of writing makes them the best positioned and most professionally expert scholars in the academic community for the task of teaching college students to be highly proficient readers of literature and thereby stronger readers of any texts, including texts of the various academic disciplines the students will eventually enter and the texts the students themselves will be engaged in composing throughout their college careers.

Writing Teachers as Teachers of Literature

That most writing teachers have undergraduate and graduate degrees in English and can show a goodly number of literature courses on their transcripts does not constitute an argument I am willing to advance for how or why they are qualified to teach a writing course built around a reading list that consists largely of literary works. The history I have presented of teaching practices in literature undermines the reliability of any claim that might be made for the general principle that university literature courses are a good preparation for the teaching of literature. Though, of course, it is surely the case that most departments of English by now house some if not many professors who have broken out of the traditional patterns of instruction that promote a false knowledge about literature rather than any kind of genuine experience of literary texts and of the reading processes that make those texts available to a reader.

What most recommends modern writing specialists as teachers of literature, however, is their professional expertise in pedagogically sound and learner-oriented teaching practices and their working understanding of how literacy is enacted through a process that is subject to various sorts of obstructions that can be alleviated or removed through therapeutic teaching and that can also be refined and rendered more productive through properly guided practice (see C. Smith). Moreover, writing teachers are typically experienced in and understand the use of small groups and dyads in instruction. And these are all key elements to effective instruction in literature as well.

Nor should it surprise us that reading and writing instruction should proceed in similar ways. Writing and reading aren't simply reciprocal processes, but are virtually the same process, at least for process-oriented teachers who in the spirit of Rosenblatt see learning and reading and writing all as processes of text construction. Writing and reading both entail the construction of a meaning. They are also processes that entail revision (or re-reading) while a meaning is under construction, usually developing gradually, often roughly sensed at first, and then corrected, refined, reconsidered, and refined again as it is brought into being as articulated yet still tentative and provisional knowledge.

Effective writing and reading also both depend on a set of competencies or dispositions that I have elsewhere called "personal" or "performative" literacy (208–14) and that call for the more thoughtful and sophisticated acts, habits of mind, and disposition that are entailed in the reading of intellectually challenging and cognitively difficult texts that typically defamiliarize commonplace experience and involve complex nested levels of mind reading. This means that the reading of literary texts, like the process of writing, demands and rewards intense, sustained, and wide-awake attention; a tolerance for ambiguity and paradox; the sensitive reading of one's own mind and the minds of characters in fiction or the minds of other real and potential readers; and a capacity on the part of veteran, as well as inexperienced readers and writers, to endure feelings of confusion and failure that can be productively addressed through multiple re-visions and a continuing dialogue with the text and other real or imagined readers of it. Reading such texts also demands—as does the process of writing—a high degree of metacognitive awareness, an awareness of the state of one's own understanding, and with it a willingness to acknowledge and explore one's questions and to continue to entertain those questions, even after achieving what might count as a provisional (and always provisional) understanding. In other words, the reading of literature, in a supportive context for learning, is the best practice possible for the development of the dispositions and habits of mind that characterize the strongest readers of any text.

Composition Pedagogy in the Teaching of Literature

What kind of instruction, then, do students need from teachers in order to obtain a genuine and productive experience of a text and a personally authenticated interpretation of it, and to do so at the same time that they are getting an opportunity to grow in their capacity to encounter future texts with the kind of disciplined attention I have identified as personal or performative literacy? The answer is instruction that takes place (the way most successful writing instruction does) in a community of apprentices (guided by an expert teacher), where productive habits and processes in reading are cultivated through the experience of reading as a collaborative activity, entailing frequent work in pairs and in groups, interrogating texts and unpacking their language in a process of acquiring well-grounded experiences of texts and warranted interpretations of the experience they provide. Classrooms devoted to such teaching will typically be organized and orchestrated as intensely social workshops in the tradition of writing workshops, not so much for the sharing of finished readings but, even more, to enable students to engage collaboratively (in pairs and in small and large groups) in the construction of their readings, especially if they are assigned to take up the passages or problems that most frustrate and puzzle them. Such collaborations to help students productively engage in the process of making sense of a text (with strategically timed teacher assistance and interventions to articulate principles) are extraordinarily productive for most literature classrooms and crucial for classroom communities of readers where students exhibit varying degrees of competence and confidence as readers of challenging texts.

Thoughtfully orchestrated workshops can accomplish what teacher lectures and directed discussions can never achieve, not only yielding a richer reading of the text under interrogation, but also fostering the development of the dispositions and intellectual traits that characterize all strong readers. Students in collaborative groups, assigned to talk about and try to resolve the problems and difficulties they are encountering in their reading, are likely to discover the power of their questions and confusions in contributing to an emerging understanding of a difficult text. And by focusing on their own questions and problems, they will also be acquiring the crucial habit of metacognition—of thinking about their own thinking and monitoring the state of their emerging understanding, even while they are discovering and practicing discursive strategies for addressing refractory and frustrating problems in constructing meaning as readers or as writers.

If writing teachers themselves feel that their authority to teach literary texts may be compromised by their lack of expertise in the particular texts they are called on to teach, they are mistaking a problem of the traditional literature class with an advantage that is gained for any teacher who teaches literature in the kind of community of learners that the best courses of both writing and literature can become. For in teaching a text that the instructor hasn't studied, or—even better—in reading a text for the first time with students, the instructor has the best opportunity possible for doing the equivalent of what many exemplary writing teachers try to do when they write with their students—letting their students see how their teacher experiences the same difficulties and frustrations the student writers are facing. That instructor can model how the more experienced and expert writer has learned not how to avoid the difficulties encountered, but to accept the inevitability of dealing with them and to endure in the struggle to solve the problems presented by the assignment with intellectual honesty and the courage to continue noticing problems that a less accomplished writer might also sense but try to avoid dealing with in the hope that the reader won't notice.

Similarly, in reading an unfamiliar text with students, teachers who wish to help their students become more accomplished readers will be able to demonstrate as they collaborate with their students in working on difficult texts how they too encounter frustrations in reading a challenging text and treat those difficulties as evidence of the difficulty of the text and not of their own insufficiency as readers. They can in their own struggles with the text show by example how, as expert readers, they have learned to persist in the face of difficulties and how they look for rather than try to avoid problems in the coherence or logical consistency of the meaning they are constructing for the text in a process of continuing vision and revision that eventuates in a still provisional sense of a meaning.

What I have described as critical for efficacious instruction in literature is not only familiar to teachers of writing but also represents the mainstream of theory and practice for the modern field of composition studies in the United States. It can be traced directly to James Moffett's *Teaching the Universe of Discourse* (1968) and Peter Elbow's *Writing without Teachers* (1973), and to the formative practices of the Bay Area Writing Project, founded in 1974 (which grew into the National Writing Project), whose founding teachers were strongly influenced by Moffett and Elbow both. Now with two or three generations of research and instructional development in the teaching of literature rooted in Rosenblatt's transactional theory, enhanced by almost half a century of complementary scholarship and teaching practice in the field of composition, composition specialists are ideally positioned by their own intellectual and pedagogical traditions to make monumental contributions toward helping entering college students to become powerful, college-ready readers by fostering their development as skilled and disciplined readers of literature. And the first step toward that achievement must be the restoration of literary texts to a central place in the curriculum of first-year writing courses.

Works Cited

Bakhtin, Mikhail. "Discourse in the Novel." *The Dialogic Imagination: Four Essays*. Austin: U of Texas P, 1981. 259–422. Print.

————. "Epic and Novel." *The Dialogic Imagination: Four Essays*. Austin: U of Texas P, 1981. 3–40. Print.

Berlin, James. *Rhetoric and Reality: Writing Instruction in American Colleges, 1900–1985*. Carbondale: Southern Illinois UP, 1987. Print.

Blau, Sheridan. *The Literature Workshop: Teaching Texts and Their Readers*. Portsmouth: Heinemann, 2003. Print.

Bonk, Joseph. *What English Pedagogy Looks Like: A Sampling of Five Schools Across the Secondary, Post-Secondary, and Tertiary Levels*. Diss. Teachers College, Columbia U. 2016. Print.

California Intersegmental Committee of the Academic Senates of Colleges and Universities. *Academic Literacy: A Statement of Competencies Expected of Students Entering California's Public Colleges and Universities*. 2002. Print.

Common Core State Standards for English Language Arts & Literacy in History/Social Studies, Science, and Technical Subjects. *Common Core State Standards Initiative*. 2010. Web. 9 Dec. 2016.

Elbow, Peter. *Writing without Teachers*. New York: Oxford UP, 1973. Print.

Frye, Northrop, *Anatomy of Criticism: Four Essays*. Princeton: Princeton UP, 1957. Print.

————. "Levels of Meaning in Literature." *Kenyon Review* 12.2 (1950): 247–62. Print.

Graff, Gerald. *Professing Literature: An Institutional History*. Chicago: U of Chicago P, 1987. Print.

Hairston, Maxine. "The Winds of Change: Thomas Kuhn and the Revolution in the Teaching of Writing." *College Composition and Communication* 33.1 (1982): 76–88. Print.

Huber, Bettina. "Today's Literature Classroom: Findings from the MLA1990 Survey of Upper-Division Courses." *ADE Bulletin* 101 (1992): 36–60. Print.

Hynds, Susan. *On the Brink: Negotiating Literature and Life with Adolescents*. New York: Teachers College P, 1997. Print.

Langer, Judith. *Literary Understanding and Literature Instruction.* Albany: National Research Center on English Learning and Achievement, 2000. Rpt. of *Literary Understanding and Literature Instruction* (Report series 2.11). Albany: Center for the Learning and Teaching of Literature, 1991. Print.

Lindemann, Erika. "Freshman Composition: No Place for Literature." *College English* 55.3 (1993): 311–16. Print.

Marshall, James. *Patterns of Discourse in Classroom Discussions of Literature.* (Report no. 2.9). Albany: Center for the Learning and Teaching of Literature, 1989. Print.

Moffett, James. *Teaching the Universe of Discourse.* Boston: Houghton Mifflin, 1968. Print.

Nystrand, Martin. *Opening Dialogues: Understanding the Dynamics of Language and Learning in the English Classroom.* New York: Teachers College P, 1997. Print.

Pradl, Gordon. *Reading for Democracy: Literature as a Social Act.* Portsmouth: Boynton/Cook, 1996. Print.

Probst, Robert. *Response and Analysis: Teaching Literature in Junior and Senior High School.* Portsmouth: Heinemann, 1988. Print.

Purves Alan. "Toward a Reevaluation of Reader Response and School Literature." *Language Arts* 70 (1993): 348–61. Print.

Richards, I. A. *Practical Criticism: A Study of Literary Judgment.* 1929. New York: Harcourt, Brace, 1963. Print.

Rosenblatt, Louise M. *Literature as Exploration.* 1938. Forewd. Wayne Booth. New York: MLA, 1995. Print.

Salvatori, Mariolina. "Reading and Writing a Text: Correlations between Reading and Writing Patterns." *College English* 45 (1983): 657–66. Print.

Salvatori, Mariolina, and Patricia Donahue. *The Elements (and Pleasures) of Difficulty.* New York: Longman, 2005. Print.

Smith, Cheryl Hogue. "Interrogating Texts: From Deferent to Efferent and Aesthetic Reading Practices." *Journal of Basic Writing* 31.1 (2012): 59–79. Print.

Smith, Michael W. "Building Paper Houses." *Style* 48.1 (2014): 83–86. Print.

Sullivan, Patrick. "Deep Reading as a Threshold Concept in Composition Studies." *Deep Reading: Teaching Reading in the Composition Classroom*. Ed. Patrick Sullivan, Howard Tinberg, and Sheridan Blau. Urbana: NCTE, 2016. Print.

Tate, Gary. "A Place for Literature in Freshman Composition." *College English* 55.3 (1993): 317–21. Print.

Wilson, Edward O. *The Meaning of Human Existence*. New York: Liveright, 2014. Print.

Zancanella, Don. "Teachers Reading/Readers Teaching: Five Teachers Personal Approaches to Literature and their Teaching of Literature." *Research in the Teaching of English* 25 (1991): 5–33. Print.

Zunshine, Lisa. "Theory of Mind as a Pedagogical Tool" *Interdisciplinary Literary Studies* 16.1 (2014): 89–109. Print.

———. "What Reading Fiction Has to Do with Doing Well Academically" *Style* 48.1 (2014): 87–92. Print.

———. *Why We Read Fiction: Theory of Mind and the Novel*. Columbus: The Ohio State UP, 2006. Print.

CHAPTER FIFTEEN

Building Mental Maps: Implications from Research on Reading in the STEM Disciplines

REBECCA S. NOWACEK AND HEATHER G. JAMES

Marquette University

In our roles as director of our university's writing center (Rebecca) and instructional librarian (Heather), we often find ourselves traversing institutional and disciplinary boundaries. As we collaboratively offer workshops on writing effective literature reviews, as we jointly visit classrooms to talk about research and writing processes, and as we co-lead sessions to cross-train our writing center tutors and graduate teaching assistants, we hope that the joint physical presence of both "the writing person" and "the research person"—weaving together our instructional activities, affirming each other's advice—will prompt writers and instructors across our campus to recognize writing and research as intertwined, iterative, and perhaps even (on our best days) empowering processes. But where is reading in all this?

We begin this chapter by synthesizing discussions of transfer in the rhetoric and composition scholarship on reading. As will become clear, recent considerations of transfer—particularly the question of transfer beyond first-year composition (FYC)—are wrapped up with a host of other concerns about students' limited reading skills. Motivated by our own work with advanced undergrads in the STEM disciplines, we offer two re-readings of the challenges facing college-level readers. To begin, we draw on a tradition of read-aloud protocols conducted with expert readers in the STEM disciplines to argue for a revised understanding of the challenges facing so-called "novice" readers. Then, perhaps more radically, we draw on recent research by Deborah Brandt to fundamentally reevaluate the relationship between reading and writing. We conclude by using a site of our own instruction—a multidisciplinary course filled with undergraduate STEM majors writing research grant proposals—to consider how these perspectives might better inform our own pedagogies of writing, researching, *and* reading.

Readers in First-Year Writing Classrooms: Questions of Transfer and Other Concerns

Connections between Reading and Writing

Composition and rhetoric scholars interested in transfer of reading skills have focused on two central questions: Do FYC students connect what they're being asked to do as readers with what they're being asked to do as writers? And do students connect what they're learning about reading in FYC to their reading in other classes?

To answer the first question, scholars have focused on the perceptions of students and instructors. The handful of systematic studies of the connections students make between instruction in reading and in writing indicate that there is a persistent mismatch between the two. For instance, grounded in their experiences teaching a reading class linked to a first-year writing class, Sweeney and McBride conclude that writing instructors' professed values when it comes to organization, thesis, detail, vocabulary, engagement, and length are often difficult to reconcile with the essays students are assigned to read—a mismatch that understandably frustrates students. Gogan's surveys similarly indicate that FYC students "did not see the connection between the rhetorical genre awareness [promoted in a reading assignment] and more effective writing" (n.p.) and Keller offers an ethnographic account of a first-year student who struggled because "he did not have a clear sense of how the readings led to or complemented the writings in the course" (*Chasing* 130).

Perhaps not surprisingly, research indicates that instructors experience a similar disconnect. Bunn reports that while every one of the FYC instructors he surveyed believes there is a relationship between reading and writing, many fewer reported actually working to "explain or teach those connections to students" (501). Keller ("Framework"), too, argues that there is a lack of connection between instructors' pedagogies of writing (which include a significant focus on revision) and their reading practices (which almost never provide feedback on readings or opportunities to re-read). On those occasions when instructors do work to make those connections, they most often do so through the use of "model texts" (Carillo; Bunn; Keller, "Frameworks"). But if instructors *do* make such connections, Bunn argues, they can increase student motivation and success in both reading and writing (512).

Connections between First-Year Writing and Subsequent Coursework

If scholars are optimistic about the potential for increasing students' sense of connection between their reading and their writing assignments, they are much less confident that students will draw connections between reading strategies cultivated in a first-year writing course and subsequent coursework (Manarin; Carillo). Studies of how students repurpose reading strategies gained in FYC offer mixed reviews. Keller's (*Chasing*) ethnographic study of students reading at school and at home, in high school and later in college, is not encouraging. When asked about reading outside FYC, Diana reports that she got relatively good grades but was frustrated by the increasingly divergent expectations in different disciplines; she describes herself as "guessing a lot" (133), and Keller suggests that "she did not seem to have metacognitive awareness of how she adapted as a reader" (132). David describes reading textbooks to extract the right answer, with no emphasis on rhetorical reading. But Diana and David are both first-year students; other research suggests that students may recognize more connections as they get further into their disciplinary studies. When Gogan interviewed students a full year after they had finished a required composition class that emphasized rhetorical reading of genres, even students who had, in earlier surveys, dismissed that assignment as unimportant later "credit[ed] the genre awareness assignment with the development of some of their current reading practices across the disciplines" (n.p.).

Although relatively few studies have offered specific strategies for promoting transfer from FYC to subsequent coursework, Carillo elaborates a pedagogical strategy she calls "mindful reading." In this approach, a range of approaches to reading (rhetorical reading, close reading, critical reading, etc.) "become the composition course's subjects of inquiry . . . [and] instructors would focus with students . . . [on] how each type of reading works in specific ways" (120–21). Becoming meta-aware of their reading strategies, Carillo speculates, may help students "recognize at what moment in their reading process they need to relinquish a particular reading approach and introduce an alternative one and why" (123). However, the effects of mindful reading have not yet been systematically studied.

Other Concerns about FYC Readers

In addition to concerns about whether first-year students are able to make links between their reading and their writing and whether they will choose to repurpose reading strategies developed in FYC for future coursework, three persistent concerns surface about the reading abilities of readers in first-year writing classrooms.

First, FYC readers focus on facts and correct answers rather than on authors making claims within rhetorical contexts. The scholarship frequently notes a tendency in students to see right answers and "correct" readings (Bunn; Keller, *Chasing*, "Framework"; Smith; Sweeney and McBride). To some degree, this approach to reading might be understood as an alternative to "reading rhetorically"—a strategy often promoted in the FYC classroom (Carillo 34). Haas and Flower's Braddock-winning article defines *rhetorical reading* as "an active attempt at constructing a rhetorical context [including authors, readers, and motives] for the text as a way of making sense of it" (167–68). One of the major findings of Haas and Flower's comparison of the reading strategies of "experienced college readers" (four grad students) and "student readers" (six undergrads enrolled in a first-year composition class) was the degree to which readers used rhetorical (as opposed to content or function/feature) reading strategies to construct the meaning of a text. Whereas only one FYC student made a single statement that was construed by the researchers as rhetorical reading (1 percent of strategies used), expert readers read rhetorically 13 percent of the time. Although Haas and Flower compared a limited number of readers, other research supports the conclusion that compared to experienced readers, FYC readers show a marked absence of rhetorical reading.

Second, FYC readers demonstrate a striking (over)reliance on personal connections. Manarin found that students most often related course readings not to "another course, context, or concept but . . . to personal experience" (287); "instead of a close reading exploring an author's rhetorical choices," students would "declare the essay's validity based on their own experience" (288)—even when that strategy was counterproductive for an assignment that required rhetorical reading. This pattern of behavior in FYC readers—what some might identify as a type of negative transfer—is also lamented by Sweeney and McBride:

> Even with an understanding of the historical events and political climate that prompted Swift to write his proposal and an understanding that Swift intended his proposal as satire, many students could not get past their text-to-self disconnect, creating a point at which their ability to engage with the text stagnated. (607)

Finally, research from the Citation Project suggests that beginning college students struggle to understand complex sources in their entirety. In their study of papers written for a sophomore-level required research course, Howard and colleagues found that while students regularly engaged in patchwriting, paraphrasing, and even copying, they found no instances of summary, which they define as putting the main ideas of a paragraph or more of text into "fresh language" and compressing it by more than 50 percent (181). Instead, students operate at the sentence level, in one representative case plucking from a text of 240 pages sentences from only two pages (186). The lack of summary and the patchwriting of individual sentences together raise not only the question of "whether the writers understood the source itself but also whether they even read it" (186). This research is often cited (Carillo; Keller, *Chasing*, "Framework") to illustrate the ways in which students struggle to comprehend complex texts and are therefore "apt to cherrypick a few sentences that seem to bear on their topic rather than applying the meaning of the whole text" (Brent 46).

In sum, the portrait that emerges from studies of readers in first-year and early general education classrooms is rather dismal: students don't understand readings or try to read them rhetorically, they cherry-pick quotes, they connect texts to personal experiences rather than other texts. And yet our own work with students leads us to a more optimistic view. While the research we've just summarized strikes a chord, we wondered if delving further into the scholarship on reading might give us other frameworks for conceptualizing college-level reading and how to promote transfer of those reading abilities into contexts beyond FYC.

Insights (and Challenges) from Research on Expert STEM Readers

We wondered: what might we learn by looking at the practices of expert readers? Given our work with students in the STEM disciplines, we were drawn to a small group of often over-looked studies that illuminate the behaviors of expert readers in the STEM disciplines: Bazerman focuses on theoretical and experimental physicists; Charney examines both grad students and established professors in evolutionary biology; Paul and Charney examine twelve professors from physics, engineering, mathematics, ecology, and meteorology; Shanahan, Shanahan, and Misichia examine the reading strategies of mathematicians, chemists, and historians. Collectively, these studies cast valuable light on the nature of expert reading with implications not only for how we understand the "novice" behaviors of writers in FYC classrooms, but also for the broader question of whether reading is a "generalizable" skill.

What Makes Expert Readers Expert?

Across these varied studies, three interrelated behaviors emerge. First, expert readers in the STEM disciplines **read selectively**.

Because they must balance the need to stay on top of the most current findings with the need to actually work in the lab, expert STEM readers do not read journals cover to cover. Instead they use author names (to judge credibility in the field) and titles (scanning for key terms to establish relevance to their own work) to decide whether to read an article—turning to the abstract if the title and author names are indeterminate (Bazerman 241; see also Shanahan et al. 408–9).

Second, expert readers in STEM disciplines **read nonlinearly**. These scientists rarely read the article sequentially, but instead hop from section to section "seeking what they consider news" (Bazerman 243). This nonlinear reading matters because previewing an article and skimming for its most relevant bits "can undercut the rhetorical force of an article" (Charney 214), increasing a reader's ability to read for their own purposes.

The tendencies to read selectively and nonlinearly are closely related to the third identified behavior: expert readers in STEM disciplines **read with a mental map of their disciplinary field** in mind. Although the terminology these scholars use varies, all invoke a constructivist approach to reading, emphasizing that meaning does not reside simply in the text but is constructed by the individual while reading a text. Bazerman uses the term *schema* to describe "structured background knowledge" that "affect[s] both the process of comprehension and the meaning constructed from the text" (236). Importantly, these expert readers' mental maps tend to have the researchers themselves—their interests, their research projects, their commitments—at their center. Paul and Charney note that when reading the introductions to new, somewhat controversial articles, "readers' first consideration was whether they could relate the reading to their prior knowledge and to their own work" (427); in this way, the mental map is connected to expert readers' inclination to read selectively.

Having a mental map of the scholarly field on which the reader can position him- or herself *and* the reading proves crucial when grappling with difficult texts—and the absence of a fully developed map can make it difficult for readers to critically evaluate difficult texts. Charney's study of evolutionary biologists points out that when reading a particularly challenging article both expert readers (professors) and novice readers (grad students) had to expend effort to understand unfamiliar material. However, the presence of what Bazerman would call a schema and what Charney calls "a stockpile of knowledge and attitudes against which they could weigh [the authors'] claims" (216) influenced the frequency and quality of expert readers' evaluative comments. Whereas grad students were likely to merely relate the text to their prior knowledge, experts were "significantly more often engaged . . . in assessing the validity and value of the text" (217). A mental map, or schema, thus seems crucial to the behaviors of expert readers in the STEM disciplines.

How Do Novices Become Experts? The Case of Eliza

At first glance, the behaviors attributed to writers in FYC and general education classrooms seem a far cry from the reading strategies attributed to expert readers in the STEM disciplines. How could such a gap be bridged? Are we to believe that these expert readers were *always* the outliers, that they *never* quite fit the patterns of novice behavior? Perhaps. But Gogan's research suggests that students' use of their previously learned reading strategies can change over time—a finding supported by Haas's longitudinal case study of Eliza, an undergraduate student in biology.

Eliza's early experiences replicate the problem described by Keller's (*Chasing*) first-year students: although her FYC class focused on how authors made and substantiated claims, Eliza saw no connections to her chemistry and biology readings. In those contexts, Eliza "viewed her role as a reader as one of extracting and retaining information"—a strategy that was rewarded by her performance on tests. Her focus on "understanding what the book says" continued during her sophomore year, as she approached a research paper required for her cell biology course by locating sources and stringing together extracted facts the night before it was due. Haas persuasively presents this reading and writing experience as evidence of a continued disjoint with her earlier FYC class: "The attention to authors which surfaced during her reading for her English class in her freshman year had disappeared. There was no evidence that she viewed any of the texts she read as the product of an individual author's motives or actions" (63).

But, Haas notes, this approach to reading began to change during Eliza's junior year. Beginning to work in a lab significantly altered Eliza's view of reading and writing; she began to distinguish reading journal articles from "just textbook reading" (64) and began to see those articles as "manifestations of scientific action and human choices" (65). During her senior year, Eliza demonstrated nonlinear reading strategies, spent more time on figures and tables, and grew more critical of methods and results sections. Although she had "extensive writing assignments based on reading," she didn't describe them as research papers. Instead she understood them as forms of communication embedded in the life of a lab—a review article and a research proposal (65).

By her senior year, Eliza's reading activities had grown nonlinear and increasingly critical—a change not only in her discrete reading strategies but also in her identifications and motivations for reading. The importance of this identification with a community of practice is underlined by Haas's speculation that while some of Eliza's transformation might be chalked up to "natural development" or to instructional support (she was being asked to read fewer textbooks and more journal articles), Eliza's increased domain knowledge and the mentoring she received in the lab also played crucial roles. Haas's narrative of Eliza's development from a student diligently searching for facts into an emergent biologist reading critically between the lines of current research suggests that we really do need to look not just for application of discrete skills, but also at how readers read in specific contexts.

When Is a Novice Not a Novice? Or, Is "Expert" Reading a Generalizable Skill?

The critical importance of context, of background knowledge and sense of identification, for readers comes to the fore in Haswell and colleagues' replication of—and variation on—Haas and Flower's study of rhetorical reading. Hypothesizing that a reader's ability to read rhetorically might be influenced by prior knowledge or "repertoires" ("bodies of cultural value, knowledge and convention" [Haswell et al. 13])—an assumption reminiscent of Bazerman's focus on schema and what Haas refers to as Eliza's increasingly scientific "discourse"—Haswell et al. replicated the study twice. The first time they used the same psychology textbook excerpt used by Haas and Flower; the second time they used a passage from a local newspaper article on gender differences in schools, written by a college senior.

Using Haas and Flower's passage produced very similar results: graduate students once again demonstrated rhetorical reading strategies far more often than the undergraduates did (7.2 percent compared to 3.4 percent). But when asked to read the second passage, which Haswell and colleagues chose to tap into the cultural repertoire of the undergrads, *both* groups of readers used more rhetorical strategies: undergrads increased from 3.4 percent to 12.9 percent, grads from 7.2 percent to 16.5 percent. The differences between the two groups, while not eliminated, were reduced considerably. Thus, Haswell and colleagues conclude, "What appears to be a lack in reading strategy may have been a lack of prior knowledge needed to activate strategies that the undergraduates did have but therefore did not use" (12–13). Haswell et al.'s work suggests that the use of expert reading strategies is at least as contextual as it is developmental. The difference may be individuals' ability to position themselves—their knowledge and motives and identities—in relation to those readings. Expert, college-level reading isn't just about discrete reading strategies, but about the contextual knowledge that activates their use.

For researchers and teachers interested in transfer of learning, this is a crucial insight. The question of the relationship between discrete skills that can be applied and the contexts in which individuals make those "applications" has been taken up at length in the research on transfer conducted in cognitive psychology. Much of the early cognitive psychology transfer scholarship focused on what has been called the two problem transfer paradigm, in which researchers attempt to track the application of a skill from a source problem to the target problem. This tradition of research opened up debates about whether sufficiently abstract strategies would be widely transferable or whether all expertise is context bound (e.g., Anderson, Reder, and Simon; Bransford and Schwartz; Greeno). But another, more sociocultural line of studies (e.g., Beach; Lave; Lave and Wenger) suggested that the abstract/contextual dichotomy may be largely a function of research methods and thus turned our attention to the cultural contexts in which learning occurs.

To the degree that rhetoric and composition scholars have proposed reading pedagogies to promote transfer, they have focused on metacognitive awareness as a widely transferable strategy that can help individuals negotiate shifts in contexts (e.g., Carillo's mindful reading). But we'd like to offer an alternate view: selective, critical reading often depends on having a personalized map of the field. What defines novice readers is not their age, institutional position, possession of an ability to read any text rhetorically, or even a metacognitive awareness of different reading strategies—but the fact that they don't yet have a highly elaborated map on which to position themselves and the text as they engage with a particular reading. One of the challenges facing college-age readers, then, is the chicken-and-egg problem of constructing such maps for long-established and sometimes jargon-laden fields. Students need a map to guide them as they select texts, identify relevant information while reading them nonlinearly, and make critical evaluations of the content. But how does one acquire such a map? In part through reading, but also through meaningful participation in a community of learners (Haas; Gogan; Lave and Wenger).

This, then, is our more modest claim: the challenge of college-level reading resides to a large degree in the need to have a mental map of the field, a map that arises from meaningful participation in a community of learners. We turn now to our somewhat more ambitious claim: perhaps we need to understand not only the resources needed by individual readers, but also the institutional contexts in which student readers operate. Maybe we're not seeing the germs of "expert" reading because we've misunderstood the context in which reading operates within schools.

Insights (and Challenges) from Recent Scholarship

Rethinking the Relationship between Reading and Writing

When addressing the relationship between the acts of reading and writing, most scholarship assumes their compatible, mutually reinforcing qualities. Carillo, for instance, describes reading as "writing's counterpart in the construction of meaning" (7). Salvatori writes that reading and writing are related and that, in fact, improvement in writing "is the result, rather than the cause, of th[e] increased ability to engage in, and to be reflexive about, the reading of highly complex texts" (659). Smith similarly argues that "college students' ability to write is limited by their ability to read" and that students "can never outwrite their reading ability" (60). Even when unwilling to make such strong causal claims, the scholarship is rife with invocations of "reading like a writer" (Bunn 506) and "reading from a writer's position" (Keller, *Chasing* 143). The flip side of this valorization of skilled reading as a necessary foundation for strong writing is that students' reading abilities are taken for granted: when they become visible is when they have proved subpar and thus reading instruction is seen as remedial (Carillo 10; Keller, *Chasing* 18). The common thread is that reading and writing are assumed to be closely and perhaps inextricably linked abilities of the successful student.

Literacy scholar Deborah Brandt challenges those assumptions. Building on the "cultural dissociation" between reading and writing described by Furet and Ozouf, Brandt argues that we have entered into a new era of mass literacy in which "writing seems to be eclipsing reading as the literate experience of consequence" (3). Convinced particularly by her study of writing and reading in workplaces, she notes that whereas historically the value of reading has resided in its "goodness," the daily literate demands of workaday writers are redefining the reading–writing relationship: reading increasingly "occurs within acts of writing and often as an interaction between one writer and another" (13). Coming to terms with this shift in mass literacy challenges the commonsense assumption that reading is the springboard and necessary foundation for writing, "that our literacy can only develop through how we read, and that how we read will condition how we write" (159).

Furthermore, Brandt directs our attention to the ways in which schools long informed by the "confines of a reading-privileged, school-based literacy" (91) may be ill-suited for the agendas and interests of young people who identify primarily as writers rather than readers. Although in our own teaching we have often assumed that the shift to becoming producers rather than consumers is a momentous one, Brandt argues that there are pockets of students who already identify as producers—and that school structures are often not congenial to their priorities and behaviors. She uses the phrase "writing over reading" to

> indicat[e] how writing is given priority over reading in the participants' often busy lives, as the two might compete for time, attention, and mental energy . . . [and] to capture how participants pursued their orientation to writing in instructional and other social contexts where they were being construed (along with everybody else) as readers. . . . These individuals more often had to "write over" the reading bias in their environments as a measure of individual initiative, sometimes violating expectations even to the point of reprimand. (96)

Brandt deliberately distinguishes "writing over reading" from "reading like a writer," describing "writing over reading" as "a set of strategies that requires deliberate separation from the rules of reading" (96). Brandt also argues that certain educational traditions have "privilege[d] the heritage of writing over the heritage of reading" (110); these traditions include spoken word, hip-hop, and other endeavors "in connection with work, apprenticeship, professions, art, commerce, and publication" (115). We believe that the reading behaviors of expert scientists, geared as they are to the workaday practice of science, may provide another model of "writing over reading."

Brandt, then, offers a framework for radically re-seeing reading scholarship and encourages us to consider whether "writing over reading" strategies might further complicate our understanding of what it means to read at the college level. If as instructors we want students to behave as producers of knowledge, then we might (as Brandt suggests) start to look for evidence of "writing over reading" behaviors—and foster them.

"Writing over Reading" as a Frame for Reconceptualizing College-Level Reading

To speak of "writing over reading" may seem to denigrate reading, particularly when reading has so long been excluded from the central concerns of rhetoric and composition. We propose, though, that "writing over reading" may lead to some reading strategies that look like novice behaviors but may in fact be more similar to the behaviors of expert STEM readers than is initially apparent. In particular, looking for "writing over reading" behaviors casts in a different light the critiques of first-year readers as prone to cherry-picking quotes and dependent on personal connections.

What from a more traditional framework of the reading–writing connection seems like writing from sentences rather than sources, might—from the perspective of "writing over reading"—be not so very different from the behaviors of expert readers in the STEM disciplines. Such readers evaluate arguments "not with respect to the correctness of the *entire* argument, but to how the reader can assimilate *pieces* into ongoing work" (Bazerman 249, emphasis added). The difference between FYC readers and expert readers, then, may be one of degree, not kind. After all, in *their* summaries of the Citation Project research, Brent, Carillo, and Keller all chose to quote the same two or three sentences that we did: did we cherry-pick, or are there often a few passages that are the most relevant for writers who share similar mental maps of the discipline? Granted, we have also in this chapter included a great deal of summary, and that lack of engagement with larger units of text is indeed troublesome in FYC writers. However, the absence of summary may indicate not a lack of ability to read long or complex texts but the lack of a mental map that enables an individual to read *certain* long or complex texts. Without a schema (Bazerman), the discourse (Haas), or a repertoire (Haswell et al.), it's hard to get a critical fingerhold. Thus, what from a traditional reading-to-write perspective may seem like insufficiently careful reading may, from the "writing over reading" perspective, be the strategic behaviors of expert readers.

Similarly, a "writing over reading" perspective invites us to reconsider the inclination of FYC students to make personal rather than intertextual connections. If expert readers do indeed rely on mental maps—on which they strategically position their own interests and research agendas—then many of the connections expert readers make are already necessarily personal. To some degree, those "personal" connections (e.g., how does this relate to my lab?) are what make the critical, selective, evaluative readings possible.

Furthermore, Haswell and colleague's research interrogates what gets counted as "personal" for undergraduate readers. In addition to using Haas and Flower's original coding categories, Haswell et al. coded for three additional reading strategies: *personal narrative* ("commentary that interprets text via life experiences of the reader" [11]); *judgmental* ("commentary agrees or disagrees with the content of the text, or otherwise places a value on it" [11]); and *noncommittal* ("deals with content without relating the passage to personal experiences or making value judgments" [11]). Haswell et al. found that when reading the original, more challenging passage, undergrads were most likely to make noncommittal statements, doing so 93 percent of the time. However, undergrads made *fewer* personal narrative connections than the more experienced grad students (2 percent to 7 percent). The undergraduates' personal narrative comments increased only with the more familiar, second reading, jumping to 16 percent (while the judgmental statements held steady around 5 percent). What explains the small number of personal narrative connections—and the increase in the second passage?

The explanation, we believe, is the definition of what counts as personal: in the case of Haswell et al.'s study, personal connections are "interpretations of the text through the reader's life experiences" as a way of "instantiating prior knowledge schemata that are activated by information in the text" (11). To interpret a text through the writer's life experiences may be surprisingly like the behaviors of the expert STEM readers, who consistently made connections between the text and their personal knowledge of their field and their own research agendas. Might the "personal" readings that exasperate Manarin, Sweeney and McBride, and others—readings that turn away from intertextual connections and rhetorical readings—in some cases be more like the noncommittal readings that Haswell et al. establish are plentiful? If so, the problem is not personal connections but connections that *lack* a sense of a personal connection to the emerging mental map.

Taken together, the "writing over reading" perspective suggests that it may not simply be a question of whether students think it is valuable to read rhetorically, but whether they have the resources to read rhetorically. It's not a question of getting students beyond the personal, but of getting them invested and located within a conversation so that their personal connections—like the personal connections of expert readers—become a meaningful leverage for critical analysis. While we don't deny that there are many areas for improvement in the reading strategies of college writers, we do find that Brandt's challenge to recognize the ways in which certain valorized types of reading do not always line up with the reading practices of many other active producers of text helps us to better understand the nature of active, critical reading in the STEM disciplines.

Developing a Pedagogy of Reading in the STEM Disciplines

In our capacities as research librarian and writing center director, we worked extensively with an undergraduate research seminar in the Honors Program of the College of Arts and Sciences. This seminar was designed by a psychology professor as an interdisciplinary introduction to research methods. In spring 2015, the course enrolled primarily STEM majors in their sophomore or junior year. The course is an elective, and the major assignment of the semester was to write a research proposal that would be submitted for review and possible funding by a special Honors Program grant. The psychology instructor designed the course with the expectation that, in addition to our repeated presence in the course curriculum, students would secure a faculty mentor in their discipline.

Our main focus in this course was to exemplify how information research and writing are integrated iterative processes that are fundamental to the overall research process in every discipline. Throughout our various meetings with students—in the classroom and individually—we both focused on the idea of entering into a research community. We worked with the students to develop and practice their skills in strategically searching and evaluating scholarly publications, taking notes as they read these articles, considering the "conversation" that occurs between scholars in the form of publications, and incorporating the work of published scholars into their own research proposals. However, this sense of scholarly conversation and community largely focused on intertextual connections. We realize now that we had not thought very much about how students come to build their own disciplinary maps of their fields.

As we reexamine our work through the framework we've articulated in this chapter, we're particularly pleased with two components. First, the emphasis on note taking is even more important than we'd initially realized. The majority of these students described their note-taking strategies as practices they had developed haphazardly. Many of them had trouble articulating any system of taking notes while they read, and most students felt they were able to remember the important elements of any text they read; so far they had been successful in relying on their memory and highlighted quotes to develop their research papers. Composing this research proposal was the first significant challenge to their (previously) successful habits. During our in-class workshop, we worked to model note taking and to encourage the nonlinear, rhetorical reading strategies of expert researchers. While some writers remained skeptical, for others the articulation of intentional, rhetorical reading and note-taking strategies immediately resonated—and several other students changed their perspective on note taking later in the semester.

Second, multiple times during the semester, Heather reviewed students' selection and representation of sources through multiple versions of annotated bibliography assignments. Heather's analysis of student citations offers a kind of feedback that we gather is relatively rare. Keller (*Chasing*) notes that reading can "leave a trace in the use of sources" but also asks "how much time do teachers have to respond deeply to the reading involved in source use, rather than primarily to writing aspects such as the integration of quotations?" (37). As an embedded librarian in a course, Heather focuses on students' use of sources in exactly this way. When an annotation or citation looks problematic or the overall cohesion of the bibliography seems unclear, she finds and reviews the source(s) in order to write responses that may head off students' misinterpretation of individual texts and intertextual connections as early as possible. One of the great advantages of the interdisciplinary collaboration in this STEM course—between course instructor, faculty mentors, writing center tutors, and research librarians—is the ability to offer more comprehensive support of students' reading, writing, and subject knowledge development.

In this way, then, what we've already been doing is compatible with our understandings of college-level reading. But looking back at our work through this framework also helps us to understand student struggles in new ways. Specifically, we can now see that although their work with a mentor means that these STEM students are often starting to move into participation in a community of learners, they most often have extremely rudimentary mental maps of their field. Often they are still in the early stages of trying to understand the phenomenon being studied and the techniques used in the labs: comparing the work of their labs to the methods of researchers elsewhere has not yet surfaced as a concern. Second, these honors students are students who—by and large—have thrived in the reading-to-write structures of their previous educations. To make the shift to read like an expert STEM researcher, to read selectively and nonlinearly in ways that are guided by a mental map, is a huge shift, not simply in terms of building a mental map but also in terms of experiencing a "critical incident" (Yancey, Robertson, and Taczak)—an experience that might nudge these students to explore and embrace new reading strategies.

Future Directions

As we look forward, we see several implications of this framework for our future teaching—implications that may help readers imagine their own pedagogies of reading. First, we would do more with mapping and the visualization of research communities. We would have students draw idea maps, to help visualize which scholars are clustered around which issues and methods. We might have them make timelines, to see the historical development of findings and of research methods. We might even have them writing dialogues—choosing several researchers on a map and scripting out where they'd be in agreement and where they would disagree. Additionally, we would ask students to connect these researchers and their findings with the forums where the work was shared. All of this could help students recognize that making connections and creating a knowledge gap isn't just a textual strategy for an effective literature review: developing a mental map of the discipline is crucial for understanding one's own work in relation to others' work.

Additionally, Heather would aim to extend the discussion of students' selected sources and annotated bibliographies. This feedback seems to be a critical missing component in a majority of courses where instruction needs around subject matter and/or writing techniques overwhelm the limited class time. Perhaps students could be required to discuss the annotated bibliography with their faculty mentor in order to review the cohesion of their selected sources and to hear the mentor talk through their process of testing the content against their own map of the field.

Finally, we'd like to capitalize on the budding relationships with disciplinary mentors. One possibility is getting mentors more involved in modeling the reading process, perhaps sitting with a student and reading aloud. Such a real-time read-aloud protocol might give students insight into how their mentors choose and actually read articles: What criteria do they use to select articles to read? Do they read nonlinearly? How much do these mentors think of the work of their own labs as they read? While we imagine it would be difficult to get every mentor to do this on a regular basis, even building a video archive of several read-alouds could be a powerful tool in our emerging pedagogy of reading. Another way in which we might build on the expertise of mentors is by asking them to review, perhaps with the student, a small portfolio of documents generated by the student, including an early map of the field, the annotated bibliography, and any later maps or drafts of lit reviews. Such a conversation might not only provide the student direct feedback on their project but also provide us insight into how students' maps of their fields are developing.

Beyond our own future plans, we see great potential for future research in these areas. For instance, as a field we would benefit from more systematic examination of the ways in which students' disciplinary maps or schema impact their reading habits and success. Although we have a great deal of research on students' entrance into disciplinary communities in relation to their *writing*, there is very little on how students develop their disciplinary schema through their *reading* practices. Furthermore, we've drawn in this chapter primarily on research conducted on STEM researchers/readers. Future research could turn to other disciplines and professions—building, perhaps, on existing research (like Wineburg's studies of novice and expert readers in history) and explore other, less studied areas as well. Finally, Brandt's argument that we have entered a new era of mass literacy in which writing is the primary mode of literate engagement—an era in which the traditional structures of reading and writing in schools may prove ill-suited to the activity of writing over reading—offers a profound challenge to both researchers and teachers.

Works Cited

Anderson, John R., Lynne M. Reder, and Herbert A. Simon. "Situated Learning and Education." *Educational Researcher* 25.4 (1996): 5–11. Print.

Bazerman, Charles. *Shaping Written Knowledge: The Activity of the Experimental Article in Science.* Madison: U of Wisconsin P, 1985. Print.

Beach, King. "Consequential Transitions: A Sociocultural Expedition Beyond Transfer in Education." *Review of Research in Education* 24.1 (1999): 101–40. Print.

Brandt, Deborah. *The Rise of Writing: Redefining Mass Literacy.* Cambridge: Cambridge UP, 2014. Print.

Bransford, John D., and Daniel L. Schwartz. "Rethinking Transfer: A Simple Proposal with Multiple Implications." *Review of Research in Education* 24.1 (1999): 61–100.

Brent, Doug. "The Research Paper and Why We Should Still Care." *Writing Program Administration* 37 (2013): 33–53. Print.

Bunn, Michael. "Motivation and Connection: Teaching Reading (and Writing) in the Composition Classroom." *College Composition and Communication* 64.3 (2013): 496–516. Print.

Carillo, Ellen C. *Securing a Place for Reading in Composition: The Importance of Teaching for Transfer*. Logan: Utah State UP, 2015. Print.

Charney, Davida. "A Study in Rhetorical Reading: How Evolutionists Read 'The Spandrels of San Marco.'" *Understanding Scientific Prose*. Ed. Jack Selzer. Madison: U of Wisconsin P, 1993. Print.

Gogan, Brian. "Reading at the Threshold." *Across the Disciplines* 10.4 (2013). Web. 14 September 2015.

Greeno, James G. "On Claims that Answer the Wrong Questions." *Educational Researcher* 26.1 (1997): 5–17. Print.

Haas, Christina. "Learning to Read Biology: One Student's Rhetorical Development in College." *Written Communication* 11.1 (1994): 43–84. Print.

Haas, Christina, and Linda Flower. "Rhetorical Reading Strategies and the Construction of Meaning." *College Composition and Communication* 39.2 (1988): 167–83. Print.

Haswell, Richard H., Terri L. Briggs, Jennifer A. Fay, Norman K. Gillen, Rob Harrill, Drew M. Shapala, and Sylvia S. Trevino. "Context and Rhetorical Reading Strategies: Haas and Flower (1988) Revisited." *Written Communication* 16.1 (1999): 3–27. Print.

Howard, Rebecca Moore, Tricia Serviss, and Tanya K. Rodrigue. "Writing from Sources, Writing from Sentences." *Writing & Pedagogy* 2.2 (2010): 177–92. Print.

Keller, Daniel. *Chasing Literacy: Reading and Writing in an Age of Acceleration*. Logan: Utah State UP, 2014. Print.

———. "A Framework for Rereading in First-Year Composition" *Teaching English in the Two Year College* 41.1 (2013): 44–55. Print.

Lave, Jean. *Cognition in Practice: Mind, Mathematics and Culture in Everyday Life*. Cambridge: Cambridge UP, 1988. Print.

Lave, Jean, and Etienne Wenger. *Situated Learning: Legitimate Peripheral Participation*. Cambridge: Cambridge UP, 1991. Print.

Manarin, Karen. "Reading Value: Student Choice in Reading Strategies." *Pedagogy* 12.2 (2012): 281–97. Print.

Paul, Danette, and Davida Charney. "Introducing Chaos (Theory) into Science and Engineering: Effects of Rhetorical Strategies on Scientific Readers." *Written Communication* 12.4 (1995): 396–438.

Salvatori, Mariolina. "Reading and Writing a Text: Correlations between Reading and Writing Patterns." *College English* 45.7 (1983): 657–66. Print.

Shanahan, Cynthia, Timothy Shanahan, and Cynthia Misischia. "Analysis of Expert Readers in Three Disciplines: History, Mathematics, and Chemistry." *Journal of Literacy Research* 43.4 (2011): 393–429.

Smith, Cheryl Hogue. "Interrogating Texts: From Deferent to Efferent and Aesthetic Reading Practices." *Journal of Basic Writing* 31.1 (2012): 59–69. Print.

Sweeney, Meghan A., and Maureen McBride. "Difficulty Paper (Dis) Connections: Understanding the Threads Students Weave between their Reading and Writing." *College Composition and Communication.* 66.4 (2015): 591–614. Print.

Wineburg, Sam. *Historical Thinking and Other Unnatural Acts: Charting the Future of Teaching the Past.* Philadelphia: Temple UP, 2001. Print.

Yancey, Kathleen Blake, Liane Robertson, and Kara Taczak. *Writing Across Contexts: Transfer, Composition, and Sites of Writing.* Logan: Utah State UP, 2014. Print.

CHAPTER SIXTEEN

Unruly Reading

MARIOLINA RIZZI SALVATORI
University of Pittsburgh

PATRICIA DONAHUE
Lafayette College

> *Given the nature of the reading process and the contribution of rereading and reflection to textual understanding, we can say that any reading is valuable insofar as it is the product of a student's own engaged and mindful act. . . .*
> —SHERIDAN BLAU

In this chapter we return, once again, to a question so fundamental to our theoretical and pedagogical understanding of composition as a field of study that we have been mining its possibilities in numerous ways for decades. That question: What is the relationship between reading and writing, and in what ways and to what degree are the two so deeply connected and implicated that one can only be thought and *taught* with, alongside, and through the other?

In much of our previous work, and now in this chapter, we look at the subject of reading, especially student reading, from the same perspective with which writing has been examined for many years, at least since composition became a self-defined field of study. It is puzzling to us that reading has not yet been given quite the same attention as writing. Just as students have been encouraged to reflect on and to own their moves as writers, so they should be able to reflect on and own their moves as readers. Just as student writers have been encouraged to express the "writer within," to explore, investigate, and imagine new and fresh possibilities, so should student readers be allowed to express and rely on "the reader within," their repertoire of already acquired knowledge and assumptions that can make them engage a text in ways relatively unencumbered by or contrary to a teacher's expectations.

A term we first used in our recent coedited issue of *Pedagogy* and that serves as our title here is *unruly*. In its simplest sense, an "unruly reading" is a reading liberated from certain "school rules," from prescriptive ideas about how students should both read and be taught to read. The primary aim and function of such ideas, which derive from academic and disciplinary protocols whose origin and acquisition have been forgotten, is to straighten the errant, correct the deficiency, inculcate the "right" way (the teacher's way). By validating "unruly reading," a move we understand might sound odd to some, we are directing attention away from the notion that "students can't read" and "reading is a problem" to an acknowledgement that students have capacities and abilities we have yet to pay adequate attention to. The fact is that very little is actually known about how students read, because so much energy is invested in pointing out what students do wrong, what they aren't "getting," where they fail (the recently published *Critical Reading in Higher Education* [Manarin, Carey, Rathburn, and Ryland] is a notable exception).

We also want to argue that if student readers and student reading constitute a "problem" to be fixed, the real problem is not in student failure but in constructions of reading (and, implicitly, constructions of reading pedagogy) that came to the fore in the 1980s and 1990s and continue to hold sway, albeit in distorted ways, far removed from their original and sometimes ironic aim. These constructions view reading and the teaching of reading as fundamentally "impossible" acts. To unpack that idea, we examine three ideas or myths about reading responsible for this presumed "impossibility." We then suggest how certain reading activities commonly viewed as preparatory—annotation, summary, and paraphrase—can be repurposed from an interpretive perspective that encourages, values, and validates the "unruly."

The Impossibility of Reading, or Three Myths of Reading

The first and most common myth is that deep reading or critical reading has become impossible because today's college students lack the ability and experience either to concentrate on or to comprehend detailed, complex, and hypotactic texts; for this reason, many college teachers have removed difficult (including long) texts from syllabi or have assigned either fewer of them or excerpts rather than full-length works. Popularized in the 1970s (remember *Why Johnny Can't Read?*), this myth places blame for reading difficulties squarely on students' shoulders: their incompetence, disinterest, or confusion. A variation of this myth persists today, although in a slightly different form. Now the primary target is "the digital"—the Internet, social media, e-readers, and so on—which is thought to reduce students' powers of concentration, providing too many tempting distractions and even altering their neural circuitry. If cognitive powers have indeed been physiologically changed (the jury is still out), it shouldn't be surprising that both deep reading and the teaching of deep reading become impossible.

Another myth about reading (and the teaching of reading) is a long-standing one, and one especially familiar to writing specialists, since it has often been deployed as a weapon against writing pedagogy. It is the idea that while most students may be capable of producing serviceable writing (like five-paragraph essays), only a few naturally gifted writers are capable of producing real writing, elegant writing, beautiful writing. To paraphrase Josiah Royce's argument, "great readers (and writers) are born, not made." The truth, of course, is that geniuses have been taught and they have learned, even if the only teacher is the genius her- or himself. Such immeasurably talented individuals are not ordinary people, but tend to be autodidacts who read and write voluminously. Given the smallness of their numbers, it is irresponsible not to make the work of reading and writing possible for others—as writing specialists have been telling us for years.

The third myth is one rarely discussed outside the academy and, even then, not with as much gusto as in earlier years. It is one that can help explain why so many college teachers have abandoned the attempt to teach reading and feel justified in doing so. Like the others, this myth takes various forms, but it is traceable to a misreading of certain deconstructionist ideas about the infinite proliferation of textual meaning, the infinite play of the signifier, the infinite instability of texts. What was initially offered as a hyperbolic challenge to New Critical or formalist orthodoxy—entrenched ideas about organic unity, textual coherence, and referential stability—was understood by postdeconstructionists in serious rather than provocative terms. Because "interpretation" was indeterminate, and indeterminacy posed threats to disciplinary and pedagogical authority, interpretation itself as a subject of theoretical investigation was suppressed, ignored, or marginalized. Ultimately, this attitude set up a "great divide" between "good readers," those who can manage the endless and *unruly* play of meaning, and those who cannot, the students, all too often represented as "bad readers."

This truncated history, however, is missing an important piece: the attention lavished on reading at the same time, loosely the 1970s to 1990s, by theorists of reading often called reader-response critics, including such figures as Rosenblatt, Iser, Fish, Holland, and Bleich (reception studies also deserves a nod). To varying degrees, these theorists viewed texts as meaning-proliferative: because different readers bring different experiences and bodies of textual knowledge to the reading activity, the text that emerges in the act of reading is polyvalent, capable of meaning and being understood in many different ways. The power and authority assigned to readers varied, however, depending on the theorist, with Iser instructing readers to respect the repertoire "contained" within the text (there is some "there" there) and Fish backing off from his early ideas about radically individualized reading processes to offer in their stead a set of different but limited parameters as defined and transmitted by often competitive interpretive communities. Whatever the orientation, there was nonetheless something about reader-response theory, something about the possibility of readers reading differently, that led teachers largely to abandon it as a pedagogical approach. How could teachers assess their students' learning if students could largely produce interpretations on their own, interpretations that acquired authority either through the reader's experience (could a male teacher really tell a female student how to interpret a text whose subject is female lived experience?) or the protocols prescribed by a different interpretive community? What were teachers to do, faced with such impossible situations?

With "indeterminacy" reframed as infinite proliferation and "reader power" understood as a threat to teacherly authority, it is not at all surprising that the problematic of interpretation was eventually neglected, even abandoned. Consequences of this were dire, for both humanistic inquiry (especially within English studies) and the teaching of reading. Within the humanities, an interest in interpretation was supplanted by an altogether different orientation that viewed textual meaning as obvious or transparent. That approach, cultural studies (especially in the form known as New Historicism), substituted for the vagaries of linguistic meaning the certainties of historical specificity, essentially signaling the death of the reader (in extreme and reductive versions of reader-response theory, it was the author who had to be killed so the reader could be born). No longer was it the reader who constructed meaning; it was now the "cultural context" that reproduced itself. Whether through politics, ideology, environment, milieu, or author, the context became the situated entity through which the social writes and reads itself. In the classroom, this led to a reestablishment of the teacher as the subject who knows *everything*. Having problems reading a complex text? The teacher will explain. No opportunity for students to produce the unexpected, unpredictable, unruly. And recent forms of cultural studies that claim to revive an interest in reading (such as Moretti's "distant reading," or Best and Marcus's "surface reading," or scholars working in the "History of the Book") have proposed nothing that might fill this empty pedagogical space.

School Practices as Interpretive Acts

The alternative to these negative assumptions begins, not surprisingly, with the following question: What would make reading and the teaching of reading possible? Before we answer, we should list some of the texts we have found especially useful in the classroom as we support and encourage our students in the practice of un-ruly, surprise-provoking, possible, self-reflexive, and interpretive reading. As we have learned from many teachers who have read our work, any text (or fragments of text) can be artfully and intelligently deployed for such purposes, whether it be "literary" or "informational," assigned in English studies or elsewhere in the academic constellation (including science), used in first-year composition or a graduate course in pedagogy. Nonetheless, the texts we have often leaned toward in recent years, in courses of various kinds (mainly writing courses), include Alison Bechdel's *Fun Home*, John Berger's *Ways of Seeing*, Simon Blackburn's *Being Good,* Bruce Chatwin's *The Songlines*, Ralph Cintron's *Angels' Town*, Sigmund Freud's *Dora*, Claudia Rankine's *Citizen*, Oliver Sacks's *The Mind's Eye*, Susan Sontag's *Regarding the Pain of Others*, and Raymond Williams' *Keywords*. For the specific course referred to in the following pages (The Language of Pain, taught by Mariolina Salvatori at the University of Pittsburgh), we add to the list: Roland Barthes's *Mourning Diary*, Jean-Dom-inique Bauby's *The Diving Bell and the Butterfly,* David Biro's *Listening to Pain*, Eula Bliss's "The Pain Scale," Thomas Hardy's *Unexpected Elegies*, Donald Hall's *Without*, Marie Howe's *What the Living Do*, Madelaine Hron's *Translating Pain*, Ann Jurecic's *Illness as Narrative*, Eugenio Montale's *Xenia I, Xenia II*, Susan Sontag's *Illness as Metaphor,* and David Small's *Stitches*.

To return to our question. To reclaim the complex and elusive nature of reading, we need to reflect on, recapture, and learn to disclose to our students some of the basic steps and strategies we have become so proficient at that we often forget to acknowledge them. We need also to engage students in activities that demon-strate the interconnectedness of reading and writing and make certain moves visible and thus available for understanding and improvement. Among the activities we have found especially use-ful for this purpose are annotation, summary, and paraphrase, activities typically considered preparatory, something students do *before* they write. We, however, argue and demonstrate in the following pages that annotation, paraphrase, and summary are as much acts of writing as they are acts of reading. They are acts of inclusion and exclusion, foregrounding and backgrounding, dis-covery and construction, selection. They are acts of interpretation.

Keep in mind that none of the myths described earlier allows for reading and writing to be intertwined in this way, nor do they consider reflection, either on prior reading experience or the present reading process, necessary, valuable, or interesting. Thus, whether by accident or design, such myths effectively bar students from joining the major leagues. But when such myths are demythologized, when naturalized ideas (ideas whose histories have been forgotten) about reading are denaturalized, the "deficiency" model of reading loses credibility. Students begin to own their reading practice and to understand that they already possess a rich assortment of strategies for navigating texts. Additionally, those of us interested in the processes of interpretation can acquire a deeper understanding of the operations of reading and writing, since the everyday interpretive practices of student readers allow for considerable "pushback"—theirs and ours—against disciplinary norms.

Annotation as Interpretation

For several years, we have promoted the work of annotation as a combined reading and writing strategy. Our assignments have assumed various forms, depending on the course and our students' experience, but they have typically been sequenced in the following way. First, students annotate an assigned text according to a series of definitions taken from William H. Sherman's work on early modern reading practices (*Used Books: Marking Readers in Renaissance England*), wherein reading is defined as a form of "use": gathering, choosing, overhearing, stealing, wandering, and tracking. (This is a move that allows us to introduce students to the history of these practices and to a complex understanding of what these practices make possible—what it means to "use" a text mainly on one's own, without the intervention of teacherly "rules.") Second, students reflect on the annotations themselves: why they marked x and not y. Third, students read one another's annotations (of the same text), considering similarities and differences, and hypothesizing possible reasons for both. Finally, they read classmates' written responses to a text (in the form of position papers) to figure out the annotation system that sustained their classmates' reading of the text and to consider the effects of that reading on the responses they produced in their position papers. Here is the first annotation assignment:

Annotation 1
Choose a short text or an excerpt from a text you are reading for this class. If you can, make six copies of the text. For each copy, annotate in ways that visually represent the acts of use delineated by William H. Sherman in *Used Books* (gathering, choosing, overhearing, stealing, wandering, tracking, etc.). Having performed all six activities, see if you observe any similarities or differences among them (if you're not using copies, look to see if the different reading approaches encouraged you to focus on some parts of the text more than others). Did any of these verbs produce a "use" for you that is more effective or meaningful or valuable?

Students were also asked to consider certain questions (the full list is provided in the appendix). Which of the formulations of reading identified in the first exercise (reading as gathering, choosing, overhearing, stealing, wandering, tracking) seemed most "helpful" to them as readers, in the sense that they enabled students to acquire traction (really get "into" the text) or view the text as a complex entity (made up of various and perhaps even competing threads of ideas) or engage the text as part of a conversation (between the reader and the writer, between the writer and other people)? These questions are our ways of guiding students to take ownership of their own reading moves.

For the next assignment, we turn from the idea of "reading as use" and different kinds of texts that might be "used" in different ways to the students' development of an individualized system of annotation that represents how they are responding to what they are reading, what they thought was important to the text, and what they thought their teacher would consider important. Writing was preceded by class discussion about various kinds of importance—for them, personal and academic (the context of our class, other classes, other contexts), and for us, as they imagine us to be (within the parameters of this specific class or in our general identity as "teachers").

Annotation 2
Select a section of 3–5 pages from the next text we're about
to read in this class. Ahead of time, make a list of annotation
marks you have used before. Then annotate the text based on
what you think is "important" in it (drawing from our class
discussion about "importance"). You may find yourself using
some new annotation marks. That's OK. Just add them to your
list (divide the list into "before" and "after"). Make copies of
your annotated pages (you can take pictures of the pages on
your phone and send them to me in a single file), along with
answers to the questions included in this assignment.

Once again we provided a list of questions that asked students
to describe the marks they used, what each meant, why some
passages rather than others were marked; to trace their use of a
particular mark throughout the text; to reflect on the nature of
the comments they wrote; and to think about their annotations as
mapping a journey through the text (and while we won't elaborate
here, annotation can also be examined as a type of hypertext).

These are not directives. They are questions that prompt students to reflect on their work as readers, to consider their sources
of motivation, to consider annotations as providing a visible
map "of their journey through the text." This is not "before you
write work," but work that has its own merit, generating a kind
of writing (in the forms of icons, words, sentences) that enables
student readers to better understand what they do, how they've
done, and how they might change their practice in response to
a new context.

We learned a great deal from the work students did in response to these assignments. We learned that some students make
a habit of annotating texts while others do not. We learned that
those who do annotate often view it as a time-saving device that
limits the amount of effort spent re-reading. We learned that
novels aren't annotated as often as are scientific texts because
readers get lost in the story. We learned that many students feel
that annotation slows down the reading process, making it less
efficient. We learned that for some students annotation is a way
to remember details. We learned that many students had found it
difficult in the past to annotate because they never knew what was
important. This is all valuable information that teachers can use

to destabilize entrenched habits of reading by fostering reflection on the kind of work they allow or do not allow students to do.

The construction of annotation as a reading map is a difficult one. It requires repeated attention to the forms of different kinds of assignments. One of those assignments invited students to reflect on the annotations made by their classmates as they read an especially difficult text, difficult in both emotional and theoretical terms (*The Language of Pain: Finding Words, Compassion, and Relief* by David Biro, a medical doctor who, having received a bone marrow transplant as a cancer treatment, comes to understand our innate reliance on metaphor to make pain, if not fully expressible, at least, as Roland Barthes wrote, "utterable"). In preparation for class discussion, we selected and distributed to the whole class two of the weekly position papers on that text that students had submitted and asked them to analyze and map out, in writing, the system of annotation they thought their two classmates had used to perform their reading, as well as the kind of writing that system had made possible. Here is an example of the work this assignment produced.

Writer #1

It seemed to me that writer #1 had a very good understanding of Biro's words, at least on the surface. They utilized numerous quotes and cited many examples from the text, and even made several of their own conclusions about what Biro's words could have meant. This being said they seemed to largely be retelling what was read, in a condensed and summarized fashion; restating Biro's words in their own voice.

I imagine this writer read with a pen in hand, constantly scribbling down bits of information and underlining key points or quotes for later use in their essay. This method of reading, although slightly distracting in my mind, allowed the reader to gather valuable information surrounding the many areas of Biro's work. The text was broken into several sections that answered and posed different questions, and heavily annotating offered the reader the means to break down what Biro was saying and condense it into a more understandable and eventually, a more relatable form. In this way, the reader knew what Biro said, and quite possibly, what he meant, but there is never a thought given as to why he says the things he does, and to what purpose Biro is writing in the first place.

Writer #1's approach, while lending a good understanding of Biro's ideas was obstructive in reaching any deeper revelations about the text (save a few, such as the metaphor with bridges at the bottom of page one, and the wonderful parallel with art in the last paragraph). Pausing constantly to underline, extract a quote, or paraphrase on the margins, while industrious, and in the end, quite wise, can often interrupt any connecting thoughts or deeper level analysis of the text, resulting in an almost surface level retelling and consideration of Biro's ideas.

Writer #2

There is no easy way to critique one's own work, but listening to the class was very helpful for me when it came to breaking down the strengths and weaknesses of my writing and reading. There is no need to speculate in this case as to how I read, as I can recount exactly what I did and didn't do; I'm also aware of the consequences, both positive and negative of my choice in reading. The "Unnecessary" blip at the beginning of my essay was, despite being largely unrelated, and in all honesty, conceived for the purpose of making my piece more interesting and lyrical, was none the less true, at least to some extent. I had actually begun the reading the night before, making sure to utilize the methods of annotation we had learned in class, and that I had promised myself I would attempt to implement in my future reading, alas, a road trip did ensue and I was forced to take my reading to the front seat of moving vehicle. While I believe I understand less about Biro's actual page to page message and the significance of his anecdotes, I'd like to think I came close to grasping at the text on a more personal and overarching level. as a result of my uninterrupted reading, I may not have understood the text to its full extent, or even reached a level of comprehension where I would be able to explain, in detail, the book to another, but I did understand what the text meant to me, and I was able to keep the thoughts that popped into my head while reading alive by continually pondering them. These thoughts were my opinions, my suspicions, and my speculations of what Biro meant, why he meant it, and what drove him to mean and say such things as he did. I do not know if I am better or worse off as a result of this reading of mine, but for my purposes, I prefer it to the alternative. I prefer to think rather than retell, and analyze rather than snag quotes and use Biro's words to support a retelling of Biros own words.

Writer #1 and writer #2 commentaries were authored by the same student (Kyle Uricchio). In the second commentary, he is actually reflecting on his own annotation system and its effects on his own writing, since his paper was one of the two that had been chosen and distributed for class discussion.

This student (who seems to believe in the "born reader" myth), at this point in the semester, resisted doing the work of annotation, and his critique of writer #1's response to Biro's book is clearly colored by his skepticism about the usefulness of annotation. He pushed back at an assignment he did not like, and yet he produced valuable insight into the practice of annotation. The last three lines of the critique of his own writing shed light on his preferred method of reading (keeping the thoughts that popped in his head while reading alive by continually pondering them), which is the method that leads him to be critical of his classmate's system of annotation and the resulting quality of her writing. He prefers "to think rather than retell, and analyze rather than snag quotes and use Biro's own words to support a retelling of Biro's own words."

What we find remarkable about his writing is the interrelationship he establishes, on his own (the idea had not yet been brought up for discussion), between ways of reading and ways of writing. That his view of the practice of annotation was rather reductive is irrelevant to our argument.

Summary and Paraphrase

Paraphrase. *Para*: Alongside *Phrazein*: To point out Greek: *Paraphrazein* Latin: *Paraphrasis* "Another text alongside original; stays faithful to original text with new words to match." *Oxford English Dictionary*

Paraphrase. A restatement of a text or passage in another form or other words, *often to clarify meaning*. 1. The restatement of texts in other words as a *studying* or *teaching device*. 2. The adaptation or alteration of a text or quotation to serve a *different purpose from* that of the original. *The American Heritage Dictionary*

In this section, we want to call into question what seems to be a commonplace in composition studies—the idea that paraphrase and summary are essentially acts of translation whose differences are negligible (this idea was hotly debated in an August 2015 exchange on the Writing Program Administrators listserv). In contrast, our work with student readers and writers suggests that summary and paraphrase are both interpretive practices that draw on a reader's repertoire and function a priori. Let's take another look at the student text cited earlier:

> It seemed to me that writer #1 had a very good understanding of Biro's words, at least on the surface. They utilized numerous quotes and cited many examples from the text, and even made several of their own conclusions about what Biro's words could have meant. This being said they seemed to largely be retelling what was read, in a condensed and summarized fashion; restating Biro's words in their own voice.

This was one of those unexpected moments when student work redirects a teacher's plan for sequencing class discussions. The plan was to move, in the subsequent weeks, from annotation to summary and paraphrase to eventually foreground their connections and overlaps. Unexpectedly preempting his teacher's planned move, the student, on his own, connects summary and paraphrase to annotation. In his mind, summary ("retelling what was read, in a condensed and summarized fashion") and paraphrase ("restating Biro's words in their own words"), like annotation, have similar, and limited, purposes and effects. What they do not allow, or call for, is "a deeper level analysis of the text, resulting in an almost surface level retelling and consideration of Biro's ideas."

In this student's "resistant" (or "unruly") behavior, he provides an eloquent critique of mechanical uses of summary and paraphrase, the very uses we are critical of. But his critique seems to be predetermined and, like his resistance to annotation, it suggests a certain annoyance at having to do a kind of work he thinks thwarts his tendency and desire to ponder and reflect on his thoughts as he reads. Insofar as summary and paraphrase are thought of as just a retelling and just a restatement of somebody else's words in one's own voice, his point is well taken. But to define them in this way is to ignore that they are both acts of selection and evaluation, contingent on interpretation.

Students were asked to consider, ponder, and reflect on the questions we provided (again, see the appendix), which they did, dutifully, if not at first very insightfully. Eventually, though, these questions came to fruition when, later in the term, discussing what may account for differing interpretations of a text, students were asked to identify a sequence of segments or salient points in a poem as a possible base for their interpretation. Our aim was to encourage reflection on the difference that the point of entry into a text—the selection of a textual kernel as a "salient point" to unravel—makes for interpretation. They worked on the first half of Donald Hall's poem "Letter with No Address" (available on the Internet). They were divided into two groups and were given twenty minutes to complete their task (they had also been presented with the definition of *paraphrase* from the *Oxford University Dictionary*; the etymology offered by *The American Heritage Dictionary* is even more promising). This is what they wrote on the chalkboard:

Group A

1. Peak of Jane's sickness. She is dependent on him

2. Hall describes her in her casket

3. Today 4 weeks—visits grave

4. Paradise

5. Pretty flowers—photographs

6. Absence. An empty house

7. Desolate landscapes

8. Winter weather (death)

9. Imagining her in the driveway—ghostly image

10. Tries to speak w/ghost—reconnects w/news

Group B

1. It's been 4 wks since Jane's death

2. He establishes a daily routine

3. Catches Jane up on things they would have done

4. Recaps her funeral

5. Reflects on Jane's absence in the present

6. Tells her about driving to Tilton

7. Tells Jane about what's going on that day

8. Addresses Jane directly and visits her grave

For Group A, the entry point into the poem was a segment that evoked an *image*. For Group B, it was a segment that evoked *time*. "Image" and "Time" were subsequently selected as the captions for the two emerging narratives.

Though there were points of connection (e.g., Image #3 and Time #4; Image #6 and Time #5; Image #3 and Time #8), an attentive reading of the two sequences points to remarkable differences. The Time sequence is more orderly and matter-of-fact than the Image sequence. The Time sequence, from 3 to 8, is based on acts of speech; the Image sequence, from 1 to 9 (and arguably 10), is based on the act of seeing. Interestingly, the less orderly Image sequence extends to and incorporates the driveway, an image that appears not in the first but in the second part of the poem (which students were not working on). Technically an error, this "deviation" demonstrates how that (subsequent) image had become part of students' repertoire and had affected their reading.

Few would dismiss the complexity of summary in this example: the text is a poem, and interpretive dissonance and ambiguity are the hallmarks of poetry. This is not necessarily the case with prose, especially the serviceable, instrumental, and informational prose taught in many writing courses for the purpose of communication. Wouldn't and shouldn't different readers be able to identify in such prose the same "message," the same structure of ideas, the same evidence? We disagree. First of all, Hall's poem is not particularly ambiguous. Second, while poetry might be especially difficult to summarize, prose is not as transparent as the typical summary assignment assumes. To show the complexity of prose in action, let's look at an exercise in prose summary recently assigned by Patricia in an advanced undergraduate course in rhetorical theory:

Summary 1
"Summary" is an activity you've been asked to engage in throughout your college year and before. In our class, I've often asked you to summarize a passage by "putting it in your own words" (a task that is also called "paraphrase"). Once when I asked you why teachers asked students to summarize, you responded, "to show teachers you've read the material." Fair enough.

Below you'll find the closing paragraphs from John Berger's *Ways of Seeing,* which we've been discussing the past week. Summarize these paragraphs in as many or as few words as you choose.

Bring two copies of your summary to our next class. Since this exercise won't be graded, you can identify yourself by your real name, chosen pseudonym, or L number.

"Publicity exerts an enormous influence and is a political phenomenon of great importance. But its offer is as narrow as its references are visible. It recognizes nothing except the power to acquire. All other human faculties or needs are made subsidiary to this power. All hopes are gathered together, made homogeneous, simplified so that they become the intense yet vague, magical yet repeatable promise offered in every purchase. No other kind of hope or satisfaction or pleasure can any longer be envisaged within the culture of capitalism.

"Publicity is the life of this culture—in so far as without publicity capitalism could not survive—and at the same time publicity is its dream.

"Capitalism survives by forcing the majority, whom it exploits, to define their own interests as narrowly as possible. This was once achieved by extensive deprivation. Today in the developed countries it is being achieved by imposing a false standard of what is and what is not desirable" (153–54).

The following two summaries suggest, in a basic way, how even nonfictional prose, which strives for nonambiguity, is open to different interpretations (each of which represents for a student a discovery, an invention, a creative surge, an unruly act):

Writer #1
John Berger believes that ads, what he calls publicity, plays [sic] an important function in capitalist societies. Ads have a subliminal purpose. They make us want to buy things. When we buy things, we are really buying dreams. We buy what we think our identity will be once we own the thing. Others will be jealous of us. Ads tell us what we want and who we want to be. They exploit us because their definition of identity is very narrow.

Writer #2
In the conclusion to his book, Berger makes three main points. First, ads are important in capitalist societies. Without ads there would be no capitalism. Second, ads make vague promises. Thirdly, ads provide us with a sense of identity.

In small groups students were then asked to consider the following assignment:

Having read each of your summaries, what can you say about them? Do they indicate "to the teacher" that their authors have read the text? How? Do they highlight the same features of Berger's text? Are they different from each other? If so, why do you think they are different?

Reading these summaries was illuminating, not only for us, but also for the students. Students thought that the summaries "fairly" represented the gist of Berger's ideas. They found it interesting that the summaries displayed similar absences. Certain turns of phrase that were confusing—such as "political phenomenon" and "a false standard of what is and what is not desirable"—were ignored: writers selected to summarize what they understood and essentially erased potentially dangerous complexities (those embedded in words like *political,* for example). Students also noted that in some cases their classmates had inserted into their summaries ideas they must have acquired elsewhere: such as "subliminal" (a move that is not much different from what students did in the poetry exercise with the driveway image). These assignments reveal rather clearly that in contrast to the "schooled" and "rule-dominated" definitions of summary taught to students over the years, summarizing is not a mindless activity that transcends the exigencies of interpretation.

Like summary, in our discipline paraphrase is conceptualized and taught in simplistic terms. It is defined as a specific act of translation (look again at the epigraphs that open this section) usually performed on smaller passages whereby an author's ideas are retold in terms so synonymous as to be equivalent. This definition obscures the difficulty of paraphrase (and translation), argued years ago by the New Critic Cleanth Brooks in a chapter titled "The Heresy of Paraphrase" in his book *The Well-Wrought Urn*. Brooks argued that a paraphrase of a poem, in part due to the figurative, connotative, and condensed power of poetic language, always represents a distortion of the original. We would argue that prose, while less compact than verse, poses its own challenges.

To make our point, we return again to work done by students. In The Language of Pain course, *translation* became a term often used to explain the work that metaphors can do as they move (trans-late, trans-pose) invisible pain from one plane to another, from inside one's body and mind to outside, from the ephemeral to the tangible, inevitably changing the meaning and experience of pain in the process, both for those who "invent" and those who receive the metaphors.

In an in-class assignment, students were asked to read and to paraphrase two difficult prose paragraphs from Madelaine Hron's *Translating Pain: Immigrant Suffering in Literature and Culture*. They were not offered any background or contextual information.

> Translation is particularly useful when considering the expression of pain. Expressing pain is not a transparent act; yet, neither is it ineffable. Translation does not presume transparency; yet, at the same time it does counter inexpressibility. In no case does a translation connote exact equivalency; rather, it advances notions of difference, interpretation, and mediation.
>
> Like translators, writers are faced with the difficulties of finding linguistic equivalencies for their pain—be it to describe

their pain, convey its intensity, explain its cause, or specify its location. The scarcity of a direct language of pain does not mean that there is no viable mode of expression for their pain; rather, like translators, writers must engage in a variety of representational tactics to render their suffering understandable to others. (40–41)

Three students responded to this passage in the following ways:

Writer #1

Translation is used to help others understand what is being said. It acts as a mediator but it never exactly conveys what has been said; there is usually some discrepancy. [Hron's] "translation" is like [Biro's] "the language of pain" (metaphors) which serves as a way of expression, [as] a parallel of what is being felt just like translation is a parallel of what is being said.

Writers and translators are similar because they both find ways to express pain/linguistic difficulties through parallels—metaphors and different languages. Both struggle with scarcity and must use "representational tactics" to make sense of what is said/felt. (Gina Cappa)

Writer #2

"PARAPHRASE: Another text alongside original; stays faithful to original text with new words to match."

In the sense of communicating pain, translation is key. Translating is not entirely easy, but it is still somewhat accessible and achievable. However, no one goes through pain the same way . . . and no, translation does not imply that anyone would. What it does though is draw attention to the differences everyone feels when it comes to pain.

It's hard to convey exactly what's going through your head when you're in pain . . . even for skilled writers. Lacking a language that can be learned [contributes to] the hardships of explaining pain, intensity, cause, and location; but, this doesn't mean it's impossible. What needs to happen is a comparison of ideas to create a common ground. (Victoria Maatta)

Writer #3

Expressing pain is a difficult task, so translation [of it] is not easy. When speaking of pain people often resort to descriptive metaphors, leaving translation up to an interpretation of what is trying to be conveyed.

> It seems that both writers and translators are faced with the same issue. The lack of direct words for pain causes them to use language that represents the pain. (Sabine Lavache)

If paraphrase is the crafting of an equivalent (as the discipline holds and Brooks countermands), paraphrases constructed by different readers–writers should be similar. As we can see from these paraphrases, they aren't. For writer #1, "translation," Hron's key concept, provides parallels; for writer #2, it highlights differences; and for writer #3, its effectiveness is a function of how the receiver (reader) processes the metaphors. Each paraphrase is different, and each is also defensible. Interestingly, each also demonstrates the fluid and inevitable effect of repertoire on reading. Before reading Hron, each student reader–writer had read Biro and had come to her own conclusion about how metaphors translate pain. For each, Biro functioned as aid, probe, and filter through which Hron's argument was understood. Their previous work of reading had so enriched their repertoires as to generate different understandings and different paraphrases. This is one, and we believe potent, example of how "simple" acts like paraphrase can be reclaimed as complex acts of interpretation.

Unruly Reading as Possible Reading and the Possibilities of Teaching It

We began this chapter by affirming our continued investment in exploring how reading and writing are interconnected and in constructing ways of mining that connection. We have argued that if we want our students to become aware of this connection, we must focus on the "reader within" the readings they produce, for such readings emerge from repertoires that, while possibly shared, can also be highly discrete. We must point out how the ways students read affect, indeed determine, what and how they will write in response to a particular text. And we certainly need to encourage, identify, and even celebrate the kernel of genius—in the form of invention—that the engagement in practices even as "micro" as annotation, summary, and paraphrase can reveal, a kernel that should be encouraged and allowed to germinate and grow. Just as we abandoned years ago the prescriptives of a product pedagogy, we need, with reading, to move beyond the idea of the deficient reader who needs to be "schooled" in narrowly described practices that ignore preexisting repertoires, ignore the possibility and pleasures of individual discovery, and negate the power of reading as an interpretive and fecund act of possibility.

Let us conclude by underscoring what we believe should be a significant concern for anyone interested in reading—what it is, how it is performed, how it can be taught: that what now passes for interpretation (in contrast to earlier decades) isn't really interpretation at all, but a passive process that fails to examine the conditions of its own possibility. To make the re-turn to reading also a re-turn to interpretation, it is imperative that teachers themselves craft assignments that function as "assisted invitations" (as recommended by I. A Richards, Anne E. Berthoff, and others) and perform a series of *recuperative acts,* acts of self-reflexive interpretation, that can reveal, make visible, and thus subject to further investigation and revision, if necessary, the how and why of the moves the reader within makes. When both teachers and students identify and recuperate the unruliness of reading, they can challenge the authority of commonly accepted interpretations, they can crack their seal of validity, and in the process they can unleash the pleasures and surprises of reading.

Appendix

Students were also asked to consider the following questions:

- ◆ Referring to another text you read for *this* class, which of these formulations would you have found "useful," in the ways suggested by William H. Sherman? Why? What about another text? And another?

- ◆ Referring to any of the class texts you've analyzed in terms of "use," did you find that the decision you made about "use" was in any way influenced by the text's genre (however you now understand that term)? Do you see yourself "using" a literary text differently than a nonliterary one, a novel differently than a poem, a theoretical/philosophical piece differently than a graphic novel, an editorial in the newspaper differently than Freud's text?

◆ Look at the texts listed on the syllabus that we've yet to read. Based on your knowledge about their probable genres (I say "probable" because genres aren't always distinguishable, and they can also cut across boundaries as hybrids) (fiction or non-fiction, literary or informational), what predictions might you make about your annotations, the ways in which you will "use" them?

◆ Reflecting on the work you've just done, might you find some of the formulations and practice of "use" more appropriate to some college courses than to others? Write a short reflection paper (1–3 pages) in which you thoughtfully respond to these questions.

Works Cited

Barthes, Roland. *Mourning Diary*. New York: Hill and Wang, 2012. Print.

Bauby, Jean-Dominique. *The Diving Bell and the Butterfly*. New York: Vintage, 1998. Print.

Bechdel, Alison. *Fun Home: A Family Tragicomic*. New York: Mariner P, 2007. Print.

Berger, John. *Ways of Seeing*. London: Penguin, 1972. Print.

Berthoff, Ann E. *Forming, Thinking, Writing: The Composing Imagination*. Montclair, NJ: Boynton/Cook, 1982. Print.

Best, Stephen, and Sharon Marcus. "Surface Reading: An Introduction." *Representations* 108 (2009): 1–21. Print.

Biro, David. *Listening to Pain: Finding Words, Compassion, and Relief*. New York: Norton, 2011. Print.

Blackburn, Simon. *Being Good: A Short Introduction to Ethics*. New York: Oxford UP, 2002. Print.

Blau, Sheridan D. *The Literature Workshop: Teaching Texts and Their Readers*. Portsmouth: Heinemann, 2003. Print.

Bliss, Eula. "The Pain Scale." *Harper's Magazine* June 2005: 25–30. Print.

Brooks, Cleanth. *The Well-Wrought Urn*. New York: Mariner Books, 1956. Print.

Chatwin, Bruce. *The Songlines.* New York: Penguin Books, 1988. Print.

Cintron, Ralph. *Angels' Town: Chero Ways, Gang Life, and the Rhetorics of Everyday.* Boston: Beacon P, 1998. Print.

Fish, Stanley. *Is There a Text in This Class? The Authority of Interpretive Communities.* Cambridge, MA: Harvard UP, 1982. Print.

Freud, Sigmund. *Dora: An Analysis of a Case of Hysteria.* New York: Touchstone, 1997. Print.

Hall, Donald. *Without: Poems.* New York: Mariner P, 1999. Print.

Hardy, Thomas. *Unexpected Elegies: "Poems of 1912–13" and Other Poems About Emma.* New York: Persea, 2010. Print.

Howe, Marie. *What the Living Do.* New York: Norton, 1999. Print.

Hron, Madelaine. *Translating Pain: Immigrant Suffering in Literature and Culture.* Toronto: U of Toronto P, 2013. Print.

Iser, Wolfgang. *The Act of Reading: A Theory of Aesthetic Response.* Baltimore: Johns Hopkins UP, 1980. Print.

Jurecic, Ann. *Illness as Narrative.* Pittsburgh: U of Pittsburgh P, 2012. Print.

Manarin, Karen, and Miriam Carey, Melanie Rathburn, and Glen Ryland, eds. *Critical Reading in Higher Education: Academic Goals and Social Engagement.* Bloomington: Indiana UP, 2015. Print.

Montale, Eugenio. *Satura: 1962–1970.* Ed. Rosanna Warren. New York: Norton, 2000. Print.

Moretti, Franco. *Distant Reading.* New York: Verseo, 2013. Print.

Rankine, Claudia. *Citizen: An American Lyric.* Minneapolis: Graywolf, 2014. Print.

Richards, I. A. *Practical Criticism: A Study of Literary Judgment.* New York: Harvest, 1956. Print.

Royce, Josiah. *The Philosophy of Josiah Royce.* Ed. John K. Roth. Indianapolis: Hackett, 1982. Print.

Sacks, Oliver. *The Mind's Eye.* New York: Vintage, 2011. Print.

Salvatori, Mariolina Rizzi, and Patricia Donahue. "What Is College English? Stories about Reading: Appearance, Disappearance, Morphing, and Revival." *College English* 75.2 (2012): 199–217. Print.

————, eds. *Pedagogy* 16.1 (2016). Print.

Sherman, William H. *Used Books: Marking Readers in Renaissance England*. Philadelphia: U of Pennsylvania P, 2009. Print.

Small, David. *Stitches: A Memoir*. New York: Norton, 2010. Print.

Sontag, Susan. *Illness as Metaphor: And AIDS and Its Metaphors*. New York: Picador P, 2001. Print.

————. *Regarding the Pain of Others*. New York: Picador P, 2004. Print.

Williams, Raymond. *Keywords: A Vocabulary of Culture and Society*. London: Fontana/Croom Helm, 1976. Print.

IV

LETTERS TO STUDENTS ABOUT READING

CHAPTER SEVENTEEN

An Open Letter to High School Students about Reading

PATRICK SULLIVAN
Manchester Community College

Dear High School Students,

Greetings!

A few years ago I wrote an open letter to ninth graders about college readiness, trying to provide beginning high school students with a college professor's perspective on what being ready for college really means (see "An Open Letter to Ninth Graders" in the January–February 2009 issue of *Academe*). As it turns out, "being ready" involves a lot more than taking a particular sequence of courses or achieving a certain GPA. My original letter received a very enthusiastic response from high school teachers and students. Some teachers even had their students write their own letters back to me in response to what I said. It was great getting feedback directly from high school students.

There were many areas of agreement expressed in the letters I have received from students over the years, but one rather consistent area of resistance was about reading. In my letter, I told students that if they wanted to be ready for college they needed to love reading, they needed to read for pleasure, and they needed to do a lot of reading overall. A number of the students I heard from did not like this advice one bit.

I have a few more things I'd now like to share with you about getting ready for college—and, believe it or not, they all involve reading.

This piece originally appeared in *Academe,* a journal of the American Association of University Professors. Copyright 2016 by AAUP.

In the years since I published that open letter, I have done a great deal of research on reading and learning, and I am in the process right now of coediting a scholarly book about reading, *Deep Reading: Teaching Reading in the Writing Classroom* (NCTE). As I mentioned in my first letter, I am the coeditor of two books about college readiness—*What Is "College-Level" Writing?* (2006) and *What Is "College-Level" Writing? Volume 2* (2010)—so I've spent a great deal of time thinking about what high school students need if they want to be successful in college.

My research has confirmed that "deep" reading and reading for pleasure may be the most important things you can do to prepare for college.

One study that has shaped my thinking on this subject was conducted by Alice Sullivan and Matt Brown. Their research showed that reading for pleasure produces important benefits across a variety of academic disciplines (including math) and that "reading is actually linked to increased cognitive progress over time." Obviously, these cognitive gains will help you regardless of your major or career aspirations. This study was based on data gathered from six thousand students in the United Kingdom. It may seem counterintuitive that reading can help you with math, but if we think of reading as an activity that by its very nature—regardless of what you are reading—helps us develop more sophisticated ways of understanding the world, then it makes good sense.

As the French novelist Marcel Proust noted, "It is through the contact with other minds which constitutes reading that our minds are 'fashioned.'" Exposure to new vocabulary, new ideas and conceptual understandings, new ways of forging relationships between ourselves and others and ourselves and the world, and new forms of reasoning help us do this.

Another important study that has helped shape my understanding of the importance of reading to college readiness was conducted by French sociologists Pierre Bourdieu and Jean-Claude Passeron. These researchers found that the influence of language skills developed through reading, conversation, and family life "never ceases to be felt" across an individual's life span. And the benefits go much deeper than vocabulary: "Language is not simply an instrument of communication: it also provides, together with a richer or poorer vocabulary, a more or less complex system of categories, so that the capacity to decipher and manipulate complex structures, whether logical or aesthetic," depends partly on the complexity of the language a student possesses. Some of this is passed down like an inheritance by one's family, and some is gained through effort, application, and focused attention to reading. Reading, then, can literally help determine the way we are able to think.

As I mentioned in my first letter, science has begun to play an important role in our understanding of learning, and some fascinating discoveries have been made in this regard related to reading. We now know that the brain actually *changes* as a result of engaged, effortful learning and that when we challenge ourselves to learn something new, the brain forms new neural pathways. These new pathways make us smarter. As psychologist Carol Dweck has noted, "More and more research is showing that our brains change constantly with learning and experience and that this takes place throughout our lives."

The discovery of the brain's "neuroplasticity" has important implications for you as students. New evidence suggests that intelligence and IQ are not fixed but rather can be strengthened through effort and activity. In fact, researcher Maryanne Wolf has shown that reading itself has had a profound impact in shaping human history and the development of the human brain: "Reading is one of the single most remarkable inventions in history; the ability to record history is one of its consequences. Our ancestors' invention could come about only because of the human brain's extraordinary ability to make new connections among its existing structures, a process made possible by the brain's ability to be shaped by experience. This plasticity at the heart of the brain's design forms the basis for much of who we are, and who we might become." Wolf suggests there is great value in students engaging in challenging reading activities— reading that is "time-demanding, probative, analytical, and creative." This is important research for you to know about as you think about getting ready for college and establishing the kind of approach to your work that you will choose to take in high school.

There has also been a great deal of research recently on the difference between "deep learning" and "surface learning." Much of this research focuses on how students engage the texts they read for school. A key variable in this research is how students position themselves *as readers* in classrooms. Some ways of engaging with texts provide very powerful opportunities for growth, while others provide very limited opportunities. In one study, sociologists Judith C. Roberts and Keith A. Roberts found that many students see "reading" as simply forcing one's eyes to "touch" each word on the assigned pages, and many students candidly admit that they do not even read assigned materials at all. Many students often read only to *finish* rather than to *understand* what they have read. Students may favor this kind of approach to learning because it requires minimal effort. Obviously, however, with minimal effort comes minimal rewards.

"Deep learning" and "deep reading" require a very different kind of engagement and investment from you, but they produce significant gains that can help you develop college-level skills and dispositions. Instead of memorization, recall, and shallow engagement, "deep reading" requires reflection, curiosity, humility, sustained attention, a commitment to rereading, consideration of multiple possibilities, and what the education scholar Sheridan Blau has called "intellectual generosity." These are characteristics highly valued in the workplace, and they can be of great service to you in all areas of your life. Why not start developing them now?

Reading researchers have also found that we read for all kinds of different reasons, and readers often have to adjust their reading strategies for different purposes and contexts. When we read for pleasure, we often read a text just once, and rather quickly, focusing on the enjoyment and the pleasure. When we read a complex text or sophisticated research, we may still focus on the enjoyment of encountering new ideas and challenging content, but we often have to change our approach and read more carefully, more slowly, and more deliberately. We also have to assume that we will likely need to reread key passages in order to understand them fully. I do this myself almost every day in my professional life as a scholar and teacher, even though I am a fairly skilled reader.

Strong readers expect to make situational adjustments in how they read, depending on context and purpose—and on what they are reading and why they are reading it. This understanding can be a very useful component of your repertoire of college-level reading skills and strategies.

I also have to admit, in the interests of full disclosure, that we as teachers have probably helped create some of the aversion to reading that many students feel. Educator Kelly Gallagher has called this process "readicide"—"the systematic killing of the love of reading, often exacerbated by the inane, mind-numbing practices found in schools." Gallagher suggests that readicide is caused by educational practices that value the development of test-takers over the development of lifelong readers. I'm afraid that this statement may, alas, be true. It certainly helps explain the disturbing results reported on the Nation's Report Card, an important congressionally mandated project run by the National Center for Education Statistics. In 2015, only 37 percent of twelfth-grade students in the United States performed at or above "proficient" in reading. The remainder tested below proficient, with either "basic" or "below basic" reading skills.

Two recent reports about reading from the National Endowment for the Arts—*Reading at Risk* and *To Read or Not to Read: A Question of National Consequence*—confirm the disturbing scope and nature of this problem. You need to know about this research, because it can provide guidance—and motivation—for you as you prepare for college. So much of college is built around reading. You want to be going in as strong readers who enjoy reading and can handle the volume and complexity of college-level reading material.

So what am I recommending? I recommend that you start to find a way right now to enjoy reading and to make it an important part of your life. A great deal of research has been done on the importance of free choice in building engagement with reading, so choosing what you are interested in is a great way to start. You can read whatever books or articles you want. Of course, we all enjoy reading social media, but we're not going to count that. Let's focus, instead, on books and articles. This kind of reading requires sustained concentration that will help you develop a number of important cognitive skills, including the capacity to focus your attention for longer periods of time and the ability to monitor and direct your reading processes (metacognition). These skills will be vitally important to you in college and beyond.

I wish you the very best in your high school years and great success as you transfer to college and put these essential reading and thinking skills to work. If you'd like to discuss anything that I've said here, please feel free to write me a letter or send me an e-mail. I would enjoy hearing from you.

Chapter Eighteen

Kick Back, Slide Down, and Enjoy the Cruise, or Slow Reading Is Like Low Riding

Alfredo Celedón Luján
Monte del Sol Charter School
Sante Fe, New Mexico

Slow reading is like low riding. You slide into the driver's seat, get hold of the steering wheel, slide down, kick back, and cruise down the main drag. No hurry. Take your time . . . look out the windows at the scenery. *Oralé.* Enjoy the rhythms of ride. It's not a "race to the top"; it's a cruise to somewhere. Reading, like writing, like low riding, is for getting from point A to point B, but it's also for adventure and pleasure. Simple pleasure.

I'm a slow reader and a slow writer, and I went to college, so I *must* be a college-level reader and writer, right? I am the teacher, yet I am a slow reader. I've always wondered why. After four decades of teaching and six decades of reading, I think I've finally figured it out. I focus on the writer's craft. I check out the writer's (word)smithing: his or her "heating, hammering, and forging" of words, phrases, and sentences. When I read, I pay special attention to what the writer is doing. I underline passages and make marginal notes (this slows me down, but don't blame me—blame the teacher who taught me to highlight and annotate).

I wonder, especially in first-person narratives, whether the character is simply reporting the story or whether the author is imposing her or his agenda through the narrator. I ask myself whether I can employ an author's strategies in my own writing. What can I borrow from authors, while being mindful of their intellectual property yet regardful of my own voice? What about the reading and writing of those around me? My family, my students?

I share with my students the reading habits of my family . . . only to explain that under each roof there is diversity among readers. My wife has books all around her. There's always a stack on her bedside table. She comes from a family of readers. She devours books. She can go cover to cover in one day. Ditto for my seventeen-year-old-daughter Mabel, who reads for school but enjoys it. And she also reads books of her own choosing. Like her mother, she loves to receive books for gifts. My other daughter, Amanda, has an MA in interpreting pedagogy. My son, Peter, reads too (when he has to). He's reading *The Odyssey* now. And he will read about Kobe and *Los* Lakers until he's purple and gold in the face—bios, mags, profiles, Internet articles—anything that annoys his Celtics green dad. After reading O. Henry's "The Gift of the Magi," he wrote an essay titled "Lakers Game" (boo, hiss!). However, he made his dad proud with his reader-response essay on the value of a nonmaterial gift, from which I take this excerpt:

> When I was in 5th grade, my Cousins Larry and Melanie [thanks to their friends Jerry and Linda] bought my Dad and me Los Angeles Lakers vs. Boston Celtics tickets for my birthday. I was extremely excited because I had just recently become a huge Kobe Bryant fan. I was a die-hard Laker fanatic, and my Dad has been a Celtics fan since before he was my age. It was always a huge rivalry around the house. It got especially intense on the day the Lakers and Celtics played each other on TV. It was and still is a huge part of my childhood. . . .
>
> We arrived at Staples Center, home of the Los Angeles Lakers. . . . I was shaking with excitement. . . . I saw the famous Magic Johnson and Kareem Abdul-Jabbar statues and nearly peed my pants. I was walking around with Larry . . . who also wore purple and gold . . . in the lobby, gift stores, and food court, prior to the game, when a woman walked up to us. I thought it was a little bit strange until I noticed her Laker badge. She said, "Hello, would you like come down to the court with us and give the Lakers high-fives as they run out of the tunnel."
>
> I started shaking and thought, "Could it be?!?"
>
> Then my dad walked up in his green Celtics hat and t-shirt. She paused, but then she said it: "Would you let your son come down to the court with us?" My heart combusted with excitement.
>
> Dad said, "Don't hold my green against him. Absolutely!"
>
> . . . I had never been more happy in my entire life. I lined up with about fifteen other kids who looked to be around my

age. . . . There was one thing that I noticed about every single one of them: they were all dressed in Laker apparel. I thought, *I can't be that decked out.* Then I looked at myself. I was wearing a Lakers hat, Kobe Bryant jersey over my Lakers t-shirt, purple and gold Lakers shorts, Lakers lanyard, and purple and yellow Jordan shoes. I was a walking souvenir.

Seconds later I was on the court. It was surreal. . . . We got to sit in the seats that the actual players were going to sit in later that game. At the time the Boston Celtics were warming up on the other side of the court. Then we stood up and the Lakers came through the tunnel. After about six players, Kobe Bean Bryant was getting close to me. I looked at his face and couldn't believe that he was giving me, Peter Lujan, a high five. It was the best half-second of my entire life.

This gift was way more than special to me. This gift symbolizes hope. . . . Those mere five minutes on the court are forever engraved in my memory, and that gift is priceless.

And me, well, like I said, I read for words and phrases and techniques that "jump out," though I've read some books from cover to cover in a day or two without stopping: *One Flew over the Cuckoo's Nest, Little Big Man, Black Water, When the Game Was Ours,* and *Bless Me, Ultima.* Like the low rider tortoise, I've slowly read all other books, stories, essays, articles, and poems.

So I wonder about my students. What are their reading lives like? What do they want to learn? Do they read for pleasure? "Why do you read?" I ask. They answer:

"I read to educate myself and observe. . . ."—Katrina Loffer

" . . . to learn what isn't taught in schools . . ."—Ona Archie

" . . . to get information . . ." —Sahana Nava Mendez

" . . . to get connected to the story if it's a good book . . ." —Ava Gannon

"Reading entertains me. . . . I share what I read." —Denise Terrazas Perez

"I enjoy reading, and time passes. . . ."—Harshini Vallabhaneni

"So I can get better. I'm not a very good reader. . . ."
—Emily Mueller

"I read to find out more. . . ."—Michael Apodaca

"I like to read a cool, fun story. . . ."—Robin Hart

"I read to calm me down. . . ."—Ilora Degreff

"I read to get smarter. . . ."—Yusef Morris

"I read to use my imagination."—Trevor Vorenberg

"I read to learn someone else's story."—Zoe Colfax

"I don't read because I'm kinda lazy and books are too long."
—Gabby Pineda

I ask what they specifically like to read. They write:

> As Junior [*The Absolutely True Diary of a Part-Time Indian*] says, cartoons are his life boats; reading books is one of mine. Books leave so much to the loud imagination of a quiet girl. . . .
> My favorite series, the Sammy Keyes series, is written by Wendilen Van Draanen. My favorite character from these three books/series is Ponyboy Curtis, and my favorite quote from them is from *Perks*: "So this is my life, and I want you to know that I am both happy and sad. . . . I'm still trying to figure out how that can be."—Jaymee Romero

> I don't like to read, but my favorite quote from Kurt Cobain's bio is, "I'd rather be hated for who I am than loved for who I'm not."—Daniel Rodriguez

> The thing I like about reading is I can visualize the story really well because of my overactive imagination. My favorite genres are science fiction and horror; my favorite author is Stephen King because the main character in his books always lives to tell the tale.—Jonah Singh

I ask my students to think about what they want from reading. I ask them to design reading–learning antennae at the beginning of the school year. I stick-figure sketch my own perception antennae on the whiteboard. I ask them to think about reading, not just as a requirement, but instead as a way to access what they want to learn: *what* they want to read. "I'm only your guide," I tell them. "You pay me to do my job. Where do you want me to guide you? What do *you* want to know about language arts and/or American literature?" I ask. "What will your antennae search for when you're reading? When will they vibrate with excitement?" I then ask students to design antennae that will be seeking entertainment, knowledge, and information. "Turn in your designs tomorrow."

Keep in mind that some of my students have few or no books in their homes. Their parents don't read. They don't read. But nearly all of them have a TV in their bedroom. Most have computers, but some have no Internet access.

Figure 18.1 offers some of the students' designs (and mine) that illustrate what their antennae will be in quest of, what will make them vibrate with excitement, and thus we integrate art with the study of American literature.

FIGURE **18.1.** *Student and teacher drawings of antennae in search of exciting things to read.*

College-level reading is also about being able to criticize a book, analyze it, and/or make text-to-life connections. From the reactions in my classroom when we discussed Sherman Alexie's young adult novel, I thought everyone enjoyed *The Absolutely True Diary of a Part-Time Indian*. But one day, Jonah, a relatively quiet student, said he found the book offensive due to the main character's obsession with sex. And after we read from James Baldwin's *Notes of a Native Son*, Jake Wolinsky wrote this double-entry journal:

> "Along each of these avenues, and along each major side street—116th, 125th, 135th, and so on—bars, stores, pawnshops, restaurants, even little luncheonettes had been smashed open and entered and looted." James Baldwin, *Notes of a Native Son*

> Response: The riot that occurred in the summer of 1943 in Harlem is very contemporary with the rioting/protesting that occurred in Ferguson, Missouri. Although the initial intent was to protest, eventually it just turned into a mob of people raiding businesses. This is almost exactly what happened in Ferguson. . . .

And after reading the following passage (perhaps my favorite paragraph from American literature ever) from *The Grapes of Wrath*:

> "The concrete highway was edged with a mat of tangled, broken, dry grass, and the grass heads were heavy with oat beards to catch on a dog's coat, and foxtails to tangle in a horse's fetlocks . . . sleeping life waiting to be spread and dispersed, every seed armed with an appliance of dispersal, twisting darts and parachutes for the wind, little spears and balls of tiny thorns, and all waiting for animals and for the wind, for a man's trouser cuff or the hem of a woman's skirt, all passive but armed with appliances of the anlage of movement."

> [Savannah Junes wrote] Steinbeck is describing a very dry and desolate country side. It is literal in the sense that seeds do get caught and dispersed by animal fur, and that they lay in wait for the wind to carry them off. . . . It is metaphorical in the sense that the seeds, although quiet and still, are armed with

the ability to disperse with the beginning of their migration [like the Joads].

In my humble opinion, these examples of student reading and writing are college level; at least, they're college-level bound.

I recently was a resident writer at the Noepe Center for Literary Arts on Martha's Vineyard. There were ten writers in residence, and we each found our physical and cerebral writing niche in the house. Some wrote in their rooms, others with their laptops on a recliner, some in the kitchen, others in the courtyard when the weather was good. I wrote on the dining room table, like I do at home—early, before anyone else is up.

Eventually, there was traffic in and out of the dining room each morning as writers ate breakfast. Caille Millner from San Jose, California, who grew up near poverty alongside migrant workers in the valley, now a Harvard graduate, art critic, and writer for the *San Francisco Chronicle*, was one such writer. Each day she seemed to be reading a new book as she crunched on her breakfast. One morning she laughed aloud while she read. I asked her what she was reading. It was "Settlers" from Edith Pearlman's *Binocular Vision: New & Selected Stories*.

"Are you reading for pleasure or are you reading to inform your writing?" I asked.

"Aren't they the same thing? Reading every day is more important than writing," she said.

Later, my friend Tino met me at Martha's Vineyard to accompany me home to New Mexico. Our adventure: we would cruise on the Martha's Vineyard Ferry from Vineyard Haven to Wood's Hole, then take the Peter Pan Bus to South Station, then Amtrak on the Lake Shore Limited to Chicago, then the Southwest Chief to New Mexico. He's a retired mechanical engineer and my high school best buddy. He was reading the John Sandford Virgil Flowers mystery series along the route. I was reading *Little Big Man* and *A Moose and a Lobster Walk into a Bar . . . .*

We went to the dining car at our appointed times, and at each meal we were randomly seated across from other passengers. One husband–wife couple was from Northern California, and they often rode the train across the country to see the contiguous landscape. In Chicago they would split off and take the California Zephyr. We, on the other hand, would cut diagonally to New Mexico. Another couple was traveling to their home in Orange County, California. He was a bird photographer and she was a retired public librarian. Both were writers, neither widely published. One breakfast morning we sat across from two young women, each engrossed in a book. Eventually they put their books down, and we did the introductions litany. One was Elizabeth and the other was Beth. Both were novelists. Elizabeth had an MFA in creative writing from Carlow University in Ireland. Beth had a degree in speech communication and theater from Northern Arizona University. Both novelists were reading, not writing. They were both reading *Hollow City: The Second Novel of Miss Peregrine's Peculiar Children*. So of course I asked why they were reading, not writing.

"We write every day," Elizabeth said, "but a writer not reading is like a musician not listening to music."

Beth said, "Reading is a connection to a long lineage of writers. If you wanna be a writer, you have to write, and if you wanna be a writer, you also have to read. They go hand in hand—it's a way to delight in the craft."

In 2015, I taught; I learned; I read; I wrote; I rode; I cruised; I thought—same as my students. I witnessed others reading and writing. With certainty, reader, I can say that readers write and writers read. Literacy. "Writing is in each person's storytelling neurobiology," said Beth on the train. We must give ourselves reading and writing time in which we can delight in the craft, and it shouldn't feel like an assignment. We're readers and writers, not just students and teachers. I can't stress this enough: it pays to read.

Works Cited

Alexie, Sherman., *The Absolutely True Diary of a Part-Time Indian.* Illus. Ellen Forney. New York: Little, Brown, 2007. Print.

Baldwin, James. *Notes of a Native Son*. Boston: Beacon, 1955. Print.

Steinbeck, John. *The Grapes of Wrath*. 1939. New York: Penguin, 2006. Print.

Afterword

ALICE S. HORNING
Oakland University

When Patrick Sullivan first contacted me about our book project, *What Is College Reading?*, having heard about it from a colleague, I was delighted to learn that there was more than one book in the works on reading. For the last few years, I have been on a personal campaign to put reading on everyone's agenda, in writing classrooms and beyond. Over the course of the development of our two books, we have been in occasional contact and have worked out our respective focused areas of interest: Sullivan and company have collected this excellent series of pieces on the reading–writing connection, while our collection looks across the curriculum to focus on reading in various disciplinary and cross-disciplinary venues. Between the two, we have created a solid array of essays on theory and practice in postsecondary reading. And we definitely need both collections, technological changes to books, reading, and the world at large notwithstanding.

Sullivan et al. make clear at the outset why two volumes are needed. Reading is a big topic and it is a big problem. The latest numbers from the National Assessment of Educational Progress (NAEP) reading test for high school seniors show 38 percent are proficient in reading, based on 2013 results. In the college classroom, this result means that six out of ten students don't read well enough to complete the assignments they are given. NAEP is a national sample run by the US Department of Education; the test is not administered to high school seniors every year, but the 2015 results for eighth graders show 34 percent proficient—not a good sign. Readers might well think that standardized assessments like NAEP have many flaws, and they do. They might think that standardized tests do not look at students' abilities online, and they don't. They might think that students are doing much more reading and writing now because of their constant use of smartphones and social media, and they are. But given our definition of *college reading*, it should be clear why there really is a reading problem:

> College-level academic reading can be defined as a complex, recursive process in which readers actively and critically understand and create meaning through connections to texts.

Being able to read in *this* way is essential to success in personal and professional realms as well as to full participation in a democratic society. There is a large pile of studies, both quantitative and qualitative, to suggest the need for concern about students' reading abilities (see, for instance, the ACT organization's major study in 2006, the recent study by the Stanford History Education Group, as well as the findings of the Citation Project as discussed by Sandra Jamieson).

As noted, many readers might think the reading problem "trope" is overused, but it is not if our definition is a fair one (it is derived from the definitions submitted by the contributors to *What Is College Reading?*). And readers might also think that with the technological changes unfolding in our lives, reading will be changing as well, and this will also be true. However, as Kevin Kelly, founder of *Wired* magazine and a widely respected technology writer, has pointed out, the reading we are concerned about has features we need to preserve for a number of reasons. Writing in his 2016 book *The Inevitable: Understanding the 12 Technological Forces That Will Shape Our Future*, Kelly notes that reading in the traditional sense has some advantages:

> When you are engaged in this reading space, your brain works differently than when you are screening. Neurological studies show that learning to read changes the brain's circuitry. Instead of skipping around distractedly gathering bits, when you read you are transported, focused, immersed.
> One can spend hours reading on the web and never encounter this literature space. One gets fragments, threads, glimpses. That is the web's great attraction: miscellaneous pieces loosely

joined. But without some kind of containment, these loosely joined pieces spin away, nudging a reader's attention outward, wandering from the central narrative or argument. (91)

I suggest that the reading space Kelly describes is the place we want students to be, and "screening," as he calls it, won't get them there. If we want, as I think we do, readers who can do "deep reading"—that is, readers who can stay focused and follow a narrative or argument—then yes, there really *is* a problem with reading.

Where reading and books may be going does not change the goal of our two collections. Kelly describes the long-standing quest for a universal library of all books, going back to Alexandria and forward to Google Books (96ff.). As technology advances, the possibilities for such a library increase, leading to four key developments, he claims. First, obscure works will get a larger audience, at least potentially (101). Second, the past will be much more accessible as the original documents and records are scanned and become readily available. Third, writers will have a stronger sense of authority because they will be able to access and read everything that is available on a given topic. Finally, all people will be able to participate actively in the culture in which they live because of their access to information from books, websites, and other kinds of materials (102). These changes are surely coming or are in some ways already here: just ask Siri!

However, for people to make real use of these resources, the essentials of "deep reading" or college reading will be required; helping students to develop the essential skills of deep reading is the responsibility of teachers in writing classes and across the curriculum. Donald Leu, one of the leading researchers on reading and "new literacies," made this point clear quite some time ago with his colleagues:

> It is essential, however, to keep in mind that the new literacies
> . . . almost always build on foundational literacies rather than
> replace them. Foundational literacies include those traditional
> elements of literacy that have defined almost all our previous
> efforts in both research and practice. These include skill sets
> such as phonemic awareness, word recognition, decoding
> knowledge, vocabulary knowledge, comprehension, inferential

reasoning, the writing process, spelling, response to literature, and others required for the literacies of the book and other printed material. Foundational literacies will continue to be important within the new literacies of the Internet and other ICTs. In fact, it could be argued that they will become even more essential because reading and writing become more important in an information age. (Leu et al. 1590–591)

These scholars explain why the essentials of reading will always be needed; it is worthwhile to note as well that Kelly, for all his claims about technology, makes those claims in a plain, old-fashioned paper-and-ink book.

This collection not only draws together the work of a number of respected scholars in the field of reading and writing, but it also brings in some newer scholars, along with the voices of college students and teachers working on the same issues, discussing the past, present, and future of reading and writing. David Jolliffe's opening piece, for example, looks both back and forward to clarify the nature of the "reading problem" as he defines it. Reporting on a long conversation with a number of colleagues, he comes to a series of issues that need the attention of one and all, including a good handful that the present book and our companion volume attempt to address. High school teacher Sam Morris is one of the new voices, reflecting thoughtfully about reading and writing in the high school setting. His careful critique of an Advanced Placement program echoes a number of my own concerns about how reading is treated in the AP program (as discussed in "Rethinking AP" in the *Journal of Teaching Writing* [Horning]); despite his experiences, he reports on ways he found to get students engaged with reading and writing. The future of reading will be bright if scholars like these continue to explore ways to make reading everyone's job.

Muriel Harris echoes this general line of thinking in her discussion of reading in the writing center situation. As a contributor to the planned special issue of *Writing Lab Newsletter* on reading, I find the attention to reading of a key leader in writing center scholarship heartening. She rightly (in my view) points to students' reading problems as they play out in tutorials as students work to complete writing assignments of various kinds. I believe this assembled collection and our companion book address the need for scholarship on reading in and out of the writing center as Harris suggests. But I would also point out that scholarship on reading has been appearing over the last decade (my own and others' such as David Jolliffe's); it simply needs much more attention than it has appeared to get until just the past few years.

Jason Courtmanche shows just what happens when teachers and students *do* read and *do* pay attention to texts. Though he doesn't cite Steven Pinker's *The Better Angels of Our Nature: Why Violence Has Declined*, his experience provides support for Pinker's claim that reading teaches people empathy, contributing to the decline of violence in society. Pinker spoke a few years ago at my university. When he got to the part in his talk about this book, in which he shows trend lines for increasing book publication and literacy rates next to a trend line for a decline in all types of violence, I had trouble keeping myself from standing on my chair and yelling, "You tell 'em, Stevie!" (see a YouTube clip of Pinker discussing this issue at https://www.youtube.com/watch?v=wWeh1Pam4Bc). Voices like these of Jolliffe, Morris, Harris, and Courtmanche achieve the primary goal that Patrick Sullivan, Howard Tinberg, Sheridan Blau, and I and my colleagues, Cynthia Haller and Deborah Gollnitz, have set for our books: to help all teachers understand why reading is everyone's job and why everyone should be doing the work of helping students become more efficient and effective critical readers, writers, and thinkers.

By focusing on these four specific essays included in *Deep Reading*, I do not mean to give short shrift to the other essays in the book. Given my own collaboration with a faculty member at a large urban institution (Cynthia Haller of York College of the City University of New York) and a high school teacher and curriculum coordinator for a public school district (Deborah Gollnitz of the Birmingham Public Schools), two venues very different from my mid-sized midwestern state university (Oakland University in Rochester, Michigan), I hope it is clear that I value the discussion of reading from a wide range of perspectives. Sullivan and company likewise have included a wide range of perspectives in *Deep Reading*. The best (though not the only) example appears in the second section of *Deep Reading*, where students' voices are heard, along with those of their teachers or mentors.

The student and mentor chapters present the direct experiences of students with an array of different kinds of reading and writing. Reading is crucial to students' writing experience and ability; this insight is of course not news. But students' willingness to read widely and their efforts to read well make an essential difference to their success as writers and to their success in and out of school. These chapters make for compelling reading. The students' discussions of their direct experiences with reading provide concrete evidence of the power and importance of reading as well as its impact on their lives in and out of school. The mentors' comments show how much they have learned from working with these students, both about their own teaching and about reading and writing.

Finally, the third and longest section of *Deep Reading* offers a grab bag of approaches to the teaching of reading and writing together. Prominent among these chapters is the mix, as is true throughout the collection, of experienced scholars and new voices. We get the editors themselves and others who have published regularly on reading–writing connections. We also get less well-known authors who present important insights. As a group, these chapters blend past and future, mix advice on daily work with big-picture views, and consider where reading might go in the grand scheme of US education, whether in large public universities, diverse community colleges, or anywhere in between.

We hope, as Sulllivan et al. say, that readers will see these books as companion volumes, one a handbook or guidebook for instructors in first-year writing and related courses, and the other full of theory and practice for faculty in a wide array of disciplines in the humanities, social sciences, and sciences. The many scholars who have contributed to these volumes, whether well-known in the field or not, have all spent time thinking about and writing about the "reading problem." Even readers who do not think there is a reading problem among students will get many insights into students' reading and writing from our collections. And even if readers believe that students' reading skills or lack of them will be mitigated by technology in the future, the fundamental skills of reading will always be needed, whether the reading entails traditional paper pages or computer screens. This book makes clear reading's importance to the teaching and learning of writing as well as the need for every teacher at every level and in every discipline to work on it. Ultimately, the issue comes down to the last words in this collection: "It pays to read."

Works Cited

ACT. *Reading between the Lines: What the ACT Reveals about College Readiness in Reading*. 1 March 2006. Web. <http://www.act.org/content/dam/act/unsecured/documents/reading_report.pdf>.

Horning, Alice S. "Rethinking AP English." *Journal of Teaching Writing* 31.1 (2016): 27–60. Print.

Jamieson, Sandra "What Students' Use of Sources Reveals about Advanced Reading Skills." *Across the Disciplines* 10.4 (2013). Web. 1 Feb. 2017. <http://wac.colostate.edu/atd/reading/jamieson.cfm>.

Kelly, Kevin. *The Inevitable: Understanding the 12 Technological Forces That Will Shape Our Future*. New York: Viking, 2016. Print.

Leu, Donald J. et al. "Toward a Theory of New Literacies Emerging from the Internet and Other Information and Communication Technologies." *Theoretical models and processes of reading, 5th ed.* Ed. Robert B. Ruddell and Norman J. Unrau. Newark: International Reading Association, 2004. 1570–613. Print.

National Assessment of Educational Progress. "Are the Nation's Twelfth-Graders Making Progress in Mathematics and Reading?" 2015. Web. 1 June 2016.

Pinker, Steven. *The Better Angels of Our Nature: Why Violence Has Declined*. New York: Viking, 2011. Print.

Stanford History Education Group. *Evaluating Information: The Cornerstone of Civic Online Reasoning*. Nov. 2016. Web. 1 Feb. 2017. <https://sheg.stanford.edu/upload/V3LessonPlans/Executive%20Summary%2011.21.16.pdf>.

Table of Contents for *What Is College Reading?*
Edited by Alice S. Horning, Deborah-Lee Gollnitz, and Cynthia R. Haller

13. "Integrating Reading, Writing, and Research for First-Year College Students: Piloting Linked Courses in the Education Major" by Tanya I. Sturtz, Darrell C. Hucks, and Katherine E. Tirabassi

INDEX

EDITORS

Patrick Sullivan teaches English at Manchester Community College in Manchester, Connecticut. He believes deeply in the mission of the community college. Sullivan has published work in *Teaching English in the Two-Year College, College English, College Composition and Communication, Academe,* the *Journal of Adolescent and Adult Literacy,* the *Journal of Developmental Education,* the *Journal of Basic Writing,* the *Community College Journal of Research and Practice, Innovative Higher Education,* the *Chronicle of Higher Education,* and *English Journal.* He is coeditor, with Howard Tinberg, of *What Is "College-Level" Writing?* (2006) and, with Howard Tinberg and Sheridan Blau, of *What Is "College-Level" Writing? Volume 2: Assignments, Readings, and Student Writing Samples* (2010); author of *A New Writing Classroom: Listening, Motivation, and Habits of Mind* (2014); coeditor, with Christie Toth, of *Teaching Composition at the Two-Year College: Background Readings* (2016); and currently at work on a book about community colleges, *Economic Inequality, Neoliberalism, and the American Community College* (forthcoming in 2017). In 2011, Sullivan received the Nell Ann Pickett Award for outstanding service to the two-year college. His article "'A Lifelong Aversion to Writing': What If Writing Courses Emphasized Motivation?" received the Mark Reynolds *TETYC* Best Article Award for 2012. Sullivan is currently a member of the *College Composition and Communication* Editorial Board. In addition to teaching and writing, he enjoys running, biking, hiking, reading, and spending time with his family—his wife, Susan, his children, Bonnie Rose and Nicholas, and his granddaughter, Marigold Hope.

Howard Tinberg, professor of English at Bristol Community College, Massachusetts, and former editor of the journal *Teaching English in the Two-Year College,* is the author of *Border Talk: Writing and Know-*

ing in the Two-Year College and *Writing with Consequence: What Writing Does in the Disciplines*; coauthor (with Jean-Paul Nadeau) of *The Community College Writer: Exceeding Expectations* and (with Ronald Weisberger) of *Teaching, Learning, and the Holocaust: An Integrative Approach*; and coeditor (with Patrick Sullivan) of *What Is "College-Level" Writing?* and (with Patrick Sullivan and Sheridan Blau) of *What Is "College-Level" Writing? Volume 2: Assignments, Readings, and Student Writing Samples.* He has also published in a variety of academic journals, including *College English, College Composition and Communication, Teaching English in the Two-Year College,* and *Change.* Tinberg's article "Reconsidering Transfer Knowledge at the Community College: Challenges and Opportunities" received the Mark Reynolds *TETYC* Best Article Award for 2015. In 2004 he was recognized as a US Professor of the Year by the Carnegie Foundation for the Advancement of Teaching and the Council for Advancement and Support of Education. From 2005 to 2006, Tinberg was a scholar in residence for the Carnegie Academy for the Scholarship of Teaching and Learning (CASTL), and in 2015 he was selected as a Museum Teacher Fellow at the United States Holocaust Memorial Museum. He is a former Chair of the Conference on College Composition and Communication, the premier national organization for college teachers of writing and rhetoric.

Sheridan Blau is professor of practice in the teaching of English at Teachers College, Columbia University. He is also emeritus professor of English and education at the University of California, Santa Barbara (UCSB), where he taught for nearly 40 years before his retirement in 2010. At UCSB he served as director of the South Coast Writing Project for more than 30 years, and directed the campus Writing Program from 1984 to 1990. Beyond the campus, Blau has served on the advisory board for the National Writing Project, as director of the National Literature Project, and as an adviser for statewide literacy assessment programs and national teacher assessments. He also chaired two international conferences on the teaching of language and literacy.

He is a former President of the National Council of Teachers of English (1997–1998), and in 2007 was awarded the NCTE Distinguished Service Award for service to the profession of English through professional leadership, contributions to teaching, and exemplary writing. In 2012 he was named Rhetorician of the Year by the Young Rhetoricians' Conference. He has published extensively in the fields of seventeenth-century British literature, the teaching and learning of composition and literature, professional development for teachers, the ethics and politics of literacy, and the character of academic discourse. His widely influential book *The Literature Workshop: Teaching Texts and Their Readers* (2003) won the Conference on English Education Richard Meade Award for outstanding research in English education in 2004.

CONTRIBUTORS

Linda Adler-Kassner is professor of writing studies and interim dean of Undergraduate Education at University of California, Santa Barbara. Her recent research has focused on how effective literacy practices are defined by faculty and students, and how ideas about effective literacy practices are conveyed in public policy. This interest has led her to the use of threshold concepts as a heuristic for teaching and for research. The chapter in this book came from a section of first-year writing at UC Santa Barbara where students investigated threshold concepts in another class in which they were enrolled. She also has used threshold concepts as a starting point for discussions with faculty about ideas that students at different levels need to "see through and see with" to be considered successful learners. Adler-Kassner is author, coauthor, or coeditor of nine books and many articles and book chapters. Her most recent book, *Naming What We Know: Threshold Concepts of Writing Studies* (2016), is coedited with Elizabeth Wardle and won the Council of Writing Program Administrators Distinguished Contribution to the Discipline Award in 2016. Adler-Kassner was the chair of the Conference on College Composition and Communication (CCCC) in 2017; she is also past president of the Council of Writing Program Administrators.

Ellen C. Carillo is associate professor of English at the University of Connecticut and the writing program coordinator at its Waterbury campus. She teaches undergraduate and graduate courses in composition and literature and is the author of *Securing a Place for Reading in Composition: The Importance of Teaching for Transfer* (2015). Her scholarship has been published in *Rhetoric Review*; *The Writing Lab Newsletter*; *Reader: Essays in Reader-Oriented Theory, Criticism, and Pedagogy*; *Feminist Teacher, Currents in Teaching and Learning*; and in edited collections.

Kelly Cecchini is the English department leader at Manchester High School in Connecticut and an adjunct instructor of English composition in the University of Connecticut's First-Year Writing Program as well as at Quinebaug Valley Community College and Manchester Community College. In 2002 she was chosen as an Aetna Fellow to the Connecticut Writing Project (UCONN/Storrs

Summer Institute) and is a CWP teacher consultant. In 2011 she was named Manchester High School's Teacher of the Year. In her free time, she enjoys historical fiction, excellent films, and being with her big, close, noisy Irish American family—especially her two-year-old grandson, Steven, who loves nothing more than to be read to (which pleases her no end).

Jason Courtmanche is currently director of the Connecticut Writing Project and lecturer in English at the University of Connecticut. He was awarded a fellowship from Teachers for a New Era in 2011, a University Teaching Scholar award from the Institute for Teaching and Learning in 2012, an award for Excellence in the Promotion of Literacy from the New England Reading Association in 2013, and an award for Outstanding Teaching from the Office of First Year Programs in 2016. He is a member of the Modern Language Association's Standing Committee on K–16 Alliances. He also reviews teacher education programs for the Council for the Accreditation of Educator Preparation and the National Council of Teachers of English. Courtmanche is the author of *How Nathaniel Hawthorne's Narratives Are Shaped by Sin* (2008). His most recent publications include essays and chapters in *What It Means to Be White in America* (2016), *Nathaniel Hawthorne in the College Classroom* (2016), and *Resources for American Literary Study, Volume 38* (2016). His blog on education, *The Write Space*, is popular with teachers throughout Connecticut and can be accessed at jasoncourtmanche. blogspot.com.

Jacob W. Craig is assistant professor of English at College of Charleston, where he teaches courses in composition theory and digital rhetoric. His research focuses on the relationships between writing practices, writing technologies, and locations of writing. His work has appeared, among other venues, in *Kairos* and the edited collection *The Tablet Book*.

Matthew Davis is assistant professor of English at the University of Massachusetts Boston, where he teaches graduate and undergraduate courses in literacy, composition, and new media. He also directs the Professional Writing & New Media and the Composition Tutoring programs. His research interests, which include writing transfer, multimodal studies, and writing pedagogy, have been explored, among other venues, *in enculturation, South Atlantic Review, Computers and Composition*, and the edited collections *Microhistories of Composition* and *Teaching with Student Texts*.

Patricia Donahue is professor of English at Lafayette College, where she established (and directed) a college writing program. Her work on reading and critical theory has appeared in a number of publications. She and Mariolina Rizzi Salvatori have done a considerable amount of coauthoring together, including essays and a book titled *The Elements (and Pleasures) of Difficulty*. She is also the editor of the journal *Reader*.

Muriel Harris, founder of the Purdue University Writing Lab and the Purdue OWL (Online Writing Lab), is emerita professor of English, director of the Purdue Writing Lab (retired), and founder of *WLN: A Journal of Writing Center Scholarship* (https://wlnjournal.org/), for which she continues to serve as editor. Her book chapters, articles, workshops, and conference presentations focus on writing center theory, practice, and administration, as well as individualized instruction in writing. She happily continues to be a perhaps overly enthusiastic fan of one-to-one tutoring in writing, and she has also authored two first-year composition textbooks, the *Prentice Hall Reference Guide* (currently in its ninth edition and now coauthored with Jennifer Kunka) and *The Writer's FAQs* (currently in a sixth edition and now coauthored with Jennifer Kunka). She invites friends she hasn't met yet to find her on Facebook or LinkedIn or contact her at harrism@purdue.edu.

Katie Hern is an English instructor at Chabot College and co-founder of the California Acceleration Project (CAP), a grassroots professional development network that supports California's 113 community colleges to transform remediation and increase completion and equity. Her publications focus on the need to reform placement, design principles for teaching accelerated English and math, and the movement to establish accelerated models of developmental education. She speaks nationally on remediation reform and integrated reading and writing.

Alice S. Horning is professor of writing and rhetoric at Oakland University, where she holds a joint appointment in linguistics. Her research over her entire career has focused on the intersection of reading and writing, focusing lately on the increasing evidence of students' reading difficulties and how to address them in writing courses and across the disciplines. Her work has appeared in the major professional journals and in multiple books. Horning's most recent books include *Reading, Writing, and Digitizing: Understanding Literacy in the Electronic Age* (2012) and *Reconnecting Reading and Writing* coedited with Elizabeth W. Kraemer (2013). Her forthcoming book is *What Is College Reading?* coedited with Deborah-Lee Gollnitz and Cynthia R. Haller.

Heather G. James is the coordinator for Scholarly Communication and Digital Programs at Raynor Memorial Libraries, Marquette University. She also holds liaison responsibilities to the Departments of Biological and Biomedical Sciences and Chemistry. Previously she held the role of research and instruction librarian at Marquette University, with responsibility for the library's role in First-Year English. Before becoming a librarian, James was an adjunct instructor of rhetoric and composition, and her work and research have centered on collaborations between faculty and librarians in the classroom as well as faculty perceptions of aspects of scholarly communication.

David A. Jolliffe is professor of English and, by courtesy, curriculum and instruction at the University of Arkansas, where he is the initial occupant of the Brown Chair in English Literacy. He writes about the preparation of teachers of reading and writing in high schools and colleges, and he leads community literacy projects throughout the state.

Alfredo Celedón Luján is from Nambé, New Mexico, and a graduate of New Mexico State University and the Bread Loaf School of English. He is an NEH and a New Mexico Golden Apple Award Fellow, and he has been a writer-in-residence with the multicultural artists in the schools program in Alaska and the Noepe Center for Literary Arts on Martha's Vineyard. His writing has appeared in *English Journal*; *La Herencia del Norte*; *Bread Loaf and the Schools*, *California English Journal*, and *The Southwestern Review*, as well as in the books *What Is "College-Level" Writing?* (Volumes 1 and 2); *Engaging American Novels*; *Making Sense: A Real-World Rhetorical Reader*; and *Courageous Leadership in Early Childhood Education*. Luján has taught and/or coached for the Pojoaque Valley Public Schools, Santa Fe Preparatory School, and the Native American Preparatory School. He currently teaches at Monte del Sol Charter School in Santa Fe, where his students were featured in a segment of CPB/Annenberg's *The Expanding Canon: Teaching Multicultural Literature in High School*.

Ronald F. Lunsford is professor of English, past chair of the Department of English, and past director of Graduate Studies in English at the University of North Carolina at Charlotte, where he teaches courses in linguistics, rhetoric, and composition theory. Lunsford's publications include *First-Year Composition: From Theory to Practice* (with Deborah Coxwell-Teague), *Twelve Readers Reading: Responding to College Student Writing* (with Richard Straub), *Noam Chomsky* (with Michael C. Haley), *Research in Composition and Rhetoric* (with Michael G. Moran), and *Linguistic Perspectives on Literature* (with Marvin K. L. Ching and Michael C. Haley).

Sam Morris, a doctoral student at the University of Arkansas, is working on a dissertation that will develop ways of studying and teaching young adult literature. He earned his BA in 2001 and his MA in 2003 at the University of Tennessee. Morris has taught at the secondary and postsecondary levels for fourteen years in Tennessee, North Carolina, and Arkansas, working with students ages 14 to 54.

Rebecca S. Nowacek is associate professor of English at Marquette University, where she directs the Norman H. Ott Memorial Writing Center. Her research focuses on writing across the disciplines and writing transfer. Her publications include *Agents of Integration: Understanding Transfer as a Rhetorical Act* (2011), *Literacy, Economy, and Power* (with multiple coeditors, 2013), and *Citizenship Across the Curriculum* (with Michael B. Smith and Jeffrey L. Bernstein, 2010). Her work has also appeared in *College Composition and Communication, College English, Research in the Teaching of English*, and the *Journal of General Education*. Nowacek was a Carnegie Scholar with the CASTL Program and the 2012 recipient of Marquette University's Robert and Mary Gettel Faculty Award for Teaching Excellence.

John Pekins received a BA in English and an MS in reading education/language arts from Florida State University. From 1979 to 1988, he worked as an instructional assistant and English teacher at the School for Applied Individualized Learning (SAIL), a public alternative middle and high school in Tallahassee, Florida, and from 1988 to 2014, as an English professor at Tallahassee Community College. Now retired, he works from home as a consultant, editor, and tutor.

Evan Pretzlaff graduated from the University of California, Santa Barbara in 2015 with a major in history and a minor in music. He wrote the essay included in this collection as a reflection of his work in 2012 and 2013, aided by his first-year writing professor, Linda Adler-Kassner. During the winter of 2014, Pretzlaff worked for the Scottish Parliament during the Scottish independence referendum. He is in the process of applying for graduate school in the DC area for a masters in public policy/administration. Since graduating, he has continued to keep music in his life, teaching music classes to students in his school district.

Meredith Ross began her stay in academia at Tallahassee Community College at the age of 15 and is now a doctoral student in American religious history at Florida State University. She holds a BA in English and an MLIS (masters in library and information studies), also from FSU. Her current research is in twentieth-century religion and information, particularly mid-twentieth-century church libraries.

Mariolina Rizzi Salvatori, now retired, has taught in the composition and literature programs at the University of Pittsburgh since

1981. She has done, and continues to do, research in the areas of hermeneutics, composition, literacy, and pedagogy. Her work has consistently focused on the transactions of knowledge; on the relations between teachers, students, and texts; and on the specific pedagogical technologies that different theories of reading call for and make possible.

Michael Spooner is associate director of the University Press of Colorado, including Utah State University Press. His published scholarly work has addressed such topics as collaboration in writing (with Kathleen Blake Yancey), editorial response, alternative discourse, the poetry of May Swenson, and the role of publish-or-perish in academe. Acquiring editor of more than 300 books for academic readers, Spooner is also the author of three novels and a student of second language acquisition.

Taryn "Summer" Walls, a native of Charlotte, North Carolina, graduated from the University of North Carolina at Charlotte in 2015, majoring in English and communication studies. She then attended the University of Denver Publishing Institute to pursue an editorial or publicity career in the book industry. She chose this path after falling in love with fantasy and science fiction stories, and credits her inspiration to J. R. R. Tolkien (her favorite author) and her supportive family. She hopes to one day return to London, England, where she studied abroad. When she isn't reading, she fences, plays laser tag, creates scrapbooks, and cooks.

Kathleen Blake Yancey, Kellogg W. Hunt Professor of English and Distinguished Research Professor at Florida State University, has served as the elected chair or leader of several groups, including NCTE, CCCC, CWPA, and SAMLA. Immediate past editor of *College Composition and Communication,* she has authored or coauthored more than 100 articles and chapters and authored, edited, or coedited 14 scholarly books—including, most recently, *Writing across Contexts: Transfer, Composition, and Sites of Writing* (with Liane Robertson and Kara Taczak, 2014) and *A Rhetoric of Reflection* (2016). She is the recipient of several awards, including the FSU Graduate Faculty Mentor Award, the Donald Murray Prize, and the CCCC Research Impact Award.

This book was typeset in Sabon by Barbara Frazier.
Typefaces used on the cover include Museo and Avenir.
The book was printed on 50-lb. White Offset paper
by King Printing Company.